THE
BUDH-GAYA TEMPLE CASE

THE
BUDH-GAYA TEMPLE CASE

ANAGARIKA DHARMAPALA,
JAIPAL GIR AND OTHERS

GYAN

Published by

Gyan Publishing House
5, Ansari Road
Daryaganj, New Delhi-110002
Phone: 011-47034999, 9811692060
E-mail: books@gyanbooks.com

Distribution Network
gyanbooks.com
India, USA, Canada, UK, Australia

ISBN: 978-93-6920-061-0 (HB)
First Published, 1895

2nd Impression 2025

Printed at: Gyan Press, Delhi.

THE BUDH-GAYA TEMPLE CASE
Author: ANAGARIKA DHARMAPALA, JAIPAL GIR AND OTHERS

THE

BUDH-GAYA TEMPLE CASE.

H. DHARMAPALA

Versus

JAIPAL GIR AND OTHERS.

INDEX.

H. DHARMAPALA *versus* JAIPAL GIR AND OTHERS.

(*Sections* 295, 296, 143, 506, *Penal Code, &c.*)

WITNESS FOR PROSECUTION I.

The Deposition of Hevavitarna Dharmapala (Complainant), aged about 29 years, taken on solemn affirmation under the provisions of Act X of 1873, before me, D. J. Macpherson, Magistrate of Gaya, this 8th day of April, 1895.

My name is Hevavitarna Dharmapala, my father's name is Hevavitarna Appuhami. I am a Buddhist. My home is at Colombo in Ceylon. I reside at present in Mouzah Gaya, Police Station Gaya, Zilla Gaya, where I am Honorary General Secretary of the Mahabodhi Society.

I have several times visited the Temple of Mahabodhi at Bodh-Gaya. I first visited it in January, 1891. My object in doing so was to worship the Bodhi tree and also the image of Buddha that was in the Temple. The image was on the ground floor of the Temple. The tree is to the west of the Temple, and is perhaps 30 or 40 feet from the place where the image was. I did as a matter of fact worship on that occasion. I stayed on that occasion for two months at the Temple, putting up at the Burmese rest-house, which may be about 100 fathoms of 6 feet from the Temple.

My second visit was in July, 1891, and I stayed there about a month. I also worshipped there.

I again came in October, 1891, and stayed a few days, and also entered the Temple and worshipped.

Between that visit and up to February, 1895, I visited the Temple about seven times, and on every occasion I entered the Temple and worshipped there.

My visit in February, 1895, was on the 25th, in the morning. The last previous occasion on which I visited it was about a month before in January, 1895.

Question.—Had you any special object in visiting the Temple in January ?

Answer.—Yes, I went with my mother and about 44 pilgrims—Singhalese—from Ceylon. My mother and all these are Singhalese Buddhists. We went on that occasion to make offerings and to worship the tree and the Temple. I stayed on that occasion about two days. We went into the Temple then and made offerings of flowers and candles before the image of Buddha, and performed our devotions. These offerings are made to the memory of Buddha before the image.

When I went to the Temple on the morning of the 25th February, it was with the special object of placing an image of Buddha presented by the Japanese Buddhists on the altar of the upper storey of the Temple. The image was given to me by the High Priest of Tokio in Japan and the Buddhists of Japan. It was the High Priest himself who actually handed it over to me. Along with the image were given the paraphernalia of it. The image is a sitting one of Buddha. It may be about 18 inches high and 15 inches in width, and 10 inches in depth. It is made of Japanned sandalwood, gilded over. The paraphernalia given were brass lotus flowers standing on a vase, a censer, two candlesticks, and a certificate. The certificate purports to attest the antiquity of the image. It is written in the Japanese language.

On the 25th February I got to the Temple about 9 A.M. I was accompanied by some two priests—two priests and a Singhalese layman. The priests were of the Buddhist religion and Singhalese also. When we got to the Temple, I placed the image on the altar on the upper floor with the help of these priests. We fixed a lotus flower on to the low stand, and then on the lotus we placed the image; we then placed the candlesticks and censer before the image. Having done this, I sent word to the Government custodian of the Temple, Babu Bipin Behari Banerji. He came about 6 or 7 minutes after. At the time when I was placing the image on the altar, there were two Muhammadan gentlemen present and a Muhammadan mukhtear. I did not then know who these Muhammadan gentlemen were, or their names. I have since learned who they were—Muhammad Fazalullah, Sub-Registrar of Gaya, and Muhammad Habibullah, Deputy Magistrate of Gaya. The third was Hussain Baksh. I see the latter here in Court (*points to Husain Baksh, accused*). After the custodian came, I entrusted the image to him, saying: "This present from the Japanese Buddhists is now placed in the shrine, and now it is under your control." I was then going to place the certificate on the left of the image, but the Babu said it would be better on the right side, and I placed it so. The certificate was in a frame, with a glass over it. I believe the three Muhammadans were not present at the time I had that conversation. We were then going to light the candles—the priests and myself. Then I heard a noise of people rushing in, and then about 30 or 40 people rushed in to the room, and six or seven got up on to the altar and two, who came and stood between me and the image, began to tell me to take away the image. They were saying more in vehement language, but that was all I understood. They told me to remove the image in a very imperative tone of voice. The Government custodian, who was beside me, with uplifted hands begged them not to be impatient. I understood a few words of what he said, but not all. He spoke to them in an imploring tone. The people, however, did not desist, but kept telling me to remove the image. I understood this by their vehement tone and by the gestures of the Muhammadan mukhtear, accused Hussain Baksh. The latter kept pushing me by the shoulder, telling me to remove the image. I appealed to the people who were there—the Sannyasis, Babu and all, saying, why should he, a Muhammadan, come there and interfere in such a matter? I said this in English. The principal men who were before me then went to bring some one who could speak English to me. The majority of them left, and I sat quietly on the floor and contemplated. I sat in religious contemplation—in the cross-legged posture with my hands resting on my feet, with the palms upwards. The next thing I knew was the removal of the image. All the time I sat in contemplation indifferent to what was going on. I saw people removing the image. I saw among those who touched the image to remove it, one of the Sannyasis on the dock, whose name I have subsequently learned is Mahendra Gir (*points to accused, Mahendra Gir*). Of those who got on to the altar in the first instance I can identify some. One who got on to it was the accused I point out (*points to Bhimal Deo Gir*), and the accused Mahendra Gir was sitting on the altar with his legs hanging down. The altar is about 4 feet high. There are others who got on to the altar whom I could identify, but these are the only two in Court whom I saw get on to the altar. After these people went away, they came back with a Hindu who spoke English. I see him here (*points to accused Vijayananda standing outside the dock instructing the defence*). I subsequently learned his name was Vijayananda. I was not molested on the first occasion in the way the Muhammadan mukhtear molested me, but they interfered with us, however, and did not allow us to light the candles. That was on the first occasion.

See Note at end of Examination-in-chief.

D. J. M.

Then when the Hindu mukhtear, Vijayananda, came, he brought back with him all the men who had previously left the Temple. As soon as he arrived, I appealed to him in English that we should not be disturbed in this manner. I pointed out to him the several men that were on the altar, and asked him to bring them down as it was desecration to be on the altar, and prayed him not to let them interfere with our devotions. When the Hindu mukhtear came, the Japanese image was on the shrine—on the altar.

Question.—Did the Hindu mukhtear assist you in any way when you asked him ?

Answer.—Yes. he asked the men on the altar to come down. One or two I think did come down then. Then the Hindu mukhtear and the majority of those with him retired. It was when they did so that I sat down in contemplation before the image.

To Court :—What I said before as to sitting in contemplation refers to this time—I meant after the Hindu mukhtear had retired.

The next thing that happened was the removal of the image. When that happened, I was sitting in contemplation indifferent to what was going on. I don't know how many were in the chamber at the time of the removal, as I did not look back. I observed only those in front. It was when I was sitting in contemplation like this that the image was removed. I noticed about three men taking actual part in the removal of the image. Among the accused I noticed one taking actual part in the removal—namely, Mahendra Gir. I am almost sure I could recognise the others also, if I saw them. After the removal of the image, I remained sitting as before, but not in religious contemplation, though in the same posture as before. During the time I was sitting in contemplation before the removal of the image, I noticed that the other priests with me were also sitting in the religious attitude. Sitting in that posture and contemplating is a form of Buddhist worship—the highest form of Buddhist worship. It is the chief form of Buddhist worship, but there are other forms, the offering of flowers and burning of candles being the preliminaries. Before the removal of the image, while we were contemplating, the candlesticks were before the image, but the candles had not been allowed to be lighted. The chief person who instigated the prevention of the lighting of the candles is present among the accused and his name, as I subsequently learned, is Jaipal Gir *(points out Jaipal Gir, accused.)* He pointed to the candles and said to the other man not to let them be lighted. The other man was Mahendra Gir. Mahendra Gir thereupon prevented one of my companions who was trying to light the candles. The prevention of the lighting of the candles was a disturbance of a part and parcel of our religious worship. This prevention took place previous to the contemplation and the removal of the image. At the time Jaipal and Mahendra Gir prevented the candles being lighted, I saw present also among those here the accused Shivanandan Gir *(points out this accused).* I learned his name subsequently. I did not then notice any others who are in the Court just now.

Question.—At the time when the image was removed, or before or after it, whom did you notice ?

Answer.—I noticed the four Sannyasis in the dock. They were there before I began contemplation. They were not there while I was sitting in contemplation. The majority of the people, including these, went away with the Hindu mukhtear, and it was then I sat down in contemplation. I was sitting in religious contemplation for a few minutes before the people came back when they removed the image. Among those whom I noticed when they came back and removed the image was Mahendra Gir, accused. I did not then notice any of the others now in Court. I cannot say how many entered the Temple when it was removed. When it was removed, all, except one or two, I believe, went away. I remained then sitting in the same posture, but not in religious contemplation, and a few minutes after a constable came up and called me downstairs, saying the jemadar wanted me. I did not go downstairs. I told the constable something, and he went away. Then the jemadar of police came up and asked me certain questions, in Hindustani ; but as I did not understand him, I wrote down a statement in English then and there, and gave it to him. Subsequently on, I think the 28th, I came and lodged a complaint in Court, on which the present proceedings are taking place. Before I lodged my complaint in Court, the police made an enquiry at Bodh-Gaya. I did not, while the occurrence was going on, know the name of the accused I have now named. Before I lodged my complaint, I came to know the names of some of them. During the police enquiry I pointed out Sannyasis, whom I had seen taking part in the occurrence. I pointed out all the four Sannyasis, accused in Court, Jaipal, Mahendra, Shivanandan, and the other man *(Bhimal Deo Gir)*.

I next saw the image on the evening of the same day—the 25th February. It was then in the courtyard of the Temple against the wall of the Panchpandava Temple. There were several people about it then.

According to the Buddhist religion, the image of Buddha is regarded as a very sacred object. If such an image, after being placed on the altar, is removed therefrom, it is regarded as a defilement of it—a desecration. Such an act also is regarded as the highest insult to the Buddhist religion.

Question.—Would an order given by other than a Buddhist to remove the image of Buddha when enshrined on the altar be considered as wounding your religious feelings?

Answer.—Yes, it injures the feelings of the Buddhists.

Question.—Would any Hindu removing the image, or speaking as described with respect to the removal of the image, wound your religious feelings and defile the image?

Answer.—Yes.

Question.—On all the occasions that you have been to the Temple, have you ever seen any Hindus either worshipping there or performing any religious ceremonies, and if so, when?

[Counsel for the defence objects to this question being put, on the ground that the Court had suggested that this branch of the case had better be dealt with separately after the evidence as to the actual occurrence of the 25th February had been taken—an arrangement acquiesced in by the parties, and he further remarked that he reserved till the time came a general objection he proposed to raise, as to the relevance of any evidence on this subject to the case before this Court. Counsel for the prosecution accordingly postponed going into evidence on this branch of the case, and did not press the above question].

On the ground floor of the Temple there is an image of Buddha, the same as I saw there when I first came four years ago. It is of stone.

Question.—In what state was it then, when you first saw it?

Answer.—In no way defiled. I have seen the image again several times within the last few months. When I visited the Temple in January last, I observed that the image had undergone alteration—in particular, that paint of red colour had been put on the forehead and the whole body covered up with cloth so as to conceal its Buddha appearance, and flowers placed on its head. When I saw the image four years ago, it had no paint on the forehead, no flowers on the head, and it had only on a cloth occasionally and that of plain yellow colour, such as Buddhist Bhikshus (monks) wear. The cloth I have now seen on it is not a mere cloth, but a regular dress for the image and of orange colour—a little lighter than the colour which the Sannyasis, accused, wear *(points to a bright orange colour a spectator is wearing on his puggree)*. All these changes are certainly such as defile the image of Buddha. Any Buddhists who went to the Temple and saw these changes would have his feelings greatly hurt. Besides that I have, since January last, seen a Hindu *pujari* (priest) officiating at the image—that is, ringing a handbell before the image, painting the forehead of the image, and putting flowers on its head. I don't recognise any person in Court as that *pujari*. If I were to see him, I should certainly recognise him.

Counsel for the defence reserves cross-examination for the present, and this is allowed.

Deposition read over by witness in presence of accused. He says that it is correct, except that on page 2 there is something out of order as it was after the Hindu mukhtear had come and retired, *i. e.*, after the second retirement of the people—that he sat in religious contemplation.

D. J. MACPHERSON,

Magistrate.

9th April, 1895.

WITNESS FOR PROSECUTION I.

H. Dharmapala, re-called by prosecution as arranged yesterday, and examined on solemn affirmation by Counsel for the prosecution.

Question.—On all the occasions you have spoken to as having visited the Mahabodhi Temple at Bodh-Gaya and worshipped there, did you ever on any of those occasions see any Hindus either worshipping or performing any ceremonies in the said Temple ?"

[Counsel for the defence objects to this question, and puts in a petition protesting against the reception of "any such ecclesiastical evidence" in this case, and stating that it will be impossible, at this early stage of the trial, to discuss the question of the relevance of this evidence without disclosing the case for the defence, while claiming at the same time to hold all evidence as to the possession of the Temple to be relevant. The question of admitting such evidence at the present stage was argued, and it was decided by the Court that it should be admitted subject to objection hereafter. See separate note of argument.*]

See page 126, Post.

Witness's examination continued.

(*Above question being repeated*).

I had never on any occasion seen any Hindus performing worship or religious ceremonies at the Temple.

Question.—Did you yourself ever place anything on the altar of the ground floor ?

Answer.—In the year 1891, in July, I put two hanging lamps above the altar, one on each side, and my companion priest in my presence put a small canopy over the image of Buddha there. No ever raised any objection to our doing so. We did not get the sanction of the Mahanth before we did so. We did it openly as a part and portion of the ceremonies connected with our worship.

Question.—According to the Buddhist religion, does the placing or setting up or offering of images on the altar form part of your religion ?

Answer.—It forms one of the highest forms of Buddhist worship to enshrine or place an image of Buddha on the altar of a Buddhist Temple. Buddhists are undoubtedly in the habit, when they go to worship at a Buddhist Temple, of placing images of Buddha on the altar, and they do the same thing also in the precincts or compound of the Temple. Beside images, Buddhists also place in the Temple other religious objects (*adds*) and also within the precincts of the Temple. Such objects are artificial and natural flowers, candlesticks, flower vases, curtains, flagstaffs and flags, banners, garlands, bells, and other docorations. They also place lamps and censers.

The cross-examination is reserved. Read over and admitted correct.

D. J. MACPHERSON,

Magistrate.

1st May, 1895.

WITNESS FOR PROSECUTION.

H. Dharmapala, re-called by prosecution and examined on solemn affirmation on 1st May, 1895, states:—

Question.—You stated in your evidence that when the police head constable came up to where you were in the Temple, you made a statement to him which you reduced into writing there and then. (*Shown the statement in question*). Is that the statement you made?

[Counsel for the defence objected that this statement was not admissible in evidence as it was made to a police officer in the course of an investigation under Chapter XIV, Criminal Procedure Code, and is, therefore, under Section 162, Criminal Procedure Code, not admissible in evidence against the accused. He contended that the information given at the outpost by Hussain Baksh was information of an unlawful assembly—a cognizable offence—and that even if it were not, the statement of Dharmapala himself was information of the offence of an unlawful assembly, and therefore inadmissible. In support of the contention, the case of *Empress* versus *Madho* (Indian Law Reports, 15 Allahabad, 25), is quoted.

Counsel for the prosecution claim to put the statement in under Section 157, Evidence Act, and also under Section 8 (*vide* illustration *k* of that Act,) and say he does not, in puting it in to corroborate the witness, use it as evidence of any particular fact against the accused. He also contends that the statement was not made in the course of a police investigation under Chapter XIV, Criminal Procedure Code, that Hussain Baksh's statement was not information of an offence, but a general statement intended to secure the intervention of the police to prevent Dharmapala's design being carried out, and that having regard to the witness's statement at pages 14 and 15 of his deposition in this case, the statement sought to be put in was information given by him of an offence of unlawful assembly.

Counsel for the defence enlarged in reply on the points already noted, reading the ruling cited, and stated that the statement, were it admitted, would neither enhance the case for the prosecution or harm that for the defence, and would be valueless, inasmuch as if it be not made evidence, the assumption would be that it was in accordance with the deposition relating to the same facts made before the Court, he having said he had made such a statement.

On reading the statement of Hussain Baksh before the head constable, I find that it amounts to information that as several persons had come to put an image in the Temple contrary to order, there was a danger of a breach of the peace. It does not amount to information of a cognisable offence, nor was it treated by the head constable as such, as it was not signed by Hussain Baksh nor recorded on the form prescribed by Government as required by Section 154, Criminal Procedure Code. It purports to be an extract from the station diary book; but the head constable, from the remarks at the end of the entry, appears to have left it to be entered in that book by the writer constable. I cannot hold that the statement sought to be put in was made in the course of an investigation under Chapter XIV, Criminal Procedure Code, and Section 162, Criminal Procedure Code, does not therefore override the provisions of Section 157, or Section 8 of the Evidence Act, making it admissible. Apart from the legal point involved, it is desirable to have on record what was stated at the time by those concerned, as much in the interest of the accused as of the prosecution; it can hardly, as Counsel for the defence admits, injure the accused. Further the objection to admitting statements recorded by the police does not attach to this statement.]

[*Statement handed to witness, who said*]: This is the statement I made to the head constable and recorded by myself at the time (*admitted and marked Exhibit I.*)

[*Shown photograph of an image*]. This is a photograph of the Japanese image which forms the subject of dispute in this case (*admitted and marked Exhibit II.*)

Read over to witness and admitted correct.

The prosecution say that this closes their case, except that they will, if they can procure it, put in a translation of the Japanese certificate or the certificate itself.

Defence say they will have no objection to this going in.

D. J. MACPHERSON,
Magistrate.

3rd May, 1895.

WITNESS FOR PROSECUTION I.

H. Dharmapala, complainant, recalled and cross-examined on solemn affirmation :—

I was educated in Colombo. I left college in 1883. I began life as a religious student. My father supports me. I took to no profession. Since then I have been all along a religious student. The Mahabodhi Society was first established in May, 1891. That was in Ceylon. I am practically not the founder of that Society. I am not a founder of it. The idea originated with Sir Edwin Arnold. I first made his acquaintance in 1893. I had communications with him before that. He was in London. I started the correspondence.

Question.—What led you to start the correspondence?

Answer.—After the formation of the Society I had to write him informing him of its formation. That is the first time I ever wrote him. I had no communication with him before the formation of the Society.

Question.—Is it not the principal object of your society to recover the possession of the Mahabodhi Temple from the Mahanth?

Answer.—I am unable to give a decisive answer to that question. The Society was principally founded with that object.

Question.—Has that object been yet accomplished ?

Answer.—Not yet.

Question.—Is this prosecution intended to secure that object ?

Answer.—No. I can say that it is not the object of this prosecution.

Question.—Will you swear that it is not even one of the objects of this prosecution ?

Answer.—No, it is not one of the objects.

Question.—If the Mahanth were to give you up the Temple to-day, would you go on with the prosecution ?

Answer.—Yes.

Question.—Do you or do you not admit that the Mahanth is the proprietor of this Temple ?

[Question objected to by the prosecution on the ground that the question of who is proprietor of this Temple is irrelevant and would be a question of law as well as of fact, and, secondly, that even if it were relevant, the witness's opinion on the matter would not be relevant, as it would be for the Court to decide that. The defence argue that it is relevant on the ground that the whole question turns on whether the Mahanth (whether rightly or wrongly it does not matter so far as this prosecution is concerned) believed himself to be the proprietor of the Temple, and therefore the defence have a right to ascertain whether the prosecution admit that view. It is a question purely of fact whether the Mahanth is proprietor and whether the prosecution have all along regarded him as proprietor. There would be other grounds on which the relevance could be based, but for the present purpose the defence are entitled to know if the position is to be admitted.

The question whether the Mahanth himself believed himself *bonâ fide* to be proprietor, would be relevant to the question of criminal intention in this case, assuming that the present defendants intend to shelter themselves behind the view the Mahanth entertained of his position, but whether the witness's individual opinion is that the Mahanth is proprietor or not, could not be relevant as indicating the Mahanth's view of his own position. It might become relevant if it was intended to show that the Mahanth was induced to take up that view by reason of an admission on the point by the witness.—D. J. M.]

Question.—Did you ever describe the Mahanth as proprietor of this Temple or cause him to be so described?

Answer.—No, I am sure of that. I am Editor of the monthly Journal of the Mahabodhi Society. I do not consider myself responsible for the articles that appear in that Journal. I do not read all the articles that appear in it before they appear. I did not write the article that appeared in January last on Sir Charles Elliott's visit to Bodh-Gaya. I don't remember having read that article. I have other work to do, and cannot remember whether I have read it or not. I am not the sole Editor of the Journal. Several friends are also Editors. There are no Joint-editors. I advertise myself as the Editor of the Journal. I produce the Journal of January, 1895. On looking to the article on Sir Charles Elliott's visit to Gaya, I can say I have read it. I swear I did not read it in manuscript or in proof. I took exception to it when I read it. I took exception to the whole article, and thought it unnecessary.

Question.—Do you remember taking exception to any particular portion of it?

Answer.—I took exception to the whole article.

Question.—When you read the article, did you take exception to any statement of fact in it?

Answer.—I took exception to the whole article.

[N.B.—*The witness was directed not to read the article at all before answering any of the above questions* —D. J. M.]

I have not up to date, to my knowledge, published any repudiation of any portion of that article.

Question.—Read the article and say now whether you take exception to any statement of fact as erroneous.

Witness reads the article, and says: I object to the whole of the first two paragraphs, *i.e.*, the one on page 73 and that on page 74. They commence at the word "when" and go on to the word "below" on page 74. I object to the whole leaderette.

Question.—In the editorial portion of the article or leaderette, is there any statement of fact in particular to which you take exception?

Answer.—I object to each and every statement in it.

Question.—Is there any particular statement to which you object more than another ?

Answer.—I don't draw any distinction. I object to the whole. I first read this article after my arrival in Calcutta I cannot say when, but it was long after its publication. I believe it was in the month of February. It was before the present occurrence. I have told my friends that I object to that article. I told it to my Bengali friends. They are friends who came to see me. I do not remember the names of any. I cannot mention any single friend in particular, as I objected in the midst of several friends. That was in Calcutta, at 2 Creek Row, which is the office of the Society. I did not remark to them that it was an article that should be contradicted or repudiated in the Journal.

D 1.

SIR CHARLES ELLIOTT AT BUDDHA-GAYA.

When the head of a Government, Supreme or Local, is out touring in a province or in a district, the expectations of the people are high that he would see things for himself and redress their grievances, if any. This is why addresses are presented, memorials are sent in, and neat speeches are made in reply condemning this or that, and upholding a lot of other things. And during a viceregal or a gubernatorial tour, it should not be omitted. Falsehood assumes the veneer of Truth. It is therefore left for the mastermind to detect it in its repulsive native nudity. When the recent tour in Gaya of Sir Charles Elliott, the Lieutenant-Governor of Bengal, was arranged and notified in the official Gazette, Self-interest looked to him. We were no exception. We were, as we still are, humbly of opinion that justice would at last be meted out to the aggrieved Buddhist world. The present Hindu *Mahant*, proprietor of our temple at Buddha-Gaya, expected in all likelihood that his interests would remain intact, confirming him, as His Honour would, in his proprietary rights. Consequently, measures were adopted to present to Sir Charles a Hindu aspect of the Temple. Some fifty Hindus were engaged in offering *pindas* to the names of their departed ancestors. In this connection it should be noted here that it is popularly believed that Buddhism is entirely antagonistic to their own faith. It has no more affinity to Hinduism than Mahomedanism has to Hinduism. The Bengali populace believe that death occurring at Buddha-Gaya results in rebirth in the animal world, assuming, as it does, the form of a donkey. Be that as it may, things do not improve a whit better in other provinces. We do not know whether or not they subscribe to the belief as it obtains in Bengal. But it is pretty certain that they look at it in no better light. Had the contrary been the fact, they would have thought it worth while to pay a visit to Buddha-Gaya, which is profitably dispensed with, and to Hindu-Gaya as well. It is the educated few, who know what Buddha is and what Buddhism is. Supposing there is some injunction or rather provision made in the *Shastras* for offering *pindas* or furneral cakes at Buddha-Gaya, how many do ever care to do that? Not one among a thousand. It will be thus seen that the *pinda* offering pretext does not hold water. How far the theory is tenable we leave it to His Honour the Lieutenant-Governor himself to determine. An English-knowing Buddhist should have attended on him, and placed before him the bare facts. We therefore deplore more than any body else the absence of any such person. We hope His Honour would see through the whole scheme, and give the lie direct to the garbled accounts communicated to the Press, which are duly contradicted by the *Behar Times* in its issue of December 7th last in a leaderette, for which we make room below :—

"It seems that during the recent visit of the Lieutenant-Governor to Buddha-Gaya, the *Mahant* or his advisers made an attempt to improve the occasion by getting up a show to impress upon His Honor the alleged Hinduistic character of the Temple. But they overdid the thing ; and a correspondent

[Article in question tendered as evidence. The prosecution say they have no objection to its going in as the article referred to by the witness, but object to its being admitted as evidence of any facts stated in it The defence tender it as explanatory of the cross-examination. Admitted accordingly, as the article to which the witness's cross-examination referred, but not as evidence of facts in it. Put in and marked D 1. D. J. M.]

Question—Do you consider the description in the article of the Mahanth as the "proprietor of our Temple" a false one ?

Answer.—It is erroneous.

Question.—Is that your present opinion, or have you all along entertained it ?

Answer.—I am unable to say that.

In Feburary and March, 1893, I think I was in Gaya. I did not send any telegrams to the press in these months. I did not cause any to be sent. I did not revise any before they were sent. I saw telegrams before they were sent. I am unable to say who sent them. I cannot say who showed them to me. I don't quite remember where or in whose house I saw them.

Question.—What was the occasion ?

Answer.—When the priests were assaulted, I came to see the telegrams, when some newspaper correspondents were discussing the subject. I am unable to say their names. I don't quite remember the identical parties. They showed them because the priests in whom I was interested were assaulted. I did not pay the cost of the telegrams. I don't remember if I wrote an article on them in my Journal. I don't remember having written an article headed "Our Indian Shrines."

writing to one of the Calcutta papers on behalf of the *Mahant*, under cover of giving a descriptive account of the Lieutenant-Governor's visit to the place, makes exaggerated efforts to bolster up the *Mahant's* claims to Buddha-Gaya as a Hindu Temple. One can easily see through the letter. For instance, he asserts that the Temple was renovated "partly at the expense of the Bengal Government, while Sir Ashley Eden was the Lieutenant-Governor, and partly with funds supplied by the late *Mahant*," but he forgets to tell the world in what proportion the credit of the renovation is due to the *Mahant* and in what proportion to the Bengal Government. Out of a lakh of rupees spent over the renovation, if the *Mahant* supplied a few hundred or even a few thousand rupees, he surely deserves to share the honor of the renovation, with the Bengal Government. Further on the correspondent says that during the Lieutenant-Governor's visit, "some forty or fifty Hindoos were employed in offering the *pinda* to their ancestors under the celebrated Bodhi tree near the Temple." Ah! "employed," to be sure—but by whom? Or, was the time of the Lieutenant-Governor's visit in any way specially auspicious, according to the canons of the Hindoo religion, for the offer of *pinda* at Buddha-Gaya, that so many as thirty or forty Hindoos should be found engaged in that description of devotion on that particular day? An answer to this question ought to be forthcoming for the enlightenment of those who have visited the Temple a dozen times, and found never a trace of thirty or forty Hindus engaged in that way under the Mahabodhi tree. The correspondent is at some pains to controvert the opinion of Sir Edwin Arnold that it is only "Mahratta peasants" who in their ignorance are now and then found to offer *pinda* at Buddha-Gaya. But these thirty or forty Hindus, who were there on the occasion of the Lieutenant-Governor's visit, we are willing to believe the correspondent, could certainly not be "Mahratta peasants," because possibly their domiciles might be discovered not a hundred miles from the *Mahant's* house. Further, we are told by the correspondent that "when His Honour entered the Temple, some Brahmans were occupied in reciting their scriptures." Possibly, the Lieutenant-Governor's visit quickened the devotional instincts of the Brahmins of Buddha-Gaya in some mysterious but irresistible manner. Brahmins reciting *their* scriptures in the Mahabodhi Temple must have been a sight indeed for the gods —and Sir Charles Elliott. We have been half a dozen times to Buddha-Gaya, and we have been invariably shown over the place by Hindu attendants, who did not seem to be over-oppressed with reverence for the places, did not scruple to go with their shoes on up to the very central shrine—causing us to shudder at the sacrilege, although we are not followers of the Lord Buddha We repeat the *Mahant* has overshot the mark.

(Mahabodhi Society's Journal, January, 1895, pp. 73, 74.)

D. 2.

OUR INDIAN SHRINES.

The correspondence published in our official columns, about the shrines of Buddha-Gaya and Sarnath, will be read with profound interest throughout the Buddhist world. It seems almost a romance of the dark and bloody days of the olden time, that a company of peaceful, unoffending Bhikshus and Samaneras engaged in their usual evening devotions at Buddha-Gaya, should have been murderously assaulted by lawless men, the company put to flight, and one monk whose gentleness and inoffensiveness is recognized by all, beaten about the head and body so severely that his blood stained the floor of the Burmese rest-house, and for days he lay in Gaya Hospital in a precarious condition. The dastardly act has naturally awakened wide sympathy even among the most orthodox Hindu community, and excited general resentment against the assailants, who whether rightly or wrongly, are alleged to be of the party of the Mahant who claims Buddha-Gaya as his private property.

Question.—Look at the first column of the number for March, 1893, page 3, as I have folded it down so that you may not look at the second column, and say if that was not written by you.

Answer.—No, it was not. I read the article. That was before it appeared. I did not approve of all the article contained. I can't remember if I struck out any portion of the manuscript article. I do not strike out from articles all that I disapprove of in all cases. I sometimes only glance at them.

Question.—If you disapprove of any passages in an article, would you allow the entire article to appear as an editorial?

Answer.—Any thing I disapprove of after serious consideration, I do not put in. Unless I read the article now, I shall not remember whether I disapprove of any part of it, as it is.

(*Given whole article to read.*)

Question.—Did you make any alteration, addition or correction in the article before it appeared?

Answer.—No, I made no correction in it. I do not remember having disapproved of any portion of the article before it appeared. I did not give much thought to it. On reading the article now, I repudiate the passage from the sentence beginning "His present attitude," to the end of the paragraph ending with the word "offering."

[Article put in and admitted as Exhibit D2 on same understanding as Exhibit D1—D. J. M.]

I don't remember ever before to-day repudiating that passage.

I know Colonel Olcott. He is a friend of mine. He is not a member of the Society. He holds the nominal rank of a Director. He was never to my knowledge the chief adviser of the Society. He holds the nominal rank of chief adviser; but practically he never was the chief adviser. I have been advertising him in the Journal as chief adviser. I was with him when he was in Gaya in Feburary, 1893. I accompanied him on his visit to the Mahanth.

His present attitude is to refuse to part with his proprietary rights in any way, but the immediate issue of the matter cannot be predicted at this early stage of the negotiations. That it must ultimately turn in favour of the resumption of their ancient rights by the followers of Buddha's Arya Dharma, would seem most probable, since it is inconceivable that the Government of Her Majesty, at least, under either of the two great political parties, could suffer a private person to hold so holy a shrine as Buddha-Gaya for his private profit, in defiance of the moral sentiment and the active sympathies of the whole world. If the Mahant will not voluntarily sell or give the Buddhists of the several Buddhist nations the privilege to station their monks there to guard the shrine from desecration, practise their devotions, and meet and encourage pious pilgrims from distant lands, then, in the exercise of its sovereign right, the Government would be quite able and justified in compelling him to part with the property on terms of equity—the only ones which our co-religionists have ever dreamt of offering.

(Mahabodhi Society's Journal, March, 1893, p. 3.)

Question.—Did Col. Olcott, in your presence, give the Mahanth to understand that the Mahábodhi Society would not take or countenance the taking of any step which could infringe any proprietary right which he or his organization might lawfully claim in the shrine?

Answer.—Not in my presence. I became aware of the alleged terms said to have been proposed by Col. Olcott, after reading a letter, from which the Counsel for the defence seems to have just now read out. I was not aware of it until the letter was drafted—I mean written—by him.

[Defence Counsel had not used the word letter at all, but read out from something in putting the question quoted above.—D. J. M.]

I read the letter when Col. Olcott wrote it out in Gaya on that occasion. That was before it was sent to the Magistrate. I don't recollect taking exception to any portion of that letter. I cannot say if it contained a correct representation of what passed between him and the Mahanth. I gave no thought to the matter then, as to whether it did contain a correct representation. In my presence Col. Olcott proposed no such terms to the Mahanth. I did not, when I read the letter, ask Col. Olcott whether that was correct or not. The letter in question is published at page 7 of the Journal for March, 1893. The leaderette headed "Buddha-Gaya" on that page is not written by me. There is a letter addressed to the Venerable H. Sumangala, President of the Mahábodhi Society, Colombo, on page 8, signed by Col. Olcott and myself. This is not the Sumangala who is a witness in this case. I cannot say at this moment whether I personally published or caused the publication of these letters in the Journal. I cannot say if I approved of their publication at the time. There is nothing in the letter to the Magistrate which I have just now read to which I now take any personal objection.

Question.—Am I therefore to understand that you now approve of what Col. Olcott says in that letter, commencing from "I gave the Mahanth to understand," down to the word "equity"?

Answer.—I agree personally in the passage, "we should endeavour to act with him in a spirit of equity"; but I repudiate the alleged proprietary right now. I repudiate that.

Question.—When did you first repudiate the alleged proprietary right of the Mahanth?

Answer.—All along I have repudiated it.

Question.—Where did you repudiate it?

Answer.—Wherever I went.

Question.—Do you repudiate the fact that the Mahanth has, rightly or wrongly, set himself up as proprietor, apart from the question of whether he has a right to be recognised as proprietor?

Answer.—I am unable to answer that question.

Question.—Do you admit that the Mahanth has been in actual possession of the Temple for more than a century?

Answer.—I do not admit it.

D. 3.

BUDDHA-GAYA.

THE Buddha-Gaya movement has assumed a new and startling phase during the past month, as the subjoined correspondence will prove. Although the Mahant of Buddha-Gaya seems disposed to behave in a truculent manner, yet we consider the question as but opened by the occurrences of the murderous assault upon our inoffensive and blameless Bhikshus, and the preliminary interview of Colonel Olcott with the Mahant. The services of Counsel have been retained, and the necessary legal investigations are proceeding. Following are the letters of our Director to the Collector of Gaya, and the joint report of himself and the General Secretary to the Venerable President of our Society:—

GAYA, *6th February*, 1893.

D. J. MACPHERSON, ESQ.,

Collector, Gaya.

SIR,

FOR your information I beg to report my arrival, in my capacity of Honorary Director and Chief Adviser of the Maha-Bodhi Society, in company with Mr. H. Dharmapala, Honorary General Secretary of the same, for the purpose of inspecting the Buddha-Gaya Maha-Bodhi Temple property, and of negotiating with the Mahant for the acquisition of the religious custody of the shrine for the Buddhists of the several nations professing that religion. I had a preliminary talk with the Mahant yesterday, through Babu Bireswar Singh, of Patna, as interpreter, and regret to say that I received no encouragement to hope that he would either sell or lease the property, or consent to the erection of a monastery or rest-house for the use of Buddhist Bhikshus or pilgrims. I gave the Mahant to understand that the Maha-Bodhi Society, as the representative of the Buddhists, would not take or countenance the taking of any step which could infringe any proprietary right which he or his organization might lawfully claim in this shrine, but that we should endeavour to act with him in a spirit of perfect equity. This same assurance I wish to give yourself and your official superiors.

As it was evident that the further stay of the Bhikshus in the Burmese King's Buddhist rest-house was not approved of by the Mahant, and that to keep them there after the murderous assault made upon them on Friday evening last by parties until now unidentified, would subject them to its repetition, perhaps to the peril of their lives, I have arranged for their removal to safer quarters in Gaya, under reservation of any legal rights which the Buddhists may be found to have for the peaceful pactice of their religion at their most hallowed shrine.

I am glad that the issue is a purely personal one of the Mahant's proprietary interests, and that a good understanding exists between the Buddhists and the leading Hindus of Gaya.

I am, Sir,

Your obedient servant,

H. S. OLCOTT.

(Mahabodhi Society's Journal, March, 1893, p. 7.)

Question.—Have you ever described or caused to be described the Mahanth as in possession of the Temple?

Answer.—I have described him as a usurper of the temple. I cannot say how long the Mahanths have been usurpers of the Temple. I cannot say that. If he has set himself up as a usurper in opposition to the Buddhists, the first time he has done so is the 25th February last. Before that I had never anything to do with him, and he never showed any hostility. I do not consider him a usurper until the 25th February. I consider him as a usurper all along, but not until that date as a personal opponent. By "all along," I mean the time since I took an interest in the Temple, that is, since 1891.

Question.—Am I to understand that from 1891 you consider the Mahanth had wrongly and improperly taken possession of the Temple?

Answer.—I cannot answer that question. I always considered him a usurper.

Question.—What did you consider that he usurped?

Answer.—He usurps the position of a Buddhist.

Question.—How did he usurp the position of a Buddhist?

Answer.—I can't say. What I meant is that he sets himself up as a Buddhist, or as a follower of Buddha. To my knowledge he first did this last January. I do not consider him as having usurped the position of a Buddhist before that. I cannot say it before last January I described or caused him to be described as a usurper.

[*Shown letter of Colonel Olcott, dated 6th February,* 1893, *to the Collector of Gaya, published at page 7 of the Journal for March,* 1893.]

That is the letter referred to above. (Admitted on same understanding as D. 1, and marked Exhibit D. 3).

D. 4.

GAYA, *7th February*, 1893.

VENERABLE H. SUMANGALA,

PRADHANA NAYAKA MAHA STHAVIRA,

President, Mahâbodhi Society, Colombo.

VENERABLE SIR,

THE undersigned have to report the following facts :—

We arrived here on the evening of the 4th instant, and on the 5th proceeded to Buddha-Gaya to inspect premises, and consult with the Hindu Mahant about the acquisition of the Maha-Bodhi Temple for the Buddhists. Upon arrival at the Gaya station we were met by Chandrajoti Bhikshu and the Hindu servant, and informed that on the evening of Friday last a violent assault had been made upon our two Priests, their Hindu servant and Chandra Dutt, the Sinhalese boy, at the Burmese King's rest-house, whilst peacefully engaged in reading Vinaya and religious conversation, by a party of men armed with sticks, who beat Sumangala Bhikshu severely about the head and body, and put the other to flight. The assailants are supposed to have been servants and tenants of the Mahant ; but have not yet been identified. The attack was apparently meant to drive our religious party off the premises ; but the assailants upon leaving carried away the cash box containing several hundred rupees given by Buddhist pilgrims and also some brass utensils. At Buddha-Gaya we made inquiries and found that no provocation had been given by our priests and saw stains of blood on the floor of the verandah, where Sumangala was struck down. This priest had been removed to hospital, where we have twice visited him and found him doing well. One of the blows upon his head would have killed him if it had not glanced.

Several eminent legal Hindu gentlemen accompanied us to Buddha-Gaya. We were received in *durbar* by the Mahant, in his Monastery, and after much general discussion Colonel Olcott, with Babu Bireswar Singh, of Patna, acting as interpreter, had a private interview with the Mahant, in which he informed the latter that the Buddhists did not seek to do anything that could prejudice in the slightest degree any lawful rights he might have over the Maha-Bodhi as proprietor of the land or otherwise : that we were ready to treat with him either for the purchase or lease of the premises upon equitable terms. He refused to either sell or lease on any terms. Colonel Olcott then asked if he would grant permission with necessary guarantees of protection to the Buddhists to build a Pansala or a rest-house or both. He refused. Colonel Olcott then told him that he put himself in this position, *viz.*, that being a Hindu *Sanyasi*, and forbidden by his religion to officiate in a Buddhist Temple, he prevented the Buddhist monks from taking the religious charge of the chief temple of their religion, and caring for the spiritual wants of Buddhist pilgrims. He replied with the false assertion that his religious books did not forbid his charge of a Buddhist temple, as Buddha was an Avatar of Vishnu. The interview then terminated, and we withdrew. We are now about making a strict inquiry into the legality of his tenure of Maha-Bodhi, and have engaged the services of a respectable pleader for that purpose. We have also talked with some of the local Governmental authorities, and Colonel Olcott has addressed to the Collector of Gaya the letter, of which a copy is enclosed for your information.

We are happy to say that the violence used towards the Bhikshus is condemned by the whole Hindu community, and that we have the sympathy of many highly influential European officials throughout India as well as in Europe, in our attempt to recover possession of the four most sacred shrines known to Buddhists.

We have removed the Bhikshus and Samaneras into a house we have hired in Gaya city, where they will be under police protection, and where they can

The letter on page 8 of the same Journal is the one referred to me, addressed to the Venerable H. Sumangala. (Admitted and marked Exhibit D. 4, on same understanding as before).

Question.—Is this passage in Exhibit D. 4 true : " We were ready to treat with the Mahanth either for the purchase or lease of the premises upon equitable terms ; he refused to either sell or lease on any terms ? "

Answer.—Personally I cannot say, as the letter was written by Colonel Olcott. I attested it by my signature.

Question.—Was it a joint letter to the President or not ?

Answer.—I cannot say whether it was, but I attested it.

Question.—What did you mean by attesting the letter ?

Answer.—As General Secretary of the Society, I attested it as an official document.

Question.—Did you join in the letter as a writer thereof ?

Answer.—When I attested it, I gave no thought to that. I signed it as Secretary, forwarding it to the President. I cannot say at this distance of time that I read it before signing it. I certainly recollect seeing it in print. Looking at the phrases in it and the use of the plural throughout, I may be regarded theoretically as a joint-writer of it ; but as a matter of fact I did not write it, and merely signed it. I could, as Secretary, have signed it without agreeing in what was said in it. It is not true that prior to the date of the letter in February, 1893, I treated with the Mahanth—not with the present Mahanth. I did treat with the late Mahanth. That was not for the purchase or lease of the premises. Col. Olcott had not to my knowledge any interview with the late Mahanth.

Question.—Is it true that the present Mahanth received Colonel Olcott and you in durbar in presence of Bireswar Singh of Patna ?

Answer.—He did receive me individually. He received the Colonel, and I was give hospitality to pilgrims, pending the final settlement of the question of our right to take over charge of Mahâ-Bodhi either as tenants or as principals. To have allowed them to stop on the premises of the temple might have endangered their lives, and would only have prejudiced our cause, whereas by removing them we have aroused wide public sympathy. Events have proved that the opposition arrayed against us is the selfishness of the alleged owner of the ground upon which Mahâ-Bodhi stands, and not any combined unfriendliness of the Hindu community or any hostility of the Government, which keeps perfectly neutral.

Our next visit will be Benares, where we shall treat for the shrine of Sarnath at Isipatana, and report the result to you in due time.

H. S. OLCOTT,
Honorary Director and Chief Adviser, M. B. S.

H. DHARMAPÂLA,
General Secretary, M. B. S.

(Mahabodhi Society's Journal, March, 1893, pp. 7, 8.)

present. Bireswar Singh of Patna acted as interpreter on that occasion.

Question.—On that occasion is it true that Colonel Olcott told the Mahanth that the Buddhists were ready to treat with him either for the purchase or lease of the premises on equitable terms ?

Answer.—I was not present on that occasion. I was not present at the private interview. I was there, but what talk he had with the Mahanth I do not know.

Question.—Did he speak in English ?

Answer.—The interview was not in my presence, and I don't know. I was in an open hall, and Colonel Olcott and the Mahanth were in a room. I did not notice when they left the hall. I did not ascertain from Colonel Olcott what passed between him and the Mahanth at that interview. It is so long ago. I cannot say if he told me. The reference in the letter is to the present Mahanth. Individually I do not believe that the present Mahanth was spoken to on our behalf for the purchase or lease of the Temple. Col. Olcott did make some representations on behalf of the Buddhists. "The premises" in the letter refers to the Temple and the adjoining grounds. I do believe that Colonel Olcott in February, 1893, did make the proposal, but I have no personal knowledge of it. Except from reading the letter, I did not hear from any one that the Mahanth refused to sell or lease the premises. From that letter I believe it to be true that he did refuse.

Question.—Did you never have any talk with any human being about the proposed sale or lease of the Temple by the Mahanth ?

Answer.—So far as my recollection goes, I myself had no talk about that with any one.

Question.—Did you ever think of buying or taking a lease of the Temple from the Mahanth on behalf of the Buddhists ?

Answer.—Personally I did not, but I have suggested to the Buddhists that the place should be restored and occupied by the Buddhists. No talk ever took place in my presence with the Mahanth about it. I cannot say if any such talk ever took place in my presence with any one else. I may have had a talk about it, but I cannot remember with whom—it is a general vague thing. I have seen the late Mahanth. I had a talk with him through an interpreter, but not regarding the restoration or purchase or lease of the Temple.

I cannot say whether I ever described the Mahanth as a usurper before January last. I may have described him as such before that, but on the strength of what I saw in the newspapers. It was in the newspapers that I first saw that he was a usurper. I read this in the *Daily Telegraph* of London. I believe I first read it in 1886. That was before I had visited the Temple. I do not think I made any inquiry to verify this, after I visited the Temple in 1891. I had visited the Temple prior to July, 1893, about five or six times. It never, I think, struck me to verify the fact of the Mahanth's being a usurper before that, except on the occasion of Col. Olcott's visit in February, 1893. Even then I did not verify it, as that was the Colonel's interview, and I was not personally interested.

Question.—Although you visited the Temple five or six times after reading the article in the *Daily Telegraph*, it never struck you to inquire whether as a matter of fact the Mahanth had usurped possession of the Temple ?

Answer.—I never wanted to inquire. I did not care to inquire who was in actual possession, as the facts were so apparent, as I saw an inscription on the Temple that it had been restored by the British Government and under the custodianship of the Government itself.

Question.—Prior to July, 1893, did you believe that the Mahanth was not in actual possession ?

Answer—Certainly I believed he was not in actual possession.
[Witness asked why the date July 1893 was specified. Shown an article entitled "Progress of the Maha-Bodhi Movement" on page 1 of the Journal for July, 1893, with the second column turned down so that witness could not see it.]

Question.—Was that written by you ?

D. 5.

THE PROGRESS OF THE MAHA-BODHI MOVEMENT.

THE usefulness of such an organisation as the Maha-Bodhi Society is being realized by the Buddhists of different countries, if we are to judge of their sympathetic attitude towards it. No other international Society has been so much widely appreciated as the Maha-Bodhi Society, and the reason is simple, for our object is one that commands the sympathy of every educated man. Already we have co-adjutors in England, Spain, Germany, Austria, Sweden, United States and other countries in the West, and in Asia. All the Buddhist countries, with the exception of Cambodia, have promised us their co-operation. The Japanese Buddhists are working in earnest, and when the time comes, we hope they will take a large share in the glorious work of the Maha-Bodhi Society. Burma, the land of pious priests and good Buddhists, just now is prominent in giving her help to the work. A more generous, devoted people than the Buddhists of Burma could not be found. Every poor man and woman there is willing to contribute their mite to the Society's fund, and they have only to be appealed to. The sweet name of the Maha-Bodhi has a charm in the Buddhists' ear, and the very mention of the sacred Tree, under the lovely shade of which our blessed and merciful Tathagata sat and meditated, brings tears into the eyes of the pious Buddhists.

He who shows respect to the Bodhi Tree and worships it, is greatly reverential. He, as it were, worships Budho himself, and thereby gets rid of all sorrow. The site is sacred to the Buddhists, for it is under the great Tree that Prince Siddharta sat in calm meditation on the jewelled throne, the Vajrasana, which was created by the power of his moral merits.

This most blessed spot is now in the hands of a *Saivite* Mahant. Who as a *Saivite* has no more right to the place than he has over a Muhammedan shrine ; but, defying public opinion, he occupies the site, simply because he believes that the Government of Bengal is in his favour.

Are the Buddhists ready to buy up the sacred site? Decidedly so, and I am happy to announce that there are individual Buddhists ready to sacrifice their wealth to rescue this sacred spot from the hands of its usurpers.

On the 14th of May last I visited Burma, and returned to Calcutta on the 20th June, and during my visit to that land of pious Buddhists, I visited Mandalay, Myinmu and Moulmein, and called on the Buddhist Archbishop, the *ex*-Prime Minister of the late King Theebaw and other great officials, who have given me the assurance of their hearty co-operation in the work. In my interview with the ex-Prime Minister, he said that the late King Theebaw's father King Mindoon-min, had deputed him with presents to the great shrine at Maha-Bodhi, worth over Rs. 3,00,000, and that they were offered to the Tree, and that this offering is recorded in the marble inscription at Buddha-Gaya.—*H. Dharmapala.*

(Mahabodhi Society's Journal, July, 1893, pp. 1,2.)

Answer.—[*After glancing at first column.*] That first part was written by me. [*Shown the concluding portion of the article on page 2 and asked if he signed it.*] That is my signature on it. [*Shown whole article.*] The whole article is mine.

Question.—Did you in July, 1893, when you published this article, believe what you wrote : "This most blessed spot is now in the hands of a Saivite Mahanth?"

Answer.—I wrote that on hearing the reports.

Question.—Did you believe it or not ?

Answer.—It is a newspaper article based on newspaper reports.

Question.—Did you believe it or not ?

Answer.—I cannot say.

Question.—Could you have written what was untrue in your belief ?

Answer.—I can't say.

Question.—By the word "spot" in the passage, "The Buddhists are ready to sacrifice their wealth to rescue the sacred spot from the hands of its usurpers," did you mean the physical spot or the position of the Mahanth as a worshipper of Buddha ?

Answer.—I meant the physical spot. I cannot say that at the time I wrote the article, I believed the Mahanth to be in actual physical possession of the Temple.

Question.—Is it simply because you read an article to that effect in the *Daily Telegraph* in 1886 that you wrote that ?

Answer.—I can't say that. I do not know whether the explanation that I based my statement as to the Mahanth being a usurper on the article in the *Daily Telegraph* is true or not.

Question.—Read the article and say if in July, 1893, you believed the Mahanth was in physical possession of the Temple?

Answer.—I cannot give a decided answer. I individually never believed that he was in actual possession of the Temple. The article was merely a newspaper one.

Question.—Are you capable of writing in a newspaper article what you don't believe to be true?

Answer.—I should not write what individually I knew to be untrue.

Question.—Did you individually know this to be untrue?

Answer.—That is a complicated question, and I can't say. What I write is based on reports I hear at the time, and I have often contradicted myself.

[*Article put in and marked Exhibit D 5 as understood before.*]

Read over and admitted to be correct by the witness.

D. J. MACPHERSON,

3rd May, 1895. *Magistrate.*

4th May, 1895.

H. Dharmapala, further cross-examined on solemn affirmation, states:—

Since the Court adjourned yesterday, I have had a talk with one of my pleaders about my cross-examination, namely, with Babu Nand Kishore Lal, who asked me to find out all the passages in the Journal relating to Maha-Bodhi. He is my pleader. I have had no talk regarding the answer I gave yesterday. I have had no talk with any one regarding the answers and explanations I gave yesterday. I have since yesterday been going through the Journals, and marking passages. I have not taken advice as to what explanation I should give, if asked about other passages.

D. 6.

MAHA-BODHI SOCIETY.

PATRON.—Lozang Thub-dan Gya-Tcho, Grand Lama of Tibet.

PRESIDENT.—H. Sumangala, Pradhana Nayaka, Maha Thero, Ceylon.

VICE-PRESIDENTS.—The Thathanabaing of Mandalay, Burmah. The Lord Abbot Unsiyo Vajo, Tokio, Japan. Veligama Sri Sumangala, High Priest. Sri Dharmarama, High Priest. W. Subhuti Thero.

HONORARY DIRECTOR.—Colonel Henry Steel Olcott.

GENERAL SECRETARY.—H. Dharmapala.

HONY. LEGAL ADVISER.—Babu Nanda Kishore Lall, M. A., B. L.

OBJECTS OF THE MAHA-BODHI SOCIETY.

The moral, spiritual and intellectual state of the world's thought at the present moment has led to the founding of the Maha-Bodhi Society, which was formed at Colombo, in the Island of Ceylon, May 31st, 1891. Its object is to make known to all nations

[*Shown the cover of the last number of the Journal, namely, for April, 1895, pages II and III.*] That represents in a general way the object of the Maha-Bodhi Society. That was drafted by me, but corrected later on, not by me. The corrections were not made with my approval. I left the manuscript in the office in Calcutta and went away to Ceylon, and when I came back I found a corrected statement printed on the cover of the Journal. (*Witness asked not to read the document.*) The person who made the corrections was either Dr. J. Bowles Daly or the Manager of the Journal. I can't say who. I did not inquire which it was. They were made probably in September or October last, as I left Calcutta in August last. I have no actual recollection when I saw them first. I believe it was in September or October. I do not think I have before to-day expressed disapproval of the corrections made. The prospectus has been appearing in its altered form in the Journal monthly since November, 1894.

Question.—Is there any passage on page 2 or 3 of the cover which you did not write, but which you disapprove?

the sublime teachings of the Buddha, Sakya Muni, and to rescue, restore and re-establish as the religious centre of this movement the holy place Buddha-Gaya, where Prince Siddhartha attained supreme wisdom. At this sacred spot stands the Bodhi Tree, under whose shade the gentle Teacher sat, when the sunlight of spiritual truth dawned upon him.

From the time of Asoka, the great, until it was destroyed by the Muhammedans under Bhaktiyar Khiliji in 1202 A. D., there is an unbroken record showing with what veneration the Temple and the great Tree was held by the Buddhists. A stream of pilgrims from distant Corea, China, Tibet and from the nearer countries of Ceylon, Burma and Arakan flowed into this central shine during the fourteen centuries of Buddhist rule. Since the destruction of Buddhism in India by the Muhammedan Conquerors, it fell into decay until it was restored, after seven hundred years, by the British Government in 1880 at a cost of Rs 1,30,000.

At this thrice sacred spot it is proposed to re-establish a monastery for the residence of Bhikkhus Tibet, Ceylon, China, Japan, Burma, Siam, Cambodia, Chittagong, Nepal, Corea, and Arakan ; to found a College for training young men of unblemished character, of whatsoever race and country, for carrying abroad the message of peace and brotherly love promulgated by the divine Teacher twenty-four centuries ago.

". . The Saviour of the World,
Lord Buddha Prince Siddhartha styled on Earth—
In Earth and Heavens and Hells Incomparable,
All honored, Wisest, Best, most pitiful ;
The Teacher of Nirvana and the Law"

has enjoined on His devoted followers to proclaim His word. In the *Mahavagga*, He says : "Go ye, O Bhikkhus, and wander forth for the gain of the many, the welfare of the many, in compassion for the world, for the good, for the gain, for the welfare of gods and men. Proclaim, O Bhikkhus, the doctrine glorious. Preach ye a life of holiness, perfect and pure." Sir William Hunter, K.C.S.I., C.I.E., in his "Indian Empire," a volume of 850 pp. 8vo., mentioning the objects of the Maha-Bodhi Society, says : "A revival of Buddhism is, I repeat, one of the present possibilities in India. The life and teaching of Buddha are also beginning to exercise a new influence on religious thought in Europe and America."

International in its character, having its basis on no dogmas, entirely unsectarian, the Maha-Bodhi Society has carried on its work so far with the help of its sympathising friends. The accomplishment of the two great objects is the grand consummation which we hope to achieve before the dawn of the twentieth century. This could only be done by the co-operation of the Buddhists throughout the word. The Christians of England alone, have contributed last year to the following Christian Missionary Societies the enormous sum of £895,811.

British and Foreign Missionary Society...	£234,284
Church Missionary Society ...	252,226
Wesleyan Missionary Society	112,211
Society for the Propagation of the Gospel	113,079
London Missionary Society ...	117,572
Baptist Missionary Society ...	56,439

Buddhists, whether in Siam, Japan or Ceylon, have localized their energies, and that spirit which actuated the early Buddhists to spread abroad the teachings of their beloved Master is dormant in them. This I have observed during my travels in Japan, Burma, Siam, Arakan and Ceylon. That burning desire to "seek and save" should be again implanted in the minds of the young generation of priests and laymen. Of all charitable offerings the distribution of the wealth of Buddha's teachings is said to be supreme. Then why should we not unite and carry out the programme of the Maha-Bodhi Society ?

The restoration of the Temple, the building of Monastery, the founding of the International Buddhist College, it is estimated, will cost about 200,000 rupees. The time is ripe to sow the seed of Buddha's teachings on Indian and American soils. We want labourers, and these must be trained in India. They have to study the Indian vernaculars, Hindi and Bengalee, and also English. The idea of restoring the central shrine and transferring it from the hands of the usurping Saivite Mahants to the custody of Buddhist monks was suggested by Sir Edwin Arnold in 1886. Since the organization of the Maha-Bodhi Society, he is taking every possible interest in the work.

Subscriptions and Donations will be gratefully received by the undersigned, or they may be sent to the Representatives of the Society, whose names and addresses are given below. All moneys are deposited in the Bank of Bengal, Calcutta.

MEMBERSHIP.

Admission into membership of the Society is open to all without distinction of caste, creed or sex, the only pre-requisite being the candidate's sympathy with the Society's objects and willingness to help its work.

Membership is either *Active, Corresponding* or *Honorary*.

Corresponding Members are persons of distinction and learning who are willing to furnish information of interest to the Society.

Honorary Members are persons eminent for their knowledge of Buddhism or for their services to Humanity.

Active members are expected to occupy themselves as far as their circumstances permit, in the propagation of the Arya Dharma and all meritorious works.

SYMPATHIZERS.

For the encouragement of the poor who may wish to contribute something towards this noble work, the group of "Sympathizers" formed is hereby of all who may pay into the Fund not less than the sum of **8 annas** or its equivalent in any currency.

DIPLOMAS, FEES AND DUES.

It is the duty of all good Buddhists throughout the world to contribute as liberally as their means will allow towards the expenses of management and the permanent establishments of Buddha-Gaya and Calcutta. An Entrance Fee of **five rupees** must be paid by each candidate upon making application for membership, and a yearly subscription of **two rupees** is payable by each active member. The first yearly subscription is to be paid in advance upon admission to membership.

Answer.—I see nothing to disapprove of. The whole prospectus has my approval.

[Put in as general evidence of the objects of the society. The prosecution object that the whole cross-examination on the above points is irrelevant and the document now put in irrelevant also. Document admitted in evidence, and marked Exhibit D. 6.—D. J. M.]

A diploma of membership will be issued to each member.

General suggestions for useful Budhistic work will be issued from Head Quarters from time to time, and local officers and Secretaries of the Society are expected to direct and supervise the work in their respective countries.

DOGMAS.

The Society representing Buddhism in general, not any single aspect of it, shall preserve absolute neutrality with respect to the doctrines and dogmas taught by sections and sects among Buddhists. It is not lawful for anybody, whether a member or not, to attempt to make it responsible, as a body, for his own views. Membership being open to all, whether professed Buddhists or not, the Society is bound to guarantee them their rights as neutrals. It will be equally ready to publish expositions of all Buddhistic sects, but without committing itself to any one.

REPRESENTATIVES :

England.—Sir EDWIN ARNOLD, 225, Cromwell Road, Kensington, London, S. W.
" Professor T. W. RHYS DAVIDS, Chairman, Pali Text Society, 22, Albemarle Street, London, W.
" J. M. PARSONSON, Esq., 26, Moorgate Street, London, E. C.
" C. W. LEADBEATER, Esq., 17, Macfarlane Road, London, W.
" Dr. GEORGE WILLIAMSON, Guildford, Surrey.
Siam.—H. R. H. Prince CHANDRADAT CHUDADHAR, and H. R. H. Prince RAJASAKTI, Bangkok.
Japan.—S. HORIUCHI, Esq., Secretary, Indo-Busseki Kofuku Kwai, 1, Hachijo, Shiba Park, Tokio.
" THE SECRETARY, THE SOCIETY OF BUDDHIST AFFAIRS, Jokoji Teramachi dori, Shojo Sagaru, Kioto.
" Rev. D. S. MIZUNO, Buddhist Society, Nagoya.
" Mr. S. P. HIROSE, 3, 4 chom, Koamicho, Nihonbashi Ku, Tokio.
" Revd. S. YAMASHINA, Daianrakuji, Kodenmacho, Nihonbashi, Tokio.
Ceylon.—A. ULUWITA, Esq., Secretary, Lanka Maha-Bodhi Society, 61, Maliban Street, Colombo.
" D. B. JAVATILAKA, B.A., Head Master, Buddhist High School, Kandy.
Singapore.—TAN TEK SOON, Esq., *China Daily Advertiser* Office, Singapore.
Mandalay.—MOUNG BAW THAW, Judicial Commissioner's Court, Mandalay, Upper Burma.
Sweden.—Mr. TONNES ALGREN, C. E. Linnegatan, 25, Stockholm.
Burmah.—MOUNG HPAY, Extra Assistant Commissioner, Myinmu, Sagaing, Upper Burma.
" MOUNG PO KIN, K. S. M., President, Upasaka Society, Thayetmyo.
Arakan.—CHAN HTOON AUNG, Advocate, HTOON CHAN, B.A., B.L., KAUNG HLA PRU, } Secretaries, Arakan Maha-Bodhi Society, Akyab.
Darjeeling (India).—Lama UGEN GYATSHO, Rai Bahadur, Chief Interpreter, Secretary, Darjeeling Maha-Bodhi Society.
Australia.—MR. D. L. SIMAN HAMI, Homebush, Mackay, Queensland.
Austria.—DR. F. HARTMANN, Hallein.
California.—PHILANGI DASA, Editor, *Buddhist Ray*, Santa Cruz, Cal., U. S. A.
New York.—CHAS. T. STRAUSS, 466, Broadway, New York.
France.—Baron HARDEN HICKEY, Secretary, Propagande Bouddhique, Andilly par Montmorency, Seine-et-Oise, France.
" Prof. LEON D'ROSNY, 47, Avenue d'quesny, Paris.
Germany.—HERR FRIEDRICH ZIMMERMANN, Hohenheimerstr, 62, Stuttgart.
" DR. ARTHUR PFUNGST, Gartnerweg, 2, Frankfort-on-Maine.
All communications to be addressed to—

H. DHARMAPÂLA,
General Secretary, Maha-Bodhi Society,
2, *Creek Row, Calcutta, India.*

D. 7.

THE TEMPLE OF MAHÂ-BODHI.

IT is here ! Beyond the little village of mud-huts and the open space where dogs and children and cattle bask together in the dust, beyond the Mahunt's College, and yonder great fig tree which has split with its roots that wall, twelve feet thick, built before England had ever been discovered, is an abrupt hollow in the surface, symmetrical and well kept, and full of stone images, terraces, balustrades and shrines. It is oblong—as big perhaps, altogether as Bedford-square, and surrounded on its edges by small houses and buildings. From one extremity of the hollowed area rises with great beauty and majesty a temple of very special style and design. The plinth of the temple is square, with a projecting porch, and on the top of this soars to the sky a pyramidical tower of nine storeys, profusely embellished with niches, string courses and mouldings, while from the truncated summit of this an upper pinnacle rears itself of graceful form with a gold finial, representing the amalaka fruit. A smaller pyramidical tower stands at each corner of the roof of the lower structure, and there is a broad walk round the base of the Great Tower. Over the richly-worked porch which fronts the East, a triangular

(*Shown an article printed on pp. 2-4 of the Journal for July 1893, and headed "The Temple of Mahabodhi".*) I ordered the article printed there to be reproduced from the London *Daily Telegraph*. The author of it is Sir Edwin Arnold.

Question.—At the time you reproduced it, did you, so far as you know, believe it to contain a correct account of the history of the Temple ?

Answer.—I did not give the matter much thought, knowing Sir Edwin Arnold's sympathy with the movement. That *Daily Telegraph* was not sent to me, and I do not know if he sent it to the person I got it from. I read the article with interest and pleasure.

aperture is pierced, whereby the morning glory of the sun may fall through upon the gilded image seated in the sanctuary within. That image, you will perceive, is of Buddha, and this temple is the holiest and most famous, as well as nearly the sole surviving shrine of all "those eighty-four thousand erected to the Great Teacher by King Asoka two hundred and eighteen years after the Lord Buddha's *Nirvana*."

Yet more sacred even than the cool, dark sanctuary into which we look, to see the sun-beams kissing the mild countenance of the Golden Buddha inside; moie intensely moving to the Buddhists who come hither, and richer with associations of unspeakable interest and honour than King Asoka's stately temple and those stone railings carved with mermaids, crocodiles, elephants and lotus flowers, which the King himself commanded, and which still surround the shrine, is yonder square platform of stone, about a yard high from the ground, out of which a tree is growing. That is the Mahâ-Bodhi tree—in the opinion of superstitious votaries the very original Bodhi tree, miraculously preserved—but more rationally that which replaces and represents the ever-memorable shade under which the inspired Sidhartha sate at the moment when he attained *sambodhi*, the supreme light of its gentle wisdom. It is a fig tree—of the *ficus Indica* species—with the well-known long glossy leaves. Its stem is covered with patches of gold leaf, and its boughs are hung with streamers of white and coloured cloth, while at its root—frequently watered by the pious with sandal oil and attar of roses—will probably be seen sitting a Brahman priest of the Saivite sect intoning *mantras*. You will hear him say, "*Gayâ! Gayâ Sirse, Bodhi Gayâ*," for though he is praying on behalf of Mahratta pilgrims, and does not know or care for Buddha, the ancient formulas cling to the spot and to his lips. And, beyond all doubt, this is the spot, dear and divine, and precious beyond every other place on earth to all the 400 million Buddhists in China, Japan, Monogolia, Assam, Cambodia, Siam, Burma, Arakan, Nepaul, Tibet and Ceylon. This is the authentic place, and this the successor-tree, by many unbrokenly cherished generations of that about which my "Light of Asia" says:

> Then he arose, made strong by that pure meat,
> And bent his footsteps where a great Tree grew,
> The Bodhi tree (thenceforward in all years
> Never to fade, and ever to be kept
> In homage of the world), beneath whose leaves
> It was ordained the Truth should come to Buddh,
> Which now the Master knew; wherefore he went
> With measured pace, steadfast, majestical,
> Unto the Tree of Wisdom. Oh, ye worlds,
> Rejoice! Our Lord wended unto the Tree!

There is no doubt, in fact, of the authenticity of the site. The four most sacred places of Buddhism are Kapilavastu (now Bhüila), where Prince Sidhartha was born; Isipatna, outside Benares, where he first preached; Kusinagara, where he died, and this site, marked by the tree, whereat "in the full moon of Wesak," 2,480 years ago, he mentally elaborated the gentle and lofty faith with which he has civilised Asia. And of all those four the Tree-place here at Buddha-Gaya is the most dear and sacred to Asiatic Buddhists. Why, then, is it to-day

Question.—Before yesterday did it ever strike you the article contained anything you do not or ought not to approve of?

Answer.—No. I read the article yesterday after leaving Court.

Question.—Is there anything in it you now disapprove of?

Answer.—I think there are things to disapprove of in it.

Question.—Can you from memory, without looking at the article, say what these particular matters are?

Answer.—No, not from memory. I don't think I can remember what they refer to.

Question.—Did you mark in the book passages you disapproved of?

Answer.—No, but I marked some passages I considered striking.

(*Shown the article and asked whether the pencil marks on the margin are his*). Yes, these are marks I made.

[Article put in and marked D. 7, and marked passages as (*a*), (*b*), (*c*), (*d*), (*e*) and (*f*).]

Question.—Read these particular passages, and say if you disapprove of any statement or suggestion of fact in them.

Answer.—I cannot express approval of all that is stated in them unless I go into and study the history of all the facts.

Question.—Is there any statement of fact in these passages which is untrue to your present knowledge?

Answer.—There is one passage I disapprove of, namely (*f*), for I say the Mahanth has no control over the Temple. That statement is untrue. The other passages are practically a repetition of that one to which I object.

a { in the hands of Brahman priests, who do not care about the temple, except for the credit of owning it, and for the fees which they draw? The facts are these. } Until the thirteenth century—that is, for more than 1,400 years—it was exclusively used and guardianed by Buddhists, but fell into decay and neglect, like other Buddhist temples, on the expulsion of Buddhism from India. Three hundred years ago a wandering Saivite b { ascetic visited the spot, and settled down, drawing round him gradually the beginning of what is now the College of Priests established there. So strong have they since become in ownership that when the Bengal Government in 1880 was repairing the temple and its grounds, and begged for its embellishment from the Mahant, a portion of Asoka's stone railing, which he had built into his own house, the old Brahman would not give it up, and Sir Ashley Eden could not or did not compel the restoration. }

The Buddhist World had, indeed, well nigh forgotten this hallowed and most interesting centre of their faith—Mecca, the Jerusalem, of a million Oriental congregations—when I sojourned in Buddha-Gaya a few years ago. I was grieved to see Mahratta peasants performing *shraddh* in such a place, and thousands of precious ancient relics of carved stone inscribed with Sanskrit living in piles around. I asked the priest if I might have a leaf from the sacred tree.

"Pluck as many as ever you like, sahib," was his reply, "it is nought to us."

Ashamed of his indifference, I took silently the three or four dark shining leaves which he pulled from the bough over his head, and carried them with me to Ceylon, having written upon each the holy Sanskrit formula. There I found them prized by the Sinhalese Buddhists with eager and passionate emotion. The leaf presented by me to the temple at Kandy, for example, was placed in a casket of precious metal and made the centre of a weekly service, and there and then it befel that talking to the gentle and learned priests at Panadurè—particularly Sri Weligama—I gave utterance to the suggestion that the temple and its appurtenances ought to be, c and might be, by amicable arrangements with the Hindu College and by the favour of the Queen's Government, placed in the hands of a representative committee of the Buddhist nations.

I think there never was an idea which took root and spread so far and fast as that thrown out thus in the sunny temple court at Panadurè, amid the waving taliputs. Like those tropical plants which can almost be seen to grow, the suggestion quickly became a universal aspiration, first in Ceylon and next in other Buddhist countries. I was entreated to lay the plan before the Oriental authorities, which I did. I wrote to Sir Arthur Gordon, Governor of Ceylon, in these words : "I suggest a Governmental act which would be historically just, which would win the love and gratitude of all Buddhist populations, and would reflect enduring honour upon English administration. The temple and enclosure at Buddha-Gaya are, as you know, the most sacred spots in all the world for the Buddhists. . . . But Buddha-Gaya is occupied by a college of Saivite priests who worship Mahadeva there and deface the shrine with emblems and rituals foreign to its nature. That shrine and the ground surrounding it remain, however, Government property, and there would be little difficulty, after proper and friendly negotiations, in procuring the departure of the Mahant with his priests, and the transfer of the temple and its grounds to the guardianship of Buddhists from Ceylon and elsewhere. I have consulted high authorities, among them General Cunningham, who thoroughly sympathises with the idea, and declares it entirely feasible. . . . I apprehend that a certain sum of money might be required to facilitate the transfer of the Brahmans and to establish the Buddhist College. In my opinion a lakh of rupees could not be expended by either Government in a more profitable manner."

Sir Arthur, who had just been exploring Buddhist remains in Ceylon, was very well disposed to the idea. Lord Dufferin warmly received it, at Calcutta ; Lord Connemara, in Madras ; and at that time, if only the Home Government had been more alive to a grand opportunity, it would have been easy to make satisfactory terms with the Brahmans, and to have effected the transfer of the Holy place to a representative committee—at one stroke delighting and conciliating all Buddhistic Asia.

But two or three years passed by, and while the idea was spreading throughout Asia, and a large society had become established with special purpose of acquiring the guardianship of the Sacred Site, the Mahant growing more exacting in his expectations, clung closer to the possession of the temple. The letters which I received from the East showed that the old Brahman had memorialised the Government, in his alarm or avarice, and that local authorities had for quiet's sake reported adversely to the negotiation. I think the Mahant is a good man. I have never wished any but friendly and satisfactory arrangements with him. Yet if we walked in that spot which all these scores of millions of our race love so dearly, you would observe with shame and grief in the mango groves to the east of Lilajan statues plastered to the walls of an irrigating well near the village Mucharin, identified with the "Muchalinda" tank. Stones carved with Buddha's images are to be found used as weights to the levers for drawing water. I have seen ryots in the villages surrounding the temple, using beautifully carved stones as steps to their huts. I have seen 3 feet high statues in an excellent state of preservation, buried under rubbish to the east of the Mahant's Baradari. A few are plastered into the eastern outer wall of the garden along the bank of the Lilajan, and the Asoka pillars, the ancient relics of the site—indeed "the most antique memorials of all India"—which graced the temple pavement, are now used as posts in the Mahant's kitchen ! To rectify the neglect, and to make the temple what it should be, the living and learned centre of purified Buddhism, money was not and is not lacking. If the Home Government had seen its way to make the Mahant well disposed, I could have commanded any sum which might have seemed fair and necessary. But the idea was too intelligent for the official grasp, and the golden moment went by.

Nevertheless, Asia did not abandon its new desire, and I received so many and such pressing communications that I went at last to the new Indian Secretary of State, Lord Cross, always intelligent, kindly and receptive, and once more pleaded for the Great Restoration.

"Do you wish, Lord Cross," I asked, "to have 400 millions of Eastern peoples bless your name night and day, and to be for ever remembered in Asia, like Alexander, or Asoka, or Akbar the Great ?"

"God bless my soul, yes," answered the Minister, "how is that to be done ?"

Then I repeated all the above facts, and produced so happy an effect upon the Indian Minister's mind that he promised to consult the Council, and to write—if the idea were approved—to Lord Landsdowne. In due time the Viceroy replied that the idea was legitimate and beneficial, and that so long as no religious d ill-feeling was aroused, and no pecuniary grant asked from the Indian Treasury, the Calcutta Government would be inclined to favour any friendly negotiations. Thus the matter stood at my last visit to the East, when I was astonished and rejoiced to find how firmly the desire of this Restoration had taken root, and how, enkindled with the hope of it, Ceylon, Siam, Burma and Japan had become. The Mahâ-Bodhi Society, established to carry out the scheme, is constituted as follows :—

* * * * * * * * * * * *

To give some faint idea of the interest felt in this matter even among such remote communities as those of Japan, I will speak of a scene in Tokyo still vivid in my memory. Last summer, in the Japanese capital, the Buddhist High Priest, with certain of his fraternity, begged me to come to the Temple in Atago-shita and speak to the brethren about the Holy Places in India, and especially about the prospects of acquiring for the Buddhist world the guardianship of the Temple of the Tree. In the cool, dark inner court of that Japanese Tera, the priests and their friends sate on the white mats in concentric circles, eagerly listening while I told them about three or four hundred miles of Indian country lying between Busti in Oudh and Buddha Gayá in the Lower Provinces, which is the Holy Land of the "calm brethren of the yellow robe." I spoke of the birth-place and death-place of the Gentle Teacher, and showed them pictures which I had myself taken of the ancient building at Isipatana, outside Benares. The hot day, beating upon the hillside beyond the temple garden, shone upon the scarlet azaleas and the lotus-buds in the garden lake, and render it warm enough, even in that vast shadowy apartment, for a constant flutter of fans, while now and then a young priest from the outer circle would glide away for drinking water. But, when I came to paint for them that site of the stately Temple—which, from its hollow beside the Bodhist-tree, looks over the hills of the "Thousand Gardens," and marks the spot where the religious history of Asia was transformed, and its manners for ever stamped with the merciful tenderness and indestructible hopes of Buddhism—those hundreds of priests and novices sate like rows of little children lost in a fairy story. The fans were laid aside, the shaven heads were craned forward in intense desire to hear every word ; old men laid their hands to their ears, and young ones leaned towards me with clasped palms, to learn all about the Tree, and the Temple, and the broken statues, and the Hindu priests who do not care for the spirit of the place, e and who ought, in a friendly way, to yield it up—on proper conditions—to Buddhist guardianship. Every man present would have given all he possessed, I think, to help towards such an end. As for their unworthy guest, they lavished upon me marks of pleasure and gratitude; they spread me out an outrageously elaborate feast table in the Temple pavilion; and sent with me back to my lodgings servants carrying presents of books and boxes of beautiful Japanese silks and embroideries. Since then the High Priest writes to me thus from Tokyo:

"Since your regretted departure from Japan the Indo-Busseki Kofuku Society has not been idle, and now I am glad to inform you that we are trying to buy a certain piece of land near each of the sacred sites according to your kind advice to us. Mr. Dharmapâla, of the Mahâ-Bodhi Society, is doing all he can to help us in India, and if everything goes as intended, a certain number of Japanese monks will start for India within this year."

Thus is this new and great idea spreading, and the world will not be very much older before Buddhism by this gateway goes back to its own land, and India becomes the natural centre of Buddhistic Asia. I suppose there are some people who will ask why should the British public take any concern in such a movement. But these will be of much the same as those who go about inquiring, "What is the British Empire to Batter sea?" Apart from the immense historical, religious and social importance of Buddhism in Asia, here is an opportunity for the Government of India to gratify and conciliate half that continent by the easiest and least costly exercise of good-will. The Mahant and his college will, no doubt, have to be bought out, and rather expensively, now that delays have made him master of the bargaining. But if an enlightened Minister and Viceroy will—as they may—facilitate the arrangement, all must end well, and grateful Buddhists would furnish whatever cash is
f requisite. No orthodox Hindus will be wounded in sentiment, because by strict truth, the Mahant, as Brahman and follower of Sankarâcharya, goes against his *shastras* by keeping control of a Buddhist temple. However, it brings him so much personal dignity and so much money that these things must be compounded for, no doubt; yet a well-disposed Collector and a farseeing Government could find a score of pleasant ways to make him willing to give up his tenure. There is no room left me to dwell upon the happy consequences which would flow to the Indian Viceroyalty and to India herself from the good-will stirred in Burmah and Siam. Buddhism would return to the place of its birth, to elevate, to spiritualise, to help, and enrich that population. It would be a new Asiatic Crusade, triumphant without tears, or tyranny, or blood; and the Queen's Administration would have the glory and benefit of it. The *Hindu* of Madras, a leading native journal, writes: "If there is anything in the intellectual and moral legacies of our ancient forefathers of which we may feel proud, it is that sublime, pure and simple conception of a religious and moral system which the world owes to Buddha. Educated Hindus cannot hesitate in helping Buddhism to find a commanding and permanent footing once more in their midst, and to live in mutually purifying amity with our Hinduism itself." It is, indeed, for an enlightened British Minister, "a splendid opportunity."—*Daily Telegraph.*

(Mahabodhi Society's Journal, July, 1893, pp. 2-4.)

I know Babu Narendra Nath Sen. He is not a Buddhist. He is a personal friend of mine. The firm Narendra Nath Sen and Co. are my attorneys in Calcutta. I see in his paper that he is editor of the *Indian Mirror*. He has been advocating the part of the Buddhists in regard to the Temple in that paper. At page 6 of the Journal for March 1893 is an article headed "The Buddhist Mission in India and the duty of the Hindus towards it," extracted from the *Indian Mirror*, of which I ordered the reproduction.

Question.—Did you at that time approve of all that was in it?

Answer.—Its general tone was so sympathetic that I ordered its reproduction. I did not at the time give serious thought to it, as to whether there was anything in it I disapproved of. Consequently it did not strike me then there was anything to disapprove of. I cannot just now without reading it say from memory whether there is anything in it that to my knowledge is untrue.

(*Asked to read the article.*)

Question.—Is there any statement of fact in it untrue to your present knowledge?

Answer.—I take objection to two passages, namely, the one relating to Buddha being revered by Hindus as one of the ten incarnations of Vishnu, and the other as to the claims of the Mahanth as in charge of the Temple being satisfied.

[Article put in, marked Exhibit D 8 and the passages as (*a*) and (*b*).]

D. 8.

THE BUDDHIST MISSION IN INDIA, AND THE DUTY OF THE HINDUS TOWARDS IT.

THE Mahâ-Bodhi Society of Calcutta, which may now be said to be established on a firm basis, is an unique institution, the first and only one of its kind in India. It represents, in a word, the Buddhist Mission in this country. With the spread of European education and influence, and the consequent awakening of a spirit to work, and attain progress among some of the Asiatic nations, that have been, as it were, sleeping for ages, the followers of the prevailing religions in Asia are showing signs of making strenuous efforts to put forth the merits of their respective faiths before the world, and claim adherence to their doctrines and principles. The Hindus have been preaching the peculiar merits of their faith; the Mahomedans have established Missions in some English and European towns. Why should the Buddhists, then, remain in the background? The Mahâ-Bodhi Society is a sign of the renewed health and activity of Buddhism. The Society's objects are few and simple. Firstly, to train Missionaries for the spread of the Buddhist faith, secondly, to establish a college for the teaching of the Buddhistic Shastras in Pali and in Sanskrit; and, thirdly, to restore to the Buddhists the absolute control of the temple at Buddha-Gaya, and several other sacred Buddhistic sites in India. The Society is under the patronage of the Buddhist High Priest in Ceylon, and has the support of some of the leading oriental scholars of Europe, who have made Buddhism their special study.

India is the birth-place of Buddhism, and though practically driven out of its limits by the Hindus, and for a long time flourishing as the prevailing religion of other Asiatic countries, both far from and near our shores, the influence of that cult is yet visible on Hindu religion, Hindu thought, and Hindu practices. Nor can it be said that the Hindus regard with any very deep animosity the founder and followers of Buddhism. Buddha, as is well known, is revered

a as one of the ten incarnations of Vishnu, and for aught we know, there is not a single Hindu, who underrates the greatness and majesty of the character of that religious reformer. We cannot, therefore, account for the ill-feeling, that seems to have been excited in some parts of the country at the attempt, which is now being made by some enthusiastic Buddhists of Ceylon, China and Japan to revive Buddhism in this country. The Hindus claim for themselves the credit for a spirit of religious toleration, and if there be any system of faith in the world, the followers of which can count upon the sympathy of the Hindus, it is Buddhism. For it was born and nurtured in India, was, in fact, an offshoot of the Hindu religion, and has always inculcated truths, which, far from being foreign to Hinduism, are, as it were, of it. Under the *pax Brittanica*, every religionist in India has the fullest liberty and the widest scope to disseminate the doctrines of his own faith. The Christians and the Mahomedans have their own Missions, and generally speaking, they have not to contend against any marked

b Hindu opposition. Why should not Buddhism be treated with the same charitable spirit of high-minded toleration? Why should not the Buddha-Gaya temple be restored to the Buddhists, after the *just* claims, if any, of the Mahant, in charge of the temple, have been satisfied? Why should not leading Hindus come forward to arbitrate between the Hindu Mahant and the Buddhist Missionaries, and bring about a compromise, satisfactory to both? Is it not against the principles of true Hinduism to give offence to the religious instincts of the followers of another faith by refusing to them the possession and absolute control of a temple, which contains the image of their prophet, and includes a site which is held sacred by them? We feel that it would be to the lasting shame of the Hindus, if a contest is allowed by them to be raged over this question of the restoration of the Buddha-Gaya temple to the Buddhists. It is the duty of the leaders of Hinduism of the day to rise above all petty feelings and narrow prejudices, and offer evidence of magnanimity by deciding the matter in a manner that would be consonant with their professed love for toleration and charity on occasions, when a fellow-man's religious feeling is in danger of being hurt and wounded.—(*Indian Mirror*).

(Mahabodhi Society's Journal, March, 1893, p. 6).

I do not object to anything else. I say that after having read the whole article. I may have myself written long ago things without proper information to which I should now take exception. Before yesterday it did not strike me that I may have done so.

D. 9.

THE RESTORATION OF OUR INDIAN SHRINES AND THE WORK OF THE MAHA-BODHI SOCIETY.

THE four sites associated with the divine memory of the Tathagato are sacred to the Buddhists. At the close of His career of blessed usefulness, extending for a period of 45 years, while resting for the last time under the *sâl* trees in the "Salavanodyana" park of the Molliyan Princes at Kusinara, addressing Ananda. He said: "There are four places whose sight will gladden the hearts of my devotees, *viz.*, the birth-place of the Tathagato, the place where He attained supreme knowledge, the place where He first promulgated the Dharma; and the place where He attained the *anupâdisèsa* Nirvana. The sight of these four places, Ananda, will gladden the hearts of my Bhikkhus, Bhikkhunis, Upasakas and Upasikas, and they who pass away from this world with pure thoughts while visiting them, will be reborn in the happy realms of Swarga (heaven)."

These four hallowed sites are Kapilavastu, Uruvela in Buddha-Gaya, Isipatana in Benares, the present Sarnath, and Kusinara,—all within an area of four hundred miles between Busti in Oude and Buddha-Gaya in Lower Provinces. During seven centuries of Moslem rule, from 1200 A. D. to 1830 A. D., the holy land of the Buddhists was forbidden ground to them; and since the advent of the British, they have again turned their attention for the recovery of these places.

Since the destruction of the Buddhist Empire in India, and for the first time in the history of modern Buddhism, an organised effort is being made by the several Buddhist nations to restore these shrines to their legitimate custodians.

Sir Edwin Arnold, the author of that incomparable epic, the "Light of Asia," was the first to draw public attention to their neglected state. In the latter part of the year 1885, in a letter to the Government of India, he wrote: "It is certainly painful to one who realizes the immense significance of this spot in the History of Asia and of Humanity, to wander round the precincts of the holy tree and to see scores and hundreds of broken sculptures lying in the jungle or on brick heaps scattered: some delicately carved with incidents of the Buddha legend, some bearing clear and precious inscriptions in early or later characters." Later on, in a letter to Sir Arthur Gordon, the then Governor of Ceylon, he wrote: "I am venturing to suggest to you a Governmental act which would be historically just, which would win for you the love and gratitude of all your Buddhist population, and would

Question.—In the number of April 1893, did you write the article headed "The Restoration of our Indian Shrines and the work of the Maha-Bodhi Society?"

Answer (*before waiting to hear the title*). Yes.—I may have visited Bodh Gaya twice before writing that article.

Question.—Was the following statement in it true to your knowledge:—'But Budh Gaya is occupied by a college of Saivite priests who worship Mahadeva and deface the shrine with emblems and ritual foreign to its nature?"

Answer.—These are not my words, they are an extract incorporated into it. I did not know the facts then, and simply quoted the words. I had not verified them by then. I quoted the words as expressing sympathy with us; I entertained at the time no belief on the subject. I wrote the words in the article, "The imperishable associations of the place........made me stay there and do all that was in my power for the restoration of the place to its legitimate custodians."

Question.—Did you at the time believe that to be true?

Answer.—I wrote these words as a journalist writes what information he gets at the time and what strikes him, but the information may or may not be true. He writes the current information of the day, but this may be liable to rectification subsequently. I did not as a journalist correct that.

[Article put in: marked Exhibit D9; and passages quoted (*a*) and (*b*).

reflect enduring honour upon your administration. It is this : The temple and enclosure at Buddha-Gaya are, as you know, the most sacred spots in all the (a) world for the Buddhists. But Buddha-Gaya is occupied by a college of Saivite priests who worship Mahadeva and deface the shrine with emblems and rituals foreign to its nature. That shrine and the ground surrounding it remain, however, Government property, and there would be little difficulty after proper and friendly negotiations in procuring the transfer of the temple and its grounds to the guardianship of Buddhist monks."

No action was taken in the matter until the formation of the Maha-Bodhi Society on the 31st of May, 1891, in the island of Ceylon, under the presidency of the Venerable H. Sumangala, Pradhana Nayaka Sthavira.

In the Ceylon *Buddhist* of May 29th, 1891, I wrote: "During my sojourn in this venerable spot made sacred by him whom we adore as our Master, it was my happiness to have revived the subject mooted by Sir Edwin Arnold. I visited the place in company with a Japanese Priest (Kozen Gunaratana) the (b) would-be successor of the High Priest of the Shingon-su sect, on the 24th January last. The imperishable associations of the place influenced me so much that a strange impelling force came over me and made me to stay there and do all that was in my power for the restoration of the place to its legitimate custodians—the members of the holy Sangha—I held communications with my co-religionists in Japan, Burma, Siam, India, and with my countrymen in Ceylon— ———" Thanks to my Sinhalese brothers, without whose help I could not have commenced the work, the pioneers of the Buddha-Gaya Mission started for India on the 10th July, 1891, by the P. and O. Company's steamer *Rosetta*. On the 21st of that month—the full-moon day of Asalha—four Bhikshus were permanently stationed there for the first time, since the extirpation of Buddhism from India, by the Maha-Boddhi Society, and the Buddhist flag hoisted. Three months later—on the 31st October—an international Buddhist Conference was held on the spot, the proceedings of which I now put on record :—

"Present : Japanese Delegate—Y. Ato, C. Tokuzawa ; Ceylon—Kozen Gunaratana Bhikshu and H. Dharmapala ; China—Lama To-Chiya of the Yung-Ho Kung temple, Pekin ; Chittagong—Mr. Krishna Chandra Chowdhry and Girish Chandra Dewan, Chakma Sub-Chief, Hill Tracts, and Amal Khan Dewan.

"The Secretary read letters from Prince Chandradat of Siam, Moung Shoung, Secretary of the Burmese-Pali Text Society, Rangoon, Sir Edwin Arnold, Baron Harden Hickey of France.

(c) "Mr. Tokuzawa said that he is authorised by the Nishi Honganji temple authorities to announce to the Conference that they are willing to buy the Temple from the Mahant.

"Y. Ato, the Japanese Delegate, said that he has come to make inquiries about the temple, and that if the Mahant gives a written document, stating the amount he wants for the temple, that all the sects of Japan would then raise funds for the purpose.

After long discussion, it was resolved that a deputation should not wait on the Mahant to make any proposal about the purchase of the Buddha-Gaya temple. It was resolved to call for subscriptions from all Buddhist countries to build the Monastery.

(Mahabodhi Society's Journal, April, 1893, p. 3.)

I think I must adhere to the statement I made yesterday that I had no talk with any person about the sale or lease of the Temple.

Question.—Have you tried to raise money for the restoration of the Temple ?

Answer.—I am doing so for the movement. The restoration of the Temple is mingled with the general object of the Budh Gaya movement, and it is impossible to distinguish particular objects. I ordered the publication in the Journal of the passage shown me at page 1 of the number for June, 1893. It is a translation from Singhalese papers, but I don't know if I made it myself.

D. 10.

THE CEYLON PRESS AND THE MAHÂ-BODHI MOVEMENT.

THE leading Singhalese papers—the *Lakminipahana, Sarasavisandaresa* and the *Dinakaraprakasa*—have in powerful leaders, cordially commended the work initiated by the Maha-Bodhi Society. The amount that we require for the restoration of this sacred site is only a lakh of rupees—50,000 dollars. The possession of this glorious spot means the rehabitation of the Arya Dharma in India. Ye who call yourselves S'ákya putra Sramanas, arise from your lethargy and try to avail of the splendid opportunity now given to you.

(Mahabodhi Society's Journal, June, 1893, p. 1.)

[Paragraph put in and marked Exhibit D10.]

I keep a diary. I do so in my private capacity. It may be I may write in it things I don't believe to be true, as I write what I may hear. On pages 6-8 of the number of the Journal for December, 1893, I published my diary leaves which I sent from Chicago. I wrote the passage contained in the first two sentences of the last paragraph on page 7, about Rs. 100,000 being required for getting the Temple into our possession.

Question.—Did you at that time believe it to be true ?

Answer.—I wrote what I had heard. Whole paragraph put in and marked Exhibit D11.] By "the parties concerned" there, I meant the Tikari Raj and not the Mahanth. I swear that. I wrote the passage at the end of the paragraph about the presents made by the King of Burmah to the Tree and entrusted to the Mahanth. When I did so I wrote what I had been told by a gentleman, and I at the time believed what he said to be true.

D. 11.

* The momentous subject to the millions of Buddhists is the acquisition of the Central Shrine at Buddha-Gaya by them, and when I formally accepted the invitation of Dr. Barrows to attend the Parliament of Religions, never did I anticipate of coming events of the greatest significance in connection with the Temple question. A friend, who takes the deepest interest in our cause, confidentially informed me that the payment of one hundred thousand rupees to the parties concerned will bring the Temple into our possession, and only three months were allowed

to us to raise the money. On the 31st of March I received this intelligence, and by the end of June I was to start for Chicago. A hundred thousand rupees for a great work in a Christian country could be raised within a few hours, and here was an important case to test the generous nature of the Buddhists. I wrote to my friends in Japan, Siam, Arakan, Burma and Ceylon to lose no time in the work of collection, and that the money must be ready before the time allowed to us. Two and a half years of uninterrupted work by a strange coincidence reached its climax at a crisis. If the lakh of rupees was ready, I could undertake my mission with ease; and the uncertainty of getting the money was a source of deep anxiety to me. "Will not the Buddhists" I thought, "rescue the sacred site, the blessed spot where Buddha attained wisdom to gain which he had for æons of ages, birth after birth, made himself a sacrifice for the sake of Humanity?" Time was approaching near, and yet there was no hopeful response from any Buddhist country. Burma, the country of good priests and pious people, was the nearest place where I could go to make the appeal, and on May 13th I left Calcutta for Rangoon and arrived there on the 16th. During my stay in Rangoon I called on all the influential Buddhists and explained to them the situation of affairs. At a meeting held on the 21st May, they decided to raise the money, and assured me of their loyalty to the cause. This was good but still I was not satisfied, and leaving these brothers I went to Mandalay at the request of my esteemed colleague Moung Hpay to confer with the Archbishop of the Buddhists Church in Burma. This venerable chief prelate showed his hearty sympathy with the work and promised to take urgent measures regarding the work. I called on the ex-Prime Minister of Burma Kin Woon Mengee, and he expressed his regret that he could not help the movement for he had no influence over the people since the fall of the Burmese government; and that if the king was on the throne of Burma, the required lakh of rupees could be got from the Royal Treasury at a moment's notice, and he said that the late King Mindoon Ming had sent presents to the great Temple valued about three hundred thousand rupees and that he was head of the Mission that went to Buddha-Gaya taking these presents, and that they were entrusted to the Mahant after they were offered to the Tree, and that an account of the Mission was engraved on a marble stone slab and set up within the Temple premises.

I have delivered lectures in different parts of Asia and America.

Question.—What you say in them do you believe to be true?

Answer.—At times I give in them reports of what others say. I delivered a lecture in the Royal Library at Bangkok in February, 1895. A report of that lecture appeared in the *Bangkok Times*, and I sent a copy of that newspaper to the Managing Editor of the Maha-Bodhi Journal, and I am not responsible for its publication in the latter. I do not think I read the report in the *Bangkok Times* carefully before sending it. I may have glanced at it after it appeared in the Journal. The report appears at page 5 of the Journal for February, 1893.

D. 12.

The Mohammedans and Christians have not forgotten their sacred sites in Mecca and Jerusalem. To restore the Holy Sepulchre the Christians in their devotion to Christ sacrificed not only gold but blood which is more than gold, and life which is more than blood. Two hundred thousand human beings perished in their attempt to restore the sacred site. After seven hundred years we are called upon to restore the site sacred to the Buddhists, and we want not blood; but only fifty thousand dollars. To our unutterable grief the Buddhists are not allowed

a { to even sojourn in the place dearest to them; and unless we purchase the land which belongs to the temple there is no hope of our ever getting back the guardianship of the holy spot.

b { For the first time in the history of modern Buddhism an attempt is being made by the Maha-Bodhi Society to bring about the religious unification of the Buddhist countries of Asia, and to re-establish Buddhism in India. So far the movement has received the sympathy of all Buddhist nations.

c { These extracts from the *Bangkok Times* will give the lie to the announcement in certain newpapers that the *Arnold-Olcott* venture to restore the Maha-Bodhi Temple to the Buddhists has been abandoned. (Mahabodhi Society's Journal, December, 1893, pp. 6-8).

(*Shown the paragraphs at page 6 and 7 beginning "The Mohammedans," "For the first time," and "These extracts" respectively: reads them.*) The first two of these are reports of what I said. I may have used the words in the last paragraph, but, if so, I did it in my ignorance. I take exception to them. (Put in and marked Exhibit D12, (*a*), (*b*), and (*c*.)

D. 13.

The Maha-Bodhi Society has accomplished so far quite a unique work. To the Buddhists of Burma, Ceylon, Tibet, Sikkhim, Chittagong, Arakan, Japan and China, I have personally delivered the great message to restore the sacred sites at Buddha-Gaya, Benares, Kapilavastu and Kusinara, and resuscitate Buddhism in India.

On page 4 of the same number of the Journal is a paragraph beginning "the Maha-Bodhi Society" which I wrote. (Put in and Marked Exhibit D13.)

D. 14.

INSULT TO THE BUDDHISTS OF JAPAN! THE MAHANT OF BUDDHA-GAYA REFUSES TO ALLOW THE IMAGE OF LORD BUDDHA TO BE PLACED IN THE TEMPLE.

THE following article is reprinted from the *Indian Mirror* (Calcutta) of May 25, 1894, and will, with the correspondence following, fully explain itself; and we

At page 10 of the number for June, 1894, is an article headed "Insults to the Buddhists of Japan," which reproduces another extracted from the *Indian Mirror*, which I caused to be inserted in the Journal. The editorial part of it was written in my presence, and may be taken as mine. At the time I approved of the article. (Put trust, with this effect, that all Buddhists will protest against the highhanded action of the Mahant, and not rest until full reparation is accorded to them. We also expect that the British Government will give us that protection which is justly due to us, by enforcing the Mahant to compliance with the wishes and rights of the Buddhists.

in and marked Exhibit D14; witness did not read the article.) Immediately after is a letter I wrote to the *Indian Mirror*, which I caused to be reproduced in the Journal. (Put in and marked Exhibit D15.)

THE BUDDHISTS AND THE HINDU MAHANT OF THE MAHA-BODHI TEMPLE AT BUDDHA-GAYA.

VERY bad news has reached us from Buddha-Gaya. It appears that Mr. Dharmapala, Secretary to the Maha-Bodhi Society, accompanied by the High Priest of Japan, went recently to Buddha-Gaya for the purpose of setting up a sacred image of Lord BUDDHA said to be seven hundred years old, in the historic, Maha-Bodhi temple there. Mr. Dharmapala had previously communicated with the Collector of the District, and obtained through him the consent of the Hindu Mahant, who is in possession of the temple, for the enshrining of the image. The ceremony was to have taken place on the 19th instant, a day considered to be very sacred by the Buddhists, but at the eleventh hour, the Mahant changed his mind, and refused permission to have the image set up in the Maha-Bodhi temple. If the Buddhists had insisted upon their rights, there would have been a sanguinary riot, for, we are told, several thousand men had been got together by the Mahant to enforce his churlish refusal. A detailed account of the occurrence has been sent to us by Mr. Dharmapala, and we have given it a prominent place in another column, so that Government may know exactly its duty in the matter. Let it be known that the image was the gift of all Japan to the holiest of Buddhistic shrines, and that the Buddhist Archhishop of Japan came all the way to India to set it up with befitting pomp and ceremony in the Maha-Bodhi temple at Buddha-Gya. We can, then, well conceive the magnitude of the insult, given by the Mahant in the name of the Hindu nation to not only the Japanese, but also to all the Buddhistic races in the world. The duty of the Hindus is clear, they must repudiate both the Mahant and his utterly unjustifiable attitude towards the Buddhists of late. Several comparatively unimportant images have been set up before now by the Burmese Buddhists in the temple at Buddha-Gya, and the Mahant did not once object. Buddhists have always worshipped in that temple, and brought rich gifts, and the Mahant has thriven fat, and this is the sort of gratitude with which he has repaid them! The present insult to Japan is such that whatever reparation the man may be compelled to make, cannot be considered too much. The Buddhists have hitherto dealt much too indulgently with him, so that there seems to be no limit now to his sauciness. The Maha-Bodhi temple is not a Hindu temple, though it has passed into the possession of a Hindu Mahant. The temple by right belongs to the Buddhists; it is their holiest shrine, and when they are ready and willing to make adequate recompense to the Mahant to forego his possession, why should they not get back their own? Are Hindus so intolerant and rapacious as to encourage the Mahant in his unjust and violent acts? We think not, and we are sure all enlightened Hindus deeply sympathise with the Buddhists in their pious attempt to re-obtain by all lawful means the possession of their holiest shrine. But the armed resistance of the Mahant to the setting up of an image of BUDHA in the Maha-Bodhi temple, and that after he had once definitely consented, is an event from which very serious complications are likely to arise. It cannot be that Japan will quietly bear the gross insult, offered by this Hindu priest, and not only the Japanese, but every Buddhist, will consider the insult as given to Gautama's entire flock. When the news of the outrage reaches Japan, her indignation will be something which we would not like to picture to ourselves. The insult will be considered as given not only by a Hindu priest or the Hindu people, but also by the British Government of India. If the Government take no immediate action in the matter it will at once alienate the sympathy of Japan, China and Siam, and political consequences may ensue, for which it is not prepared. After the recent occurrence at Buddha-Gaya, the continued possession of the Maha-Bodhi temple by a Hindu Mahant will lead to dreadful results. Let the Mahant have whatever compensation is just under the circumstances, but he must go. The Maha-Bodhi Society was established by Buddhists to get back their temple. We understand that Government at one time sympathised with the principal object of that Society. But the cow riots have apparently unnerved it, and the Buddhists are left to the mercy of the Mahant. That priest has now taken the law into his own hands. But let the Government of India reflect what it all means. We assure it that the number of Hindus would be very small who would not be glad to see the restoration of the Maha-Bodhi temple to the Buddhists. Let the Government ascertain the fact for itself and it can easily satisfy itself. But Government must know that this last act of the Mahant is no less a disgrace to itself than it is to him, or to the Hindus on whose behalf he pretends to speak.

D. 15.

THE BUDDHISTS AND THE HINDU MAHANT AT BUDDHA-GAYA.

[TO THE EDITOR OF THE "INDIAN MIRROR."]

SIR,—Things have come to a crisis. The Mahant did not allow the Buddhist to set up the image in the Maha-Bodhi temple, brought from Japan, as had been previously arranged. Several months' notice was given to the Collector that a holy image would have to be placed there; and a month ago, the Collector, after having consulted with the Mahant, wrote to me to say that the image could be enshrined in the temple on the 19th instant, the full moon day, being the anniversary of the birth and of enlightenment of Lord Buddha. Every preparation was made, and a lot of expenses incurred to celebrate the festival, as it was the first of the kind after the expulsion of the Buddhists, 700 years ago. Two days previously, the Mahant became aggressive, and refused to let us have the image set up in the temple. His arguments were that the temple is Hindu, and that unless he consulted the Hindus, he could no allow us to set the image up, and that if they consented thereto, then a *pranpratishta* ceremony should be performed. Nearly a dozen of images have been set up by the Burmese in the temple, but no objection, was ever raised; and for the first time, this aggressiveness is shown by the Mahant. The Mahant after having organised his people to attack us, came to Gaya, and then went to Patna to see the Commissioner. As the District Magistrate, Mr. Macpherson, feared a riot, I had to put off the ceremony of placing the image, sent by the great Japanese nation; an image, 700 years old, full of historic interest, and presented by the nation to be enshrined in the Central Temple of the Buddhists. And when the Buddhists, according to precedent, go to set it up, nearly 5,000 men, armed with *lattis*, &c., are prepared to resist this benevolent action! A great nation is insulted, and the Buddhists who have the right and freedom to perform worship in their own temple, are coerced by an aggressive mob, and yet the British Government take no action. The image could not be placed in the temple; and I am at a loss to know what to do with it. If I return it to Japan, it will be an insult to the nation, and it is so historic that I cannot keep it here to decay.

On account of the selfishness of one man, several millions of Buddhists are put to pain.

Yours, &c.,

Gya, the 21st May, 1894. (Mahabodhi Society's Journal, June, 1894, pp. 10-11). H. DHARMAPALA.

D. 16.

THE HINDU MAHANT AND THE BUDDHA-GAYA TEMPLE.

THE Central Shrine of the Buddhists, the hallowed spot where Prince Sakya Sinha attained supreme Enlightenment and elaborated that system of faith, which has for 24 centuries swayed the destinies of millions upon millions of Asiatic peoples, has by an irony of fate gone out of the hands of Buddhists. For 17 centuries it remained under Buddhist sovereigns of India, until it was destroyed by the Musulman Conquerors of India about 700 years ago. Since the destruction of Buddhism in India in 1200 A. D. until the advent of the British, the great temple remained neglected. It was in the early part of the present century that Archæologists first turned their attention in making researches into the history of the temple.

In 1509 A.D. the founder of the *Sanaysi* Math of Buddha-Gaya took up his residence somewhere near the temple, and it was then a "sylvan solitude." The village of Taradih whereon the ruins of the temple stood was given by a *firman* to the Sanyasi Lal Gir about the year 1711 A.D. by His Majesty Muhammad Shah Padshah Gazi "*so that all produce of the said property be used by him for his own livelihood and that of the itinerant faqirs.*" It is evident that the temple was then not the scene of either Buddhist or Hindu pilgrimage.

In 1822 the first Burmese Embassy arrived in India and worshipped the Bodhi Tree and since then the place again began to be visited by the Buddhists.

In 1874 the King Mindoon Min of Burma sent an Embassy and commenced the restoration of the great temple; but His Majesty's lamented death prevented the Burmese Commissioners to complete the work. Fortunately His Honor Sir Ashley Eden, the then Lieutenant-Governor of Bengal interfered, and in the interest of Archæology, took up the work of restoration, in 1880 and at a cost 1,30,000 rupees, completed it. The Burmese rest-house which now stands to the west of the temple, was erected by the Burmese Commissioners for the permanent residence of Buddhist priests who were sent to live there by the King.

The Mahant is a Hindu Sivite, and as such could not co-operate with the Buddhists in their worship, and the temple remained always Buddhistic. Since the establishment of the Maha-Bodhi Society, the whole Buddhistic world has turned its attention to the temple, and the Mahant now attempts to convert it into a place of Hindu worship. He is using his wealth and influence to accomplish his ignoble ends; but he will not succeed. The Buddhists have perfect faith in the British Government, and they hope that His Honor Sir Charles Elliott, Lieutenant-Governor of Bengal, will enforce on the Mahant not to interfere with the Buddhists in their worship in the Maha-Bodhi temple.

(Mahabodhi Society's Journal, July, 1894, p. 20).

D. 17.

Magah to the present day is a Buddhist country. It is covered with ruins of temples, and, in frequent fields, Buddhist images are turned up by the plough. It is still affected by strange Buddhist customs, and though Buddhism has disappeared from India, its inhabitants still worship a so-called incarnation of Vishnu, whom they call *Baudh Deo*. (p. 3.)

* * * *

Bodh Gaya, which is situated a few hundred yards to the west of the river Phalgú or Lílajan, is without doubt one of the most interesting historical sites in the world. It was under the sacred fig-tree here that Sakya Sinha received enlightenment, and became "the Buddha" (or "enlightened one"). The village is hence the birth-place of the Buddhist religion, and the holiest place in existence to one-third of the inhabitants of the earth. The writer avoids any detailed description of the famous temple built over the spot where the Buddha sat when the divine message came to him, for any account which could be contained within the limits of these notes would necessarily be incomplete and give a wrong impression. Dr. Rajendra Lal Mittra and General Cunningham have each devoted a whole volume to its history and architecture, to which those interested must be referred. A brief account will also be found on pages 53 and ff. of the Statistical Account of Gaya. Suffice it to say here that the present temple is undoubtedly the same as that seen and described by the Chinese pilgrim, Hiuen Tsiang, in the seventh century A.D., and was probably built a century before him. The special

I have been trying to make enquiries regarding the early history of the Temple. I think I published an article entitled "The Hindu Mahanth and the Buddha Gaya Temple" in the Journal for July, 1894. (*Shown the article on page 20.*) It was written by me. (Put in and marked Exhibit D16.) I have read parts of Mr. Grierson's book called "Notes on the District of Gaya," published in 1893, but not till the last three or four days I did not read the portion of the book shown to me on page 3. My information does not tally with what Mr. Grierson states in the last paragraph on that page.

[The defence tender the book. The prosecution object to the admissibility of any statement of fact made by Mr. Grierson or any opinion expressed by him in that book, but do not object to quotations in it from historical works. The defence say they put in the passage referred to above, and also pages 16 and 17 containing the early history of the Monastery, as showing statements made by a responsible public officer in 1893 before this case was thought of, as explanatory of the claim put forward by the Mahanth, whether that claim be well-founded or not. The book is allowed to be put in, as a whole, subject to the qualification that the relevance of any particular passage that may be relied on or the evidential value to be attached to it may be discussed at a later stage when the defence come to deal with these pages. (Marked Exhibit D. 17.) D. J. M.]

I have read a publication called "A Brief History of Bodh Gaya Math," compiled by Rai Ram Aungrah Narayan Singh Bahadur, under order of Mr. Grierson, and published in 1892. I object to the correctness of certain passages put into it. I distinctly remember one passage in it to which I object, namely, the insertion of the word "Maha-Bodhi Temple." (*Shown book*). I object to the words 6 lines from the foot of page 1: "in which the Buddhistic Maha-Bodhi Temple is situated." I read the book about two years ago.

attention of the visitor may be directed to the famous Asoka railings, some of which are still in position, which date from the third century B.C., and originally surrounded an older temple, on the site of which the existing one was built. Some of the sculptures on the pillars of this railing show distinct traces of Greek art.

Independently of the great Buddhist temple, the *math*, or Sivite monastery close by, and in whose land it stands, demands more than a passing notice. It is inhabited by a sect of *Dasnami Sannyasis*, the ten orders of which were founded by Sankara Acharya. The Bodh Gaya sect is styled *Gir*. The founder is said to have been Gosain Ghamandi Gir, who came here in the year 1590 A.D., and, attracted by the beauty of the spot, built a small monastery. He was the first *mahanth* or abbot. The present mahanth, Gosain Krishna Dayal Gir, is twelfth in descent from him. Among his predecessors may be mentioned the third mahanth, Gosain Mahadeva Gir (1642—1682). Tradition says that he worshipped Anna Púrna, the Goddess of Plenty, who, pleased by his devotion, presented him with a wondrous cup for the distribution of grain, the virtue of which was such that so long as alms were distributed by the mahanths from it, the monastery would never lack. Moreover, its contents were always sufficient to exactly satisfy the appetite of the recipient of the alms dealt from it, be he man or woman, child or adult, full or hungry. This cup (*Catora*) is still in existence, and is used daily for the distribution of alms to the numerous pilgrims who pass by the monastery. It was during the time of this mahanth that the present large monastery was built. Subsequent mahanths received valuable presents of land from the Emperor of Delhi and others, for which *farmans* are still shown.

The tenth mahanth Gosain Bhaipati Gir, rendered service to the English in the mutiny of 1857. He died in 1867 and was succeeded by Hem Narayan Gir, a learned man, who managed his important trust with liberality and discretion. In consideration of his services in the famine of 1873-74, he was granted a Certificate of Honour on the occasion of the proclamation of Her Majesty's title of Empress of India. He died at Benares universally regretted, on the 27th December, 1891, when he was succeeded by the present mahanth, Gosain Krishna Dayal Gir.

The succession to the see of the mahanthship is according to custom, determined by election. When a mahanth dies five of his followers are nominated as *panches*, or electors, by the general body of disciples. These select as the successor, the disciple whom they consider most learned, most pious, and most capable. The person chosen is then formally installed on the *gaddi* or throne of the monastery, and each disciple presents him with a sheet in token of acceptance of his supremacy.

The following is a list of the mahanths of Bodh-Gaya, since the foundation of the monastery in 1590 :—

(1) Ghamandi Gir (1590—1615).
(2) Chaitanya Gir (1615—1642).
(3) Mahadeva Gir (1642—1682).
(4) Lala Gir (1682— ?).
(5) Keshav Gir (? —1748).
(6) Raghav Gir (1748—1769).
(7) Ram Hit Gir (1769—1806).
(8) Balak Gir (1806—1820).
(9) Siv Gir (1820—1846).
(10) Bhaipati Gir (1846—1867).
(11) Hem Narayan Gir (1867—1891).
(12) Krishna Dayal Gir (1891, now living). — Mr. Grierson's Notes on the District of Gaya pp. 16-18.

D. 18.

A BRIEF HISTORY OF THE BODH-GAYA MATH.

THE Bodh-Gaya Math is an ancient Monastery of the Hindu Sannyasis, styled *Girs*, who belong to one of the ten orders of Sankara Acharya's Sivite school. It traces its origin back to the middle of the sixteenth century of the Christian era. It is said that as early as *Magh* of the Fasli year 997 (corresponding with 1590 A.D.), one Gosain Ghamandi Gir, a holy devotee of this order, while on a pilgrimage tour, became so very fond of the sylvan solitude of the neighbourhood of the place where the *Math* now stands, that he selected it as the place of his religious devotion, and subsequently built a small monastery there for the accommodation of the itinerant members of his order. He was the first Mahanth, and the founder of the monastery. He was succeeded by his disciple, Chaitanya Gir, in 1022 Fasli (corresponding with 1615 A.D.). Mahanth Chaitanya Gir was much renowned for his learning and austere piety, and spent his time in worship and religious devotion. He died in 1059 Fasli, and his remains were interred in the enclosures of the great Buddhist temple, and a small temple was built thereon. Mahanth Chaitanya Gir was succeeded by his disciple, Mahanth Mahadeva Gir, who led a very pious and austere life. He worshipped *Anna Purna Devi* for several years and his *dhuni* (place of worship) and *samadhi* (tomb) of pucka masonry work stands in front of the *Mahabodhi* temple, where also a temple was built by him in honour of his Ishta (tutelary) goddess *Anna Purna*. The tradition is that the goddess *Anna Purna Devi* was so much gratified that she presented him a *katora* (cup) for distribution of grain, with the *ashirbad* (blessing) that if the mahanths of the Asthan would continue freely distributing *sadabarat* (alms) out of this *katora*, they would never be in want. It is said to hold exactly enough to satisfy the appetite of whoever receives its contents, be he man or woman, child or adult.

(Book put in and admitted as Exhibit D18, subject to same qualification as above, the prosecution having the same objection as to Exhibit D. 17.)

Question.—Are you aware that the Mahanth claims to hold the land on which the Maha-Bodhi Temple and surrounding temples stand as revenue-free?

Answer.—I am aware that he claims to be Zemindar of the land on which the Maha-Bodhi Temple stands. I do not know if he claims also the surrounding lands. To my mind they belong to the Tikari Raj. Since reading the book last shown me I am aware he claims to hold the land under a farman of the Moghul Emperor.

This talismanic cup is still in the monastery, and grain is doled out daily with it. It was under the auspices of this goddess, the presenter of the inexhaustible cup, that he was enabled to build the large monastic building, the present *Math* of Bodh-Gaya, which is situated on the bank of Lilajan river (another name for the sacred Phalgu), in the midst of a garden extending over an area of about 52 bighas, and surrounded by a high masonry wall. He also founded an alms-house, which has been much extended by the later mahanths, where rice and pulse are daily distributed to three to five hundred persons up to the present time.

He died in 1089 Fasli (corresponding with 1682 A.D.), and was succeeded by his disciple, Lal Gir.

Mahanth Lal Gir is said to have been much favoured by the Emperor of Delhi, and the villages of Mastipur and Taradih, in which the Buddhistic *Mahabodhi* temple is situated, were made over to him by a Royal firman. A jagir of six villages was presented to the *Math* by Wazirul-Mumalik Qamaruddin Khan. He was followed by his disciple, Keshava Gir, who was so well known for his piety and devotion that before he ascended the Mahanthi Gaddi of Bodh-Gaya, and in the lifetime of his guru, he got a present of Antarin and other villages from Emperor Farukh Siyar of Delhi, and in the Royal firman he was styled as *Faqir Kamil wa Haq Parast* (a monk who had reached the highest degree of talismanic powers and of the merit of holy orders). He was succeeded by Mahanth Ragbava Gir in 1155 Fasli (corresponding with 1748 A.D.), who was followed by Mahanth Ramhit Gir in 1176 Fasli (corresponding with 1769 A.D.). Mahanth Ramhit Gir contributed greatly to increase the wealth and prosperity of the *Math*. He obtained lakhiraj lands and villages from the Maharajas of Tikari and Ichak. He died in the holy city of Benares, and his *dharam samadhi* (tomb) was built by his successor in the Bodh-Gaya *samadhi* (family burial-ground). He was followed by his disciple, Mahanth Balak Gir, in 1213 Fasli (corresponding with 1806), who obtained a few villages from Maharaja Ramsingh of Jaipur, and was succeeded by his disciple, Shiva Gir, in 1227 Fasli (corresponding with 1820). Mahanth Shiva Gir, who was equally noted for his personal beauty, generous heart, and religious devotion, and who made no less than 1,400 *chelas* (disciples), brought the condition of the *Math* and its properties to a most flourishing condition.

It is said that in his time some of the *Math* properties were resumed under Regulation II of 1819 and Regulation III of 1828, and that they were all released after due enquiry being held. The Mahanth, it is said, was thus also acknowledged as Mahanth of Bodh-Gaya by the British Government. After his death in 1253 Fasli (corresponding with 1846 A.D.), his disciples, following the custom which had been prevalent in the *Math* since the very beginning, selected Bhaipat Gir, one of their own body, as the Mahanth of Bodh Gaya. Mahanth Bhaipat Gir was at the helm of affairs for 21 years. He is said to have distinguished himself for his conspicuous loyalty by helping the English Government in the dark days of the Indian Sepoy Mutiny. He died in 1274 Fasli (corresponding with 1867 A.D.), and after him his disciple, Hem Narayan Gir, succeeded to the Mahanthi Gaddi of Bodh-Gaya.

Mahanth Hem Naráyn Gir was a great Sanskrit scholar, and collected a large library of original Sanskrit manuscripts. He built a large house at Benares at a cost of about fifty thousand rupees for the benefit of those *gosains* of his order who wished to pass the last days of their life in the holy city of Kashi (Benares). He also built many temples in his zemindaries, and established a *dharamsálá* and excavated a tank at Zindápur on the Hazáribagh road. This Mahanth rendered valuable assistance to the Government during the famine of 1873-74, and in recognition of his services he was presented with a Certificate of Honour in the name of the Queen-Empress of India on the 1st January, 1877, the day of the proclamation of the title of Empress of India. He was known to be one of the most influential and respectable zemindars of the district, and was held in great reverence by the entire native community. The Government of India, as a mark of personal distinction, exempted him from his attendance in the civil courts under Government orders, dated the 22nd February, 1876.

He was very religiously inclined, and spent a great portion of his time in worship and religious devotion. In 1882 he went out on a *(tirtha jatra)* pilgrimage, with the intention of passing the remainder of his days in mere austerity. He therefore executed a registered deed of gift (*hibba*) on the 25th of August, 1882, in favour of his disciple (*chela*) Krishna Dayal Gir, who was more familiarly called Brahmacharji on account of his pious habits. He stated in this deed that as, in consequence of his old age, he wished to retire from the worldly life, he desired to abdicate his mahanthship in favour of any of his disciples who would be the most eligible, and as a panchayat consisting of five of the most respectable *gosains* of the *Math* had unanimously selected Krishna Dayal Gir as the fittest amongst the disciples, he, agreeing with the *panches*, appointed him as his successor, and made an absolute and free gift of all his properties in favour of the said Krishna Dayal Gir. Krishna Dayal Gir thus obtained possession of all the properties appertaining to the Math, and reigned as mahanth, *de facto* for nearly four months. During the short period he showed good capacity for work, and ruled over the Math in a verly liberal spirit. He also contributed Rs. 2,500 towards the expenses of repairs of the Mahabodhi temple. However, Mahanth Hem Narayan Gir, who had set out on pilgrimage, returned again to Bodh-Gaya and, at the most earnest solicitation of his disciples and other *gosains*, consented to take up the onerous and responsible duties of the mahanthi of the *Math* once again. A registered deed of relinquishment (*bazidawa*) was therefore executed by Krishna Dayal Gir on the 22nd December, 1882, who most gladly and cheerfully gave up and abandoned all the right and title he had derived under the above-described deed of gift (*hibba*) in fovour of his guru and donor. During his lifetime Mahanth Hem Narayan Gir thus once more assumed the management of the estate, and managed it with great prudence. Mahanth Hem Narayan Gir died at Benares on the 12th Paus, corresponding with the 27th December, 1891. His *dharma samadhi* (temple) is built in the Bodh-Gaya *samadhi* (the family burial-ground).

The Mahanth, as well as his disciples (*chelas*) are pledged to a lifelong celibacy, and, according to the time-honoured custom of the *Math* and the rule of their order, when a disciple of the *Math* dies his properties, moveable or immoveable, revert to the monastery.

Succession to the mahantship of Bodh-Gaya is governed according to custom. When a mahanth dies, all his disciples nominate five *gosains* of their own *Math* as panches or arbitrators to select a worthy and fit successor to the *gaddi* out of their own body; and all the disciples abide by the decision of the panchayat so constituted. Accordingly, a *panchnamah* was executed on the 13th of Magh 1299 Fasli, corresponding with 1892 A.D., by all the disciples of the late mahanth, by which they empowered *gosains* Bishun Dhari Gir, Raghubar Sahay Gir, Ramkaran Gir, Mohan Gir, and Jairam Gir, to elect a mahanth for the Bodh-Gaya *gaddi* out of their own body, and all these five gosains gave their written and unanimous verdict in favour of the same Krishna Dayal Gir, in whose favour the late mahanth had made a gift. Mahanth Krishna Dayal Gir was considered most eligible, being the most learned, the most pious, the most religious, and the most capable of all his fellow-disciples.

The formal ceremony of ascending the ancient and holy *gaddi* of the Math was performed with great *eclat* on the 21st Magh 1299 Fasli, corresponding with the 4th of February, 1892, on which day, after the usual *pujas*, *homa* and sacrifices, the present mahanth, Krishna Dayal Gir, was declared Mahanth of Bodh-Gaya in the presence of the principal officials and other residents of the district of Gaya. When the new mahanth was formally installed on the *gaddi* as the Mahanth of Bodh-Gaya, all the numerous disciples presented him each with a sheet in token of their acceptance of his supremacy. This concluded the ceremony of installation. Mahanth Krishna Dayal Gir is the 12th mahanth of Bodh-Gaya. His present income, which is derived from presents offered to the great *Mahabodhi* temple, personal presents made by disciples to him and to the holy shrines in the *Math*, and the landed property, amounts to upwards of a lakh of rupees a year. The expenses of the monastery under head *sadabarat*, or daily alms-giving, feeding the *gosains*, or members of the fraternity of all the subordinate *maths*, and the expenses on occasion of the principal festivals, such as Dasahra, Tilsankranti and others, are said to be on a grand scale. Among other items of expenditure the one under *bhandara* is noteworthy. Some time after the death of a mahanth and subsequent to election of a new mahanth, a grand feast is given, to which as many members of the fraternity throughout India as can possibly be asked to join, are invited. They are fed on very richly, and highly spiced cakes called "*mal pua.*" This feast, it is said, costs nearly a lakh of rupees.

The assets of the estate are always in a very solvent state owing to good management. One peculiar feature in the management of the domestic and foreign affairs of the estate is that all the posts in and outside the monastery are reserved for the members of the order. All persons employed,—from the grass-cut to the highest priest, or biggest village agent,—are *gir gosains* of the Saivite school, disciples of His Holiness the Mahanth of Bodh-Gaya.

The present occupant of the *gaddi*, Mahanth Krishna Dayal Gir, is a young man of very pious habits. He has shown great application for business, and seems to have the affairs of the monastery well in hand. He has shown good public spirit and liberality in the right direction by subscribing Rs. 5,000 to the "Grierson Well and Public Gardens Fund," and seems to possess the entire confidence of the members of his order, by whom and the native community (both Hindus and Musalmans) he is held in high esteem and regard.

English translations of the *sanads* or royal grants form appendices to this report. A statement showing the details of property held by the Math is also enclosed.

D. 19.

Sanad granted under the seal of His Majesty Muhammad Shah Padshah Gazi.

Muhammad Shah Padshah Gazi. Era 6th Muhammad Shahi. Seal of Nasrat Jang Itmadu'd-daulah Wazir al Mumalik Qamaru'd-din Khan, Khan Bahadur.

Seal of Muhammad Shah Padshah Gazi. (In Togra character.)

Be it known to all present and future gumáshtas and mutsaddís of pargana Maher, Sarkár and Súbá Bihár, that according to the order of His Majesty the King of all lands and time, Khalífá of strict justice and means of preservation and comfort to all beings (may God preserve him), who is the minister of the God of Gods, on whom is the special mercy of the Almighty Father, and who is the sole means of livelihood to the whole world, the roots of all laws and regulations, and the preserver of the throne of the *khalafat*, written on the 27th day of Ziquád in the 9th year of his Jalus (accession), mauzas Mastipur, Taradih, are conferred upon Lál Gir Sannyasí as *madad mash*, without any restriction of names and divisions from the middle of *bijiail*. You all, in obedience to this order, should leave the said mauzas in his possession, without making any change or alteration therein, and you should in no way be overcome by any kind of temptation, and should in all respect look upon the order as just and right, so that all the produce of the said property be used by him for his own livelihood and that of the itinerant faqírs; for which act of benevolence, he should ever pray for the stability of the wealth (of His Majesty). You all should not take notice of other properties belonging to the grantee. You all should take great care in carrying out this order.

Written this day, the 11th day of Rabiulawal in the 9th year of the August Jalus (accession).

(Corresponding to A. D. 1727).

[Defence tender the farman in evidence without proof as purporting to be more than 30 years old. Prosecution object that it has not been shown to come from proper custody. Counsel for the defence say that the Mahant's servants are the accused and the document is produced from their custody by their counsel.

Accused Jaipal Gir was questioned at this stage, and stated that he is a servant of the Mahanth and that he has brought the document in question from the *Sarishta* of the Mahanth. Document admitted and marked Exhibit D19. D. J. M.]

I am not aware whether the Magistrate and Collector of this district asked the Mahanth's permission in 1875 to allow the King of Burmah to repair the compound of the Bodhi tree.

[Letter in Persian purporting to be signed by "A. V. Palmer, Magistrate and Collector" and bearing a seal, dated 15th January, 1875, tendered in evidence, as admissible without proof on the ground that it is a document purporting to be the official act of the chief executive officer in the district and under his seal and signature, *vide* clause *(iii)* section 74 of the Evidence Act. As to its relevancy, defence argue that it explains the state of mind in which the Mahanth has been making his present claim, as it shows that a predecessor of his was long ago asked his permission for the repair of the Temple.

The prosecution object to its admissibility. They contend that as regards proving it, if it be assumed to be a public document within the meaning of Section 74, it could not be proved except under Section 78 by producing the whole of the records of which the document forms a part. As regards its admissibility, prosecution contend it is irrelevant, as there is absolutely nothing to show on what grounds the Collector of the day formed the opinion that he should ask the Mahanth's permission: it is, therefore, a mere expression of his opinion.

In reply, it is said that the fact of its being merely an isolated document out of a mass of others affects only the weight to be attached to it, and, as a matter of fact, the defence have applied for copies of the whole papers and will only be too anxious to put them in: while it is sufficient for their case that the Mahanth had the opinion—whether a right or wrong one it is not for this Court to consider—that his permission was necessary for the repair of the Temple.

D. 20.

SEAL

By order of the Magistrate of Gaya.

MY DEAR MAHUNTH OF BODH-GAYA.

MAY YOU LIVE COMFORTABLY.—

IN sending herewith an extract from the letter of the King of Burmah to His Excellency the Viceroy in Council regarding the wishes of the King of Burma to have the compound of the Bodhi Tree repaired and the deputation of two men near the said Tree for the purpose of its daily worship, and also as regards the sending of articles of worship to be offered to the Tree once or twice a year, I request you to let me know whether you approve of and agree to the same. Be it known that an early reply to this is required.

Dated 15th January, 1875.

A. V. PALMER,
Magistrate and Collector.

Extract translation of a letter from the Foreign Department, Mandalay, to the address of the Secretary to the Government of India, Foreign Department.

As in 1234 corresponding with 1872 A.D., His Excellency the Governor-General of India sent a delegate (envoy) with presents to the King of Burmah, the King of Burmah has now in return ordered a royal letter with presents to be sent by way of friendship, and also that his delegates do see the Bodhi Tree in Hindoostan. As under this Bodhi Tree, which has been very sacred and incomparable during three Jugal (ages), the all knowing Buddha had his Buddha dominion under it, the King therefore wishes that religious offerings to God be made before the sacred tree on the understanding as if Buddha is in existence. With this view the King has ordered that articles of offering be made over to the delegates. The following four persons have been appointed delegates :—

(1). Andok Mahe Manhila Zethoo.
(2). Tarini Dogi Nimboo Mandar Rithoo.
(3). Ajud Dogi Nimboo Mandar Kayoogong.
(4). Noorthe Dore Tisi Thod.

The articles of offering have been made over to the above-named person for offering to the Bodhi Tree and their being sent to Hindoostan. It is hoped that on arrival of the delegates, the Secretary by way of friendship will do his best towards the realization of their object, and after helping them in delivering the letter and the royal presents, will render every assistance in their visit to the Tree in Hindoostan, and also in making offering and worshipping the Tree on behalf of the King. The King further desires that the compound of the Tree, which may have been burnt on account of age, be repaired. It is also his wish that two persons be deputed near the Bodhi Tree for daily worship. He also wishes that one or twice a year his people may take offering to the Tree, as he may desire ; and it is hoped that the Secretary will lay before His Excellency the Viceroy the objects of the King and help in their fulfilment.

D. 21.

I am Dharmapala Hevavitarana, son of D.C. Hevavitarana, Secretary, Bodh-Gaya Mahabodhi Society at Colombo in Ceylon, otherwise called *Lanka Dwipa.*

Whereas one bigha and ten cotthas of land situate within the compound of Fortress (killa) Juggunnath in Mahabodhi, Pergunnah Maher, District Gaya, belongs to Mahanth Hem Narain Gir as his ancestral Lakhiraj property. That land I have taken lease of for erecting a house from Mahanth Hem Narain Gir, disciple of Mahanth Bhaipat Gir, resident of and *Gadi Nashin* of Math Bodh-Gaya, by profession Zemindar and mendicant, on a rental of Rs. 8 per bigha, which for the portion of the land comes up to Rs. 12 annually. I therefore promise and do

The Court postponed decision on the question of the admissibility of the document and the nature of the proof of it required, in order that the cross-examination of the witnesses may proceed. Document marked Exhibit D20 for purposes of identification only. D. J. M.]

I first learned that the surrounding lands belonged to Tikari in the beginning of 1893. I was given to understand then that the land on which the Maha-Bodhi Temple stands also belonged to Tikari. I was told this by Babu Nand Kishore Lal, my pleader. I made his acquaintance in the beginning of the year 1893. I don't think I had ever seen him before that. To my knowledge I never acknowledged the Mahanth as landlord of the place. I acknowledged the late Mahanth as landlord of some land outside the Temple. That was in 1891, soon after I came in July or August. I executed then an agreement in his favour. I cannot say if it was read out to me before I signed it. I believe I was not made fully acquainted with its contents. I trusted to my interpreter. I have reason to suppose that the proper contents were not given to me. The document was registered. I have complained to my pleader and also to Durga Shankar Bhattacharjya, who is my witness in this case, about that. I complained when I remitted the first year's rent, about a year after the execution. It was then I became aware of the contents—the contents were not in accordance with the first arrangement. The rent I remitted was refused by the Mahanth, and that is how I came to know the document was faulty.

Question.—Has that land been taken away from you by the Mahanth ?

Answer.—It has not been taken away, but we have had to leave the place. I don't know who took it after that. I sent the money for the second year's rent to my pleader ; I inquired from him as to whether he had paid it, but he told me better not to trouble about it just now, as it was a small matter. He did not pay the rent, and the money must be with him still. (*Shown a document.*) This is the agreement I executed : the signature on the face and back of it are mine. (Admitted and marked Exhibit D 21.)

execute this *Kabuliat*, otherwise called *Sarkhat Kerainama*, that I will erect a house on the land and will either remain in the house myself or will settle tenants therein, that I will not do anything against the order of the proprietor, the *Jagirdar*, so that any injury may be done to the *Malik*. I also promise that I will pay the rent every year to the *Malik Jagirdar*. In case of default in the payment of the above rent and in case of going against (the orders) of the *Malik Khairatdar* (*Jagirdar*), the said *Malik* has and will have the right to take possession of the land with the house either himself or through the assistance of a competent court, and may settle the same with whomsoever he likes. In that case I or the proprietors of the Committee or any body else will not have any objection. In case it is objected, then we may pay the rent, remove the materials and vacate the land without any objection. This *Kabuliat* is, therefore, executed that it may be of use, when required.

Land rented 1 bigha 10 cottahs *khairat* land in the compound of fortress (killa) Jaggurnathji, situate in Mahabodhi, Pargana Maher, District Gaya.

Annual Rent ... ... Rs. 12 0
Half of which ... ... Rs. 6 0

Division of Registry	Collectorate	Jagir No.	Sudder Jama.
Gaya	Gaya	3160	Rs. 28,024-12

NORTH. Land of Budhan Gowala.

WEST. Near the ditch land of Budhan Gowala.

Land according to Government measurement 1 Bigha 10 Cottahs.

EAST. *Dhela* tree.

SOUTH. Public Road.

Dated 24th August, 1891, *Corresponding to Bhadon* 1298, *F.S.*

DHARMAPALA HEVAVITARANA,
Secretary, Budh Gaya Mahabodhi Society of Colombo, Ceylon.

Scribe —Ramsaran Lal, resident of mouza Adampore Fazhaha, Pargana Sonoret, District Gaya, at present residing in Sahebgunj. On the admission of the executant.

Witness.—Champat Lal, resident of M. Bukrour, Pargana Maher, District Gaya. On the admission of the executant in my own pen.

Witness.—Baijnath Sahay, resident of Maher, Pargana Maher, District Gaya. On the admission of the executant in my own pen.

Witness.—Bhikhori Shunker Bhattacharyya, resident of Benares, residing at present at Gaya Muhullah Uperdit. In my own pen.

Stamp of Rs. 1 purchased on 24th August, 1891, Monday, by Babu Bhikhori Shunker, son of Babu Tara Shunker Bhattacharyya, Bengali by caste, residing at present in Sahebgunj-Pargana and District Gaya.

No. 52.

JUGGURNATH SAHEY,
Stamp Vendor, Gaya.

Presented for registration between the hours of 1 and 2 P.M. on 29th August, 1891, by Dharmapala Hevavitarana, son of D. C. Hevavitarana of Ceylon, Colombo, by caste Buddhist, by occupation merchant.

HASSON KULY KHAN,
Registrar.

Execution admitted. Registered on 29th August, 1891.

In April, 1894, I wrote a demi-official letter to the Private Secretary to the Lieutenant-Governor of Bengal about the Mahábodhi Temple, but I am not sure of what its contents were.

Question.—Can you swear that you did not in it apply for the transfer of the Temple from the Mahanth's possession to you or to your Society ?

Answer.—I have no recollection. I cannot swear. I got a reply to it from the Chief Secretary to the Government, which I have produced in answer to the call of the defence.

D 22.

No. 6 P. D., Political Branch.

FROM

H. J. S. COTTON, ESQ., C S.I.,
Chief Secretary to the Government of Bengal.

TO

H. DHARMAPALA, ESQ.,
General Secretary, Mahabodhi Society, Gaya.

Dated Darjeeling, 5th May, 1894.

SIR,

I AM directed to acknowledge the receipt of your letter, dated 14th April, 1894, and, in reply, to inform you that the Bengal Government is not in a position to give encouragement to any negotiations for effecting the transfer of the Bodh Gaya Shrine to the Maha-Bodhi Society. There is perfect freedom of worship for all Buddhists at Bodh Gaya, and the Hindu Sannyasis, who have held the place for over five centuries, are ever ready to meet all reasonable requirements of worshippers. Any well-grounded complaint that difficulties were imposed, would meet with ready attention and redress at the hands of the Bengal Government, but the Lieutenant-Governor can undertake no measures for the furtherance of the general objects of the Maha-Bodhi Society.

I have the honor to be,
Sir,
Your most obedient Servant,

H. J. S. COTTON,
Chief Secretary to the Government of Bengal.

(*Shown a letter, No. 6PD., dated 5th May*, 1894). This is the letter I got. Looking to the contents of the reply, I cannot yet remember whether I applied for the transfer of the Temple or not. (Put in and marked Exhibit D 22.)

Question.—Last year did you or did you not request the Lieutenant-Governor to exercise his influence on the Mahanth to permit you to place this Japanese image in the Temple ?

Answer.—I do not understand exactly what is meant by the word "influence."

(*Question explained as meaning that the Lieutenant-Governor should exercise his control as ruler of the Province.*) I did not ask him to use his influence. I remember writing a letter to the Private Secretary in which I mentioned that the Mahanth objected to the Japanese image being placed in the Temple.

Question.—Did you in that letter ask the Lieutenant-Governor to help you to put the image in the Temple ?

Answer.—I did not ask any help.

Question.—What did you ask him to do ?

Answer.—I complained that the grievance should be redressed about the Japanese image not being allowed to be put into the Temple. I have no recollection if I asked the way in which he was to redress the grievance. I think I have kept a draft of my letter. It is in Calcutta.

(*Shown a letter No.* 654, *P. D., dated 22nd June*, 1894.) This is the reply I got from the Lieutenant-Governor.

Question.—Did you on receiving it write to the Lieutenant-Governor, and say you had not asked him to exercise his influence with the Mahanth ?

Answer.—I don't think I sent any reply. (Letter put in and marked Exhibit D 23.)

D. 23.

No. 654 P. D., Political Branch.

FROM

H. J. S. COTTON, ESQ, C.S.I.,
Chief Secretary to the Government of Bengal.

TO

H. DHARMAPALA, ESQ.,
General Secretary, Mahabodhi Society, Gaya.

Dated Darjeeling, the 22nd June, 1894.

SIR,

WITH reference to your letter, dated the 15th June, 1894, to the Private Secretary to His Honor the Lieutenant-Governor, I am directed to inform you that the Government must decline to exercise any influence with the Mahanth of the Bodh-Gaya shrine, and can pass no other orders than those already communicated to you in my letter No. 6 P.D., dated the 5th May last.

I have the honor to be,
Sir,
Your most obedient Servant,

H. J. S. COTTON,
Chief Secretary to the Government of Bengal.

Deposition read over by the witness and admitted correct, except that he says with reference to page 55, that he is not sure whether it is from November, 1894, the altered prospectus has been appearing.

D. J. MACPHERSON,
Magistrate.

6th May 1895.

WITNESS FOR PROSECUTION, I.

H. Dharmapala, further cross-examined on solemn affirmation, states:—

I know Mr. J. D. M. Beglar. I have known him since 1893. In that year I appointed him Consulting Archæologist to the Mahá-bodhi Society. I have several times had conversations with him regarding what he knows about the Temple. I am aware from reading historical works that he was appointed by Government to superintend the repairs to the Temple about 15 or 16 years ago. I have heard he resided on the premises for some years during the repairs. I announced his appointment as Consulting Archæologist to our Society at page 2 of the Journal for April, 1893. I identify the passage. (Put in and marked Exhibit D24.)

D. 24.

THE CONSULTING ARCHÆOLOGIST OF THE MAHA-BODHI SOCIETY.

FROM the correspondence printed in our official column, it will be seen that we have succeeded in securing the services of Mr. J. D. Melick-Beglar, C.E., Pensioner of the Department of Public Works, as Consulting Archæologist and Engineer to the Maha-Bodhi Society. This news is of the highest importance, as Mr. Beglar was associated for more than sixteen years with Major-General Sir Alexander Cunningham, K. C. I. E., Director-General of the Archæological Survey of India, in his explorations of the historical Buddhist and Hindu shrines and ruins. Mr. Beglar under his supervision and by the order of the Government of India, repaired and restored the Maha-Bodhi temple to its ancient magnificence, to accomplish which he stopped at Buddha-Gaya between four and five years and expended for the Government about Rs. 1,20,000. General Cunningham having retired to England, Mr. Beglar is now the most experienced of Indian Archæologists, and his aid will be indeed precious to us in the work that we shall have to do at our four most sacred shrines.

(Mahabodhi Society's Journal, April, 1893, *p.* 2.)

I may or may not have asked him if the Mahanth was in possession of the Temple. I don't know if I ever asked him whether during his residence he ever saw Hindus come to the Mahá-bodhi Temple. *(adds)* He mentioned to me distinctly that he had given permission to a gentleman from Ceylon to put up a marble slab with an inscription for offering flowers from the Bodhi tree, and he mentioned his name, *viz.*, Mr. E. R. Gunaratna.

Question.—Did Mr. Beglar ever tell you that he was in the habit of asking the Mahanth's permission in regard to all that he did?

Answer.—He told me that he got certain Asoka pillars which were in the *math* (that is, the monastery,) and that all the rest of the work he did at his own discretion. He never told me that he consulted the Mahanth in regard to his work. He said he did everything at his own discretion, and that the Bodhi tree even was planted by him. I don't remember asking him who appropriated offerings to the Temple.

Question.—Are you now aware that the Mahanth has for years appropriated the offerings?

Answer.—I knew that he has almost by force been taking away the offerings made to Buddha. I hear he has been doing so for years, he being a powerful zemindar and there being no one to protest, and I believe that.

Question.—Are you aware that Mr. Beglar brought the big image of Buddha, which is now on the ground-floor of the Temple, from the Mahanth's monastery with the Mahanth's consent?

Answer.—I am aware that it had been lying in the Mahanth's *math*, and that it was set up by Mr. Beglar. I am not aware that the Mahanth performed any ceremonies on the occasion on which he set up the image. I did not ask him if any ceremonies had been performed on that occasion. So far as I am aware, no Buddhist performed any ceremonies on that occasion. The image on the altar in the chamber of the upper story, beside which I put my image, is the image, so I have heard, of Mayadevi, the mother of Buddha. I never cared to inquire how that image was set up there, as it was all apparent the whole thing had been set up by Mr. Beglar. I am not aware that in setting up these images, Mr. Beglar invariably consulted the Mahanth. On the contrary I know he did what he thought best to bring the Temple to its ancient splendour. I never asked him whether, in placing these big images, he ever consulted the Mahanth. I remember that the image of Mayadevi has gold-leaf fixed on to it. Buddhists do put gold-leaf on their images in that way. I am not aware that the big image, before Mr. Beglar set it up, used, while it was in the monastery, to have a *sindur tilak* on its forehead. I am not aware that, when the excavation was going on, the Mahanth claimed all the bricks from Mr. Beglar, or that he had to explain to the Mahanth that they would be used only *boná fide* for the purposes of the Temple. I do not know whether he could give material evidence in this case. I did not think of citing him as a witness for the prosecution. I do not think I discussed his name with my pleader when drawing up my list of witnesses, as that list had nothing to do with him. I mean he was not a witness to the occurrence of the 25th February. I cited a number of witnesses who had nothing to do with the occurrence. It was not to prove possession and prior occupation of the Buddhists, but simply, if necessary, to prove that the Temple was a Buddhist one. I cannot say that I would have cited Mr. Beglar as a witness, had I been advised his evidence would be material.

Question.—Can you suggest any reason why you have not examined Mr. Beglar on behalf of the prosecution?

[Counsel for the prosecution remarks that the defence must know perfectly well that counsel are responsible for all matters of that kind, and that it is prolonging the cross-examination into most minute detail to question witnesses about this: but he does not positively object to the question being put. The defence say they will show it is most relevant to have witness's own answer. Question allowed to be put, as it will only prolong proceedings further to discuss the relevance of such matters.]

Answer.—I thought it was unnecessary. There was no other reason. I consider Mr. Beglar to be a witness of truth and honour.

The idea of enshrining a new image in the Mahábodhi Temple first struck me when I was in Japan in the year 1893. (*adds*). I suggested the idea to the Japanese. The idea was my own, suggested by reading a passage in the *Vinayapuspamala*. That is an old Buddhist book, several centuries old. I read it for the first time in Japan. It was quoted in the Mahábodhi Journal.

Question.—Thereupon you requested the Japanese, Mr. Asaki, to give you the image?

Answer.—I suggested to the Buddhists there and to the Right Reverend Asaki, High Priest, that it would be better if an image be sent to the Mahábodhi Temple at Gaya, as there was no proper image of Buddha. The Japanese were not unwilling to part with the image. They gave it with great delight and at the same time sorrow. I was not on that occasion collecting subscriptions for my Society. I did not go there to collect any, nor did I try to.

Question.—What was the object of your visit to Japan?

Answer.—To tell the Japanese about the objects of the Mahábodhi Society and the Mahábodhi movement. The expenses were partly my own and partly the Society's.

Question.—Did you get any money from any one in Japan on that occasion?

Answer.—A friend gave me a small subscription unasked.

D. 25.

A HISTORIC JAPANESE IMAGE OF BUDDHA.

WHEN I was in Tokio last November, I told the Rev. Mr. S. Asahi, Chief Priest of the Tentokuji Temple, that the image of Maya Devi which is now enshrined on the altar of the upper storey of the Great Temple at Buddha-Gaya could be replaced by a statue of Buddha if we had one from Japan, and am glad that he was successful in getting a historic image of the Great Teacher about seven hundred years old. This beautiful image, two feet high, re-

[*Shown an article entitled "A historic Japanese image of Buddha," at page 5 of the Journal for January,* 1894.]

That is a letter that I wrote.

(Put in and marked Exhibit D25.)

The image arrived in Calcutta on the 31st March, 1894. I brought it to Gaya about the 16th or 17th May, 1894.

presents Buddha sitting on the lotus seat in the attitude of expounding the Law. It was carved by the order of the great general who erected the famous Kamakura statue of Buddha, and it remained enshrined these seven hundred years in the temple in Kanagawa near Yokohama.

The good people of Kanagawa were put into a dilemma when they were asked to present their much-loved statue to the greatest Buddhist shrine. For generations there people worshipped it, but they thought it was their duty to cement the bond between Japan and India by presenting it; and the presentation scene was indeed a touching one. All the people assembled in the temple, and when it was being removed under great ceremony from the shrine, men and women actually wept. The custodians of the temple, Messrs Niuemon Asaha and Sentaro Asaha, father and son, members of their family escorted the image to Tokyo, where I took charge of it. The image is valued one thousand rupees.

(Mahabodhi Society's Journal, January, 1894, *p.* 5.)

H. DHARMAPALA.

D. 26.

THE BUDDHA-GAYA TEMPLE.

THE historic image of Buddha presented by the Buddhists of Japan through the Rt. Rev. S. Asahi, of Tentokuji Temple, Shiba, Tokyo, to the great Temple at Buddha-Gaya, will be placed there by Mr. H. Dharmapala on the 19th instant, (the full-moon-day of Wesak) in the presence of Mr. D. J. Macpherson, Collector of Gaya.

(Mahabodhi Society's Journal, May, 1894, *p.* 3.)

Question.—Did you, before doing so, consult the District Collector regarding putting it up in the Mahábodhi Temple?

Answer.—I brought a letter from Japan addressed to him, and on its basis I consulted him.

Question.—Did you receive the Collector's permission to announce in your Journal that the image would be placed on the 19th of May in the presence of the Collector of Gaya?

Answer.—No. (*Shown an editorial paragraph headed "The Buddha-Gaya Temple" at page 3 of the Journal for May,* 1894.)

The paragraph is mine.

[Put in and marked Exhibit D26.]

Question.—At the time you made that announcement, did you suspect. or had you any reason to think, that the Mahanth would object to the placing of the image?

Answer.—I had not the least suspicion that any objection would be brought. On the contrary I was perfectly sure.

Question.—With the Mahanth's consent?

Answer.—I did not care to consult the Mahanth. Even the possibility of his objecting never occurred to me.

Question.—When did you first learn that the Mahanth objected to your placing the image?

Answer.—At the last moment, when all arrangements had been made, the day before the day fixed, I think. I learned this first from the Collector. I believe the date was the 18th of May.

Question.—Did you meet or did you not meet the Mahanth on the night of he 17th of May at about 9 o'clock at a house in Gaya?

Answer.—I met the Mahanth at about that time in a house. I learned from him then that he objected, that is, he objected merely to this extent that he promised to put the image if it was given to him. The meaning was that he would place it. He insisted on the performance of a Hindu ceremony called, I believe, the *Pranpratistha*.

Question.—On or about the 19th May did you receive any order or communication from the District Magistrate of Gaya, forbidding you to place the image as you intended?

Answer.—I received a demi-official letter from him. I received no order under Section 144, Criminal Procedure Code. I have been asked to produce such an order, but I have no recollection of receiving such.

D. 27.

IN THE COURT OF THE DISTRICT MAGISTRATE, GAYA. ORDER UNDER SECTION 144 C.P.C.

TO—THE MAHANTH OF BODH GAYA AND HIS CHELAS.

WHEREAS complaint has been made to me to-day by some Buddhist pilgrims from Ceylon that you have given instructions that Buddhist pilgrims, who may go to Bodh-Gaya to-night, the fullmoon night, are to be prevented by force from going to the Temple, and whereas such may occasion a breach of the peace, I hereby direct you to abstain from taking any action which will prevent any Buddhist pilgrims of any country whatever from worshipping in the shrine of Mahabodhi this night, according to custom, on pain of prosecution for disobeying order of a public officer. It is mentinned at the same time that no Image will be set up in the Temple to night except with your consent, and the pilgrims referred to do not intend to do so.

Given under my hand and seal of the court of this day, the 19th May, 1894.

K. M. MITTER,
For *District Magistrate.*

(*Shown an order under Section 144. Criminal Procedure Code, addressed to the Mahanth of Buddha-Gaya and his Chelas, dated 19th May 1894. and signed by K. M. Mitter, for District Magistrate*)

I have no recollection if receiving any order of a character simllar to that.

(Put in and marked Exhibit D27.)

In consequence of the demi-official communication I received from the Magistrate on the 19th May, I obeyed his instructions, and I desisted from placing the image.

Question.—The Mahanth locked the Temple ?

Answer.—I don't know myself. I heard from the Buddhist priests who went that day under Police escort, that the Temple door had been locked, and that it was afterwards opened to them for worship.

Question.—Where was the image from the 16th May, 1894, to the 24th February, 1895 ?

Answer.—I think it was brought to Gaya on the 17th May. After I received the order that it could not be placed, I put it in a house I rented from Babu Bhikari Shankar Bhattacharjya. He is a brother of my witness, Babu Durga Shankar Bhattacharjya He is the same person who did not give me fully to understand the contents of the *Kabuliyat* already put in (Exhibit D21). I never imputed fraud to him about that (*this added because the question originally contained the word "misinterpret."*) Between the 19th May and 24th February I made no attempt to enshrine the image, as I was not here and went away to Ceylon. I was in Gaya in June, 1894. I left Bengal in, I think, the early part of August, 1894. I next came to Bengal in January, 1895. In September, 1894, I was in Ceylon.

Question.—Did you or did you not receive, when you were in Ceylon, a communication from the Commissioner of Patna ?

Answer.—I received a communication from the Commissioner through the Magistrate of Gaya in Ceylon. I have not that communication with me. On being called on to produce it, I searched for it and could not find it. [*Shown certified copies.*] These are copies of the communication I received. (Put in and marked Exhibit D28 (*a*) and Exhibit D28 (*b*).) The petition of mine referred to in it was presented to Mr. Macpherson, the Magistrate of Gaya, by me. It was immediately after I presented it that Mr. Macpherson went away to Europe on leave, and Mr. Drake-Brockman acted for him. I went to see Mr. Drake-Brockman in his office room in his private house. I saw him once only.

Question.—I suppose that was with a view to get him to help you to place the image ?

D. 28. (a.)

No. 240G.

FROM

A FORBES, ESQUIRE, C.S.,
Commissioner of Patna,

To

THE MAGISTRATE OF GAYA.

Bankipore, the 23rd July, 1894.

GENERAL.

SIR,

WITH reference to your No. 1575, dated 12th instant, forwarding copies of a petition filed by Mr. Dharmapala before your predecessor and of Mr. Macpherson's note thereon, I have the honor to say hat the questions involved are not such as it is competent to the local authorities to deal with. If Mr. Dharmapala wishes to pursue the subject you should refer him for orders to Government.

I have the honor to be,
SIR,
Your most obedient Servant,

BIPIN BIHARI MUKERJEE,
Personal Assistant to Commissioner,
For Commissioner.

D. 28 (b.)

No. 2297.

Copy forwarded to Mr. H. Dharmapala, 2 Creek Row, Calcutta, for information with reference to his petition, dated the 12th June, 1894, to the Magistrate of Gaya, on the subject of placing an image of Buddha obtained from Japan in the Temple of Mahabodhi.

D. J. MACPHERSON,
Magistrate.

September 27th, 1894.

Answer.—No, but to give him a translation of a Japanese letter connected with the image.

Question.—Did you receive anybody's authority or sanction between June 1894 and the 25th February, 1895, to place this image in the Temple ?

Answer.—No.

Question.—Did you ask for anybody's consent or permission, the Mahanth's or anybody's ?

Answer.—No.

Question.—Did you inform any one in Gaya that you were going to place the image on the morning of the 25th February ?

Answer.—I did not fix the date, but I informed the Collector that I would place the image in the Temple, as I had a duty to perform to the Japanese.

Question.—When did you give this intimation to the Collector ?

Answer.—I sent it from Calcutta in a letter about four or five days before.

Question.—When you wrote that letter, did you or did you not apprehend that the Mahanth would object ?

Answer.—I did write in the letter that if the Mahanth wants he may remove it, but that I would place the image in the Temple. I should free myself from the responsibility, and if any one wanted to remove it he might do so. I wrote that because I knew from experience that any thing offered to the Temple is robbed and removed from it by the Mahanth or his men.

Question.—Did you then contemplate, by placing the image on the 25th of February, defying the Mahanth ?

Answer.—Oh no, not at all.

Question.—What do you mean by the words, "He may remove it if he likes ?"

Answer.—I meant that, as it was usual to rob everything that was placed there, I was utterly indifferent whether it was removed by the Mahanth or by any body else.

Question.—Then you would not have considered its removal hurtful to your religious feelings ?

Answer.—Oh certainly. It would hurt not only my religious feelings but those of Buddhists. When I said I was indifferent, I meant if it was clandestinely removed without our knowledge. When I was going to Buddha-Gaya on the morning of the 25th February, I did not expect to meet with opposition in placing the image. I think I can swear that.

Question.—Did you take writing materials on that occasion?

Answer.—Such as are always in my despatch box which I always carry with me. I carried the despatch box because I had in it a very sacred relic of Buddha. It is supposed to be part of the remains of the Buddha. The technical name is *sarire dhatu*. It is about the size of a coriander seed. That was the only reason I took the box with me.

Question.—Did you do anything with the relic?

Answer.—No, it remained in the box. I had the two letters from Government which I have put in the box.

Question.—Did you during the occurrence show to the mukhtear or any one the Government letter to show that you had authority to do it under that?

Answer.—I did not show it to the mukhtear, but I showed it subsequently to the police jemadar when he came upstairs. I have no knowledge of any Buddhist having tried to enshrine any image on the upper floor. The stage at which I first noticed any of the Mahanth's men was when we were going to light the candles ceremoniously. At that time several of them rushed in together. Before that I had seen of the accused the Muhammadan Hussain Baksh. The first rush of the Mahanth's men was before I sat in contemplation. When they came, I thought it was to oppose me, as they did oppose. I knew that Hussain Baksh was the Mahanth's Mukhtear. I did not suspect that he was there watching the Mahanth's interests in this matter.

Question.—Then it is the fact that after you knew the Mahanth's men were opposing you, you sat down in contemplation?

Answer.—When I sat down in contemplation I felt perfectly assured no opposition was meant, and that I was perfectly free, as they had retired. They were away for, I think, about 15 minutes or so.

Question.—Did they all go away or did any of the Mahanth's men remain?

Answer.—Those who opposed me went away, but some remained. I could not say where the latter remained, as I was in contemplation. When I was going to sit down in contemplation I saw, I think, a few standing to my right. Those who remained were not talking to me. When I sat down none of them spoke to me.

Question.—After the first batch retired and before you sat down in contemplation, did any of those who remained speak to you?

Answer.—None of them spoke to me after the others had retired.

Question.—Did you actually see the faces of the men who took down the image from the altar, while in the act of taking it down?

Answer.—Yes, when I raised my eyes I think I saw one. I think I am sure I saw one. When I was contemplating I had my eyes down-cast, but not actually shut.

Question.—When you were contemplating, will you swear that not even the existence of the Mahanth occurred to you?

Answer.—I sat down with the perfect delight that no opposition was again meant, and from that time I was in pure religious contemplation. The reason I thought no oppostiion was meant was that one batch had retired. I was contemplating on the compassion of Buddha, his great self-sacrifice to humanity, and was concentrating on the virtues of love and peace. It was not on peace with the Mahanth in particular, it was on the subject of peace with all—universal peace.

I am not aware that in June, 1894, the Mahanth in a letter to the Collector of Gaya made a claim to take all the votive offerings of the Mahábodhi Temple as proprietor thereof. I have never heard of his having made such a claim before.

[The defence here asked for the production of a letter No. 7 E., dated 18 June, 1894 from the Mahanth to the Collector of Gaya. The letter was allowed by the Collector to be produced and shown to witness.]

Question.—Did you ever see that letter or a copy of it?

Answer.—No.

On the 25th of February there was nothing on the altar of Mayadevi in the upper storey of the Temple, except the image of Mayadevi, including the pedestal and every thing. I think the Japanese image is almost the same height as the image of Mayadevi. The image of Mayadevi is in the centre of the altar. I have worshipped that image. I think I did so several times on my previous visits. If I ever go to the upper storey, I worship it. I have gone several times. How often I cannot say. I have never sat in contemplation there before.

Question.—Did you ever make any offerings to Mayadevi there before?

Answer.—I have lighted candles, but not made offerings. I brought the Japanese image in a box.

Question.—Would coolies carrying the image from one place to another defile the image?

Answer.—Not when enclosed in a box.

Question.—If masons were to repair a temple and remove a figure of Buddha for the purpose of repairing the Temple, would you consider that a defilement of the image?

Answer.—According to Buddhist rites images are always removed by priests and *upasakas* or authorized laymen, not by masons. If masons were authorized by Buddhist rites and performed the necessary oblutions, they would not be masons for the time being, and for them then to remove an image would not be defiling it.

Question.—Would you worship an image that had been touched by unauthorized masons?

Answer.—If masons removed it from the altar, it would not again be worshipped until it had been replaced.

Question.—If any unauthorized mason were to touch an image at all, whether on the altar or not, would that defile the image?

Answer.—If he touched it when it was on the altar with a malicious motive, that would be defiling it. If the image were in an unsanctified place, such as under a tree, the image would not be the object of worship or considered sacred, and so we would not care. By malicious motive, I mean with intent to defile the image or insult the religion of the Buddhists.

Question.—If an unauthorized person were to touch an image without that intention, but in the ordinary discharge of his work, for instance, in cleaning the room or accidentally, would that be defiling the image?

Answer.—No, it would not be defilement.

Question.—Then you do not consider that, when Mr. Beglar and his men brought the big image of Buddha from the monastery and placed it in the temple without Buddhistic rites, the image was in any way defiled?

Answer.—If it was done with a good intention, in the interests of the Buddhists, then there is no defilement, because there has been no destructive motive meant. From my knowledge of the facts, and knowing it was done with a constructive motive, I do not consider that what Mr. Beglar did was any defilement.

Question.—If Mr. Beglar had placed that image solely in the interests of archæology, irrespective of any "constructive motive," would it be defilement?

Answer.—Not placing it upon the altar: if it was put on the altar simply with archæological motives, it was not defilement.

Question.—If he has placed any image of Buddha anywhere, not on the altar, in the interests of archæology and without any malacious motive, has he defiled that image?

Answer.—With respect to an image in an unsanctified place, it does not matter.

Question.—Supposing that there was an image of Buddha from ancient times on the altar of the Temple or in any sanctified place in it, and Mr. Beglar removed it for purely archæological purposes, and placed it anywhere he chose, would the image have been defiled thereby?

Answer.—If it was an object of worship for the time being, and if it was removed purely in the interests of archæology to another important or historical sanctified place, then it is not defiled.

Tathagata is a synonym for Buddha.

Question.—Have you ever heard that Modern Hindus regard Buddha as Vishnu?

Answer.—I have heard that.

Question.—When did you first hear it?

Answer.—I learned it from my studies. I learned it before I came to India.

(*Shown an Editorial paragraph on page 2 of the Journal for September* 1893). I did not write that or cause it to be published I was away at the time. I don't agree in the remark made in the sentence there, to the effect that the Brahmans, versed in the Vedas, worship the Tathagata's image.

D. 29.

The Brahmans who are versed in the Vedas and the Tantras, and also the Buddhist Mahatmas living at all times in those holy places, but in a manner unseen and unperceived by the unbelievers, worship the Tathagata's image.

(Mahabodhi Society's Journal, September, 1893, *p.* 2.)

It is quite contrary to the Hindu *shastras* as I know them. Vedic Brahmans can never worship the image of Tathagata.

(*Passage put in and marked Exhibit D29.*)

Question.—Do you consider Puri one of the places where Buddhists have been ousted by Hindus?

Answer.—No, the Buddhists have nothing to do with Puri.

Question.—Do you want to get the Jagannath Temple back?

Answer.—The Buddhists do not put forward any claim to that.

D. 30.

THE JAGANNATH TEMPLE REPAIRS FUND.

THIS historic place of worship, which contains relics of Buddhism and rock-cut temples, where still the influence of the gentle Tathagata is felt, is being embellished by the restoration of the old temples now in ruins. A strong Committee, consisting of eminent Hindus, set to work to collect funds about a year ago, and now they have collected over Rs. 1,00,000 from all parts of India. For the two hundred millions of Hindus Jagannath Temple is the central shrine and hundreds of thousands of pilgrims from all parts of India flock thither to commemorate the festival which is held yearly on the full-moon day of May—June. The temple is situated at Puri, in Orissa, on the north-east coast of India.

What an irony of fate that the central shrine of the Buddhists, 475 millions in number, has gone into alien hands. The time is come to rescue it, and everything is in our favor; given a lakh (1,00,000) of rupees, and the temple shall revert to the hands of its legitimate custodians, the Buddhists.

(Mahabodhi Society's Journal, June, 1893, *p.* .)

(*Shown a paragraph headed "The Jagannath Temple Repairs Fund" at page* 3 *of the Journal for June,* 1893.)

That paragraph was taken from one of the newspapers. I think I took it from a paragraph that was going round the newspapers of the day. The comment in the last paragraph of it was not takon from the newspapers. I am the author of that.

(*Put in and marked Exhibit D30*).

The last paragraph there refers to the Mahábodhi Temple.

D. 31.

SRIMAT CHAITANYA, THE APOSTLE OF JAGANNATH.

THIS great reformer of Bengal was born in the year 1485 A.D. He commenced his religious career in 1513. The following is taken from Dr. Rajendralala's "Orissa Antiquities:"—

"Chaitanya found the temple of Jagannath the best adapted for the purpose. The old Buddhistic character of the place had been preserved to a great extent. The images that were there were those of divinities

(*Shown an extract headed "Srimat Chaitanya the Apostle of Jagannath" at page 8 of the Journal for May,* 1894.)

I extracted that from Dr. Rajendra Lal Mitra's work on Orissa Antiquities. I did not consider it true at the time; but I inserted it on account of its sympathetic tone.

(*Put in and marked Exhibit D31*).

There are several *Samadhis* (tombs) east of the Mahábodhi Temple. They who were as yet no members of the Hindu pantheon by analogy, the name of the principal divinity was of so unsectarian a character that it left a wide room for innovation; and caste distinctions, which elsewhere raised insuperable barriers against a wide system of proselytism, had been long since destroyed by Buddhism and never been revived. These were exactly the conditions which suited his purposes best, and he did not fail to take advantage of them to the utmost extent possible."

* * * * *

Looking moreover to the history of Buddhism in other parts of India, and the way in which the Buddhist doctrine of the identity of the human soul with divinity was appropriated by some of the Vedantins, the Buddhist belief of the sanctity of the Bo Tree made a part of the Hindu religion, the Buddhist repugnance to animal sacrifices taken up by Vaishnavas and Buddhist emblems, Buddhist temples, Buddhist sacred places and Buddhist practices appropriated to Hindu usages, it is impossible to resist the conclusion that Puri was like Gaya, a place of Buddhist sanctity, gradually converted to Hinduism." (p. 107.)

(Mahabodhi Society's Journal, May. 1894, p. 8.)

are said to be tombs of Hindu Mahanths. The nearest is within about 4 feet of the Mahabodhi Temple. There is a small temple to the east of the *samadhis* with a figure in it which, I think, Hindus call Annapurna, but which I don't recognise as that. I do not think it is a figure of Buddha, but it may be a figure of a Bodhisatva, *i.e.*, one who aspires to become a Buddha. It means a Buddhist who aspires to Buddhahood. Ever since I came to Gaya I have known of the Hindus worshipping that image as Annapurna.

Question.—When did you first come to know that the Hindus had put a dress to which you have objection, on the great image of Buddha on the ground floor?

Answer.—I think I came to know it first when I was in Ceylon last year in October, after the visit of the Lieutenant-Governor to Buddha-Gaya. I heard then there had been an attempt to convert the image into a Hindu one.

Question.—When did you first hear that images of Buddha anywhere about Buddha-Gaya had been objectionably clothed by the Hindus?

Answer.—Two or three years ago, I saw several Buddhistic images in the Mahanth's monastery, which had been painted and clothed in such a manner as to destroy their Buddhistic character. I do not think I went to the monastery on the occasion of my first visit to Buddha-Gaya. I may have gone round the enclosure. I think I may have entered the enclosure then. I did enter the enclosure, but whether I went into the monastery I cannot remember. I have seen several Buddha images plastered against the wall of the monastery and some buried under rubbish. In the outer enclosure, to which I went on the occasion of my first visit, I think I then saw red paint on some of the Buddhistic images. That was in the outer enclosure where the well is. I can't remember whether I saw any such images clothed. I thought they had put on the red paint for the purpose of Hindu worship—the Buddhistic aspect was entirely obliterated. That visit was before the foundation of the Mahábodhi Society.

Question.—Did you, on the occasion of your second visit, see any images any where about Buddha-Gaya, which you considered had at one time been Buddhistic images, clothed in a manner that you considered objectionable?

Answer.—I cannot say that I saw any such. I saw some images all covered up, but I could not say if they had once been Buddhist images. My second visit was in July, 1891. My third was, I believe, in October, 1891. I think my fourth visit was about February, 1892.

Question.—When did you first see any image of Buddha clothed in what you consider an objectionable manner anywhere in Buddha-Gaya?

Answer.—The first time I saw an image which I knew to be one of Buddha objectionably clothed was in January of this year. I swear I never saw a true image of Buddha so clothed before. I wrote an article headed "The History of the Great Temple of Buddha-Gaya" in the Journal for December, 1892. (Shown a paragraph at page 5, beginning "The images of Buddha and the Bodhisatvas have undergone transformation in having clothes put on them.")

D. 32.

The images of Buddha and the Bodhisatvas found in the Mahant's *baradari* have undergone transformation in having clothes put on them; but the unconverted statues found outside his garden are allowed to rot and be trampled by cattle.

(Mahabodhi Society's Journal, December, 1892, *p.* 5.)

(Paragraph put in and marked Exhibit D. 32).

Question.—Did you believe that to be true at the time you wrote it?

Answer.—It was a descriptive article, and I wrote it without accurate investigation, that is, I presumed that they were images of Buddha, not being able to go to the spot where they were. I saw them from a distance of 20 or 30 feet. It was in the day time. The article was hurriedly written, and I did not get all the details accurately.

When the above was read over the witness said he had two corrections to make, first on page 76 to the effect that what he said was that "Mr Beglar was appointed by the Society," not that it was witness who appointed him, which he did not; and, secondly, at page 83 to the effect that his expenses were paid partly by himself and partly by others—not partly by the Society. With the above corrections, witness admitted the deposition to be correctly recorded.

D. J. MACPHERSON,

6th May, 1895. *Magistrate.*

7th May, 1895.

Witness for Prosecution, I.

H. Dharmapala further cross-examined on solemn affirmation, states:—

I was never present anywhere when any proposal was made to purchase the Temple from the Mahanth.

Question.—Were you present on the 31st October, 1891, at what you call an International Buddhist Conference?

Answer.—I was.

(Shhown a passage now marked (c) in Exibit D9 already put in.)

D. 9(*c*).

Mr. Tokuzawa said that he is authorized by the Nishi Honganji Temple authorities to announce to the Conference that they are willing to buy the Temple from the Mahant.

Y. Ato, the Japanese delegate, said that he had come to make enquiries about the Temple, and that if the Mahant gives a written document, stating the amount he wants for the Temple, that all the sects of Japan would then raise money for the purpose.

After long discussion it was resolved that a deputation should not wait on the Mahant to make any proposal about the purchase of the Buddha-Gaya Temple. It was resolved to call for subscriptions from all Buddhist countries to build the Monastery.

(Mahabodhi Society's Journal, April, 1893, p. 3)

The statements here mentioned were made at that Conference in my presence. I took part in the Conference. I was not present at a meeting held at the Mahinda College Hall in Ceylon, in May 1893.

(Shown a report under the head "Correspondence" at page 6 of the Journal for August, 1893.)

I am not sure if I caused that report to be inserted. I was not in India at the time. I may have read it later, after my return, that is, several months later. I cannot remember in what month I returned. The thanks of that meeting were never communicated to me as stated in the report. I was away, and I never got them. I have no recollection of ever having written to those who reported that meeting to say the Mahanth was not in possession, and that it was unnecessary therefore to raise money to purchase the Temple from him.

Report put in and marked Exhibit D33. The prosecution remind the Court that their general objection made as regards anything that appeared in the Journal being exhibited in this case applies. D. J. M.

D. 33.

CORRESPONDENCE.

On the 7th May last, a grand meeting was held in the Mahinda College Hall. There were present, among others, Dr. J. Bowles Daly, Messrs. E. R. Goonaratna, G. C. A. Jayasekera, G. P. Weerasekera, D. O. D. S. Goonasekera, D. E. A. Jayasingha and O. A. Jayasekera.

Mr. E. R. Goonaratna was voted to the Chair, and Mr. O. A. Jayasekera as the Secretary of the meeting. The Chairman opened the meeting, explaining at length the importance of the Buddha-Gaya premises to the Buddhists. The inexhaustible treasures which the buildings on the spot give to the historian, the philosopher, the poet and the traveller; the history of the ruins which on his visit he found to be so great as to be able to fill up about 10 houses like the College; the attention paid by the Indian Government in repairing the temple at the expense of about a lakh of rupees; how he was kindly shown all the noteworthy things on the spot by Mr. Beglar, the Superintendent of the Works, and how his attention was drawn to an inscription on a slab which

Question.—When did you first engage pleaders in regard to contemplated litigation about the Temple?

Answer.—There was no contemplated litigation, but we engaged a pleader in February or March, 1893, as our legal adviser, namely, Babu Nand Kishore Lal. To my recollection that was the first time I ever engaged a lawyer. I think was to the effect by King Kasup of Lanka; how he was treated by Mahanta, and what accommodations are opened to the pilgrims by Mahanta, and how his resources grow in proportion to the visits of pilgrims and the offerings made. Then he concluded his glowing address by appealing to the assembly to do what they can possibly do to ensure the success of the laudable object of the Mahâ-Bodhi Society, whose indefatigable worker is Mr. H. Dharmapala.

Mr. D. O. D. S. Goonasekera, addressing the meeting, said that he regretted very much for his inability to speak in such glowing terms as the Chairman has done, who has seen the place. To allow such a sanctified spot as Buddha-Gaya to be desecrated is, to say the least, most deplorable and most culpable on our part. Mr. H. Dharmapala, the head of the Theosophical Society and other kindly disposed gentlemen are now trying hard to secure the free use of the place for the Buddhists, and, on our part, if we do not co-operate with them thereby, we become miserable and disdainful. Therefore, let us not deny our help, the more so, because it is the very spot where all the great souls become Buddhas. Then the following resolution having been moved by him, was carried out :—

"That this meeting is convened for the purpose of making arrangements to collect subscriptions from the Southern Province to enable the Mahâ-Bodhi Society to purchase the most sacred shrine of the Buddhists."

Mr. D. L. Dhanayaka said that Buddhism is destined to be in the world for 5,000 years, and not even half of the period has expired. The spot of ground on which the great sage became Buddha, and the spot on which the great Bo-tree stood, most undoubtedly demand the admiration and love of all the Buddhists. Therefore now it is time to help Mr. Dharmapala to enable him under the sound advice of the Mahâ-Bodhi Society to secure the place for the Buddhists. Then the following resolution proposed by him was carried out :—

"That it is most disadvantageous to the interest of the Buddhists and Buddhism, and that it is a reflection on those professing this religion that their most sacred shrine should be in the hands of aliens, and consequently all present are kindly requested to cooperate in collecting subscriptions."

Mr. G. C. A. Jayasekera said that although he was in bed up to this moment, being attacked with rheumatism, yet his enthusiasm gave wings to his feet to attend the meeting; and that he was sorry as his ailment denies him the free use of his breath. He proposed the following resolution which was carried out :—

"That for this purpose a Committee be formed in Galle of the undermentioned gentlemen to collect subscriptions to be forwarded from time to time. Messrs. E. R. Goonaratna, Arthur Jayawardena, Dr. J. B. Daly, with power to add more to the number."

Mr. G. P. Weerasekera moved the following resolution which was carried out :—

"That this meeting tenders its acknowledgments to Mr. H. Dharmapala for the unfeigned interest he evinces in this undertaking, and that its thanks be conveyed to him by the Secretary with the proceedings of the meeting."

O. A. JAYASEKERA,
Secretary.

(Mahabodhi Society's Journal, August, 1893, p. 6.)

EXHIBIT I.

I, H. Dharmapala, General Secretary of the Maha-Bodhi Society, on this 25th day of February, 1895, in the presence of two Sinhalese Bhikshus (Priests) and one Sinhalese lay Buddhist, enshrined on the altar of the second storey of the Maha-Bodhi Temple, the image of Buddha brought from Japan, and which was presented by the Japanese Buddhists to be enshrined therein.

that Col. Olcott took legal advice about the assault on the priests, but that was in the same month. I think I can swear that, until then, we did not consult any lawyer anywhere or take any legal opinion. Babu Nand Kishore Lal was the first to be appointed our regular pleader. Before the arrival of the Japanese image, I engaged no other lawyer either on my behalf or on behalf of the Society. There was no contemplated litigation in connection with the Temple in February, 1893, but there was a case in connection with the assault on the Buddhist priests.

Question.—Will you swear that in February, 1893, Babu Nand Kishore Lal was not appointed for the purpose of inquiry into the validity of the Mahanth's tenure of the Temple?

Answer.—He was appointed in connection with the general work of the Society, and that matter was included in it.

Question.—Repeated.

Answer.—He was not appointed for the specific purpose, but that was included in the appointment, so to speak.

(*Read a passage now marked* (*a*) *in Exhibit D4*).

I have before said that that report was drawn up by Col. Olcott.

Question.—When did it first strike you that you would have to come into Court, civil or criminal, in connection with the Temple?

Answer.—After the 25th February last.

Question.—Is it a fact that you have retained barristers in Calcutta?

Answer.—I have engaged counsel in Calcutta. It is in connection with this case.

Question.—Is it a fact that no counsel in Calcutta was retained or consulted by you or your Society before the 25th February last?

Answer.—I have no recollection whatever of any such thing before this case.

My statement to the Police (Exhibit I.) was written out by me in the Temple, the whole of it, in presence of the Police Jemadar.

There were present at the time the Mukhtear and two other Musulman gentlemen. After setting the image up, I requested the custodian of the Temple, Babu Bepin Behari Banerjee, to be present, and then I told him that I have freed myself from the responsibility of care taker of the image, and that the image is now under the control of the authorities, and that if the Mahanth wishes he can do anything with it. About a quarter after ten o'clock, when the priests were going to light the candles, a few of the Sanyasis with some laymen and the Muhammadan Mukhtear came up and threatened me and ordered the removal of the image. I insisted on my right and freedom of worship and begged them to leave me alone. They interfered and did not allow the priests to light the candles. The Lieutenant-Governor of Bengal, in his letter No. 6 P. D., Political Branch, of 5th May, 1894, assured the Buddhists that "there is perfect freedom of worship for all Buddhists at Buddh-Gaya"; this freedom of worship has not been allowed; we were insulted when we were at our devotions; the image and other things that were placed before it, as well as the Japanese letter, were forcibly removed from the altar by the Mahanth's men. I spoke not a word, but kept perfectly still.

A policeman came up to me, and then I requested him to send for the *Jamadar*, and then at his request and before him I have written this statement.

H. DHARMAPALA,
General Secretary, M.-B. S.
M. SUMANGALA,
Signature in Sinhalese Character
Signed "Devananda."
N. P. D. SILVA.

(Put in by prosecution on May 1 : see p. 6, *ante*.)

Question.—Did he ask you to write that statement, or did you offer to do so ?

Answer.—He put me questions in Hindustani, and I did not understand them all, and he gave me that paper and I wrote my statement down.

Question.—Did you intend this to be a complaint to the Police or not ?

Answer.—I do not think I gave it as a complaint to him. I intended it in general to be a statement of what had just taken place. (*adds*). I did not go into full details as I was surrounded by an angry mob, and my mind was not then in a calm state.

Question.—Why do you add of yourself that you did not go into details ?

Answer.—Because it is the truth.

Question.—Will you swear that no one has drawn your attention since that statement was made, to the fact that it does not contain all that you have since alleged ?

Answer.—I swear that no one has suggested to me what I have said just now.

Question.—Repeated.

Answer.—I am unable to say.

Question.—Between the 25th February and the presentation of your complaint before the Magistrate, did you consult any legal adviser on the subject of the case ?

Answer.—I did. I had to consult in order to get the complaint drawn up. I presented the petition two days, or perhaps three, after the occurrence. During the interval, I think, I had only one interview with any legal adviser. That may have been on the 27th, or on the evening of the 26th, after my arrival from Bodh-Gaya I returned from Bodh-Gaya on the evening of the 26th. I saw my pleader that evening. I do not think I saw him again on the 27th, but I may have. I remember I saw him on the evening of the 26th.

Question.—When did you first learn that the Viceroy was likely to come to Gaya this year ?

Answer.—I think about a fortnight before his arrival. I have no recollection of hearing it before that—it did not concern me. To my knowledge, my Society has not tried to approach the Viceroy or the Government of India on this subject, and I do not think any one on behalf of our Society has attempted to do so. I have no recollection of any attempt of the kind to my knowledge.

I know the Reverend W. Subhuti of Ceylon. He is one of the Chief Priests of the Buddhist religion in Ceylon. I have known him for a long time, since my youth. I am not very intimate with him. I do not think he knows English, but he signs in English.

(Shown the signature on a letter : letter itself not shown.)

That is his signature. I know P. N. M. W. Subhuti. He is the same person who signs himself W. Subhuti. I am familiar with the stamp he uses. *Shown an envelope.*) The stamp on this I know as his.

Question.—Do you know whose handwriting this is on the envelope, "Forward this to the Mahanth of Budh Gaya?"

Answer.—I think it is Mr. Grierson's.

D. 34.

WASKADUWA KALUTARA,
CEYLON, *4th September*, 1891.

MOST RESPECTED SIR,

I AM glad to say that I received your letter, dated the 12th ultimo, which has been sent by Mr. Grierson, Government Agent, who is ready to render me his favor jointly with you, and rejoiced at the information therein that the graft will reach me in about three months. The branch, when separated from the tree, should in my opinion be planted in a tub to take root before sending it here. I have to request of you some other aids which will not trouble you much, *viz.*, one or two stone statues of Buddha and some pieces of relics of saints found in the ruins of the old monuments. If this is possible they should be accompanied with the branch of the sacred Bo-Tree. Major-General Cunningham, who had been appointed to repair the ruins at the spot, sent me some relics which I doubt to be those of the saints of the faith. Rajendra Lala Mittra, L. L. D., had sent a stone statue, and also promised to send me a stone having the sacred footprints of our Lord found in the very spot, which is at present in his possession and placed at his residence, but unfortunately his unexpected death did not permit him to keep his word of honor.

I am in great anxiety to have a pilgrimage to the holy site should my health permit me, when I expect to see you.

I am always willing to procure for you, as soon as I am informed, anything you require of me from this Island that lies in my power. It is easy for me to understand if you will write to me in Sanskrit.

I am now in good health and sound, and hope that you also are the same.

With constant fidelity,
I AM,
Your faithful and sincere friend,
W. SUBHUTI.

[The above letter and envelope are tendered in evidence to show how the Buddhist Priests long prior to this litigation regarded the Mahanth. Counsel for prosecution object on the ground that the evidence is irrelevant. Defence say it is relevant and important, as showing that in 1891 the Buddhists regarded the Mahanth as having control over the Temple, and that the Mahanth has therefore acted in good faith. The prosecution say there is nothing to show that the letter in question is addressed to the Mahanth, and that there is nothing to show that the letter came in the envelope produced. The defence admit they cannot prove that the letter came in that envelope, and therefore they are willing to tender them separately, but contend it is enough they come from their custody. Documents allowed to be put in for what they are worth as evidence of the point mentioned above, and marked Exhibits D34 and D35.]

D. 35.

MAHANT

THE PRINCIPAL IN CHARGE OF

BUDDHA-GYA TEMPLE.

Forward this to the Mahanth of Budh-Gaya.

G. A. G.—18-9-91.

I have seen several maps of Mastipur Taradih. I have seen a map of the Government Revenue Survey of Taradih.

[*Shown a certified copy of the Revenue Survey Map of mauza Mastipur Taradih, Pargana Maher, Season* 1842-43.]

I have never seen a map like that. I did not last year make a comparison with a Revenue Survey map, in order to see whether the Temple is included in the Mahanth's *farman*.

Question.—Did you make such at any time?

Answer.—I have made a comparison with the Survey map of Buddha-Gaya, but I am not sure if I have made one with the map of Taradih. That was in 1893. The object was to ascertain the actual facts of the survey, to see what the map contains and what it does not. The month was, I believe, May, 1893. I did not make the comparison myself. I showed it to Mr. Beglar. I was present when the comparison was made.

Question.—In the map itself was the Temple marked ?

Answer.—There was no mention of the Temple in it. It is merely a survey of the land of Buddha-Gaya.

Question.—Was it one of the objects of the comparison to find whether the Mahanth's claim was legitimate or not ?

Answer.—It was to find out what the survey map of the Maha-Bodhi land contains. I had not thought of the legitimacy of the Mahanth's claim. (*Question repeated*).—I did not go into the question. It is impossible to answer the question in the way it is put. My principal object was what I have stated.

(*Revenue Survey Map of Mastipur Taradih put in and marked D36.*)

I sent copies of the Journal of the Maha-Bodhi Society to the Mahanth. I remember sending the first two or three numbers, but I then discontinued doing so. I remember sending several numbers. I do not think I sent all the numbers of 1892.

D. 37.

THE BUDH-GAYA TEMPLE.

MR. H. DHARMAPALA, Secretary to the Maha-Bodhi Society of which the chief aim is to get back the Budh Gaya Temple from the hands of its present Brahmin custodians, writes to us as follows : "I have to work single-handed in this great Empire, for the Buddhists have no idea of the tolerant spirit of the Hindus. They seem to think that we shall be treated unkindly by them. We solicit the sympathy of your people, and you will be doing us the greatest favour if you will call upon your people to show their sympathy with our work. We want to get back our Central Shrine in Budh-Gaya ; but the Government fears that the Hindus will raise objections if the temple be transferred to us. The King of Siam does and the late King of Burma did support the Brahmans ; and in Siam, the Buddhists get the Brahmin priests to perform all Vedic ceremonies. The Brahmans have always been supported by the Buddhists, and so there could be no hostility between the two great families." We remember there was at one time last year every prospect of the Temple being restored to the Buddhists, as the result of an amicable arrangement with the present Mahant of Budh-Gaya. But the negotiations ultimately failed, for reasons which we do not know. So far as the general body of Hindus are concerned, we believe there is no serious objection to the temple being restored to the Buddhists. Indeed, such a course would be most natural and proper ; but then the Mahant's private or prescriptive rights cannot be altogether ignored, although it is not impossible for some satisfactory settlement of these rights to be made.—*Behar Times.*

(Mahabodhi Society's Journal, June, 1894, *p.* 16).

(*Shown a paragraph at page* 16 *of the number for June,* 1894, *headed* "*The Budh-Gaya Temple.*")

Question.—Did you cause the reproduction there from the *Behar Times* ?

Answer.—Yes, I wrote a letter to the Manager of that Journal, not for the purpose of publication, and there is an extract from it in the Journal as reproduced from the *Behar Times.*

(*Article put in and marked Exhibit D 37.*)

I am not the Treasurer of the Maha-Bodhi Society. The Treasurer is Babu Nilcomul Mukerjee He is not a Buddhist, but a Hindu. He is Honorary Treasurer. He is a Hindu by religion, not merely by birth. He is in the firm of Messrs. Graham and Co., and is a respectable gentleman. The money is spent at times under my direction, at times under the Society's direction. I have appealed to the Buddhist public for funds in connection with this case, and have got money.

Question.—Have you been telling them that the local officials are on your side ?

Answer.—I am not in a position to say so. I have, I think, in my letters stated that I believe the local officials see the justice of our case, I mean the assault case.

Question.—Have you ever gone the length of telling any body that Mr. Macpherson, Collector of Gaya, has expressed indignation at this desecration of the Temple, meaning thereby the occurrence of the 25th of February ?

Answer.—I did say so, but I immediately contradicted it, as it was merely on hearsay information that I stated it. I contradicted it in the papers.

Question.—Did you contradict it voluntarily?

Answer.—Certainly, I did so entirely of my motion.

Question.—What led you to contradict it?

Answer.—On hearing it was not true. I heard it in open court from the Magistrate that it was not true. It was that that led me to contradict it, the hearsay report being found false.

Question.—Was it not your object in circulating this hearsay report to enlist the sympathy of your people and get money for this case?

Answer.—No.

Question.—Did you so far back as March, 1893, state at page 5 of your Journal, " Mr. Macpherson in his individual capacity expressed his cordial sympathy with the Buddhists?"

Answer.—I wrote that on my own responsibility, but I was immediately rebuked by Mr. Macpherson the first time after that, that he saw me. I have not published any contradiction of it in the Journal. The object in my saying this was not in the least in order to get support from the Buddhists.

After the occurrence of the 25th February last, I sent a telegram to the press.

(*Shown a telegram purporting to come from the General Secretary of the Maha-Bodhi Society in the " Statesman " of the 28th February*, 1895.)

That is the telegram I sent; it is the one I contradicted. I don't know whether my contradiction has appeared. I did not take the trouble to see whether the contradiction appeared or not.

(*Put it and marked Exhibit D* 38.)

(*Shown an article at page* 93 *of the Journal for April*, 1895, *headed* " *Desecration of the Maha-Bodhi Temple.*")

I issued that appeal on my individual responsibility. It is not an appeal for funds—not specially so.

(*Put in and marked Exhibit D* 39.)

D. 38.

(TELEGRAMS.)

DISTURBANCE AT THE BUDHA-GAYA TEMPLE.

(*From General Secretary, Mahabodhi Society.*)

GAYA, *27th February.*

WHEN the Buddhist Priests were performing worship in the Mahabodhi Temple of Budha-Gaya, some Mahanths and Sanyasis with Mohamedan retinues, entered the sanctum, insulted the priests and snatched away the great Japanese image of Buddha. A police investigation is proceeding. The Collector has expressed indignation at the desecration.
[*Extract from the " Statesman," February* 28, 1895.]

D. 39.

DESECRATION OF THE MAHA-BODHI TEMPLE.

THE following petition which I have presented to the District Magistrate of Gaya will speak for itself, and the facts therein stated will show the high-handedness of the Mahânt's *chelas* and retainers who desecrated the Temple and outraged the feelings of unoffending, peace-loving followers of BUDDHA.

Now that an attempt has been made by the Mahânt claiming the sacred site and the historic Temple as places of Hindu worship, it is high time that the Buddhists should wake up. He asserts that BUDDHA is a Hindu god, and that the Temple is Hindu, and that to put an image of BUDDHA in the Temple by Buddhists is a sacrilege, and therefore that no Buddhist can enshrine any image therein.

The Mahânt is a Saivite Hindu, a follower of Sankarâcharya who, if we are to believe that apocryphal work, the " Sankara digvijaya ", should be the last man to claim a Buddhist Temple as his own and BUDDHA as his God! But we are living in the Kali-Yuga, and nothing selfish is therefore impossible.

Two years ago, when the Mahânt's *Sanyâsis* severely assaulted the Buddhist priests then living at Buddha-Gáya, and when the Police authorities instituted a case against the assailants, I did all that was in my power to stop legal proceedings; and the priests declined to give evidence against the men, and the case had to be withdrawn. Then only personalities were concerned; in this instance, the religious feelings of millions of people have been wounded, a historic image sent by the Japanese Buddhists as an offering to their shrine, has been desecrated. The image was enshrined in the Temple on February 25th, 1895, in the presence of the Deputy Magistrate of Gáya; and now that we have been dragged into the court, we shall have to fight to the last. Individually I deplore that this incident has occurred. My mission is one of peace, and this beautiful image was brought by me as a token of love, devotion and loyalty of the Japanese Buddhists to India, their motherland.

The image is now lying outside the Temple, exposed to the East winds; but it is under the custody of the Police.

The case is now before the Magistrate of Gáya, and as it has to go through several stages before it is decided, there will be a drain on the Society's exchequer. Eminent Counsel has been retained, and the case has to be pushed on to its conclusion. Funds are wanted, and I ask all loyal Buddhists to send help at once.

[NOTE.—Here follows the petition to the Magistrate of February 28, 1895, on which the present proceedings are being taken. See *post*, among the Documentary Evidence.]

(Mahabodhi Society's Journal, April, 1895, p. 93).

(*Shown a passage at page 8 of the Journal for December, 1893, about the money-loving British.*)

I am the author of these words. They were simply my impressions.

D. 40.

Under the Burman kings the Burmese people were happy; under the British Raj, they have been made the slaves of selfishness. The impartial historian of the future will decide whether it was a blessing for the people to have been made the slaves of vice and drunkenness by the money-loving British. They were better off under their own Kings. Drink was unknown, beef-eating was done only by the outcast, and the slaughtering of animals was prohibited. But what a change now! Crime is daily increasing, and poverty is stalking about: Western liquor has been introduced, and with it opium.

(Mahabodhi Society's Journal, December, 1893, p. 8.)

[Passage put in. Counsel for prosecution object to its relevancy. Defence say it indicates complainant's character as an adventurer trying to get up an agitation. Allowed to be put in; defence say they have no more of the kind to put. Admitted and marked Exhibit D 40.]

I am living in Gaya at present with Babu Durga Shankar Bhattacharjya, my witness. That has been since about the 28th February last. I have several times, when visiting Gaya on previous times, stayed with him. His brother Gadadhar is not a member of the Maha-Bodhi Society. I swear that. He shows sympathy to me. He is in court just now and has been here throughout the trial. He and his brother do not eat with me. I always eat separately. They never take me when they eat, as their caste rules prevent it. Durga Shankar is not a particular friend of mine, but he has been very kind to me ever since I brought letters of introduction to him in 1891. Dr. Haridas Chatterji is a brother-in-law of his. I came to know him through Durga Shankar. I cannot say whether I came to know Gangadhar Pandit through Durga Shankar. I don't know how I came to know him.

I have never seen a book published by the Government of Bengal, headed "A List of Objects of Antiquarian Interest in the Lower Provinces of Bengal." I have never seen any edition of that.

[Pages 125-7 of the above publication, edition of 1879, tendered in evidence to show that the Mahanth has been regarded by the Government of Bengal as proprietor of the Temple, and that the Temple had then been considered as appropriated to Hindu worship. Prosecution counsel objects that this has no concern with the witness's cross-examination, and that he objects to its relevancy except in so far as the Mahanth may have been led by it to entertain a *bonâ fide* belief as to his right to the Temple. Defence say they are going to put in also the edition of 1887, expected to-day. Allowed to be put in and marked Exhibit D 41. Defence put in from pp. 125-133 inclusive, and say the prosecution can refer to any part of the book.]

NOTE.—D41 is printed separately among the documentary evidence. See *post*.

Re-examined :—

This is the first time in my life I have ever given evidence in a court of Justice.

(*S hwn a report on page 1 of the Journal of the Maha-Bodhi Society for May, 1892.*)

That is a report of the first meeting of the Society, and that is also the first number of its Journal. That meeting was held at Colombo. I was present at it. On that occasion, officers were elected and their names are given in that report. Not one of the officers is a paid one. They are all honorary. That has been the case all throughout, and is so still. I have never been paid by the Society. On the contrary I pay out from my own pocket. My father is alive, and lives in Ceylon. He is a landholder, merchant and the sole proprietor of the firm "H. Don Karolis and Son." His annual income will be about Rs. 70,000 or Rs. 80,000 net income. He has a very large cocoanut plantation. He also has a furniture and upholstery business, the firm mentioned, and it is the largest business of the kind in Ceylon. At the first meeting of the Society a resolution was passed as to what the object of the Society should be. The general purport of it is published on page 1 of the Journal above referred to. Since the first meeting the number of officers has increased and representatives of the Society. The representatives are not confined to Ceylon, but belong also to other countries, which are Buddhist countries.

EXHIBIT III.

The Maha-Bodhi Society has commenced its mission for the resuscitation of Buddhism in the land of its birth, and within these eleven months the movement has been received with great sympathy. Since the commencement of our labours only words of encouragement have been received from all parts of the learned world.

"The hope of man is man,
"I would not let one cry whom I could save,"

said Sakya Muni. The encouragement we have received gives us hope to push forward.

The Society will have its Head-quarters at Buddha-Gaya, and it is hoped in time to establish on that sacred spot a monastery and a college. Translations of the Dharma into English and Indian Vernaculars have to be made. For the interchange of news between the Buddhist countries and Buddha-Gaya this Journal will serve as a vehicle. I hope that the Buddhist Societies of China, Japan, Siam, Burmah, Ceylon, Chittagong and Arakan will send for publication a monthly budget of Buddhist news. This would help to unite the Buddhists together in one common cause.

The Journal will, for the present, be issued monthly. Eminent Buddhist Bhikshus of Ceylon will, from time to time, write for the Journal. Colonel Olcott, the benefactor of the Buddhist people, will be a frequent contributor. Under his experienced leadership who shall say that the Buddha-Gaya movement can be a failure?

THE BUDDHA-GAYA MAHA-BODHI SOCIETY.

Established at Colombo, May, 31st, 1891.

OBJECTS.—The establishment of a Buddhist Monastery and founding a Buddhist College, and maintaining a staff of Buddhist Bhikshus at Buddha-Gaya representing the Buddhist countries of China, Japan, Siam, Cambodia, Burma, Ceylon, Chittagong, Nepal, Tibet, and Arakan.

The publication of Buddhist Literature in English and Indian Vernaculars.

To carry on this important work a sum of rupees one hundred thousand is required, which will be invested in Government Securities. Buddhists all over the world are invited to contribute liberally.

CONSTITUTION.

PRESIDENT.—Pradhana Nayaka, H. Sumangala, Maha Thera.

DIRECTOR AND CHIEF ADVISER.—Colonel H. S. Olcott.

GENERAL SECRETARY.—H. Dharmapala.

REPRESENTATIVES.

SIAM.—His Royal Highness, Chandradat Chudatdhar, Prince of Siam, Bangkok, Siam.

JAPAN.—Rt. Rev. Shaku Unsiyo, Shincho-ko-kuji, Mejiro, Tokyo, Japan. The Committee of Buddhist Sects, Jokyoji, Tera Machi Dori, Shojo Sagaru, Kyoto, S. Horiuchi, Esq., Secretary, Indo-Busseki Kofuko Society, Atago Shita, Tokyo.

CEYLON.—G. P. Weera Sekhara, 61 Maliban Street, Colombo.

BURMAH.—Moung Hpo Mhyin, K. S. M., Hon' Secretary, Maha Bodhi Society, 38, Commissioner's Road, Rangoon.

CALCUTTA.—The Secretary, Calcutta Maha-Bodhi Society, 20-1 Gangadhar Babu's Lane. Calcutta.

CHITTAGONG.—Krishna Chandra Chowdry, Secretary, Buddhist Aid Association, Raozan, Chittagong.

(*Page* 1 *of the Journal for May*, 1892, *put in and marked Exhibit* III.)

Since May, 1892, I have visited the following countries in connection with the Society:—Ceylon, Burma, Arrakan, Chittagong, Siam, Japan, Shanghai and Hongkong in China, and Singapore; and I met the Tibetan Buddhists at Darjeeling. I think these are the only countries I have visited in connection with the Society. I also visited America, but it was not in connection with the Society, but as the special delegate of the Buddhists at the Parliament of Religions in Chicago. I also visited England on my way to America and lectured in London. Since May, 1892, I have received lots of articles from different people from different countries which have been inserted in the Journal.

(Defence have objected to the last answer as not arising out of the cross-examination, but it was allowed as the cross-examination tended to make witness responsible for all views expressed in the Journal.)

The Journal has all along been published in Calcutta. Since May, 1892, I have visited Calcutta about eight or nine times, my head-quarters being there.

Question.—What was your longest stay in Calcutta during any one of those visits?

(Objected to by defence as irrelevant. Allowed on general ground indicated above.)

Answer.—My longest stay has been six or seven months. Whilst I am travelling in other countries, the publication of the Journal continues. When I am not in Calcutta the person who receives all articles for publication is the Acting Manager, and the Journal is conducted at different times by different Acting Managers.

Question.—As a matter of fact, are all letters and articles sent to your Journal for insertion first perused by you in manuscript or in proof before they are printed and published?

(Objected to as not arising out of cross-examination. Seeing that the latter asked specific information in regard to every article put in, the prosecution would have a right in re-examination to ask information in regard to the above point, in regard to every article put in in cross-examination, so that it tends really

ARAKAN.—Kaung Hla Pru, Asst. Commissioner's Office, Akyab.

All communications to be addressed to, H. Dharmapala, General Secretary, Maha-Bodhi Society, 22, Baniapooker Road, Entally, Calcutta.

(Mahabodhi Society's Journal May, 1892, p. 1.)

to shorten the re-examination to put the general question, and if specific information has already been given in cross-examination in regard to each article put in, the answer to the question now put cannot affect the matter much. Question allowed.)

Answer.—Not all.

(Shown Exhibit D 9 (*c*).*)*

Question.—Why was it resolved that a deputation should not wait on the Mahant with the proposal for the purchase of the Temple ?

Answer.—I pointed out to the delegates that the Temple is absolutely under the control of the Government and that the custodian looks after the Temple; and therefore that there was no use in approaching any body but the Government.

(*Shown telegrams printed at page* 3 *of the Journal for March,* 1893, *regarding the assault on the Buddhist priests.*)

Question.—Are these the telegrams which you were asked about in cross-examination and which you said you had sent about the assault ?

EXHIBIT IV.

The following telegrams appeared in the Indian Press :—

GAYA, *6th February*, 1893.

"Some Buddhist priests stationed at Buddha-Gaya by the Mahâ-Bodhi Society, were assaulted on Friday by the people in Mahant's interest, as alleged, while engaged in their evening devotions. One priest, peculiarly inoffensive, badly bruised, and wounded, is in the Gayá hospital. The police are investigating in the matter."

THE PERSECUTED BUDDHIST PRIESTS IN BUDDHA-GAYA.

[FROM A CORRESPONDENT.]

GAYA, *7th February*, 1893.

"The wounded Buddhist priest in hospital is convalescent. Apprehending further violence, the Mahâ-Bodhi Society has removed all Buddhist monks to Gaya. The cowardly attack has no sectarian basis, and is condemned by all respectable Hindus."

(Mahabodhi Society's Journal, March, 1893, p. 3.)

[Question objected to on the ground that the witness was only asked in general way whether he was in the habit of sending telegrams. The prosecution claim to put the telegrams in, in view of the detailed questions about them on page 9 of the cross-examination, and in reply to the attempt made in such cross-examination to make out that the witness has been in the habit of sending bogus telegrams. Telegrams allowed to be put in, but not as proof of the facts of the assault. Put in and marked Exhibit IV.]

Question.—Amongst those priests referred to in these telegrams, can you name any one ?

[Objected to as irrelevant, no question having been asked about the assault in cross-examination. The prosecution explain that this was to be followed by other questions to explain why no complaint of the assault was laid, as it was open on the evidence given about it for the defence to argue that in spite of this assault no complaint was laid because the priests knew that the Mahanth was in possession. The defence say that they will not argue whether a complaint of the assault was laid or not, or refer to the assault at all, as the sole object of the questions at page 9 was to test the veracity of the witness: for all the defence are entitled to say, they say, there may have been not only a complaint, but a conviction. Question accordingly disallowed.]

The objection I have to the passage on page 1 in Exhibit D 18, as quoted at the bottom of page 26 of my deposition, is that it is impossible to say what is there said unless the whole place is surveyed. I knew that the village of Bodh Gaya or Mahabodh belongs to the Tikari Raj.

The purport of the passage in the *Vinaya Pushpamálá* that gave me the idea of bringing the image from Japan was, that, when the Muhammadan conquerors invaded India, the Buddhist priests of the Maha-Bodhi Temple, fearing the destruction of the image of Buddha that was in it, took it away and hid it in the forests of Rajgir. When I said the Japanese in giving the image felt sorrow and also delight, I meant that they felt sorry at parting with an image so historical, and at the same time delight that it was to go to be enshrined in so holy a place as Maha-Bodhi.

The Hindu ceremony called *pranpratishta* is never performed by Buddhists.

The relic of Buddha I had in my despatch box was set in a small locket.

All the matters I said I was contemplating on, after the first rush of people disappeared, are strictly enjoined by the Buddhist religion as objects of religious contemplation.

The reason I never contemplated on the upper floor until the 25th February, is that there was no image of Buddha there. Buddhists do not sit down and contemplate before the image of Mayadevi.

Read over and admitted by witness to be correct.

D. J. MACPHERSON,
Magistrate.

8TH MAY, 1895.

WITNESS FOR PROSECUTION, I.

H. Dharmapala recalled for further re-examination on solemn affirmation.

[THE prosecution propose to put in a passage from the article at page 5 of the Journal for December, 1892, (of which another passage, Exhibit D 32, has already been put in), containing a copy of an inscription over the Temple door-way, to the effect that the Temple was repaired by the British Government in 1880, and an addition to the effect that since then it has been under the guardianship of Government. It is contended that this arose out of cross-examination, inasmuch as the defence had endeavoured to show in it that the witness entertained the belief that the Temple belonged to, and was in the exclusive possession of, the Mahanth. The defence object that it does not arise out of cross-examination, as they carefully abstained from going into the question of the alleged rights of Government in the Temple, as this could not be relevant to the present case.

EXHIBIT V.

On the marble slab over the main door-way leading to the adytum of the Temple, the following inscription stands prominent :—"This ancient Temple of the Maha-Bodhi, erected on the holy spot where Prince Sakya Sinha became Buddha, was repaired by the British Government under the orders of Sir Ashley Eden, Lieutenant-Governor of Bengal. A. D. 188c." Since then the Temple has been under the guardianship of the Government of Bengal.

(Mahabodhi Society's Journal, 1892, December, p. 5.)

The witness, at page 15 of his deposition, in answer to a question by the defence, seeking explanation of an answer given by him, to the effect that he never cared to inquire whether the Mahanth had, as a matter of fact, usurped possession, stated that he did not care to inquire, as the facts were apparent from the inscription referred to, showing the Temple had been restored by the British Government and was under the guardianship of Government. In view of this answer, and in explanation of the views expressed by him at various times as to the possession and control of the Temple which the defence sought to elicit, I consider that the passage sought to be put in does explain a matter referred to in cross-examination, and I allow the question to be put and the passage to be put in, subject to the qualification applying to all paragraphs put in by the defence not written by the witness himself, that it is not proof of the substantive fact, but merely explanatory of the witness's belief.]

Question.—Looking at the passage referred to, is that a copy of the inscription referred to in your cross-examination, and have the words "since then the Temple has been under the guardianship of the Government of Bengal" been written by you?

Answer.—Yes.

(*Passage put in and marked Exhibit* V.)

[The defence ask leave to put questions as to when and from whom and how the witness got the idea that Government was guardian and possessor of the Temple. The Court does not think that the question put by the prosecution has introduced new matter, and at the same time does not regard the sources of the witness's information on this point (apart from the inscription) as material so as to justify new matter being brought in now.]

Read over and admitted by witness to be correct.

D. J. MACPHERSON,
Magistrate.

11TH MAY, 1895.

WITNESS FOR PROSECUTION, I.

H. Dharmapala, complainant, recalled by Court and examined on solemn affirmation by it.

Question.—What were you doing between the time the people went to fetch an English-knowing Mukhtear and his coming?

Answer.—I was standing surrounded by some of the men. At that time I could not do anything. We did not attempt to light the candles again after the Hindu Mukhtear left. That was because the Sannyasis had removed the candles. I don't know whether they had taken them altogether away from the place or not. When the image was taken away, everything with it, the candle-sticks, &c., were taken away. The reason I did not obey when the Police came to call me was that I was then sitting in the same position as I had been in before.

Question.—Were you then contemplating?

Answer.—I was then in a very sorrowful state. (*Question repeated.*) I was partly sorrowful and partly in contemplation. I do not think I remained throughout the Police enquiry.

Question.—When did you come away?

Answer.—On receiving an order from the Collector. I left Buddha-Gaya about 4 P.M. on the 26th February.

Question.—You did not see any one till the image was actually being removed, you said. Was it that that disturbed your contemplation or the people coming?

Answer.—I was disturbed, I think, by the rush of the people coming up.

Question.—But you did not see who were there till the image was actually being removed?

Answer.—No.

I went away from India in August last. I next returned to Calcutta in January. I placed the image on this occasion without the Collector's permission. The letter I wrote was not in reply to one I got from the Collector. I remember that.

Question.—Did you write a letter to the Collector and ask him when he would be in from camp and be able to see you?

Answer.—I did so. I got a reply to that letter to the effect that he was in camp, but would be glad to see you.

Question.—Was any date fixed for seeing the Collector?

Answer.—About the 20th or 21st February. I think I did not go to see the Collector on that occasion. I did not go to see him before placing the image. That was because I thought he was not in town. *(adds)* I arrived in Gaya on the Sunday by the noon train. I placed the image the next morning, Monday. I did not then arrive in Gaya in time to see the Collector on the 20th or 21st, the time when he said he would be in Gaya and might see me.

I left India on the occasion I went to Japan and America, in June, 1893, and I returned on March 31st, 1894. I went to Japan in November, 1893, that was on my way back from America. The reason why the passage in the *Vinaya Pushpamala* to the effect that the image of Buddha had been removed to the forest of Rajgir suggested to me the idea of bringing this image from Japan, is that there was no historic beautiful image. No proper image of Buddha is in the temple.

Question.—Why were you dissatisfied with the great image on the ground floor?

Answer.—I was not dissatisfied with it. Everything about it was right.

Question.—Was it not a proper image then?

Answer.—What I mean is that there was not a proper one of Buddha on the upper floor, as the image there was of Mayadevi. I thought that the passage referred to an image that was in the upper floor, as if it was carried away it must have been a small one, and I thought the upper floor chamber was the *sanctum sanctorum*, Holy of Holies, which is always in an upper chamber.

Read over and admitted correct.

D. J. MACPHERSON,
Magistrate.

13TH MAY, 1895.

WITNESS FOR PROSECUTION, I.

II. Dharmapala, recalled by Court and examined on solemn affirmation by it.

[*N. B.*—I had not finished perusing the deposition of this witness when, for convenience of parties I stopped questioning on the last occasion—Saturday evening. The witness is accordingly recalled just now. The defence wish it to be recorded, in the event of any answer prejudicial to them being given, that they have already filed their written statement and closed their case and the prosecution have obtained copies of the statement.—D. J. M.]

Question.—What is the difference between a votive image and an image set up for purposes of worship?

Answer.—There is no difference. It is one of the matters enjoined in the Buddhist religion to offer or rather enshrine images in a Temple. There is no difference.

Question.—When an image is placed in a Temple, can you worship it, whatever image it may be?

Answer.—Yes, any image placed in the altar can be worshipped. All are images presented to the Temple.

Question.—Does it matter whether it is an image placed beside an existing image of Buddha or the first image of Buddha placed on an altar ?

Answer.—There is no difference. Once an image is placed on the altar, it becomes an object of worship.

Question.—You said that, when you came with your mother and other pilgrims in January last, you worshipped the image on the ground floor. Was there any harm in worshipping it after it had been changed by Hindus in the way you have described ?

Answer.—So long as the marks and clothes are there, you can not worship it, but if they are removed you can.

Question.—Had the marks, &c., been removed by them ?

Answer.—They were there when we came, but the Buddhist pilgrims on that occasion removed the marks. They must have been put on again afterwards, for I saw them there on the 25th February again. We remained at Buddha-Gaya two days on that occasion in January, and I worshipped inside the Temple on the first day, but I do not think I did so on the second day.

Question.—What is it that you found unsatisfactory with the Temple, before you brought the image from Japan, that led to the formation of the Maha-Bodhi Society and to your various proceedings in connection with it, such as visits to other countries ?

Answer.—It was painful for Buddhists to see it in a neglected state.

Question.—In what respect was it neglected ?

Answer.—From the point of view of Buddhists, there being no priests, no offerings, no festivals, no celebrations, everything that was required for the central shrine of the Buddhists was wanting. I believe the present Mahanth succeeded in January or February, 1892.

Question.—Did you see either the Hindu or the Mahomedan Mukhtear in the Temple at the time the image was actually removed from the upper story ?

Answer.—No. I did not observe.

Exhibit A.

TENTUKUJI, KWOMYOSAN,
TOKIO, JAPAN,

November 27th, 26th of Meiji (1893.)

TO

MR. H. DHARMAPALA,
Genl. Secy., Maha-Bodhi Society,
India.

MOST reverently I present herewith the sacred Image of Buddha Amitabha, in sitting attitude, to the great temple in Buddha-Gaya, India. [The old Sanskrit reads " Buddha Amitabha."]

" The True Reality of all beings is great and grand ; and those whose positions are in either of the five vehicles, do not know how it is so great and grand ; and the real nature of all things is great and profound ; and those holy men who are in either of the ten degrees do not know how it is so great and profound. The quality and quantity of the True Reality of all things is not different even from those

Question.—Have you succeeded in obtaining a translation of the Japanese certificate that was placed with the image ?

Answer.—A translation of it appeared in the Maha-Bodhi Journal for May or June, 1894. The translation was made in Japan. It was sent to me by post from there after I had left. I do not know Japanese, and so I can not say if it is a correct translation, but I believe it to be so. It was sent by the translator, Mr. Ohara, a Japanese. I know him personally. He knows English. In my presence, before I left Japan, a copy of the Japanese certificate was given by the priests to him to translate while I brought the original along with me.

I point out at p. 11 of the Journal for

of the mind of trembling animal (when seen from the spiritual point of view). The real nature of all things is infinite; that infiniteness and quality is, from eternity, in the state of unmovedness and free from all impurities. The state of things is always same and perfect, though there appears (to the spiritually ignorant men) the difference of holy and unholy; pure and impure. It silently comprises all souls and all the virtues of all things and beings. But covered by the temporal veil of impurities, the virtues contained in it are not apparent. Hence, the Buddha has, out of his great and infinite compassion, appeared upon this planet, and dropped the sweet heavenly dew upon the thirsty lips of living beings. His great light and wisdom illumined or chased the darkness of long, long, weary night. Well and completely the Three Secrets were comprised in Himself, and the Four ways of conversion, too. He opened and showed to us the cause of our long, long, sufferings from eternity, and made us ready to enter the Infinite Bliss and Eternal Life."

Deeply and heartily believing in the statement above mentioned, Minamoto Yoritomo (1200 A.D.) highly revered the Buddhist Triple Gem. He had enshrined the Image of Buddha Amitabha, which was made by the famous Buddhist sculptor Sadatomo of Nanto, now Nara, in the Province of Yamoto. The Court of Kamakura was changed afterwards, and then this sacred image was removed into a far-away mountain valley, after which event this was again transmitted into the hand of the chief priest of Kwomyogi, in which temple this was enshrined.

In the third year of Meiji, period (1890), this image was placed in the new built temple, Kai-ko-ji, Furosan, Miura-gori in the province of Sangami, and from this time this was made the chief Holy Image of Buddha Amitabha of that temple.

Now in the twenty-sixth year of Meiji (1893) our Ceylonese Brother, Mr. H. Dharmapala, came to this Empire, on his way home from America and addressed us concerning the work of restoration of the Buddha-Gaya Temple. We have been deeply impressed by our learned and good Brother's earnest address, and feel very sorry to learn that there is, at present, no Buddhism in India; much less the perfect image of our Lord, the Buddha. Hereupon I determined to present this Holy Image of Buddha Amitabha to be enshrined in the second story of the Buddha-Gaya temple. This was encouraged by those who have heard my determination. Mr. Niemon Asaha, an ardent lay adherent who belongs to this temple, has also assisted me very much. Here we have performed the sacred ceremony of "Presenting the Holy Image of Buddha Amitabha to India." Buddha-Gaya is the Holy place where our Lord Buddha Sakyamuni attained the perfect state of enlightenment while there is at present, not one image in perfect from, but mostly destructed, for which we Buddhists feel very sorry. Now, the Holy Image of the Buddha which I present here is the good sign of the future prosperity of Buddhism, Northern and Southern, in perfect harmony, and for the success of the restoration of the Buddha-Gaya temple. Full of respect and reverence, I herewith present the Holy Image of Buddha Amitabha, heartily wishing and praying for eternal prosperity of our great Doctrine of Buddha in India and Japan, and in all other countries in the world.

May the Holy Triple Gem and all the good devas guard this Holy Image, rejecting every evil which comes near, and arrive safely to the Holy Place, Buddha-Gaya.

Again, may this Holy Image be reverently enshrined in that holy place, and diffuse abroad the ray of infinite compassion and save every being that remember the Amitabha's name from sinfulness.

May blessings abide with us, the Buddhists.

May the seed of the Good Law grow and increase gradually in the field of worlds, present and coming; and may the Buddha stretch out His all-merciful hands to all living beings; again, may we with all beings, be born again in the Buddha's Holy Land.

Fraternally yours,

BHIKSHU SHUKO ASAHI,

High Priest, Tentokuji, Tokio.

(Mahabodhi Society's Journal, June, 1894, p. 11.)

June, 1894, the translation of the certificate that I had inserted in the Journal.

It is a correct reproduction of the translation except as regards one or two corrections in grammar I made.

(Put in and marked Exhibit A.)

Defence say they have no questions to put to the witness in regard to this matter, which is a new one, and apparently a revelation to every one, the Court included.

Read over by witness and admitted to be correct.

D. J. MACPHERSON,

Magistrate.

WITNESS FOR PROSECUTION, II.

The deposition of Bipin Bihari Banerjee, aged about 37 years, taken on solemn affirmation under the provisions of Act X of 1873, before me, D. J. Macpherson, Magistrate of Gaya, this 8th day of April, 1895.

MY name is Bipin Bihari Banerjee, my father's name is Sridhar Banerjee, I am by caste a Brahmin, my home is at Calcutta. I reside at present in Mouzah Bodh Gaya, Police Station Mufassil Gaya, Zilla Gaya.

I am custodian under the Public Works Department of Government of the Maha-Bodhi Temple. I took over charge of the Temple on the 21st July, 1890. I am custodian of the Temple and also of its precincts. My duty is to look after the Temple, prepare estimates for repairs, see to its repair and look after all relics in the Temple and its surroundings. I reside, since I have been custodian, about 100 feet from the Temple compound and 300 feet from the Temple itself. In the discharge of my duty, I constantly visit the Temple. I am a Hindu, and a Brahmin of the Kulin or highest caste. I never worship in the Temple.

Question.—" Did you ever see other Hindus worship in the Temple ?"

[Counsel for the Defence protested against this matter being gone into. For the prosecution it was contended that it was a necessary part of the case that this matter should be gone into, as introductory to, and explanatory of, the action of the accused on the 25th February, and as throwing light on the probability and improbability of the story for the prosecution. The Court considered that to go into this seemed a departure from the arrangement come to on the 13th March, as it was then understood. At any rate this was what the Court meant in making the suggestion to divide the case into two branches, namely, that the evidence to be given to-day was to be confined to the question of what actually occurred on the 25th, and what changes had actually taken place on the image on the ground floor, forming the other count charged in the complaint. Counsel for the prosecution said they had understood the arrangement only referred to the subsequent calling of witnesses who were not to depose to the actual occurrence, and that if it extended to the witnesses now present, they must claim that the defence be likewise prevented from going into any questions regarding possession in cross-examination in regard to which some hints had been thrown out. Counsel for the defence, however, contended that they could not abstain from going into this question of possession in dealing with the actual occurrence, but would contend that this was quite different from going into any religious question as to whether the Temple was Hindu or Buddhist, and that it was not competent for a Criminal Court to go into that aspect of the case. He was not, however, prepared in the absence of his senior who had been expected by now, to argue the question of the relevance of this latter part of the evidence proposed to be given, which the prosecution pressed should now be gone into from the beginning, as they considered it essential to their case, seeing that the defence were not prepared to abide by the understanding come to The terms of the order recorded in adjourning the case on the 13th March, were then read out, and it was then arranged that the case should be adjourned until to-morrow to enable the defence to argue any objections it might raise to the relevance of the evidence now proposed to be gone into. Deposition postponed accordingly.]

D. J. MACPHERSON,
Magistrate.

9TH APRIL, 1895.

WITNESS FOR PROSECUTION, II.

Bepin Behari Banerjee re-called and examined-in-chief on solemn affirmation.

Question.—Did you ever see other Hindus worship in the Temple of Maha-bodhi ?

Answer.—I never saw any Hindu worship in the Temple according to their religious rites or *Shastras.*

Question.—What worship, if any, have you seen performed at the Temple by Hindus ?

Answer.—Only a few Hindus bow their heads before the image of Buddha. I saw the image of Buddha on the ground-floor when I first went to the Temple as Government custodian.

Question.—Have you seen any change in the appearance of the image recently ?

Answer.—Yes, recently. The changes I have noticed recently are paint put on the forehead of the image, and worship commenced by the Brahmin employed by the Mahanth.

Question.—When did you first notice this ?

Answer.—I went on three months' leave in April of last year, and after I returned from leave I noticed it first.

Question.—Before this time, this form of Hindu worship did not go on at the Temple, did it ?

Answer.—Flowers.—

Question.—repeated.

Answer.—Since I came to the place as custodian I never noticed the above, form of Hindu worship at the Temple till I returned from leave.

[*Questions are now put in Hindustani : so far they have been put in English which witness does not understand very well*].

I knew the predecessor of the present Mahanth. He died about three and a half years ago. I never saw the old Mahanth either doing *puja* to the statue of Buddha on the ground-floor or bowing before it. The times when he used to come to the Temple were when any Government officer would come to the Temple. I know the present Mahanth. I never saw him doing any *puja* or bowing before this image on the ground-floor. There are many disciples of the Mahanth in the monastery (*math*). I never saw any of them doing *puja* or bowing before the image.

Question.—What kind of servants sweep the Temple ?

Answer.—There are two servants—one a woman, who is a Dosadhin by caste, and there is a Chatri, Jagarnath Singh, who sweeps inside the Temple.

I remember the 25th of February last. After returning to my house from paying my respects to the Mahanth that morning, my chaprassi came to me saying, Dharmapala had called me, and I went to the Temple. It was then about 8-30 or 9 A.M. I saw Dharmapala there. He said to me in English, " This is the Japanese image I have brought from Japan and I have placed it here : you shall take charge of it." That was in the upper storey of the Temple. I saw the Japanese image there by the side, to the south side, of the old image already there on the altar in the upper story. When I saw Dharmapala there and he said as above, I saw two Bhikshus with him and a layman, and perhaps (*hoga*) a *gariwala*. Then a number of persons came up into the Temple, and there were a lot collected in the courtyard. About 30 persons came up into the upper story. I know the names of some of them, namely, Jaipal Gir, Bhimal Deo Gir, Mukhtear Hossain Baksh, Mahendra Gir, and others. (*Identifies all the above among the accused.*)

When these men came up, they said, " We will not let you set up this image here ; take it down and take it away." Some said this in soft (*ahiste*) language and others with vehemence (*zor*). Dharmapala said he would not remove the image; and then when I saw the Gosains getting much enraged, I implored them with folded hands, saying. " What you want to do, do with full consideration (*bichar.*)" They said, " No, we will not let the image remain ; we will not prevent worship at the old image, but on no account (*halat*) will we let this new image be set here." Then when a priest with Dharmapala, Sumangala, went to light the candles for the purpose of worship, they snatched the candles out of his hand. That *Sadhu* Sumangala was a Singhalese. *(Called in and identified)*. Hossain Baksh Mukhtear was also joining with the rest in saying the image must be removed. Dharmapala said to Hossain Baksh, " You are a Musalman ; why have you come here ? What right have you in this temple ? We have a right to worship and we will worship here." He said all this in English.

Question.—Did he say any thing as to why he placed the image ?

Answer.—He said that he had the order of Government to worship in the temple.

(Question repeated).

Answer.— He said he had set up the image in order to worship it. I translated all this into Hindustani to Hassain Baksh Afterwards an English-knowing Mukhtear whose name is something like Vidyanand came. (*Identifies accused of that name*). When he came there was a conversation between him and Dharmapala. I don't know all that happened afterwards, as I was going in and out, and seeing the Gosains getting enraged, I sent word to the Police.

Question.—Meanwhile what happened to the image ?

Answer.—It was forcibly removed. It was taken downstairs and put into the courtyard. Amongst those who took part in removing the image were Jaipal Gir, but he did not touch it with his hands, and Mahendra Gir whom I saw take it up with his hands, and four or five other Gosains who carried it away.

Cross examination reserved.

Read over and admitted correct.

D. J. MACPHERSON,
Magistrate.

9TH APRIL, 1895.

WITNESS FOR PROSECUTION, II.

Bipin Bihari Banerjee recalled by prosecution for questions omitted by oversight to be put to him and examined-in-chief on solemn affirmation.

Since I have been Government custodian of the Temple I have seen images of Buddha placed in the Temple. I have seen three or four white marble images placed in it by Burmese pilgrims. These, I mean, were placed after I became custodian. They were placed on the altar on the ground floor since I have been custodian. I have seen European gentlemen, officials, and others, visit the Temple. I have seen them enter the shrine in the ground floor, both ladies and gentlemen. They went in with their shoes on, and I frequently go into the Temple leaving my shoes outside.

Read over and admitted correct.

D. J. MACPHERSON,
Magistrate.

10TH MAY, 1895.

WITNESS FOR PROSECUTION. II.

Bipin Bihari Banerji re-called and cross-examined on solemn affirmation on 10th May 1895:—

I have been summoned to produce certain documents, and have brought them to Court. (*Shown two documents*).

These are two which I have produced.

The documents referred to are letters, No. 1005, dated 24th March, 1891 and No. 1726, dated 9th May, 1890, from the Superintending Engineer, Sone Circle, to the Executive Engineer, Eastern Sone Division.

I received the first mentioned letter, No. 1005, on 3rd April, 1891. The endorsement of receipt of it is by me. I joined my appointment on the 21st July or June, 1890—that is the date I took over charge of the Temple. I read the letter, No 1005, when I received it.

Question.—Did you since 1891 know and regard the Mahanth as proprietor of the Maha-Bodhi Temple ?

[Question objected to on the ground that this witness's opinion is quite irrelevant. Allowed for the purpose mentioned when similar questions were objected to in the case of the complainant.]

D. 53.

No. 1005.

FROM

THE SUPERINTENDING ENGINEER,
SONE CIRCLE.

To

THE EXECUTIVE ENGINEER,
EASTERN SONE DIVISION.

Dated Arrah, 24th March, 1891.

SIR,

I HAVE the honour to say that on the 21st I inspected the Buddha-Gaya Temple in company with the Collector. The sites selected for the custodian's house and the small museum are approved. Care should be taken that a ditch and fence round them, where not otherwise demarcated, are kept up. I have instructed the Sub-divisional Officer to build the pillars of the museum as far as possible after the pattern of the Asoka pillars now in the temple, and I think stone capitals might be procured from Dehree. I should be willing to sanction Rs. 50 or Rs. 60 extra, which I think would suffice. Before the pillars are built, large scale drawings should be submitted for your approval.

2. An estimate should be submitted early next year for ordinary repairs to the temple, and should include removing grass from the masonry. Very special care should be taken to prevent *peepul* trees taking root there.

3. I request that you will cause the custodian to be very fully informed of the peculiar, and, in some respects, delicate position he occupies. The building is not the property of Government, and is only taken charge of, with the consent of the Mahant. The custodian must at all times treat the Mahant with the greatest respect and deference, and it would, I think, be well for him to pay the Mahant a monthly official visit, so that he may be informed of any matter in which the Mahant desires any special course to be taken. It would be absolutely impossible to retain the custodian in his office, if he gave any reasonable cause of offence to the Mahant or the temple officials, and the fact should be thoroughly impressed on the custodian, who can with ordinary carefulness maintain a good understanding with

Answer.—From the letter which I got from the Superintending Engineer, I learned that the Temple was not the property of the Government.

Question.—Did you regard the Mahanth as *malik* of it ?

Answer.—I did not consider the Mahanth the absolute *malik*. I regard him as somewhat (*thora thora*) of a *malik*.

Question.—Since you received the letter, did you regard any one else than the Mahanth as proprietor ?

Answer.—I also regarded the Government as something (*kuchh*) of a proprietor. That is since I received the letter in question.

[*Shown the letter, No. 1005, above referred to, containing a forwarding memo., No. 240, dated 31st March, 1891.*]

Question.—Are these the instructions you received at the time for your guidance ?

[The prosecution contend that, while they have no objection to anything in the letter going in, that contains instructions as to what he is to do as part of his duties ; they object to any opinion, expressed by the Superintending Engineer on any matter, being put in evidence. Document allowed to be put in according to question put above.]

them. This efficiency will be largely judged by his remaining on really good terms with the temple authorities.

4. The Collector, as you are aware, retains his former position of guardian on the part of the state of the temple. He should be constantly referred to by the Sub-divisional Officer in case of doubt as to touching any part of the temple, and his advice taken in all matters connected with its preservation. I am quite certain that the Collector will render you whatever assistance you may require in connection with your duties on maintaining the building.

I have the honour to be,
Sir,
Your most obedient Servant,

C. W. ODLING,
Superintending Engineer,
SONE CIRCLE.

No. 240.

Dated Gaya, 31*st March* 1891.

COPY forwarded to the custodian of the Bodh-Gaya Temple for information and guidance.

G. C. MOOKERJEE,
Supervisor,
GAYA SUB-DISTRICT.

D 54.

No. 1077.

FROM

G. A. GRIERSON, ESQ., C. S.,
Offg. Magistrate, and Collector, Gaya,

To

THE MAHANTH OF BODH-GAYA.

Dated Gaya, 3rd April, 1889.

SIR,

IT has been brought to my notice that visitors to Bodh-Gaya are in the habit of carrying away images and carved stones, which they find lying about on land in your possession.

I am sure you would not permit this if you knew it. On your letting me know that you wish me to do so, I shall tell the Police not to allow it.

I would suggest that you should collect all these carved stones and put them in a safe place in charge of the Bungalow chowkidar, as they are very valuable.

I shall be obliged by an early reply.

I have the honour to be,
Sir,
Your most obedient Servant,

G. A. GRIERSON.
Offg. Magistrate, and Collector

D. 55.

No. 2282.

FROM

G. A. GRIERSON, ESQ., C. S.,
Offg. Magistrate, and Collector, Gaya,

To

THE MAHANTH OF BODH-GAYA.

Dated Gaya, 8th July, 1889.

SIR,

IT appears from the report of the chowkidar of Bodh-Gaya that the Burmese Bungalow at Bodh Gaya requires immediate repair.

Answer.—This letter contains the instructions I received as to my duties; (*adds*), but I also got some verbal instructions.

(*Letter put in and marked Exhibit D* 53.)

Question.—Then in spite of its being said in that letter that Government was not proprietor of the Temple, you regarded Government as somewhat of a proprietor?

Answer.—I understood that from other matters. When Mr. Grierson, the former Collector, accompanied Prince Damrong of Siam to the Temple, he said in my presence that the Temple was the property of Government. Mr. Grierson said that once or twice verbally in my presence. I don't remember in what year that was, but I think it was in 1892 that Mr. Grierson said so. He said it not only when he went with Prince Damrong, but also when he came on an inspection. The last time he said so would be within 1892. I did not mention or show the above letter to him, nor had I any talk with him about the letter.

Question.—Read paragraph 3 of the letter, and say whether up till now you have always acted according to that letter?

Answer.—I have always acted, until now, according to these instructions.

(*Shown a letter, No.* 1077, *dated* 3*rd April* 1889.)

Question.—Is that Mr. Grierson's signature?

Answer.—I believe that is his signature.

[*Shown another letter No.* 2282, *dated* 8*th July*, 1889.]

I believe the signature there also to be Mr. Grierson's.

[Letters tendered in evidence as showing that the Collector of the District treated the Mahanth at the time as proprietor of the Temple and of its relics. Counsel for prosecution object that the signature is not proved, as the witness has not shown he is acquainted with the signature of Mr. Grierson, under section 47 coupled with section 67 of the Evidence Act. Prosecution also object that it is not admissible without proof under Section 74 on the ground of being a

I would suggest the propriety of your repairing it, and shall be obliged by your doing so.

I have the honour to be,
Sir,
Your most obedient, Servant,
G. A. GRIERSON,
Offg. Magistrate and Collector.

public document, as it is not a document forming an act or record of an act of Mr. Grierson as Collector. Defence reply that it is the act of an officer in his public character, and so admissible without proof, but even if it did require proof, it is sufficient that witness believes it to be Mr. Grierson's signature. The Court held that the witness had not, as required by Sec. 47, proved that he was acquainted with Mr. Grierson's hand-writing. Thereupon defence put questions to which the following answers were given.]

I have received two or three letters from Mr. Grierson, which I considered to be signed by him These came both in connection with official business and also privately. He did not write to me frequently privately. I used to answer his letters, but I never got answers from him to letters written by me. I received letters from him during about two years while he was here as Collector.

Question.—Have you any doubt that that is his signature?

Answer.—I have not seen his signature for a long time, and all I can say is, I believe it is like his signature.

[The Court held that the signature was not proved under Sec. 47 of the Evidence Act. The defence then tendered them as public documents admissible without proof. The prosecution objected that the documents are not admissible under Sec. 57 unless they are public documents as defined under Sec. 74. The Court holds that Sec. 57 is not confined to public documents as contended by the prosecution, and that under clause (7) it is bound to take judicial notice of the signature and office of Mr. Grierson as a gazetted officer of Government. The documents in question are therefore admissible as documents bearing his signature. Counsel for the prosecution then objected to their being admitted on the ground that they are not relevant. The discussion of this question was postponed till to-morrow, it being too late to go on further to-day. The documents are marked for identification as Exhibits D 54 and 55.]

Deposition read over and admitted by witness to be correct.

D. J. MACPHERSON,
Magistrate.

11TH MAY, 1895.

WITNESS FOR PROSECUTION, II.

Bipin Bihari Banerji, further cross-examined on solemn affirmation states.

(*Shown para. 3 of Exhibit D 53.*)—By "the Temple officials" that were not to be given offence to by me, I understood the Sannyasis and the *Pujari*. There was then only one *pujari*, but now there are two. The *pujari* was Jagarnath Singh, a man of the Mahanth. Both the present *pujaris* are the Mahanth's men.

Question.—Since you have been in Bodh-Gaya, who has been taking the offerings given to the Temple?

Answer.—Cloth and costly articles that are presented the Mahanth has been taking, and pice and rupees Jagarnath Singh has been taking.

Question.—Does this apply to all sorts of pilgrims, Hindus and Buddhists both?

Answer.—It applies to all offerings made by all sorts of visitors, but all don't make offerings. I understood that was the practice from before the time I came.

Question.—Have you ever since you came, seen Hindus throwing flowers by way of offering at the great image on the ground-floor ?

Answer.—I have never seen any Hindu pilgrims offering flowers to that Image. Occasionally I have seen Jagarnath Singh, the *pujari,* placing two or three flowers on the *singhasan* (altar). I have seen him do that before the new *pujari* came. I have seen Jagarnath Singh do that occasionally since the time I came here, that is, since 1890.

Question.—Have you ever since you came to Bodh-Gaya, heard that the Hindus regarded Buddha as one of the Hindu *avatars* ?

Answer.—When Hindu pilgrims used to come to offer *pindas* at Bodh-Gaya, and they expressed wish to go and see the image in the Temple, the Brahmans accompanying them used to prevent their going into it, saying to them it was a Jain Temple, and that it was forbidden to enter it. Since Dharmapala came here and has been asking Government for the right to worship there, I have heard it said that the Gautama Buddha is a Hindu *avatar ;* but I understood myself all along that one of the Hindu *avatars* was Buddha. It is since 1892 only that I have been hearing them say the Gautama Buddha is a Hindu *avatar.* It is the Mahanth and his Sannyasis who have been saying this. They have been saying there is proof of this in the *Shastras.* I don't go inside the Temple every day, but I go round about its compound. I go actually inside the Temple on twenty or twenty-two days in a month about. On some days I go inside two or three times, and sometimes only once a day ; but when there are many pilgrims I remain there all day sometimes.

Question.—Do you remember, in 1893, a form coming to you to fill up about ancient monuments at Bodh-Gaya ?

Answer.—I remember one coming. I remember there was a heading in it called "Tomb or monument to the memory of."

Question.—Do you remember writing in that column "Prince Sakya Sinha of ancient Kapilavastu or Buddha, *avatar* of the Hindus ?"

Answer.—I remember writing that. I understood at the time that that was correct.

Question.—Do you remember if in the fair copy you sent in, you cut out the words "Buddha *avatar* of the Hindus ?"

Answer.—I do not exactly remember that.

[*Shown a communication No.* 1748 *from Gaya Magistracy, dated 25th August,* 1893 *containing the above form.*] I produced that yesterday among the papers I brought to Court. Looking to the entry in column 5, I do not remember when I struck out the words. I cannot say if it was before or after I sent the fair copy.

Question.—Can you remember the reason for cutting the words out ?

Answer.—At first I wrote it, but then on reading I found that it was not correct.

Question.—When did you read ? What made you correct it ?

Answer.—After I had written that, I made a fair copy, and I must have corrected it before sending the fair copy. No one told me to correct it, but I did so of myself. I cannot remember if it was all done in one day or in several days.

(*Shown the form*). I see that the date I put on the form is 2nd September, 1893, and from the character of the handwriting I consider that I wrote the words about the *avatar* at the same time as I wrote the date. The correction is made in red ink. From looking at it I believe I made the correction on the same day as I wrote the original.

D 56.

COLUMN 5.
"Tomb or Monument to the Memory of"
~~Late~~ Prince Sakya Sinha of ^ancient Kapilavastu ~~or Buddha avatar of the Hindus.~~

B. B. BANERJEE,
Custodian.
2-8-93.

D. 57.

No. 1134.

FROM

G. A. GRIERSON, ESQ., C. S.,
Magistrate and Collector, Gaya.

TO

THE COMMISSIONER
OF THE PATNA DIVISION.

Dated Gaya, 6th May, 1891.

SIR,

I HAVE the honor to forward herewith an extract from a letter written by the Superintending Engineer to the Executive Engineer regarding the Bodh-Gaya Temple :--

"I request that you will cause the custodian to be very fully informed of the peculiar, and in some respects, delicate position he occupies. The building is not the property of Government, and is only taken charge of with the consent of the Mahant. The custodian must at all times treat the Mahant with the greatest respect and deference, and it would, I think, be well for him to pay the Mahant a monthly official visit, so that he may be informed of any matter in which the Mahant desires any special course to be taken. It would be absolutely impossible to retain the custodian in his office, if he gave any reasonable cause of offence to the Mahant or the Temple officials, and this fact should be thoroughly impressed on the custodian, who can, with ordinary carefulness, maintain good understanding with them. His efficiency will be largely judged by his remaining on really good terms with the Temple authorities."

2. Personally I entirely agree with these instructions, which also accord with the tradition handed down from Magistrate to Magistrate as to the position held by Government with regard to the Temple, and have indeed reason to believe that the instructions are founded on information given by me to Mr. Odling.

3. I should be glad to communicate the tenor of these instructions to the Mahanth himself with whom I am on excellent terms, but before doing so I wish to be certain of my ground.

4. I can find no paper in the office defining the position of Government in regard to the Bodh-Gaya Temple.

5. The tradition is that as Government has spent two lakhs on the Temple, it has a certain undefined right to see its preservation and protection, the Mahanth remaining the proprietor, and all that we do being done with his consent.

6. I am not prepared to condemn this state of affairs, which has grown up naturally and works smoothly.

7. The only thing I want to be certain about is whether it exists.

8. There must have been some negotiations between Government and the Mahanth, when the repair of the Temple was first undertaken, and probably the rights of Government in the matter were then defined.

Question—Can you now say, on seeing the thing, what occurred on that day to lead you to pen the word through ?

Answer.—I entertained a doubt. I got to know Dharmapala first in 1891.

Question.—When did you first learn that he wanted possession of the Temple ?

Answer.—When he first started the Journal, which he sent to me at first.

Question.—Before you received the Journal, had you any doubt that Buddha was an *avatar* of the Hindus ?

Answer.—I had no doubt that Buddha was an *avatar* of the Hindus.

[*Passage in column 5 in the form put in and marked Exhibit D 56 as explaining the cross-examination.*]

The Mahanth's man used to keep the key of the door of the Temple. I have always till now seen it in his possession.

Question —Did he not open the door on the arrival of pilgrims and again shut it when he pleased?

Answer.—Yes.

Question.—If any pilgrims might arrive when the door was locked, it would be necessary to call the man with the key to open it ?

Answer.—Yes.

Question.—Is it your duty to look after loose relics, such as movable images and pillars, lying about in the compound of the Temple ?

Answer.—Yes. I have had a sculpture-house built where loose relics are arranged by me. No rent is paid for the sculpture-house to the Mahanth. Rent is paid for the inspection bungalow to the Mahanth. It also is in my charge. I live in a house to the east of the bungalow. It is in a different compound. It is my duty to see that visitors and pilgrims, or any one, do not carry away any relics or loose image.

I have twice seen the Mahanth sign his name in my presence. [*Shown a letter No. 7 E., dated 13th June.* 1894, *from the Mahanth to the Collector of Gaya.*]

Question.—Can you say whether the signature there is the Mahanth's or not ?

9. There are no papers that I can find on the subject in my office, and I shall be obliged if you will enquire from Government as to what arrangement, if any, was come to, as to the right of Government

(i.) In regard to the Temple itself.
(ii.) In regard to its precincts.

10. You can understand that while hitherto acquiescing in the traditional arrangement, I am unwilling to give the Mahanth a written document confirming it, till I am certain that no other arrangement has been previously made.

I have the honour to be,
SIR,
Your most obedient Servant,

G. A. GRIERSON,
Magistrate and Collector.

D. 58.

No. 297 G.

FROM
A. FORBES, ESQ., C. S.
Commissioner of Patna Division,

TO
THE GOVERNMENT OF BENGAL,
PUBLIC WORKS DEPARTMENT.

Dated Bankipore, 21st May, 1891.

SIR,

I HAVE the honour to forward copy of a letter from the Magistrate of Gaya on the subject of certain instructions proposed to be issued at the instance of the Superintending Engineer to the custodian of the Bodh-Gaya Temple.

Before issuing these instructions, Mr. Grierson wishes to know what arrangement, if any, was come to as to the rights of Government in regard to the Temple itself and its precincts. There are no papers in his office or in mine, which can throw light on the subject. I therefore, submit the matter for the orders of Government. It seems very desirable that the position of Government in regard to the Temple and its precincts should be carefully defined.

I have the honour to be,
Sir,
Your most obedient Servant,

DHANESH CHANDRA ROY,
Personal Assistant to Commissioner for Commissioner.

D. 59.

No. 1336 AY.

FROM
GOVERNMENT OF BENGAL,
PUBLIC WORKS DEPARTMENT.

TO
THE COMMISSIONER
OF THE PATNA DIVISON.

Dated Calcutta, the 7th July, 1891.

SIR,

WITH reference to your letter No. 297G., dated the 21st May, 1891, with which you forward copy of a letter from the Magistrate of Gaya on the subject of certain instructions proposed to be issued to the

Answer.—I cannot say. The times I saw him signing his signature it was in larger letters than these.

Question—You said yesterday that Mr. Grierson orally told you that the Temple was the property of Government. Do you remember the exact words he used?

Answer.—I remember them.

Question.—What were they?

Answer.—I remember distinctly that he said the Temple belonged to Government, but what the actual words he used were I cannot remember. The conversation was in English.

Question.—What was the occasion on which Mr. Grierson said that?

Answer.—When Prince Damrong and Mr. Grierson and I were coming away from the Mahanth's house, and we were close together. Prince Damrong asked and Mr. Grierson said that. He did not say it to me on that occasion, but to the Prince.

Question.—But when did he say it to yourself?

Answer.—At an inspection. He said it then in English. As nearly as I remember the conversation was going on in English. I told him first that some pilgrims are in the habit of breaking the Temple and the *stupas* for obtaining some bricks which they think sacred, and they also are in the habit of taking them off to their home, and that if they are allowed to do so, the Temple will be ruined in a short time. Then the Collector, that is, Mr. Grierson, said: "This is Government property: you should take proper care of it, and I will make some other arrangement for the preservation of the Temple" *(adds.)* After a few days, I got a letter through the Sub-Divisional Officer of my Department to the effect that Mr. Grierson had said a constable would be deputed to guard the place, daily, and this also I reported to my Department. That would be in the year 1892, as far as I remember.

[Defence here tender the following correspondence received from the Commissioner's Office:—

(1) Mr. Grierson's letter, No. 1134, dated 6th May 1891, to Commissioner.

(2) Draft letter of Commissioner, forwarding above to Government, No. 297G, dated 21st May, 1891.

custodian of Bodh-Gaya Temple, and requesting that the position of Government in regard to the Temple and its precincts should be clearly defined, I am directed to say that the question has never yet been decided, and that the Lieutenant-Governor would like the case brought before him whenever he visits Gaya.

I have the honour to be,

Sir,

Your most obedient Servant,

F. J. JOHNSTONE,

Joint-Secretary.

MEMO. No. 333G.

Patna Commissioner's Office,

Dated Bankipore, 14th July, 1891.

COPY foward ed to the Magistrate of Gaya for information and guidance, with reference to his No. 1134, dated 6th May last.

DHANESH CHANDRA ROY,

Personal Assistant.

D. 60.

No. 2498.

FROM

G. A. GRIERSON, ESQ.,

Magistrate and Collector of Gaya,

TO

THE COMMISSIONER
OF THE PATNA DIVISION.

Dated Gaya, the 4th November, 1891.

SIR,

WITH reference to your letter No. 333G., dated 14th July, 1891, I have the honour to say that I have had the honour of discussing the subject with His Honour the Lieutenant-Governor during his late visit at Gaya, and His Honour is of opinion that it is not advisable to take any action at present in the matter to disturb existing arrangements.

I have the honour to be

Sir,

Your most obedient Servant

G. A. GRIERSON,

Magistrate and Collector.

(3) Reply of Government to above letter, No. 1836 A. Y., dated 7th July, 1891.

(4) Mr. Grierson's letter No. 2498, dated 4th November, 1891, to Commissioner.

[Counsel for defence tender these without proof as being public documents (being acts of the executive) with a view to show that the Government refused to disturb existing arrangements and that the Mahanth was left in possession of the Temple and regarded as owner of it at that time, such evidence being relevant as regards the *bonâ-fide* of the Mahanth.

Counsel for prosecution raised the same objection, as regards proof, as he had already done to similar documents, and likewise repeated the objection as to relevance raised in regard to such. He further contended (as he has already intimated at previous stages of this case, *e. g.*, when the defence intimated they would call for production of official correspondence) that if the documents are admitted in evidence, the whole correspondence on the subject should be put in, remarking that what is material is not what the Mahanth may have believed in 1891, but what he believed at the date of the occurrence, 25th February, 1895.

The Court held that the documents (except possibly the Commissioner's draft No. 297 G., dated 21st June, 1891, which bears only initials) are admissible without proof of signatures under clause (7) Section 57 Evidence Act. It was, however, understood that no objection to the admissibility of official documents in this case on the ground of their being merely initialled and not signed in full should be made, Counsel for the defence contending that initials are presumptive proof of signature, and Counsel for the prosecution not pressing any objection on this ground.

It was arranged that the question as to the relevance of the documents should be determined after the evidence of witnesses has been concluded. The documents were therefore marked for identification as D 57, D 58, D 59 and D 60 respectively.]

(*Shown book entitled Revised List of Ancient Monuments in Bengal,* 1886.) I have seen the book handed to me just now.

[Book tendered in evidence, whole passage relating to Bodh-Gaya put in from page 119 to end of page 124, to show that the Government after the repairs published to the world that the Mahanth was the custodian and proprietor of the Temple and that the repairs were done with his consent. Counsel for prosecution say they

For D 61, see among the documentary evidence. See *post*.

have no objection to the book going in for archæological purposes, such as the history of the Temple, but they objected to any expression of opinion in the book regarding question of proprietorship and the like. Marked Exhibit D 61.]

In December, 1892, or January, 1893, I had no sort of difference or dispute with the Mahanth's *chelas.*

Question.—Did the Government ever call upon you for an explanation with reference to an article in the *Sanjibani* newspaper ?

Answer.—Yes, but that was not about a dispute with the Mahanth's *chelas.* It was about a dispute with some Burmese and a Singhalese person.

Question.—When that was sent to you, were you not warned to be careful in future to carry out the instructions given to you on your appointment ?

Answer.—I was to act properly towards every one. I was reminded of the instructions. I cannot remember about what month it was. I cannot remember whether it was February, 1893. It was about the year 1893.

There is a tank on the south of the temple. It is called the *Buddha Kunda.* There is an inscription on a stone on it, to the effect that it was repaired by Gosain Belpat Gir in, I think, 1882. Gosain Belpat Gir is still living. He is not a disciple of the present Mahanth, but he was of the next predecessor but one of the present Mahanth.

The Brahmans who used to tell pilgrims not to enter the Temple as it was a Jain one, were servants of the Gayawals of Gaya.

Question.—Is there good feeling between the Gayawals and the Mahanth ?

Answer.—With some of them there is, and they come to see the Mahanth.

Question.—But is there generally as a body ?

Answer,—I cannot say.

Question.—Do you know of there being any dispute between the Mahanth's *chelas* and the Gayawals regarding the offerings made by Hindus when they offer *pindas* at the tree ?

Answer.—There is no dispute between them. (*adds*) The Mahanth's men take the pice put at the tree, but the Gayawal Brahmans take the other offerings made with the *pindas.*

Re-examined—

The first time I saw the second *Pujari* in the Temple was on my return from three months' leave in July, 1894, last year. Since I came to Bodh-Gaya, I have seen Jagarnath Singh place flowers on the altar of the great image about twenty or twenty-five times in all. The reason he placed them was not by way of *puja*, but on behalf of pilgrims who would come there in order to get paid for it. My work is not confined to looking after the loose relics about. I have also to prepare estimates for the repair of the Temple, to look after every thing that is in the compound of the Temple, to repair the Burmese rest-house and keep it in my charge (*hifazat*), to repair and look after the inspection bungalow and sculpture-house, to repair the portico of the *ghat* of the *Buddha Kunda*, and look after the tank and clear the drain under it. It is also my duty, if the inside of the Temple is not clean, to see that it is cleaned. The images that are inside are also in my charge.

Question.—If the Mahanth or any one were to take away any image from inside the Temple to your knowledge, what would be your duty ?

Answer.—To report the matter.

The reason I regarded the Mahanth as only somewhat of a proprietor, but Government also as something of a proprietor, is that officers who would come used to say so with reference to letter marked Exhibit D 53 (*shown*). The repairs to the Temple have been made by Government and their expense met by Government. All the duties I have said I have to perform I always perform without reference to or permission of the Mahanth. The inspection bungalow for which rent is paid is outside the Temple enclosure. The Mahanth has never employed any one to look after the relics lying about to see no one takes them away. After I complained to Mr. Grierson, and he said he had deputed a constable daily, a constable was, as a matter of a fact, deputed, and remained for some days, but whenever I report to the Police for assistance, the Police give it to me. It has never occurred, although the Mahant's man has the key of the door, that the Mahanth has refused to have it opened when pilgrims came, on the ground that he is proprietor of the Temple. Jagarnath Singh, the Mahanth's *Pujari*, is a *Kshattri* by caste.

To Court—

Question.—You said in your examination-in-chief that you did not see all that went on on the 25th February last, as you were going in and out. Did you see Dharmapala and his Bhikshus do any *puja* at all that day?

Answer.—I saw it.

Question.—What sort of *puja*?

Answer.—They were sitting down with their hands across their knees (*shows how*) and contemplating (*dhyan karta.*) The reason I went to the Mahanth on that day was to pay my respects as I was going on ten days' leave to bring my family, and to ask him to have the kindness to look after things and see that no *golmal* should occur in my absence. The second *pujari* who has been appointed is Bishun Misser. He is a *Sukaldipi* Brahman by caste. He is the one who has been the second *pujari* ever since July last till now.

Question (*at suggestion of defence.*)—Do the Bodh-Gaya Sannyasis recognise any distinction of caste among themselves?

Answer.—Since I came to Bodh-Gaya I have learned that the Bodh-Gaya Sannyasis are formed from three castes only, but when they become Sannyasis, no caste distinction is observed.

I have never seen Hindu pilgrims offering any things to the image, whether flowers or not. When I said I knew all along that one of the Hindu *avatars* was Buddha, I don't know whether that is the Gautama Buddha or not. I don't remember whether Dharmapala was in Bodh-Gaya when I filled up the form referred to in cross-examination or not. It was Jagarnath Singh who used to keep the key of the Temple door, and up till now it is he who does so. Not only do I prepare estimates for repairs of the Temple, but I carry out those repairs. The sculpture-house was built in 1892. The sculpture placed in it were not only those that were lying about outside the Temple enclosure, but also some selected from among a lot collected on a platform in the Temple enclosure. (*adds*) I also asked the Mahanth for two images that were in his house, and he let me take them to the sculpture-house, and one of them is inside it and the other, a heavy one, just outside it. I never saw the Mahanth take images from the Temple compound or from inside the Temple. I don't know whether the Brahmans, who come with pilgrims on behalf of the Gayawals, are Vaishnavas or Saivites.

The above was read over and admitted by the witness to be correct, except that he forgot to add that on the occasion of the explanation called for from him at page 66 of his deposition, he got a certificate from the Mahanth of his good conduct.

D. J. MACPHERSON,
Magistrate.

11TH MAY, 1895.

WITNESS FOR PROSECUTION, II.

Bipin Bihari Banerji re-called by court and examined by it on solemn affirmation.

THE place where the Hindu pilgrims brought by Brahmins offer *pindas*, is on a platform beneath a *pipal* tree to the north of the Maha-Bodhi Temple. The distances from the Temple will be 30 or 40 feet—that is, the platform. The tree itself will be about 80 feet off. I never saw Buddhists worshipping at that tree. The *pipal* they do worship at is west of the Temple quite contiguous *(ek dam satte hue)* with it. I have seen Hindus go to see *(darsan karna)* that tree, but not to perform any other kind of worship at it. By *darsan* is meant bowing the head.

The new sort of worship I have seen at the big image on the ground-floor since July last is of the following kind:—*Tilak* marks have been placed on the forehead, a light is passed in front of it by way of *arathi*, and at the time the light is passed bells, etc., are sounded, and the image and altar are both bathed with water. That is all the innovation I have seen since July last. I never saw any one of these things before July last. That constitutes Hindu worship, but not completely so. Both a bell and a gong are sounded. I don't hear a conch sounded.
Read over and admitted by witness to be correct.

D. J. MACPHERSON,
Magistrate.

9TH APRIL, 1895.
WITNESS FOR PROSECUTION, III.

The Deposition of Muhammad Fazalullah, aged about 44 years, taken on solemn affirmation under the provisions of Act X. of 1873, before me, D. J. Macpherson, Magistrate of Gaya, this 9th day of April, 1895.

My name is Muhammad Fazalullah, my father's name is Moulvi Mohiuddin. I am a Muhammadan. My home is at Mouzah Erki, Police Station Jahanabad, Zila Gaya. I reside at present in Mouzah Gaya, Police Station Gaya, Zilla Gaya.

I am Special Sub-Registrar of Gaya.

On the 25th of February last I had occasion to go to Bodh-Gaya. Moulvi Habibullah, a Deputy Magistrate of this place, accompanied me. I went to Bodh-Gaya to receive a document for registration from the Mahanth and to record his admission to its execution. We reached Bodh-Gaya about 8 A.M. On that occasion we went into the Maha-Bodhi Temple, and the accused Hussain Baksh accompanied us into it. We visited both the ground and upper floor. There was a person, an ordinary man, whom I took to be the keeper of the Temple, who accompanied us to the upper storey. Hussain Baksh also came upstairs. We went upstairs between 8 A.M and 9 A.M When we got upstairs, we saw a person whom I subsequently came to know was Mr. Dharmapala (*identifies him*), taking pieces of an image from two or three boxes, and fitting them together. He had not completely put the things together when we left. There was a pedestal, and something like a lotus flower on the pedestal, and then on the lotus flower an image. Then he took something from a box which looked like a back piece to the image, but he had not fitted it on to its place when we left. When he was putting them together, the things were on the altar, where there is an image of Buddha, and he put them together on the altar. When we left, the things were actually on the altar. It was a gilded image, and in a sitting posture. I did not know what the image purported to be, and did not enquire. Before we left, Hussain Baksh said something to the man who came with us, the man I took to be the keeper of the Temple. I did not hear what he actually said to him. That man was a Hindu. He had on the sacredotal thread. When we left, we went to the Mahanth—that is, Moulvi Habibullah, Hussain Baksh and myself. We all went together. We saw the Mahanth. We had some talk with the Mahanth as to what Dharmapala was doing in the Temple, but I don't remember what the exact words were.

Question.—Did either you or the Deputy Magistrate or Hossain Baksh inform him that Dharmapala had placed an image on the altar ?

Answer.—The Mahanth appeared to have been informed of this before we got there. The Mahanth was somewhat excited.

Question.—Did you offer any advice to the Mahanth in presence of Hossain Baksh ?

Answer.—I cannot say, if Hussain Baksh was present all the time, but we advised him to inform the Magistrate or the Police of what was being done. When we went to the Mahanth on our return from the Temple, we saw with the Mahanth among those in Court the Mukhtear Vijaya Nanda. The Deputy Magistrate and I stayed with the Mahanth on that occasion about half-an-hour or three-quarters of an hour.

Cross examination reserved.

Read over and admitted correct.

D. J. MACPHERSON,
Magistrate.

8TH MAY, 1895.

WITNESS FOR PROSECUTION, III.

Moulvi Muhammad Fazalullah, recalled and cross-examined on solemn affirmation, on 8th May, 1895 :—

I am not familiar with the signature of Mahanth Krishna Dayal Gir. I have seen him sign only once.

(*Shown a letter No. 7 E., dated* $\frac{13}{18}$*th June,* 1894 *from the Mahanth to the Collector of Gaya, produced from the Collectorate*). I cannot say if that is his signature.

Read over and admitted by witness to be correct.

D. J. MACPHERSON,
Magistrate.

9TH APRIL, 1895.

WITNESS FOR PROSECUTION, IV.

The Deposition of Muhammad Habibullah aged about 29 years, taken on solemn affirmation under the provisions of Act X. of 1873, before me, D. J. Macpherson, Magistrate of Gaya, this 9th day of April, 1825.

My name is Muhammad Habibullah. My fathers' name is Haji Abdul Karim. I am a Muhammadan. My home is at Mouzah Monghyr, Police Station Monghyr, Zilla Monghyr. I reside at present in Mouzah Gaya, Police Station Gaya, Zilla Gaya.

I am a Deputy Magistrate and Deputy Collector of Gaya.

I accompanied Moulvi Fazalullah, Special Sub-Registrar of Bodh-Gaya, on the 25th of February. I had no business to take me there, but as I had not seen the

Temple since I came to Gaya, I took the opportunity of his going there to go and see it. I accompanied him. I went into the ground floor and looked at the great image there from the threshold, remaining there for some minutes; but I did not go inside that shrine. There was with us at the time the Mahanth's Muhammadan Mukhtear (*points out to Hussain Baksh, accused*). We all, the Mukhtear, Fazalullah and myself, went upstairs. When we got there, I saw a gentleman fitting up certain pieces of an image and placing them on a raised place like an altar inside the room on the upper storey. (*Identifies the complainant as the person referred to*). The image they were putting together was a gilded one, the figure being in a sitting posture immersed in devotion. After the pieces were put together, we came away, and went to the Mahanth, accompanied by Hussain Baksh. When we got to the Mahanth, the Mukhtear standing here (*points to accused Vijaya Nanda*) was with the Mahanth. We did not speak to the Mahanth about the placing of the image, but the Mahanth appeared to know about it already, as he asked the Mukhtear Hussain Baksh to go to the Temple and see about it. The Mahanth seemed anxious about this. I gave the Mahanth advice, saying there was no necessity for anxiety, and that he should refer the matter to the District Magistrate and to the Police, if necessary, and I also said that the mere placing of the image did not create any possession, and told him not to do anything against the law.

Cross-examination reserved.

When witness read over his deposition, he said it was correct, but that when they went upstairs they were accompanied also by a man of dark complexion whom they took to be the warder of the Temple.

D. J. MACPHERSON,
Magistrate.

[NOTE: *This witness was not cross-examined by the Defence.*]

9TH APRIL, 1895.

WHEN the prosecution tendered as witness, Sumangala the Singhalese priest, they stated that he know neither English nor Hindustani, but that there was in Court a Mr. Harrison who would be able to interpret the evidence. This Mr. Harrison had come up from Ceylon being sent by the Singhalese to watch the case and help Mr. Dharmapala in it, and was himself a Buddhist.

There is no one else in the district, so far as is known, capable of interpreting the evidence, and so the above gentleman was sworn as interpreter. The defence merely wish it recorded what he is and under what circumstances he comes here. When he was called up to be sworn, *the defence stated that they objected to his being allowed to interpret in this case owing to his being a Buddhist and having come here to help the prosecution.* There would be no other alternative than to postpone the evidence of these witnesses until an interpreter is obtained from Calcutta or elsewhere. The prosecution stated Mr. Dharmapala of course could also interpret, but this, of course, is still more objected to.

It was decided that an interpreter should be telegraphed for from Calcutta, the evidence of the Singhalese witnesses being, therefore, postponed.

The prosecution stated they considered it unnecessary to multiply evidence by calling Nirghin Ram, the Government Custodian's Chaprassi; and the *gariwan* who had been summoned by the Court, though not cited by the prosecution.

(Sd.) D. J. MACPHERSON,
Magistrate.

11TH APRIL, 1895.

A. R. LEWIS, a Singhalese interpreter sent up at my request by the Commissioner of Police, Calcutta, took the oath as an interpreter in this case. He says he is a native of Ceylon and a Christian by religion, but has, for the last seven years, been in Calcutta as an assistant in shops and the like. He seems to know English sufficiently well. He has travelled all night from Calcutta and arrived here 1½ hours ago.

(Sd). D. J. MACPHERSON,
Magistrate.

11th April, 1895.

11TH APRIL, 1895.

WITNESS FOR PROSECUTION, V.

The deposition of Mahtali Sumangala, aged about 34 years, taken on solemn affirmation under the provisions of Act X of 1873, before me, D. J. Macpherson, Magistrate of Gaya, this 11th day of April, 1895. Evidence given in Singhalese and interpreted by A. R. Lewis.

My name is Mahtali Sumangala. It is against religion for me to mention my father's name. I am a Buddhist priest. My home is at Mouzah Mahtali, Ceylon. I reside at present in Mouzah Bodh-Gaya, Police Station Mutassil Gaya, Zilla Gaya, where I am a worshipper at the Maha-Bodhi Temple.

Question.—How many times have you been to the Maha-Bodhi Temple?

Answer.—The first time I went was the 17th July, 1891. I stayed there for seven months on that occasion. When I came there I was accompanied by four Buddhist priests, that is, including myself, there were four altogether. None of them are here to-day. I entered inside the Maha-Bodhi Temple when I came in July, 1891.

Question.—Was anything done inside the Temple according to your religion? (*This question was translated.*—Was anything done then inside the Temple against your religion?)

Answer.—Nothing was then done against my religion. I met Burmese pilgrims there on that occassion. I saw them put two marble images of Mayadevi inside the Temple. The images were first kept at the Mahanth's *baradari* (reception-house). Then they put them at the place where the Japanese image is now. That place is just opposite the Great Temple, in the compound of the Temple. It was outside the Great Temple itself, about three yards from the steps. That spot where they put the images is a sanctified place. That was on the 18th July, 1891, the day after I arrived myself. There came with me to Gaya on that occasion Mr. Dharmapala and two boys. During the seven months I was there I stayed in the Burmese rest-house. It is about 50 cubits from the Maha-Bodhi Temple. After July, 1891, I saw other pilgrims come to Bodh-Gaya. Some came in November, 1891, namely, four Burmese priests and twenty-five Burmese pilgrims, being Buddhists. When at Bodh-Gaya, the four Burmese priests stayed at the same place as I stayed. I accompanied them inside the Temple.

Question.—Did you and they do anything inside the Temple?

Answer.—We offered (*literally* "placed by way of *puja*") two marble images of Buddha. We placed them on the same altar as the great image of Buddha is now on, on the ground floor. Besides that we stretched 80 yards of silk cloth upstairs. There is a place upstairs round which one can walk, and we stretched the silk round that. We did not ask the permission of the Mahanth before doing all that. The images we placed were there in the Temple, when I was there last a week ago. Again in the next month, December, I saw more pilgrims. They were Burmese Buddhists, without priests. I saw them inside the Temple, and they offered two marble images of Buddha, placing them on the same place where the great image of Buddha is. They did not take the Mahanth's permission before offering these images. The Mahanth then was the predecessor of the present Mahanth. I don't know his name.

This year, in February last, I went to Bodh-Gaya. It was on a Monday, the 25th. There went with me then, Devananda priest, Dharmapala and Palis Silva. We went there in order to enshrine (*tabanda*) the image from Japan. We wanted to enshrine it on the second floor of the Temple. We took it up on to that floor. We went and enshrined it. I put the brass lotus flowers beside it, and we were going to worship it. After placing it we sent the chaprassi for Bepin Behari Babu. We placed it on the altar. Bepin Behari came. Those who took part in placing the image on the altar were Devananda, Palis Silva, and Dharmapala and myself. The image itself was placed on a carved lotus flower, which rested on a pedestal. When we were placing the image on the altar, I noticed three respectable Muhammedans there. There were two gentleman I saw. I do not see either of these in Court just now (*looks round the Court, but not to the dock*).

Question.—Do you know any of the people in the dock ?

Answer.—I know the names of three persons in it,. namely, Jaipal Gir, Shivanandan Gir, and Mahendra Gir. I don't know the names of the others.

Question.—Have you ever seen the Muhammadan who is in the dock before ?

Answer.—That is the man who hit Dharmapala on the shoulder and spoke to him. After we placed the image on the altar, we sat down for our devotion. Before we sat down to our devotion, Bepin Behari Babu came. Some conversation took place between him and Dharmapala in English, which I did not understand, but Dharmapala explained it to me. After that we sent for some candles and were about to light them. We fixed one candle up in one of the candlesticks. I put one with the candle in it on the altar, and had the other candle* in my hand. I did this myself. We also placed on the altar a Japanese letter, which was in a frame. We put two candlesticks there, but one had not a candle in it. I had its candle in my hand. I was about to light that candle when Mahendra Gir, the accused, (*identifies him*) snatched it out of my hand. My intention was, after lighting it, to put it in the candlestick on the altar, and then worship before it. Mahendra Gir was accompanied into the Temple by the four persons in the dock, and about fifteen others. Among those who came with Mahendra Gir I recognise four of those in the dock (*points out Jaipal, Bhimal Deo, Shivanandan and Hussain Baksh*). They came into the Temple in a very rowdy way. They spoke in Hindi. I understood some of the words they said. I understood the following that they said: *Tumhárà hukum nahin, jáo. jáo; murti rahne ko nahin degá: badmash. marega: báhir nekal karegá; hamara panch sau admi hain.* They were making a tremendous noise, and these were the only words I understood. I saw the Muhammedan defendant hitting Mr. Dharmapala on the shoulder (*makes a gesture showing that accused pushed him with his fist on the side of the shoulder*), and he spoke to Dharmapala very harshly in Hindustani. On account of the noise I could not catch anything he said. After that a Mukhtear of the Mahanth came. The other people were there where we were before he came. I see him in Court (*points out defendant Vijaya Nanda*). When he came he spoke to Dharmapala in English. Then the Sannyasis got up on the altar and began interfering with the image that was placed there. Of those who got on to the altar I recognise the accused Mahendra and Bhimal Deo (*points them out*). Jaipal and Mahendra were very rowdy. The old Sannyasi (*meaning Shivanandan*) was there, but was not noisy. Others got on to the altar, but only the two I have pointed out, out of those in Court. About ten others got on to the altar—Sannyasi boys (*Kolho*). After the Hindu Mukhtear came, Dharmapala, on seeing these two Sannyasis and the boys on the altar, stretched out his hand to it and said something to the Hindu Mukhtear. The Hindu Mukhtear then warned the boys and some of them got down from the altar. Then some went out of the place, and it got quiet. Thereupon we again sat down to our devotion. Our hands were crossed with the palms upward in the attitude of Buddha. We remained on religious contemplation (*bhavána.*) That was just below the altar, in front of the Japanese image which was on it. Those who were thus worshipping were Dharmapala, Devananda and myself. Silva was standing. We were then engaged in religious worship of the highest form in the Buddhist religion. While we were so worshipping, about fifty Sannyasis came and took away the image and the other things that were on the altar. When they entered to put their hands on the image and things, Dharmapala, Devananda and I were still contemplating. Among the Sannyasis who came then there are in Court the following. (*Points out four Sannyasis, accused, and the Muhammedan Hussain Buksh*). Among

* This word "candle" was added when the deposition was read over to witness.
D. J. M.

those actually touched the imge on removing it I recognise these two (*points out Mahendra Gir and Bhimal Deo Gir*). These two and a third person actually removed the image and carried it out. When they did this Dharmapala and Devananda still remained sitting in contemplation, but I got up and followed them. I went out on to the terrace of the upper floor and looked down, and I saw them take the image outside the Temple and place it in the sun to the east of the Temple. That would be about half-past ten, I think.

Question.—Did any one all the time from the very beginning till they took the image out speak to restrain them ?

Answer.—Bepin Behari Babu kept imploring them with folded hands.

Before the image of Buddha on the ground floor, I used to sit in religious contemplation, but I don't do so now. I have ceased doing so since November last.

Question.—Why have you since then ceased doing so ?

Answer.—Because they have added on many embellishments to the image of Buddha. They have painted something like a snake's head on the forehead, and put garlands of flowers on the head, and put on to it a dress like a lady's gown, which is "mocking" it. All that constitutes defilement of the image of Buddha so great that he who does it will, according to the Buddhist religion, be born in the lowest hell. They are all insults to our religion. The image of Buddha is a very sacred object among us Buddhists. Enshrining an image of Buddha on the altar is a very great and most meritorious act of worship. As a priest, I say that the setting up and placing on the altar of the image of Buddha, and the setting up of candlesticks and lighting the candles are ceremonies bringing innumerable blessings (*asankhyak pun.*) They are all most religious ceremonies. All the acts that the Sannyasis did on the 25th February, were great insults to the Buddhist religion, and they constituted a disturbance of our religious worship and ceremonies. All these things greatly hurt my religious feelings and pained me. The removal of the Japanese image from the altar and placing outside, was a great defilement of the image, and not only so, but a great insult to the whole Buddhist religion. I have been inside the Temple down below, where the great image of Buddha is, about twenty or thirty times. Previous to November last, I used to see Hindus go into the Temple, but only to look at it and not to worship.

Question.—Did you ever see the old Mahanth worship in the Temple ?

(Question objected to, but allowed on the general grounds stated at last hearing, namely, that the defence are not prepared to argue yet why such questions are not relevant.)

Answer.—I never saw the old Mahanth worship in the Temple. I never saw the presant Mahanth worship in the Temple.

Cross examination reserved.

Evidence read over to the witness in English, and interpreted to him in Singhalese, and admitted by him to be correct, except that he says that of respectable Muhammedan gentlemen, he saw only two and not three. The accused were present and appeared also by their pleader who understood the language in which the deposition was read out. It was agreed this would suffice.

D. J. MACPHERSON,
Magistrate.

8TH MAY, 1895.

WITNESS FOR PROSECUTION, V.

Mahtali Sumangala recalled and cross-examined by the defence, the evidence being interpreted by A. R. Lewis.

I HAVE known Dharmapala for the last ten years. The first time I came to Gaya, I came from Ceylon with him. I can talk a little Hindustani, but not very correctly. Buddhists are in the habit of offering both large and small images in Buddhist Temples.

Question.—Do they do so by way of votive offerings (*pujawa*) as distinct from enshrining images (*tábanda*) ?

Answer.—There is no distinction between *pujawa* and *tábanda*.

Question.—Is there a distinction between offering images to another image and enshrining images ?

Answer.—Images are offered to temples, not to another image.

Question.—Is there any distinction between offering (*pujakrim*) and enshrining (*tabima*) images to a temple ?

Answer.—These are one and the same thing. *Mantras* in the form of *gata* are uttered in making offerings of images. *Gata* are utterances in Pali.

Question.—When one image is placed in a new temple, are *gata* uttered ?

Answer.—*Gata* are uttered when an image is offered to a new temple.

Question.—Are the *gata* used in offering the first image to a new temple, the same as those used in offering additional images in the same temple subsequently, or different ?

Answer.—Images are not offered to images, but to temples.

Question (*repeated*.)

Answer.—Sometimes the same *gata* is used, and sometimes different ones.

Question.—You have said that on the 18th July, 1891, that is, the day after the first visit you ever paid to the Temple, you saw Burmese pilgrims put two marble images of Mayadevi inside the Temple. Were these placed in the same sacred way as you say the Japanese image was placed ?

[Prosecution object to the question as ambiguous, having regard to the context at page 71 of his deposition, which shows witness meant outside the Temple. Question allowed to be put, as follows.]

Question.—You remember the first occasion on which you visited the Temple: that was the 17th July, 1891 : you remember the day after that, the 18th July : in your deposition you have said that on the 18th July you saw Burmese pilgrims put two marble images of Mayadevi inside the Temple.

(*At this stage, witness, who had been answering in the affirmative to each portion of the above question, said*) : These images were not put *inside* the Temple ?

Question.—Did you say before in your deposition in this Court that you saw the Burmese put two marble images of Mayadevi inside the Temple ?

Answer.—I never said so.

Question.—Did you ever at any time see any Burmese pilgrims put any marble images inside the Temple ?

Answer.—I saw them do so. That was in November, 1891. I don't recollect the day. The first place I saw the Burmese place the images of Mayadevi in, which I saw placed on the 18th July, 1891, was in the verandah of the Panchpandava Temple, to the east of the Great Temple. I cannot say why they did not take them inside, as I was new to the place.

Question.—Did you see them first put them in the Mahanth's *baradari* ?

Answer.—When I arrived and heard Burmese pilgrims were there, I went to see them and found them bringing the images from this *baradari*. The *baradari* is inside the compound of the Mahanth's *math* (monastery). That was the first time I ever saw those images.

Question.—Do you or do you not know that they went to the Mahanth to get his permission about placing the images?

Answer.—I do not know whether they went to him for this.

Question.—Did the Burmese place these images in the Panchpandava Temple with the same ceremonies as you placed the Japanese image in the Temple.

Answer.—They were not placed in the same way, as they were not images of Buddha.

I have said that in November, 1891, I saw two marble images of Buddha being placed on the altar of the great image of Buddha. They were placed in exactly the same sacred way as the Japanese image was placed.

Question.—They were not then placed in a more sacred way than the Japanese image?

Answer.—They were placed in the same way, except that there were more priests on the occasion of the Burmese images. These marble images of Buddha are still in the same place as they were placed then. I last saw them a week before I was first called to this Court. They were then inside the Temple. *(adds)* They are now clothed. When I last saw the two marble images that were placed in November 1891, they were inside the Temple. They are about a cubit high.

Question.—Why did you want to enshrine the Japanese image on the second floor and not on the first?

Answer.—We thought it was the best place. We thought it was the best place, because lots of Hindus go up on the altar on the ground-floor and pour water on the altar and then come down.

Question.—That was the only reason?

Answer.—From the floor they used to throw water and flowers at the image. Before the Japanese image we did not try to place (*tabanda*) any other on the upper storey.

(*A person who gives his name as Jagarnath ingh was here pointed out to witness*).

Question.—Did you see that man on the morning of the 25th February when you went to the Temple with the Japanese image?

Answer.—Yes.

Question.—Do you know him as the Mahanth's *durwan?*

Answer.—Yes. That man did not on that morning tell us not to go upstairs. He did not speak to any of us before going upstairs. He was at the time sitting near the door of the Temple. I mean the big door. I did not see him go off to the Mahanth's before going upstairs. I saw him upstairs that morning. I saw him when we were fixing up the image, and he was looking at it. He left us and went downstairs. That was before our contemplation. He left before the Sannyasis came. They came about 15 minutes after he left. I was in Gaya in May a year ago. I then knew the Mahanth objected to the placing of the Japanese image. On the night of the 24th February before the image was set up, I slept in Gaya in the same house as Dharmapala. Devananda also was with me. I learned for the first time that night that the image was to be placed next morning. Dharmapala told me that.

Question.—Did you suspect that the Mahanth might object to its placing?

Answer.—I did not think he would object. The ruler of India had given permission for it to be placed. By ruler of India I mean the Viceroy (*rájáruyo*).

Question.—Who told you the *rájáruyo* had told you this?

Answer.—When Dharmapala applied to the *rájáruyo* for permission, the Buddhists were allowed by the *rájáruyo* to place the image. It was Dharmapala who told me that, and he showed me a letter.

[The prosecution challenge the translation of the last two questions, including the question set out above. The interpreter says he cannot now remember all the words in Singhalese the witness used. The defence then put the following question.]

Question.—Tell us all that Dharmapala told you on the night of the 24th February as to what the ruler of India had said about placing the image in the Temple.

Answer.—On the 24th February, 1895, Sunday, Dharmapala told me as follows:—"Priest, we will take the Japanese image to the Great Temple at Bodh-Gaya and place it to-morrow; with regard to this I have written the Agent (*agent*) of Gaya; last year the ruler (*andu karetuma*) of Bengal has given us Buddhists written permission to perform any ceremonies (*pinkam*), so we will place this image in the Government Temple (*andue vihar*); let us place the image there." That is all he said to me on that subject.

[*The above was all written down by the interpreter in Singhalese as given by witness*].

I did not have any talk with Dharmapala as to the possibility of the Mahanth's opposing.

Question.—Did he say he had the Agent's (Collector's) permission to place the image?

Answer.—No: he did not say he had his permission, but only that he had written a letter to him.

***Re-examined*—**

I have often seen Hindus throwing water and flowers on the great image of Buddha on the ground floor; but the first time I saw this was in November last, that is, November, 1894.

Read over and interpreted to the witness and admitted by him to be correct.

D. J. MACPHERSON,
Magistrate.

9TH MAY, 1895.

WITNESS FOR PROSECUTION, V.

Mahtali Sumangala re-called and examined by Court on solemn affirmation, the evidence being interpreted by A. R. Lewis.

Question.—You said that the two marble images the Burmese placed beside the great image inside the Temple are now clothed. Why did you make that remark?

Answer.—Because when respectable gentlemen go to see the place, the images are clothed. I saw them again last night clothed.

Question.—Do Burmese Buddhists put clothes on small images like that then?

Answer.—Buddhists do not clothe images.

Question.—Have these marble images always been clothed?

Answer.—I have seen them always clothed since November last I never saw them clothed before November last.

Question.—Do you know who put the clothes on them?

Answer.—I think the Mahanth's *pujari* (priest) did so.

Question (at suggestion of prosecution.—When *gatas* are uttered at the placing of images, are they uttered aloud or low ?

Answer.—When I utter them, I utter them so low that no one else can hear them.

Read over and interpreted and admitted by witness to be correct.

D. J. MACPHERSON,
Magistrate.

NOTE.—The interpreter, in answer to the Court, says his present occupation is Manager of the Anglo-Indian Club, Calcutta, on pay of Rs. 60 a month. He got this appointment from 1st instant.

D. J. MACPHERSON,
9th May, 1895. *Magistrate.*

11TH APRIL, 1895.

WITNESS FOR PROSECUTION VI.

The Deposition of Nahagoda Devananda, aged about 30 years, taken on solemn affirmation under the provisions of Act X of 1873, before me, D. J. Macpherson, Magistrate of Gaya, this 11th day of April, 1895. The Evidence being given in Singhalese and interpreted by A. R. Lewis.

My name is Nahagoda Devananda. It is against my religion to mention my father's name. I am a Buddhist priest. My home is at Mouzah Nahagoda, Ceylon. I reside at present in Mouzah Bodh-Gaya, Police Station Mufassil Gaya, Zilla Gaya, where I am worshipping.

I came to Bodh-Gaya on the occasion of my last visit there on the 25th of February last. On that occasion an image of Buddha was placed in the Temple on the upper floor. It was placed on the altar upstairs. Those who took part in placing it on the altar were Dharmapala, Sumangala priest, and myself. Along with the image there were placed on the altar two brass lotus plants, two candlesticks without candles, and an inscription in a frame. Sumangala priest was about to light the candle, when a Sannyasi came at the moment and snatched it away. There were other people with the Sannyasi, about forty or fifty. Just after enshrining the image, we sent for Babu Bepin Behari, and he came. He came just before the candle was snatched away. He had a conversation with Dharmapala in English, which I don't understand. Then, when the forty or fifty men came and snatched away the candle, they used harsh words in Hindi, some of which I understood. They said, *uthao, uthao, tumlok ko hukum nahin yih murti huán rakhne ke wáste, murti lejáo;* and many other words I did not understand. Among those who came and used these words, I recognise these three *(points out Jaipal Gir, Mahendra Gir and Hussain Baksh, accused).* The man who snatched away the candle was that man (*pointing to Mahendra Gir.*) Bepin Behari, with folded hands, spoke to them imploringly in Hindi. Then some of them left the place. Then we sat down there and engaged in religious contemplation (*bhávána.*) Those who sat down thus were Dharmapala, Sumangala and myself. We were sitting with our hands crossed with the palms up. Dharmapala, and I were sitting with our hands like that. I cannot say whether Sumangala had his hands like that. We were all three in contemplation The image of Buddha is a little different from the attitude we were in. We were sitting in front of the altar. We were engaged in religious worship according to the Buddhist religion. When we were so engaged, some Sannyasis came and seized the image of Buddha, and walked away with it. Among those who took away the image from the altar, I recognise of the accused only that man (*points to Mahendra Gir*). He helped the others to lift up the image and take it off. I remained when they took it away, in the same position as I was in before, but my contemplation was stopped. I saw the Muhammadan accused, when they came and snatched away the candle, digging Dharmapala on the shoulder with his knuckles. I saw many Sannyasis get up on to the altar, but I cannot say how many.

Cross-examination reserved.

Read over to the witness in English and interpreted to him in Singhalese, and admitted by him to be correct, except that the image of Buddha differed from their attitude of devotion only in respect of its having a hand raised, and that Bipin Bihari Babu arrived before the candle was lit. The other remarks recorded at close of Sumangala's deposition apply.

D. J. MACPHERSON,

Magistrate.

8TH MAY, 1895.

WITNESS FOR PROSECUTION, VI.

Nahagoda Devananda recalled and cross-examined by defence on solemn affirmation on 8th May, 1895. The evidence being interpreted by A. R. Lewis.

[*N. B.—The witness is ill with fever, and has been so since yesterday, when it was intimated to me he was in Hospital: he is evidently ill and weak. D. J. M.*]

I CAME first of all to Bodh-Gaya on the 31st March, 1894. I have been in this District ever since. I have not gone to Ceylon or Calcutta since.

Question.—Since the 31st March, 1894, where have you principally lived, in Gaya or Bodh-Gaya at night ?

Answer.—Being ill, I made a mistake—it was on the 31st May, that I came to this District. I have principally stayed at night in Gaya. That is in the house of Babu Bhikhari Shankar Bhattacharjya. That is not the same house as Babu Durga Shankar Bhattacharjya lives in. Bhikhari Shankar is Durga Shankar's brother.

Question.—How often in a week do you generally go to Bodh-Gaya ?

Answer.—I cannot say how often in a week, but I used to go often in a month. I have gone about six or seven times in a month. I have not gone there every month.

Question.—When did you go to Bodh-Gaya last before the 25th of February ?

Answer.—I cannot remember, but I know I went in November. I cannot remember if I went in December or January. When I was there in November, I went and performed ceremonies (*puja*) and engaged in religious contemplation (*bhavana*) and worship (*namaskar.*) When I went in November, the image I worshipped was the one near the Bo-tree outside the Temple. Sumangala was with me on that occasion. It was not an image but the Bo-tree I worshipped then. (*adds*) I found a difference in the image, and so I did not worship it. I do not recollect seeing any other pilgrims on that occasion worshipping or making offerings at the tree. I saw Hindus about the place on that occasion. There were both Sannyasis and other Hindus going about the place then. I did not on that occasion see any Sannyasis worshipping the great image of Buddha on the ground-floor of the Temple.

Question.—Did you ever worship the great image of Buddha on the ground-floor?

Answer.—The first time I went to the Temple I worshipped (*namaskar*) it. I do not remember if I worshipped that image after that occasion.

Question.—Then you remember only one occasion on which you worshipped it?

Answer.—Yes, I worshipped it in May, 1894, that is, on the very day I came.

I have known Dharmapala since March, 1894. I first came to know him in that month. That was in Ceylon. I came to India with him. He asked me to come with him, and I was glad to do so. I heard of the Japanese image first when I was in Ceylon; it was from Dharmapala.

Question.—Did you hear when you came to Gaya that the Mahanth objected to its being placed?

Answer.—I heard that he was opposed to it.

Question.—When you went to the Temple on the 25th February of this year, did you go of your own accord, or did Dharmapala ask you to come?

Answer.—I went of my own accord as the others were going. Dharmapala called me to go. There was talk before we left Gaya as to what floor the image was to be placed on. He said it was to be on the upper storey. I have no remembrance of any talk before we left Gaya as to whether the Mahanth might object. I don't remember any mention being made even of the Mahanth's name then. I cannot recollect when there was the first talk about the image being placed on the 25th February. I first heard that that was to be the day selected for placing it, on the previous evening. I cannot say at what time in the evening that was. Those present then were Dharmapala, Sumangala, Palis Silva and myself. I don't remember if any one else was present. I don't remember if there were any Bengalis or Beharis present. The talk was at Bhikhari Shankar Bhattacharjee's house. I have no recollection whether there was any talk with Bengalis or Beharis about placing the image. I did not count the number of Sannyasis or of the Mahanth's people who came into the Temple when we set up the image.

***Re-examined*:—**

The reason I did not worship the great image of Buddha on the ground-floor of the Temple in November last, was that I found that it could not be worshipped as it had been changed, and had on a dress, like a lady's dress, and had paint on the forehead. I don't know whether, when we stayed in Bhikhari Shankar's house, we were his guests, or rented the house. Dharmapala knows all that. I have been suffering from fever for the last ten days and am staying in Hospital and came from it to-day.

Defence asked it to be noted that the witness answered all questions intelligently. He had said in cross-examination he was not able to speak loud, being ill. He was seated during his examination.

Read over and interpreted to the witness and admitted by him to be correct, with the correction as to the month of his arrival noted in his deposition.

D. J. MACPHERSON,
Magistrate.

11TH APRIL, 1895.

WITNESS FOR PROSECUTION, VII.

The Deposition of Palis Silva, aged about 27 years, taken on solemn affirmation, under the provisions of Act X. of 1873, before me, D. J. Macpherson, Magistrate of Gaya, this 11th day of April, 1895. The Evidence being given in Singhalese and interpreted by A. R. Lewis.

My name is Palis Silva. My father's name is Raja Karuna Tilaka. I am a Singhalese Buddhist. My home is at Mouzah Kolupitiya, Ceylon. I reside at present in Mouzah Bodh-Gaya, Police Station Mufassil Gaya, Zilla Gaya.

I am a carpenter by trade, but have come here on account of my health.

The prosecution put this witness in the box, but think it unnecessary after taking so much evidence to examine him in chief, and simply tender him for cross-examination.

Cross-examination is, however, reserved.

Read over in English and interpreted in Singhalese, and admitted to be correct.

D. J. MACPHERSON,
Magistrate.

8TH MAY 1895.

WITNESS FOR PROSECUTION, VII.

Palis Silva re-called on the 8th May, 1895, for Cross-examination and sworn.

Defence stated that they would not cross-examine him.

D. J. MACPHERSON,
Magistrate.

12TH APRIL, 1895.

WITNESS FOR PROSECUTION, VIII.

The Deposition of Dr. Hari Das Chatterji, aged about 41 years, taken on solemn affirmation under the provisions of Act X of 1873, before me, D. J. Macpherson, Magistrate of Gaya, this 12th day of April, 1895.

My name is Hari Das Chatterji. My father's name is Mahesh Chandra Chatterji. I am by caste a Brahman. My home is at Mouzah Ranaghat, Zilla Nuddea. I reside at present in Mouzah Gaya, Police Station Gaya, Zilla Gaya, where I am a medical practitioner.

I am a high-caste Kulin Brahman. I have been practising as a doctor at Gaya since 1883. I had many times paid Gaya a visit before that, since 1873, when I first came. I saw the Temple of Maha-Bodhi in 1873, when I first came. It was then in a very dilapidated state. I have visited it often since it has been restored. I have seen pilgrims in it, Burmese and Tibetans. I have also seen Hindu pilgrims outside the Temple. I saw the Buddhist pilgrims making *puja* and lighting candles inside the Temple. There was an image in the Temple then, one of Buddha. I have seen offerings been made to that image On one occasion, for instance, I saw some Burmese pilgrims offering Huntley and Palmer's biscuits. I have also seen them offer earthenware saucers, such as rice, etc., are kept in. The candles I saw them burn were bazar candles, candles made of lard. From what I know of the Temple, it is a Buddhist one. The Burmese and Tibetan pilgrims must have been Buddhists. I took them to be such. As a Hindu I would never worship inside that Temple. Never on any of the different occasions on which I have been to it, have I ever seen Hindus worship inside the Temple. It would certainly be repugnant to all Hindu notions to offer Huntley and Palmer's biscuits and burn lard candles inside a Hindu Temple. The image I saw was on the ground-floor, and it was a Buddhist one, not a Hindu one. That is the one I saw the above offerings being made to.

Cross-examination reserved.

Read over and admitted correct.

D. J. MACPHERSON,
Magistrate.

9TH MAY, 1895.

WITNESS FOR PROSECUTION, VIII.

Dr. Hari Das Chatterji recalled and cross-examined on solemn affirmation on 9th May 1895.

I WAS educated at the Calcutta Medical College in the English Department. I do not pretend to be an orthodox Hindu. I do now perform daily *pujas* as orthodox Hindus do. I have been doing so for the last two or three years. I perform the *puja* of my god. I believe in one God. I am a Theist. I believe in the whole Hindu pantheon. I have been believing in it since the last two or three years. That was before Dharmapala's arrival. Prior to that it is not the fact that I did not believe in it, but that I did not care to do so. I do not take forbidden food, but I used to do so. I have given up taking any since I commenced my *pujas*. I took *mantras* from my *guru* when I commenced doing *pujas*.

Question.—Who is he?

Answer.—He lives in Bhatpara. [The Court remarked that presumably what was wanted was the name of the *guru*, but perhaps this cannot be disclosed.]

Question.—What is his name?

Answer.—I cannot mention it. We are not actually forbidden to do so, but it is a point of honour among us not to do. The god I do *puja* to is Sakti. I will not say if the god has any other name.

I began my medical practice at Gaya in 1883. When I took the *mantras* I performed the *praschit* penance. I cannot say the exact year, but it was probably in 1890. I used to partake of forbidden food while at Gaya before that. The Gayawals did not object to call me in as a doctor before I had performed the penance.

Question.—Has your practice increased among the orthodox since you performed the ceremony?

Answer.—My practice is increasing daily. My practice has increased since then. I have known Dharmapala for some three or four years. I am a friend of his. I am a brother-in-law of Babu Durga Shankar Bhattacharjya. Having married his sister, I have offered *pindas* (funeral cakes) at Gaya to the *manes* of my forefathers. I offered no *pindas* at Bodh-Gaya. I am aware that it is customary for Hindus to offer *pindas* at various places about Gaya, inclusive of Bodh-Gaya.

Question.—Is there any reason why you did not offer them at Bodh-Gaya?

Answer.—It is optional there. The year I offered the *pindas* was in 1877.

Question.—Do you dine with Dharmapala?

Answer.—What do you mean by dining with him? I have dined on the same floor with Dharmapala, but far away from him. It was in the same room with him, but it was quite far away, as he is not a Hindu. He could be regarded as a *mlechha* by Hindus.

Question.—Have you ever seen Hindu Sannyasis in or about the Maha-Bodhi Temple during your visit?

Answer.—Yes. I knew them as *chelas* of the Mahanth.

Question.—Have you ever seen these Sannyasis appropriate any *dakhina* or offerings from pilgrims?

Answer.—I have never seen them do so, but I know that offerings made by Buddhists in the Bodh-Gaya Temple have been taken by the Mahanth.

Question.—How long have you known this?

Answer.—The late Mahanth, Hem Narayan Gir, once showed me a room where he kept them. That room was within the enclosure of the Monastery. That would be about 1887 or 1888.

Question.—Do you remember what the Mahanth told you when he showed you these?

Answer.—He said these were offerings by the Buddhists.

I once took a lease from that Mahanth. It was of mouza Manshabigha. I returned the *patta* within a few days of getting the lease as being unprofitable. I thereafter told his Mukhtear to speak to him about my getting a lease of another mouza instead. I mentioned Laru as one I should like. I did not get the lease of it. I was not much anxious to get it. I was not recently anxious to get it, and in fact don't now want it.

Question.—During the last two years have you visited any person in Gaya to speak about the Buddhist claim to the Maha-Bodhi Temple, or to consult about their claim?

Answer.—No. I first knew my evidence would likely be taken in this case after Babu Kedarnath, pleader, took my statement. That was in April last. Probably he is Dharmapala's pleader.

Question.—Who were present then?

Answer.—Another pleader, the Headmaster of the Zillah School, my compounder and some others. It was at my house. I don't remember who the others were. Dharmapala or my brother-in-law was not there. I have never called myself a Theosophist.

Re-examined.

The place where Hindus offer *pindas* at Bodh-Gaya is not inside but outside the Temple. That is at a *pipal* tree to the north of the Temple. Before a Hindu sits to take his meal, he does not make a *chauka* round him. Bengalis don't do that.

Question.—Is there anything contrary to your usages in taking your food in the same room as a Muhammadan may be?

Answer.—Yes. As regards a Muhammadan, the distance makes no difference. There is no truth in the suggestion that I performed the *praschit* ceremony in order to increase my medical practice. The reason I don't mention the other name of my god Sakti is that I am forbidden to do so.

To Court.—

Beyond its being a point of honour, I have no objection to mention the name of my Guru, and I will mention it, if ordered by the Court to do so.

The defence say they do not require it.

Read over and admitted by witness to be correct.

D. J. MACPHERSON,
Magistrate.

12th April, 1895.

WITNESS FOR PROSECUTION, IX.

The Deposition of Babu Durga Shankar Bhattacharjya, aged about 46 years, taken on solemn affirmation under the provisions of Act X of 1873 before me, D.J. Macpherson, Magistrate of Gaya, this 12th day of April, 1895.

My name is Durga Shankar Bhattacharjya. My father's name is Tara Shankar Bhattacharjya. I am by caste a Brahman. My home is at Mouzah Gaya, Police Station Gaya, Zilla Gaya. I reside at present there.

I am a Zemindar here and an Honorary Magistrate, and also Chairman of the Gaya Local Board and a Member of the District Board. I have been holding these positions for over twelve years, and been Chairman of the Local Board since its institution. My Zemindari is situated in the Sadar Sub-Division of the Gaya District. I am a Kulin Brahman. I have seen and visited the Maha-Bodhi Temple at Bodh-Gaya. I had a few villages in lease about eight miles beyond the Temple. My interests in them ceased about ten years ago. In order to get them I had to pass through Bodh-Gaya. I had seen the Maha-Bodhi Temple many times before it was repaired by Government. Before it was repaired I saw an image in the same place where the great image now is on the ground-floor. It was made of bricks and mortar. It was said to be an image of Buddha.

Question.—Would you or any Hindu worship a Hindu image made of brick or mortar ?

Answer.—Never. I many times went to see the Temple while the repairs were going on. There was a contractor employed in carrying on the repairs, Gopal Chandra Mukerjee, a relation of mine. After the Temple was restored, the present great image was put by Mr. Beglar in the place where the brick and mortar one was, the latter being pulled down. I have been seeing the great image there since immediately after the repair—perhaps for the last ten or twelve years. Since the Temple has been restored, I have been inside it many times. The present great image on the ground-floor there is an image of Buddha. I have been up on to the upper storey since the restoration. I don't think that on any occasion, when I went either into the ground floor or on to the upper storey, I took off my shoes. I now remember that on one or two occasions, when I saw pilgrims performing worship and ceremonies in the Temple, I took off my shoes out of regard for the worshippers. The pilgrims I refer to were Buddhists, perhaps Tibetans. The ceremonies (*pujas*) I saw them doing were burning candles on the altar, offering something, and pouring incense—European essence, such as lavender water and other scents—and burning *dhup* (incense). On one occasion I also saw rice and *dal* cooked together *(kichheri)* placed in front of the altar, below the altar. I never believed that either of the images I saw on the ground-floor—either the old one or the present one—was an image of a Hindu god, and no Hindu would ever believe that. I have always taken the Temple to be a Buddhist one. As a Hindu I would never worship in that Temple, not unless I were to become a convert to Buddhism. I have never seen any Hindus worshipping inside the Temple. No Hindu would ever pour European scents on a Hindu shrine. That would be desecration to it.

Question.—Do you regard the Bhagwan Buddha, the ninth *avatar* of Vishnu, as the Buddha of the Buddhists?

Answer.—Until the present case we never heard of Buddha Bhagwan being the Buddha of the Buddhists. Up to this time I knew that this Buddha was not an object of worship to us Hindus. By "this Buddha" I mean not only the image in the Temple, but also the Buddha who was born in Kapilavastu. The Buddha born in Kapilavastu is said to be the son of Suddhadhan and his wife Mayadevi. The ninth incarnation of Vishnu is said to be the son of Jina, and born in *Kikat-desh*. The ninth incarnation of Vishnu is said to have been born long before the Buddhist Buddha, namely, at the beginning of the *kali-yuga*, or 4,900 years ago. The Buddhist Buddha is said to belong to the date 500 B. C.

Cross-examination reserved.

Read over and admitted correct.

D. J. MACPHERSON,
Magistrate.

10TH MAY, 1895.

WITNESS FOR PROSECUTION, IX.

Babu Durga Shankar Bhattacharjya recalled and cross-examined on solemn affirmation on 10th May, 1895.

I FIRST became acquainted with Dharmapala in 1891 or 1892. That was when he first came to my house with a letter of introduction to me from a friend of mine in Benares.

Question.—Was it a simple letter of introduction, or were you requested to lend him every help in your power in the furtherance of his object?

Answer.—I was asked simply to put him up comfortably. I was not asked to render him any help. I put him up in my own house on that occasion.

Question.—Do you consider him to be a *mlechha*?

Answer.—Yes, I have often put up other *mlechhas* in my house besides him. I have put up Japanese, Europeans, Mahomedans.

Question.—Do orthodox Hindus in Gaya generally do so?

Answer.—Yes, if they have suitable accommodation for the purpose. There is certainly objection to doing so, if there is no accommodation for *mlechhas*. I consider myself an orthodox Hindu. I have all along done so. I have never partaken in my life of forbidden food or drink.

Question.—Would you dine with a Hindu who takes forbidden food and drink?

Answer.—If he does it publicly—that is, if I know of it and see it—I would not do it. If I heard from a reliable source that a Hindu had taken forbidden food and drink, I would not dine with him; but not if I heard it by mere rumour.

Question.—Are you thinking just now of your brother-in-law, Dr. Hari Das Chatterji?

Answer.—No. I have not asked him what he was examined about. I have not seen him since his cross-examination. I heard he had been asked about his taking forbidden food. I heard he had admitted that. I knew that before.

Question.—When did you first know that?

Answer.—I saw him taking his meal at Burdwan Railway Station about ten or twelve years ago. That was after he became my brother-in-law. I ceased to dine with him. I have never dined alongside of him, but I have in the same room, of course.

Question.—Did you ever forbid him entrance to your kitchen?

Answer.—There was no occasion to do so.

Question.—Did you ever forbid him your *hookah ?*

Answer.—He never dared asked me for it, as he knows I never giv : *hookah* to any body. There was never any occasion for my forbidding him to touch water in my *kalsi.* I have a room where I keep drinking water. I keep it in an earthen pot.

Question.—Did you ever tell him not to take water out of it ?

Answer.—No, I never had any occasion to do so. I would never allow a *mlechha* to touch that earthen pot.

Question.—Did you ever tell him not to hand you over anything, such as a letter, and not to touch you when eating ?

Answer.—No. I would not let a *mlechha* hand me over a letter or touch me, when eating. I don't recollect telling Dr. Hari Das I did not approve of his taking meals at refreshment rooms. In my opinion a Hindu who takes meals at railway refreshment rooms, becomes a *melechha.* I have four brothers.

Question.—Do you all live together in the same mess ?

Answer.—Only my third brother, Gadadhar, lives in the same mess with me.

Question.—Do you or any of your brothers ever take forbidden food ?

Answer.—I never saw them. I never heard it. I don't believe it. I have not been taking an active interest in this case.

Question.—Have you been taking an interest in Dharmapala and his object ?

Answer.—I do not understand the question.

(*N B.*—The examination of this witness is being conducted in English. D.J.M.)

Question.—Have you been trying to render help to him in regard to the objects with which he has come ?

Answer.—I don't know his objects—but this time one of them is to look after this case.

Question.—Besides looking after this case, are you aware of any object with which he has come to Gaya ?

Answer.—He came once with an image to fix in the Maha-Bodhi Temple. At present I don't remember any other object that ever brought him to Gaya.

Question.—Did you never hear of any other object than the two you have mentioned that brought him to Gaya ?

Answer.—I cannot assure you that I ever heard of any other. I don't find that he had any other. I don't remember any.

Question.—Have you ever discussed or conversed with him about his objects in coming to Gaya ?

Answer.—Last time he told me he had come to fix the image, and this time to look after this case. That is all the talk I ever had with him about his objects, so far as I remember,

Question.—Did you ever hear from Dharmapala that he wished to have control and possession of the Maha-Bodhi Temple on behalf of the Buddhists ?

Answer.—I never heard that.

Question.—Did you ever hear it from any one else ?

Answer.—Not so far as I recollect. I never heard from him or any one that it was his wish that the Buddhists should have control and possession of the Temple. I believe the first time I hear such a suggestion is from the Counsel now.

Question.—Will you swear that, besides rendering him comfortable in your house, you have never tried to give him help of any kind ?

Answer.—That is a very general question. I don't deny that I may have given him some help besides making him comfortable—I am not sure.

Question.—What sort of ways have you helped him in ?

Answer.—For instance, I have taken him out for a drive to my zemindari. I don't remember having rendered him any other kind of help. I don't remember if he asked me for the drive or I asked him to come. The help that I gave him was giving him fresh air.

Question.—Have you ever been to any pleader of Dharmapala to consult about the Maha-Bodhi Temple ?

Answer.—No. I never went to Babu Sital Prashad, pleader, with Dharmapala.

Question.—Did you ever tell Sital Pershad about Dharmapala's affairs ?

Answer.—Never.

Question.—You never had any talk with Sital Pershad about Dharmapala ?

Answer.—I may have talked with him about Dharmapala—that being a general matter for talk. I did talk with him about Dharmapala. I did not request Sital Pershad to be on his side. I never wished in my mind that he should be on his side, having no occasion for wishing it. I have often conversed with Babu Nand Kishore, pleader, about this case. I do not take the Journal of the Maha-Bodhi Society. I have seen it, as the first two issues were sent me, but they discon-inued it, as I did not subscribe. I have read, glanced over, those two copies. I don't remember whether I read there about the objects of the Society.

I have seen the big figure of Hanumanji about half way to Bodh-Gaya. I have seen it only from the road in passing. I do not know if it is built of brick and mortar. I don't remember whether there are any figures of Hanumanji in Gaya built of brick and mortar. I am not aware of it. I never heard it. Hindus worship the one on the way to Bodh-Gaya. I never enquired what it is made of. I know the Kathokar Talao in Gaya. There is a big figure of Hanumanji there. Hindus worship that. I never enquired if that is made of brick and mortar.

Question.—What reason had you for saying that Hindus don't worship an image of brick and mortar ?

Answer.—According to the *Shastras* images are made of metal, wood, clay, jewels, but never of burnt clay. I think that is in the *Srimat Bhagavat*. I have read it. It may be in the 14th Chapter. I remember reading the prohibition there. That is not my only reason for making the statement—it is our common notion. I never asked any one whether there are brick and mortar images in Gaya. I had no occasion to do so.

I was not present when Mr. Beglar put up the image in the Maha-Bodhi Temple. I am not aware who takes the offerings at that Temple, but I have heard that the Mahanth took valuable offerings that were put there by the Burmese. I heard that before the restoration. That would be more than twelve years ago.

Since I came to know Dharmapala, I have not examined the *Shastras* to see whether Buddha is worshipped by the Hindus, but I have seen printed extracts from them on his side. I saw these recently—within the last ten or fifteen days. Before these ten or fifteen days, I never examined the *Shastras* in order to ascertain the position of Buddha with reference to the Hindus. I have discussed the matter before giving evidence in this case with friends. I often did so. I have done so only since the institution of this case, so far as I remember. I don't know of discussing it before. I was present at the meeting at the Collector's house, when the matter was discussed.

Question.—Is it not the fact that you have on many occasions talked with the Collector about that?

Answer.—No, only on that occasion. That was last year. I told him on that occasion that in my opinion it was contrary to the *Shastras* that Hindus should worship Buddha. I said that without any reference whatever to the *Shastras*, and without consulting any one on the subject beforehand.

Question.—Did you ever accompany Dharmapala on visiting Mr. Macpherson?

Answer.—I have no remembrance. I can swear I don't remember. I cannot swear that I never did.

Question.—Besides that occasion last year, did you ever speak to the Collector about Dharmapala or the Buddhists?

Answer.—Once or twice he enquired where Dharmapala was and his coming. That was the only thing, quite casually. I never spoke to him that Dharmapala was being badly treated, or about the Buddhists. I wish Dharmapala to succeed in this case.

My sister, the wife of Dr. Hari Das, frequently visits my house. She does not enter my kitchen. My cooking is done by a male, a *Panre*, and she is not allowed to enter it. I never saw her eating with my wife. Our females never dine before us. She may have eaten with her, but I don't know it. I dont recollect if my sister ever handed me a glass of water. *(After a pause)*. Yes, I do recollect.

Question.—What do you recollect?

Answer.—She has given me water. I did not object to drinking it.

Question.—If a Hindu man becomes a *mlechha*, is his wife forbidden to touch the food or drink of an orthodox Hindu?

Answer.—Only if he becomes outcasted. Dr. Hari Das was never excommunicated or outcasted at any time. If a Hindu takes *mlechha* food or food given by a *mlechha*, there is objection to eating with him, even if I know he is not outcasted. Whether outcasted or not, a Hindu who takes forbidden food ceases to be a Hindu, that is, for the time being.

Question.—Is not his wife under these circumstances also not a Hindu?

Answer.—No, because she does not take that forbidden food. Cohabitation of a Hindu wife with a husband who has ceased to be a Hindu, does not render her an outcast, that is, if she does not know he has ceased to be a Hindu and does nothing, forbidden to Hindus, herself.

Re-examined

My brother-in-law Dr. Hari Das does not now take forbidden food. I have known he has abstained from doing so for four or five years back. He has, since he abstained, reinstated himself as an orthodox Hindu. I know that, as I was present at the public performance of the *praschit* ceremony by him. A few Hindu friends were present there.

[*To Court*] :—That was about three or four years ago.

I have never actually seen any one taking the offerings at Maha-Bodhi. I have only heard it from the Sannyasis. Apart from reading the *Shastras*, it has all along been my personal belief that orthodox Hindus do not worship Buddha. The grounds on which I made the statement to the Collector last year that orthodox Hindus do not worship Buddha, is that almost all the other members present at the meeting said that.

[*Witness was going on when he was stopped by the counsel for the prosecution, who then asked :*]

Question.—Leaving alone what the members at the meeting said, had you any other ground for making that statement?

(Question objected to on the ground that he has already answered it. Question allowed, as witness was stopped before he finished his answer).

Answer.—I had learned it from my personal observation, from my father, from pandits, from friends, ever since my youth. There were a dozen or more people present at that meeting.

Question.—What class of persons were present at the meeting?

(*Question objected to and disallowed.*)

I did not go to that meeting of my own accord I was invited. The reason I wish Mr. Dharmapala should succeed in this case, is that I consider his cause is the right one. Mr. Dharmapala had many times come to my house before the present occasion.

To Court.—

Mr Dharmapala lives in my house now. He often lives in it when he comes to Gaya, but not always. Babu Bhikhari Shankar, my brother, is not owner of the house he stays in. When Dharmapala stays in my house, he does so as my guest My brother Bhikhari Shankar has a house where Buddhists have put up. He lets it to them on hire. It is quite separate from his dwelling-house. I have nothing to do with that house. Bhikhari is separate from me. I never saw anything on either the old or the new image on the ground-floor in the Maha-Bodhi Temple to lead me to believe Hindus ever worshipped it.

Question.—You have said you know of no objects for which Dharmapala came to Gaya except to place the image and carry on this case. What was his object in coming to Gaya when you first saw him?

Answer—He came on pilgrimage to Bodh-Gaya. The reason I did not say that object before is that I was referring only to recent times.

Question.—After the first time he came to you, did he ever come again until he brought the image last year?

Answer.—He came on other occasions with Japanese priests and also with Singhalese priests to settle in Bodh-Gaya. When the Collector sees people, he has a fixed day in the week, and all come about the same time on that occasion. The Japanese image was not kept in my house all the time it was in Gaya. It was kept in a house hired from my brother, Bhikhari Shankar. The way I know the Mahanth took valuable offerings that were put in the Temple by Burmese is, that when I went to the Temple and the monastery with a friend, the Sannyasis showed us the bells in front of the Temple, and also said that, besides that, the Mahanth had in his custody valuable jewels that the Burmese King had dedicated to the image. When I was invited to the meeting at the Collector's, it was by a general notice containing the names of the gentry.

(*At suggestion of Defence*). There was one man at the meeting who gave a contrary opinion, but I remembered that all the rest at the meeting agreed in their opinion. The point to which the opinion referred was whether it was the duty of Hindus to worship the image in the Maha-Bodhi Temple or not, and the dissentient member said that both the Hindus and Buddhists were equally entitled to worship it. That person was not a Sanskrit Pandit but a Hindu Pandit, namely, of the Gaya Zilla School, named Buldeo Misser.

Question.—Are you sure of that?

Answer.—I remember he dissented. I remember it as he discussed with me on several occasions afterwards. I have no recollection of any one else objecting.

Question (suggested by Defence): May the person who dissented have been Chander Sekhar Bhatt?

Answer.—I don't remember. I don't know the person. I never heard his name. He may or may not have been present.

When the above was read over, witness admitted it to be correct, except that he modifies certain passages as follows:—

(1) "He did not take his meal at Burdwan Railway station, but he got some biscuits from the Refreshment Room there."

(2) "I now remember that I did take Dharmapala to Babu Sital Pershad, pleader, to introduce him."

The Defence ask it to be noted that the deposition was read by witness after the ten minutes' adjournment of the Court. Witness says that he went out of Court during the adjournment only to get a glass of water, and that he came back immediately without seeing any body on Dharmapala's side or talking to any one about the subject of his examination.

D J. MACPHERSON,
Magistrate.

12TH APRIL, 1895.

WITNESS FOR PROSECUTION, X.

The Deposition of Pandit Gangadhar Shastri, aged about 38 years, taken on solemn affirmation under the provisions of Act X of 1873, before me, D. J. Macpherson, Magistrate of Gaya, this 12th day of April, 1895.

MY name is Gangadhar Shastri, my father's name is Pandit Umadatt Pathak. I am by caste a Brahman. My home is at Mouzah Arair, Police Station Daudnagar, Zilla Gaya. I reside at present in Mouzah Gaya, Police Station Gaya, Zilla Gaya.

I am Head Pandit of the Government Zillah School in Gaya.

I know the Maha-Bodhi Temple at Bodh-Gaya. That Temple is a Buddhist, not a Hindu one.

Question.—Did you ever enter the Temple?

Answer.—Before it was restored *(bana)*, I went three or four times to see it, but I never actually went inside it. I have never till now been inside it, but after it was restored also, I have seen it three or four times from outside. The reason I have never entered it is that in the *Shastras* it is written that one should not look at the face of Buddha or enter inside a Jain Temple. I know the *sloka* containing that prohibition *(repeats it in Sanskrit)*. That particular sloka does not contain the word Buddha, but it means Buddha, as there is another *sloka* from the *Bhagavat* which says that Buddha is the son of Jina, and the word "Jain" is derived from Jina. That *sloka* speaks of Jina of Kikat-desh, and Kikat-desh is Gaya. (*Repeats the sloka in Sanskrit*. Buddha, the son of Jina of Kikat-desh, was born in the begininng of the *Kaliyug*, that is 4,996 years from now. The description of the image of this Buddha the son of Jina, is given in the *Vishnu-purana*, Part III, Chapter 18, *sloka* 2. (*Witness repeats the sloka and explains the description of the image as follows*). It is naked, with head shaven, and a bunch of peacock feathers in the hand. There is another half *sloka*, the details of which I don't remember just now, but it is in my books. Even the Buddha described in these *slokas* is not worshipped by Hindus. No Hindus would ever worship the Buddha of the Buddhists, who was the son of Suddhodhan and born in Kapilavastu. He was born according to Buddhist history 2,400 years ago.

Question.—What is the reason why Hindus do not worship Buddha, the son of Jina?

Answer.—It is given in the second Chapter of the *Bhagavat* and is the following: The enemies of the gods, the Rakshasas, began to follow the Vedas, and as they did so, they acquired strength and ascending in a balloon made by Maya-daitya or Maya Asura, began to destroy people. Then Vishnu, assuming the disguise of Buddha, ordered them not to believe in the Vedas and began to teach them false doctrine in order to confound them and protect the gods. It is all described in the second chapter of the *Bhagavat*, in the 37th or 38th *sloka*. Sannyasis originated with Sankara Acharya, who was born 1,100 years ago, at a time when the Buddhist religion was spread greatly over India. Sankara Acharya waged war against the Buddhists, destroyed their Temples, and established the Hindu religion. He had ten disciples, each of whom started a separate order, one of which is the Giri, represented at Bodh Gaya by the Mahanth and his disciples.

Cross examination reserved.

Read over in Hindi and admitted to be correct.

D. J. MACPHERSON,
Magistrate.

9TH MAY 1895.

WITNESS FOR PROSECUTION, X.

Pandit Gangadhur Shastri recalled and cross-examined by deffence on solemn affirmation on 9th May 1895.

My monthly salary in the Zillah School is Rs. 30. I have known Dharmapala for two or three years. So far as I remember, the first place I ever met him in was the Indian Billiard Room in Gaya. I often go there in the evening to see billiards played. I am not a member of that Club.

Question.—Who introduced you to him then?

Answer.—The then Head Master of the Zillah School, Sura Babu, said to me that he was a person from Ceylon. I have met him since at several places, such as Hari Babu Doctor's, Durga Shankar Babu's, and Nand Kishor Babu's. I had no idea when I first met him that he had come to take possession of the Mahabodhi Temple. I do not know even yet that his aim is to take possession of the Temple. I know that his object in coming to Gaya from time to time is to worship, being a Buddhist, at the Bodh-Gaya Temple. I have also heard that he wishes to spread the Buddhist religion.

Question.—Have you heard that people say he desires to wrest the Temple from the possession of the Mahanth?

Answer.—Yes. I heard that first last year.

Question.—Where?

Answer.—In the city somewhere. Several persons asked me what were the *Shastras* bearing on Buddhism, such as I have quoted in my examination-in-chief. Among those persons were Rai Ram Narayan Lal,, Babu Chhote Lal Sijwar, C. I. E., and some pleaders whose names I don't remember. Among the latter I remember Babu Harihar Nath, senior. No pleader of Dharmapala's asked me. Durga Shankar Babu also asked me what was in the *Shastras* about it. The first time he did so was in the hot weather of last year.

Question.—Did Durga Shankar ever take you anywhere last year to get you to give your opinion on these *Shastras*?

Answer.—No. I did go somewhere to give my opinion about them. The Magistrate, Mr. Macpherson, called me. Durga Shankar Babu also went on that occasion. A notice was issued in which my name was included. I do not know if Durga Shankar Babu gave my name to the Magistrate. A chaprasi brought the notice round, that is all I know. I stated to the Magistrate something about the *Shastras*, but I cannot say if I said all I have said here. What I stated on that occasion was what the Hindu *Shastras* say about Buddhism. Dharmapala was not there. I did not see him either before going there or after that he was not here at all then. It would be in May or June last year in the hot weather.

I have read the *Vayú Purán*. (*Shown a passage in that book.*)

Question.—Is the Dharmesvar referred to in that passage Buddha or not?

Answer.—No.

Question.—Who is he?

Answer.—There is a place, Dharmarana, 1½ kos east of Bodh Gaya, where there is an image of "Dharm." After making *pranam* (bowing down) there, one ought to come and make *pranam* at the *pipal* tree at Mahabodhi. That is my interpretation of the passage shown me. Dharmraj is a synonym of Buddha in the Amarkosh Dictionary, but not in the Hindu *Shastras*. Amarkosh is a very ancient and leading Sanskrit Dictionary. Bhagwan is a synonym of Buddha in Amarkosh.

Question.—Is the word Bhagwan used for deity (*deota*) by Hindus?

Answer.—It is used both for *deota* and for *muni* (saint).

Question.—Is not Jina a synonym for Buddha—Jina not Jaina?

Answer.—Yes.

I have read *Bhavishya Puran*. It is an antheritative (*pramanik*) book (*granth*) among Hindus. [*Shown a passage in above*].

Question.—Is it said there that one ought to worship Budh Bhagwan?

Answer.—This is not the original, but a Hindi translation. I have seen the original. I saw it once at an Agarwala's in Barh, in Patna District. That would be about 20 years ago. I cannot remember if the passage I have read just now is a correct translation.

Question.—Is not the word " Buddhāya nama " quoted there from the Sanskrit ?

Answer.—It is wrongly spelt, being here *Budha* and not *Buddha.*

(*Shown a subsequent passage with the words " Buddha Bhagwan" in it.*)

Question.—" Is that correctly spelt there ?

Answer.—Yes.

In that second passage Buddha Bhagwan refers to Vishnu, because the word " Sridhar" is also quoted. The book shown me purports to have been printed in September, 1886.

[*Books referred to tendered. Admitted as evidence of the passages the witness read in Court, and marked Exhibits D42 and D43 (a) and D43 b) respectively.*]

(*Shown another passage in the Bhavishya Puran*)

Question.—Are not the ten Hindu *avatars* mentioned there as object of Hindu worship ?

Answer.—Yes.

Question.—And is not Buddha mentioned as one of them ?

Answer.—Yes.

It is not mentioned that Buddha is to be worshipped, but that the ten *avatars* are to be worshipped.

[Put in and marked Exhibit D44.]

I know the book *Nirnaya Sindhu*, which is one of the Dharma Shastras of the Hindus.

Question.—Have you read in it that it is enjoined there that the Hindus must worship Buddha in the mouth of Pous?

Answer.—Where there is mention of the ten *avatars* it is said that they are to be worshipped each on the day of his birth, and that the day for worshipping the Buddha *avatar* is the 7th day of the bright fortnight in Pous, which is the birth-day of Buddha. I read it last the day before yesterday. I read that chapter to ascertain on what day the *ekadasi* fast would fall this month. I did not refer to it for the purpose of evidence in this case. When I was examined-in-chief I knew what was contained in the *Nirnaya Sindhu.*

Question.—Does the following passage occur in the book ; " On the second day of the bright fortnight in Jaishtha Buddha was born ?

Answer.—I do not recollect. [*Shown the passage referred to.*] It is there said that Buddha and Kalki both will be born on that day.

[Put in and marked Exhibit D 45 (*a*)].

Two or three sentences after occurs the sentence to the effect that the Buddha *avatar* is to be worshipped on the 7th day of the bright fortnight in Pous.

[Put in and marked Exhibit D 45 (*b*)].

I have read the *Agni Puran.* There is mention in it of Buddha the son of Suddhodhan. [*Shown a passage in it.*]

Question.—Is it not there stated that the Buddha *avatar* is the son of Suddhodhan ?

Answer.—Yes.

I wish to explain the preceding verses, namely ; at the time when there was a fight between the Devas and Asuras, the Devas went to Vishnu for protection ; and then Vishnu took an illusive form in the shape of Suddhodhan's son, for the sake of deluding people, deceived them, and made them give up the practices of the Vedas.
[Passages put in and marked Exhibit D 46 *(a)* and D 46 *(b)* respectively.]

Question.—Do you know that in the *Agni Puran* it is stated, when the worship of the ten *avatars* is spoken of, that Buddha is to be clothed ?

Answer.—I remember that. [*Shown a passage referred to.*] The signs by which the Buddha *avatar* form is known are here described, including covering with a cloth. [*Witness went on to describe what was in the whole passage*].

[Put in and marked Exhibit D 47].

The chapter in which that passage occurs describes how an *avatar* is to be set up (*sthapan)* and worshipped, but there is no special mention of setting up any *avatar*, such as Buddha, in particular.

I know the *Lingam Puran.* It is one of the Hindu *Dharma Shastras.* [*Shown a passage in it.*] That passage says that in setting up the ten *avatars*, which included Buddha, the Gayatri *mantra* is to be used.

[Put in and marked Exhibit D 48.]

I know the *Varaha Puran.* I have some remembrance of the Buddha *avatar* being mentioned in it. [*Shown a passage in it*]. That refers to the *dwádási vrat* (feast, including fast of the twelfth day*)* of Buddha. The chapter itself does not deal with that, but the conclusion of the chapter says that it relates to the *brat* of the twelfth day of Buddha.

(Put in and marked Exhibit D 49.)

[*Shown another passage*] That chapter shows for what purpose each *avatar* is to be worshipped, and with regard to Buddha, it is said, he is to be worshipped for the sake of his *rup* (figure).

[Put in and marked Exhibit D 50.]

The *Srimat Bhagavat* does not enjoin the worship of Buddha. There is no description of such. (*Shown a passage on a leaf purporting to be from that book*). I know that passage in the *Srimat Bhagavat.* That passage speaks of bowing (*namaskar*) to Buddha. It speaks of Akrur who was sent by Kans to bring Krishna and Baldeo, finding when he was at the river Jamna that he saw both Krishna and Baldeo on looking into the water, and then on looking to the bank he saw them sitting there, and then he prayed in the water with folded hands to certain of the *Avatars*, including Buddha. That was before Buddha was born.

[Put in and marked Exhibit D 51.]

I have said that there is a prohibition in the *Shastras* that one is not to go to a Jain Temple. I have not seen that stated in any *Shastra*, but it is an oral tradition ; but there is a passage similar to it in the *Brihannardi Puran.* (*recites the passage*).

Question.—What does *Bauddhàlay* mean in that passage ?

Answer.—It means a temple (*mandir*) of Buddha. There is no difference between Buddha and Baudha. There is a difference similar to that between Siva and Saiva. Siva is different from Saiva. Siva refers to the God, and Saiva to the sect that worship Siva. The word for the English word Buddhist is also Baudh.

Auestion —Have you ever heard a Siva temple called Saivalay ?

Answer.—It is so called in Sanskrit, but people do not call it so, speaking Hindi. I do not at present remember any passage in a Sanskrit book where a temple of Siva is called *Sivalay* as distinct from *Saivalay*, but I can find them out.

Question.—In the passage "*Bauddháh páshandinah prokta*", does not the word *bauddháh* mean followers of Buddha ?

Answer.—Yes.

Páshandinah there means cheats. That is the reason, namely, that Buddhist people are reputed as cheats, given for the prohibition in the preceding sentence not to go to a *Baudhálay*, (*adds*) because they have abused the Vedas. The word *bauddha* is no doubt used in the same passage twice, but in the word "*Bauddhálay*" it means 'Buddha', and in the other '*Bauddhah*' it means followers of Buddha.

[*Shown the passage in the 'Brihannardi' : Put in and marked as D* 52.]

I do not remember a passage in the *Brihannardi Puran* relating to the worship of Buddha. That *Puran* is one of the eighteen Purans, and is not regarded as a subsequent *Puran (Upapuran)*

***Re-examined.*—**

When I went to the Magistrate's house as referred to in cross-examination, I remember there were there also Rai Baijnath Singh Bahadur, Zemindar and Honorary Magistrate of this town, Babu Beharilal Barik, Zemindar and Honorary Magistrate, Babu Harihar Nath, Senior Government Pleader, Pandit Baldeo Misser, Second Pandit, Zilla School, Pandit Chandra Shekhar Bhatt, Pandit Banidatt Pathak, Babu Durga Shanker Bhattacharyya, Honorary Magistrate, and others I don't exactly remember. The Amarkosh is by Amar Singh, who was reputed to be a Buddhist. The Hindi translation put into my hands in cross-examination of the *Bhavishya Puran* is of no authority, but the original would be in Sanskrit.

The *Nirnaya Sindhu* is the book for ascertaining on what dates various festivals are to be observed. It is intended for the use of all religions in India, not merely Hindus.

[*Shown Exhibit D* 47.] That passage means that when you are to contemplate *(dhyan)* Buddha, you are to think of him as having the various signs there mentioned, including regarding him as a clothed figure. It does not mean you are to clothe him when worshipping him.

I know of no passage in the *Purans* in which there is any mention of the worship of Buddha alone as apart from the worship of the ten *avatars.*

***By Defence with Court's Permission.*—**

One of the nine gems of Vikramaditya's Court was Amar Singh. That is the Amar Singh who was the author of the Amarkosh. Raja Vikramaditya was a Hindu Raja, not a Buddhist.

***To Court.*—**

Question.—How do you know Amar Singh was a Buddhist ?

Answer.—At the beginning of all Hindu books the name of a Hindu God, such as Ganesh, Sarasvati, Vishnu, Mahadeo, is quoted ; but in the beginning of the *Amarkosh* no name of a deity is quoted, and the first sloka begins with an invocation to whatever is indestructible and *amrita*, that is what has not attained *mukti* (salvation).

There may somewhere be used the phrase *Baudh-Bhagwan*, in which case Bhagwan would be an adjective. The word *Bauddh-Bhagwan* is used in Hindi. When used in Hindi it means the Buddha *avatar*. The words *Baudh Deo* also mean the Buddha *avatar*. When people in Hindi want to speak of the Buddha of the Buddhists, they say *Baudh-Bhagwan*, *Buddh Bhugwan*, *Baudh Deo*, or *Buddh Deo*.

In our *Shastras* Buddha is referred to, and I have said that means the *avatar* of Vishnu. The deity of the Buddhists is also spoken of in the *Shastras* as Buddha. The Buddha, which is mentioned in the *Shastras* as an incarnation of Vishnu, is the Buddha that is worshipped by the Buddhists.

Question.—Is that stated in the *Shastras* or is it only your own opinion ?

Answer.—From the *Shastras* it appears that, as the Buddhists worshipped that Buddha, the Hindus ceased worshipping Buddha.

Read over to witness in Hindi and admitted by him to be correct.

D. J. MACPHERSON,

Magistrate.

13TH MAY, 1895

WITNESS FOR PROSECUTION, X.

Pandit Gangadhar Shastri, re-called as arranged from the beginning to file the Sanskrit passages he had quoted in his examination-in chief and examined on solemn affirmation.

I POINT out the passage in the *Bhagavat* referred to at page 90 of my deposition referring to Buddha, the son of Jina of Kikatdesh (*Put in and marked Exhibit* VI).

I point out also the passsage in the 37th Sloka of the 2nd Chapter of the *Bhagavat* in the same volume referred to at page 90 of my deposition.

(*Put in and marked Exhibit* VII.)

[N.B.—Three volumes of the Bhagavat are put in.]

I point out also the passage sloka 2, Chapter 18, Part III. of the *Vishnu Purana* quoted at page 90 of my deposition. (*Put in and marked Exhibit* VIII.)

I put in correct transcripts I have made of all these originals together with what I say is their translation in Hindi and the translation into Roman character. These are all correct. [*Put in and marked Exhibits* VI. *a*) VII. (*a*) and VIII. (*a*).]

I have not written out the sloka about not entering a Jain Temple on looking at the face of Buddha.

To Court.—

I put in also correct transcripts of the original passages shown to me in cross-examination the other day with what I say is the Hindi translation of them.

(*Put in a file of* 12 *pages. Marked Exhibit B.*)

The Gayawals are priests of the Vaishnavite sect. The Mahanth of Bodh-Gaya belongs to the sect of *Giri*, one of the ten sects who follow *Sankaracharya.*

(*After an interval.*)

I have now written out from memory the *sloka* about not entering a Jain Temple or looking at the face of Buddha, and also what I say is the Hindi translation of it.

(*Put in and marked Exhibit* IX.)

Read over and admitted by witness to be correct.

D. J. MACPHERSON,
Magistrate.

NOTE.—The translation of the Sanskrit passages contained in these Exhibits D 42 to 52, VI., to IX., and B., will be found printed among the Documentary Evidence, *post.*

13TH MAY, 1895.

WITNESS CALLED BY COURT.

Bireswar Bose, Head Clerk of the Magistrate's Office. Gaya, called by Court and examined on solemn affirmation.

WHEN called on in this case to produce all the correspondence in the office relating to the Bodh-Gaya affairs, I made a careful search throughout the office, both the Magistrate's and Collector's, assisted by various clerks. I have produced all the correspondence that has been found, and indexed it in my own handwriting. (*Shown files for* 1875 *and* 1876, 1878, 1879 *and letter of 2nd August*, 1884, *from Mr. Beglar to the Magistrate.*) That is all the correspondence discoverable anywhere in the office about Bodh-Gaya affairs from 1875 to 1884, but of the file of 1884 only the first letter is put there, as that is the only one in it relating to the Temple repairs. Search was also made for correspondence of earlier years, but none was found. All B and C papers have been destroyed. B papers are those to be kept for 12 years and C paper for 2 years ; and all other papers are to be kept for ever. The flyleaf of the file of 1875-76 is not an original one, it contains only the letter still in existence. There is another sort of flyleaf in other files which is original, containing notes of B and C papers that were in them once.

I have been Head Clerk since July, 1894. My predecessor was Babu Haran Chandra Banerji. His handwriting has been continually before me in the course of ordinary business, and I am acquainted with it. (*Shown a note on the docket of letter No.* 1006, *dated 24th March*, 1891, *from the Superintending Engineer, Sone Circle to the Magistrate of Gaya.*) That note is in his handwriting (*marked Exhibit C.*) From office notes in the files I know the complete correspondence has been searched for on several occasions.

The defence have no question to suggest.

Read over and admitted to be correct.

Sd. D. J. MACPHERSON,
Magistrate.

CHARGE.

I, D. J. Macpherson, District Magistrate of Gaya, hereby charge you, Jaipal Gir, Mahendra Gir, Shivanandan Gir, Bhimal Deo Gir, Hussain Baksh and Vijayananda Barına, as follows :—

I.

That you all, on or about the 25th day of February, 1895, at the Maha-Bodhi Temple, outpost Bodh-Gaya, in this District, by entering tumultuously with other persons into the upper storey chamber of the said Temple whilst certain Buddhists, *to wit,* H. Dharmapala, Sumangala, Devananda and Palis Silva, were engaged in the performance of religious ceremonies connected with the enshrinement of an image of Buddha in the said chamber, did voluntarily cause disturbance to an assembly lawfully engaged in the performance of religious ceremonies, and thereby committed an offence punishable under Section 296 of the Indian Penal Code, and within my cognizance.

II.

That you all, on or about the said date at the said place, by entering tumultuously with other persons into the said chamber of the Maha-Bodhi Temple, whilst H. Dharmapala and other Buddhists were assembled there for the purpose of performing religious ceremonies and worship in connection with the location of an image of Buddha on the altar, did trespass in a place of worship with the knowledge that the religion of the said Buddhists would likely be insulted and their feelings wounded thereby, and thereby committed an offence punishable under Section 297 of the Indian Penal Code, and within my cognizance.

III.

That you all, on or about the said date at the said place, by entering tumultuously with other persons into the said chamber of the Maha-Bodhi Temple, whilst Buddhists, *to wit,* H. Dharmapala, Sumangala and Devananda were absorbed in contemplation, did voluntarily cause disturbance to an assembly lawfully engaged in the performance of religious worship, and thereby committed an offence punishable under Section 296 of the Indian Penal Code, and within my cognizance.

IV.

That you, the said Mahendra Gir, Jaipal Gir and Bhimal Deo Gir, on or about the said date at the said place, by removing, or, being present, abetting the removal of an image of Buddha from the altar of the said chamber whilst certain Buddhists, *to wit,* H. Dharmapala, Sumangala, Devanand and Palis Silva, were engaged in the performance of religious ceremonies and worship in connection therewith, voluntarily caused disturbance to an assembly engaged in the performance of religious ceremonies and worship, and thereby committed an offence punishable under Section 296 read, if neccessary, with Section 114, of the Indian Penal Code, and within my cognizance.

V.

That you, the said Mahendra Gir, Jaipal Gir, and Bhimal Deo Gir, on or about the said date at the said place, by entering tumultuously with other persons into the said chamber of the Maha-Bodhi Temple and removing from the altar an image of Buddha, did defile an object held sacred by Buddhists or a class of Buddhists, with the intention of insulting the religion of the Buddhists or with the knowledge that the said Buddhists would be likely to consider such defilement an insult to their religion, and thereby committed an offence punishable under Section 295 of the Indian Penal Code, and within my cognizance.

VI.

That you all, the said Mahendra Gir, Jaipal Gir, Bhimal Deo Gir, Shivanandan Gir, Hussain Baksh and Vijayananda Barma, on or about the said date at the said place, by entering tumultuously with other persons into the said chamber of the Maha-Bodhi Temple, with the intention of removing an image of Buddha that had been placed there, at a time when certain Buddhists were engaged in placing it there or in ceremonies connected with its location, did defile a place of worship with the knowledge that Buddhists would be likely to consider such defilement an insult to their religion, and thereby committed an offence punishable under Section 295 of the Indian Penal Code, and within my cognizance.

VII.

That you, the said Mahendra Gir, and Bhimal Deo Gir, on or about the said date at the said place, by going on to the altar in the said chamber at a time when Buddhists were engaged there in religious ceremonies or worship did defile a place of worship with the knowledge that Buddhists would be likely to consider the said defilement an insult to their religion, and thereby committed an offence punishable under Section 295 of the Indian Penal Code, and within my cognizance.

VIII.

That you, the said Mahendra Gir, on or about the said date at the said place, by entering tumultuously with other persons into the said *cella* in the Maha-Bodhi Temple and taking away a candle from Sumangala Bhikshu at the time when candles were about to be lighted in connection with the enshrinement of an image of Buddha on the altar there, did voluntarily cause disturbance to an assembly, *to wit*, H. Dharmapala, Sumangala, Devananda, and Palis Silva, whilst lawfully engaged int he performance of religious ceremonies, and thereby committed an offence punishable under Section 296 of the Indian Penal Code and within my cognizance.

IX.

That you, Jaipal Gir, on or about the said date at the said place, were present instigating the said Mahendra Gir to the commission of the said offence, as set forth in the last preceding head of this charge, by pointing to the said candles and saying to Mahendra Gir, and others, not to let them be lighted, and thereby committed an offence punishable under Section 296, read with Section 114, of the Indian Penal Code and within my cognizance.

X.

That you, Hussain Baksh, on or about the said date at the said place, by entering tumultuously with others into the said chamber of the Maha-Bodhi Temple, and pushing Dharmapala, a Buddhist, and signifying to him by gestures and words uttered in a vehement tone of voice, to remove an image of Buddha from the altar there, at the time when the candles were about to be lighted in connection with the enshrinement of the said image, did voluntarily cause disturbance to an assembly, *to wit* the said Dharmapala, Sumangala, Devananda and Palis Silva, whilst lawfully engaged in the performance of religious ceremonies, and thereby committed an offence punishable under Section 296 of the Indian Penal Code and within my cognizance.

XI.

That you, Hussain Baksh, on or about the said date at the said place, did use criminal force to the said H. Dharmapala without grave or sudden provocation, and thereby committed an offence punishable under section 352 of the Indian Penal Code and within my cognizance.

XII.

That you all, Jaipal, Gir, Mahendra Gir, Bhimal Deo Gir, Shivanandan Gir, Hussain Baksh and Vijayananda Barma, on or about the said date at the said place, were members of an unlawful assembly, whose common object was one or other of the following, namely :—

Either to commit the offences described in Sections 295, 296 and 297 of the Indian Penal Code and set out in heads I, II, III, and VI, of this charge.

Or else, by show of criminal force to H. Dharmapala, Sumangala and Devananda, Bhikshus, to enforce the right or supposed right of preventing the said Buddhists from accomplishing the enshrinement of an image of Buddha in the upper storey chamber of the Maha-Bodhi Temple.

And thereby committed an offence punishable under Section 143 of the Indian Penal Code and within my cognizance, and I hereby direct that you be tried on the said charge.

GAYA,
2nd May, 1895.

Seal of the Court.

D. J. MACPHERSON,
Magistrate.

On the charge drawn up to-day being read over and explained to all the accused, they all pleaded not guilty.

The accused were then called upon to enter upon their defence and produce their evidence.

The defence then said they would begin their defence by cross-examining the witnesses for the prosecution, and would mention to-morrow, if possible or else next day, what witnesses, if any, they would wish to call or require process for.

D. J. MACPHERSON,
Magistrate.

2nd May, 1895.

I may record here that, in drawing up the charges, I have not adhered to what the prosecution suggested as requisite, and that, as regards the addition of a charge under Section 143 of the Indian Penal Code, the prosecution applied that no such charge should be added until the close of the cross-examination of the witnesses for the prosecution ; as it was uncertain, in the absence of any statement made by the accused in answer to the questions put them by the Court and of what might be disclosed by the course the cross-examination might take, what would be the precise common object that should be entered on the charge, and the prosecution were unable at the time to say that such object would not merely be to commit the offences separately specified in the charge. The prosecution, therefore, made no suggestions as to the terms of any charge under Section 143. I have, however, included a charge under that section so that the defence may have notice of what is regarded as *primâ facie* the legal effect of the evidence for the prosecution, without, of course expressing any opinion as to its credibility or as to the sustainability of such charge) in the hope that it may obviate any necessity for double cross-examination of the witnesses. The charges, of course, may still be open to amendment at a later stage of the case under the conditions laid down in the law.

D. J. MACPHERSON,
Magistrate.

2nd May, 1895.

Memo. of examination of the accused Jaipal Gir on 2nd May, 1895.

Question.—What is your name?

Answer.—My Counsel will say.

Question.—Do you refuse then to answer any questions that may be put by the Court?

Answer.—My Counsel will answer.

D. J. MACPHERSON,

2nd May, 1895. *Magistrate,*

Mr. Manomohan Ghose, Counsel for accused, states that he will not answer any questions at present, because he considers that there are no facts in evidence constituting an offence and that all questions should be reserved until after the close of the cross-examination for the prosecution. This answer was made in English in reply to a question from the Court as to whether he would answer any question.

Counsel added that he had given the same advice to all the accused, and they all said their Counsel would answer for them.

D. J. MACPHERSON,

2nd May, 1895. *Magistrate.*

WRITTEN STATEMENTS ON BEHALF OF THE ACCUSED.

IN THE COURT OF THE DISTRICT MAGISTRATE OF GAYA.

QUEEN-EMPRESS ON THE PROSECUTION OF H. DHARMAPALA.

Versus

JAIPAL GIR AND OTHERS, *accused*.

Written Statements on behalf of Jaipal Gir, Mahendra Gir, Shivanandan Gir, and Bhimal Deo Gir.

1. That we are *chelas* or disciples of the Mahanth of Bodh-Gaya, and are *Sannyasis* or devotees, acting under the instructions of the present Mahanth, Krishna Dayal Gir.

2. That we have all along believed, and still believe, that the said Mahanth and his predecessors, also Mahanths of Bodh-Gaya, have been in possession from time immemorial of the Maha-Bodhi Temple and all images, figures, trees, and shrines within the premises known as Bodh-Gaya.

3. That the said Mahanth and ourselves have been informed (which information we believe to be true) that with the consent of the then Mahanth Hem Narayan Gir, His Honor the Lieutenant-Governor of Bengal caused the Maha-Bodhi Temple, which was then out of repair, to be properly repaired under the supervision of Mr. J. D. Melick Beglar, C.E., and that the present Mahanth Krishna Dayal Gir, who was then officiating as Mahanth, and one Gossain Belpat Gir, a *chela* of the Mahanth, jointly contributed the sum of Rupees 6,000, or thereabouts, towards the cost thereof, besides rendering other assistance.

4. That the then Mahanth, Hem Narayan Gir, never suspected that, beyond generously coming forward in the interests of archæology to repair the Temple, the Lieutenant-Governor of Bengal for the time being ever had the remotest intention of laying any sort of claim on behalf of Government to the possesion or guardianship of the Temple by reason of such repairs, but that on the contrary he received a distinct assurance from the Hon'ble Sir Ashley Eden himself in person that there was no intention or desire on the part of the Government to infringe upon the proprietory and possessory rights of the Mahanths in the Temple. Nor have we yet any reason to suppose that any such claim will be set up by the Government, although attempts have been made by certain officials since May, 1894, to suggest such a claim to the Government.

5. That from documents in the possession of the Mahanth, some of which have already been put in as evidence on behalf of the defence, the Mahanth, Krishna Dayal Gir, and his *chelas* had every reason to believe that he, the said Mahanth, was like his predecessors, the sole proprietor and owner of the Maha-Bodhi Temple; and, as such proprietor and owner, he, like his predecessors, had every right to receive and appropriate all offerings made by pilgrims, whether Hindus or Buddhists, whom he permitted and allowed to worship on the premises according to rules and directions which he alone was competent to frame and give.

6. That we were aware from a long time that the Secretary to the King of Burmah, who came from Mandalay in the year 1877, had on the 11th of February, 1877, executed in favor of the then Mahanth of Bodh-Gaya an agreement which was registered on the 19th of the same month, in which on behalf of the Burmese Buddhists, the said Secretary recognised fully the Mahanth as proprietor of the Temple, and undertook to make certain repairs, according to the orders and directions of the Mahanth. We pray that the said registered agreement, annexed and marked with the letter A., be taken as part of this our statement.

7. That, in addition to the documents already put in on behalf of the defence, we beg to set out as part of our statement the following letter writtten by Mr. Grierson, the Collector of Gaya, to the Commissioner of the Patna Division, a copy of which letter has been since the year 1891 in the possession of the Mahanth of Bodh-Gaya.—

No. 1134.

FROM

G. A. GRIERSON, ESQ., C.S.,

Magistrate and Collector, Gaya,

TO

THE COMMISSIONER OF THE PATNA DIVISION.

Dated Gaya, 6th May, 1891.

SIR,

I HAVE the honor to forward herewith an extract from a letter written by the Superintending Engineer to the Executive Engineer regarding the Bodh-Gaya Temple.

"I request that you will cause the custodian to be very fully informed of the peculiar, and in some respects, delicate position he occupies. The building is not the property of Government, and is only taken charge of with the consent of the Mahanth. The custodian must at all times treat the Mahanth with the greatest respect and deference, and it would, I think, be well for him to pay the Mahanth a monthly official visit, so that he may be informed of any matter in which the Mahanth desires any special course to be taken. It would be absolutely impossible to retain the custodian in his office, if he gave any reasonable cause of offence to the Mahanth or to the Temple officials, and this fact should be thoroughly impressed on the custodian who can with ordinary carefulness maintain good understanding with them. His efficiency will be largely judged by his remaining on really good terms with the Temple authorities."

2. Personally I entirely agree with these instructions, which also accord with the tradition handed down from Magistrate to Magistrate as to the position held by Government with regard to the Temple, and have indeed reason to believe that the instructions are founded on information given by me to Mr. Odling.

3. I should be glad to communicate the tenor of these instructions to the Mahanth himself, with whom I am on excellent terms, but, before doing so, I wish to be certain of my ground.

4. I can find no paper in the office defining the position of Government in regard to the Bodh-Gaya Temple.

5. The tradition is that, as Government has spent two lakhs on the Temple, it has a certain undefined right to see to its preservation and protection, the Mahanth remaining the proprietor, and all that we do being done with his consent.

6. I am not prepared to condemn this state of affairs which has grown up naturally and works smoothly.

7. The only thing I want to be certain about is whether it exists.

8. There must have been some negotiations between Government and the Mahanth, when the repair of the Temple was first undertaken, and probably the rights of Government in the matter were then defined.

9. There are no papers that I can find on the subject in my office, and I shall be obliged, if you will enquire from Government as to what arrangements, if any, was come to, as to the right of Government

(1) in regard to the Temple itself.

(2) in regard to its precincts.

10. You can understand that, while hitherto acquiescing in the traditional arrangement, I am unwilling to give the Mahanth a written document confirming it, till I am certain that no other arrangement has been previously made.

I have the honor to be,

Sir,

Your most obedient Servant,

G. A. GRIERSON,

Magistrate and Collector.

8. That a copy of the reply of the Government of Bengal to the above letter from Mr. Grierson, forwarded by the Commissioner of Patna, has also,

since the year 1891, been in the possession of the Mahanth, and that copy is as follows :—

No. 1836 A. Y.

FROM

THE GOVERNMENT OF BENGAL,

PUBLIC WORKS DEPARTMENT.

TO

THE COMMISSIONER OF THE PATNA DIVISION.

Dated Calcutta, 7th July, 1891.

SIR,

WITH reference to your letter No. 297 G., dated 21st May, 1891, with which you forward a copy of a letter from the Magistrate of Gaya on the subject of certain instructions proposed to be issued to the custodian of Bodh-Gaya Temple and requesting that the position of Government in regard to the Temple and its precincts may be clearly defined, I am directed to say that the question has never yet been decided, and that the Lieutenant-Governor would like the case brought before him whenever he visits Gaya.

I have the honor to be,
Sir,
Your most obedient Servant,
F. J. JOHNSTONE,
Joint-Secretary.

MEMO. No. 333 G.

PATNA COMMISSIONER'S OFFICE,
Dated Bankipore, 14th July, 1891.

Copy forwarded to the Magistrate of Gaya for information and guidance with reference to his No. 1134, dated 6th May, 1891.

By order,
DHANESH CHANDRA ROY,
Personal Assistant Commissioner.

9. That a copy of the reply of Mr. Grierson to the above letter of the Government of Bengal is in the possession of the Mahanth, and is as follows :—

No. 2498.

Dated Gaya, 11th November, 1891.

FROM

G. A. GRIERSON, ESQ., C.S.,
Magistrate and Collecter, Gaya,

TO

THE COMMISSIONER OF THE PATNA DIVISION.

SIR,

With regard to your letter No. 333G., of 14th July, 1891, I have the honour to say that I have had the honour of discussing the subject with His Honor the Lieutenant-Governor during his late visit at Gaya, and His Honor is of opinion that it is not advisable to take any action at present in the matter, or to disturb existing arrangements.

I have the honor to be,
Sir,
Your most obedient Servant,
G. A. GRIERSON.

10. That in the year 1894 the present Mahanth of Bodh-Gaya, suspecting and believing that the real object of Dharmapala and the Maha-Bodhi Society was to deprive him, the Mahanth, of the possession and control of the Maha-Bodhi Temple, declined to permit Dharmapala or the Buddhists to do any act without his permission, which was likely to infringe upon the rights which he possessed from time immemorial as regards worship by pilgrims in any part of the Temple and its premises.

11. That the Mahanth and his *chelas*, believing the attempt by Dharmapala in 1894 to place a new image, said to have been brought from Japan, to be a mere ruse or pretext to acquire control over the Temple, strongly opposed the placing of that image in any part thereof.

12. That believing that the Collector of Gaya, Mr. Macpherson, had been misled by Dharmapala and his supporters, and had in consequence thereof and in ignorance of the just rights of the Mahanth, been induced to question his authority over the Temple and the offerings made therein, he, the present Mahanth, Krishna Dyal Gir, wrote in June, 1894, the following letter to the Collector of Gaya, the original of which has been produced before the Court by the Collector of Gaya in whose custody it has been since June, 1894, and been shown to some of the witnesses for the prosecution. We pray that the said letter may be taken as part of this our statement.

No. 7E.

FROM

MAHANTH KRISHNA DAYAL GIR OF BODH-GAYA.

TO

THE MAGISTRATE AND COLLECTOR OF GAYA.

Dated Gaya, the 13/18th June, 1894.

SIR,

With reference to your letter of the 3rd June, 1894, intimating to me that I am not authorised to remove images or other votive offerings of any kind, not being of a perishable description, that may be placed by Buddhist worshippers in the Temple, I have the honor most respectfully to submit that I and my predecessors in office have been exercising absolute control over such images and votive offerings from time immemorial, and that my right in this behalf has never been been questioned, and that I, as proprietor of the Maha-Bodhi Temple, have such a right under the law ; and under the circumstances, I have been advised to request the favor of your kindly not interfering in matters which involve questions of civil rights. At the same time I, as a loyal subject of Her Most Gracious Majesty the Queen Empress of India, am quite willing to obey any just and equitable order that may be passed by the Government at your recommendation. Hoping earnestly that you, as my best patron, will do all that is necessary for the maintenance of my just right and title, and as a dutiful Mahanth, praying for ever for your welfare,

I have the honor to be,
Sir,
Your most obedient Servant,
KRISHNA DAYAL GIR,
Mahanth of Bodh-Gaya.

13. That the same attempt of Dharmapala to place the image in the Temple without the consent of the Mahanth having failed, and the Magistrate of Gaya, having, in May, 1894, as we believe, directed Dharmapala to desist from any further attempt, the Mahanth and his *chelas* believed that the said Dharmapala would not make a second attempt without having recourse to law.

14. That the attempt made by Dharmapala on the 25th of February last to place the image inside the temple without the consent of the Mahanth was, we believe, wholly unjustifiable and illegal.

15. That, on the morning of the 25th of February, information having reached us that Dharmapala and some of his adherents had come to the Maha-Bodhi Temple with a view to place the image which he failed to place on a previous occasion, some of the Mahanth's *chelas* went to the Temple in good faith to prevent Dharmapala from enshrining any image on the upper floor of the Temple without the consent of the Mahanth and without the requisite ceremony of *Pranpratishtha.*

16. That, accordingly and in order to protect what we believe to be the just rights of the Mahanth, we, on his behalf, came to the Temple and protested against the placing of the image by Dharmapala. In so doing we are not guilty of any criminal offence whatsoever.

17. That we believed in good faith that we had a perfect right as *chelas* of the Mahanth to make the protest on his behalf, and, in so doing, none of us had

the remotest intention of insulting any body's religion or of defiling any religious object whatsoever, or of causing any disturbance to any person lawfully engaged in the performance of any religious worship or ceremony.

18. That by entering the Temple or the upstairs chamber where a figure alleged to be that of Mayadevi is kept, both of which were under our control or possession, we committed no trespass whatsoever, nor did we enter with the intention of wounding the feelings of any person or insulting the religion of any person nor had we any reason for knowing or believing under the circumstances of the case that any person's feelings would be likely to be wounded or that the religion of any persons would be insulted thereby.

19. That our sole object in doing what we did was to prevent Dharmapala from creating evidence of some right which, we believe, he was anxious to create, and in the *bonâ-fide* exercise of a right which we then believed, and still believe, ourselves to possess, two of our *sannyasis* brought down the image set up by Dharmapala without the least intention of showing any disrespect to that image or of rendering it impure or knowing it to be likely that the removal of the image by us in assertion of our legal right be considered as defilement by any person.

20. That the two *sannyasis* who got on the altar did so without the least intention of showing disrespect to that altar, although it had previously never been treated as such. The *sannyasis*, as holy men, being in the habit of getting on all the altars in the Temple including those on which no worship is ever held, believed that they had a perfect right to get up on the altar and to remove any image for any purpose whatsoever.

21. That we did not believe that Dharmapala and his comrades were either lawfully or in a *bonâ-fide* way engaged in any worship or in the performance of any religious ceremonies. On the contrary, we regarded all his proceedings on the morning of the 25th February as *mala-fide* and colourable and intended only for the purpose of creating a right adversely to the Mahanth. In this view of the matter which the circumstances of the case fully justified us in entertaining, we acted throughout, and it never occurred to any one of us that our acts could be possibly construed as hurtful to the religious feelings of any person.

22. That we believed, and still believe, that according to the Shastras Buddha is a Hindu deity, and, as such, we treated the image with all the respect that would be due to the image of such a deity, even though it had come from a *mlechha* country.

23. That in maintaining the then existing possession and right of the Mahanth, we were not actuated by any unlawful common object whatsoever, nor did we ever use any criminal force to any one, nor did we intend to carry out any object by any show of force.

24. That we had no knowledge of the rites and practices of Buddhism prevailing in Ceylon and other Buddhistic countries, and we had no idea whatsoever that the touching or the removal of any image by any Hindu Sannyasis (who are regarded as holy men throughout India) would be looked upon as defilement of the image or as an insult to the religion of any Buddhists, especially as the Buddhists of Ceylon are regarded by us as *mlechhas*, who partake of food considered by Hindus as unclean.

25. That we were not aware that the Buddhists objected to any Sannyas's going on an altar of any kind, or that when a Buddhist is in contemplation it is improper to disturb him, nor were we aware that the mere sitting in silence constituted a worship or religious ceremony according to the Buddhist religion. Even now we are not prepared to believe the evidence of Dharmapala and his witnesses in this respect.

26. That we had never seen any Buddhist pilgrims worship the figure on the upper floor, which Mr. Beglar had placed there with the Mahanth's consent.

and we were not aware that any Buddhists had ever looked upon the masonry platform upon which the said figure is placed, as an altar or a sacred place.

27. That in acting under the general orders of the Mahanth whom we believe to possess full authority to give those orders, we intended simply to protect the rights of the Mahanth and to oppose the forcible and unauthorised act of an intruder and a tresspasser.

28. That we believe that neither Dharmapala nor the Maha-Bodhi Society in any way represent the Buddhists; but that the whole agitation, which has for its object to oust the Mahanth from the possession and control of the Maha-Bodhi Temple, is being fomented and fostered by Sir Edwin Arnold and Colonel Olcott, neither of whom are Buddhists or connected with Buddhism, and further that the sole object of the present criminal prosecution is to secure a decision adverse to the civil rights of the Mahanth, and in such manner to indirectly obtain possession of the Temple.

Dated 11th May, 1895.

Written Statement on behalf of Bijaya Nanda Barma.

1. That I have read and understood the written statement put in to-day by Jaipal Gir and his fellow *sannyasis*, who are being jointly tried with me.

2. That I pray that the said statement may be also taken and read as part of my statement in this case.

3. That I am the Ammukhtear of Mahanth Krishna Dayal Gir of Bodh-Gaya, and as such I went to the *math* on the 25th February for the purpose of getting registered a document, which the Mahanth wished to be registered that morning, before the Sub-Registrar who had also come to the *math* for that purpose.

4. That while I was in the *math*, as aforesaid, information was brought to the Mahanth to the effect that Dharmapala had come to the Maha-Bodhi Temple to place an image on the upper story of the Temple. Shortly afterwards I was sent on to the Temple, so that I might be able to interpret in the English language to Dharmapala what the Sannyasis intended to say on behalf of the Mahanth.

5. That accordingly I went and spoke to Dharmapala in English, pointing out to him the impropriety on his part in having come to the Temple without order for the purpose of placing the image. He thereupon pointed out to me the Government letters, which have been put in by the defence, as his authority.

6. That I never was any member of any assembly that morning, and I never had any illegal object or intention in saying what I said.

Dated 11th May, 1895.

Written Statement on behalf of Hussain Baksh.

1. That the written statement put in to-day by Jaipal Gir and his fellow Sannyasis, who are being jointly tried with me, has been read and explained to me.

2. That I pray that the said statement may be also taken and read as part of my statement in this case.

3. That I am in the employ as *Karpardaz* of Mahanth Krishna Dayal Gir of Bodh-Gaya, and in such capacity I was present in the Maha-Bodhi Temple on the morning of 28th February last watching the interests of my master.

4. That I never assaulted or used criminal force towards Dharmapala or any of his comrades.

5. That I do not know English. I do not understand the language of Dharmapala, nor does Dharmapala understand Hindustani. I spoke to Dharmapala in Hindustani, protesting against what he is doing, and while so speaking I gently touched him with my fingers once, when he was standing, on his shoulders in order to draw his attention to what I was conveying to him by signs. In so doing, I did not use any force whatsoever, nor did I intend to do so.

I was not even aware, nor did I suspect throughout the 25th day of February, that Dharmapala had himself supposed that by touching him, I did anything that was wrong or objectionable.

6. I had no desire whatever to show any disrespect to Dharmapala or his religion, and, in doing what I did, I had no sort of criminal intention or object, but acted *bonâ fide* in the interests of my master.

7. That finding that Dharmapala, on the morning of the 25th of February, was bent upon forcibly creating some evidence in his favor by placing the image upstairs, I went immediately under orders of the Mahanth to the Bodh-Gaya outpost and lodged information there. It was I who brought the head constable to the Maha-Bodhi Temple, and, after I brought him, Dharmapala gave him his written complaint in the English language, which has been put in by the prosecution.

Dated 11th May, 1895.

ANNEXURE A.

Copy of a registered Agreement between Mahla Chowdin Saidu, Secretary to the King of Burma, and Mahanth Hem Narayan Gir of Budh-Gaya, dated the 11th February, 1877.

TRANSLITERATION OF ORIGINAL.

Stamp Kagiz Kimati Sola Rupia.

Stamp correct under Article 37, Section II, Act XVIII of 1869.

Admissible under Sections 21, 23, 28, and 32, Act VIII of 1871.

Manka Mahla Chowdin Saidu, beta Mahan Mahla Chowdin, rahnewala Mandala Mutaaqa-i Saltanat Burma, wo Wazir Shah Burma ka hun.

Agi Shah Burma mazhab-i-Budh ke hain aur Budh Bhagwan ka Mandil Budh Gaya iane mouza Taradih men kisi zamana ka bana hua hai, magar iswaqt bemaramat wo shikasta hai, islia Shah Burma chahte hain ke, waste dharam wo kirti apne, usko maramat karain. Magar wuh zamindari men wo qabza dakhal men Mahanth Hem Narayan Gir Gadinashin Asthan Math Budh-Gaya ke waqa hai, aur ham bamujib hukum Shah Burma ke maramat kia chahte hain, aur bhi bamujib hukum Shah Burma ke, waste maramat karne mandil ke, Mahanth Bodh-Gaya mausuf se chaha. Mahanth Bodh-Gaya mausuf ne bhi waste rah jane kirti muddat ki samajh kar, waste maramat karne mandil ke bamazmun

ENGLISH TRANSLATION.

Stamp paper of Rs. 16.

Stamp correct under Article 37, Section II, Act XVIII of 1869.

Admissible under Sections 21, 23, 28, and 32, Act VIII of 1871.

I am Mahla Chowdin Saidu, son of Mahan Mahla Chowdin, inhabitant of Mandalay in the kingdom of Burma, and Wazir (Minister) of the King of Burma.

Whereas the King of Burma is of the Buddhist religion, and there is a shrine of Budh Bhagwan (God) at Budh-Gaya, that is at mouza Taradih, which was constructed from time immemorial, but which is at present out of repairs and in a dilapidated state. Therefore the King of Burma wants that he would repair the shrine for his spiritual benefit and for perpetuation of his name. But the said shrine stands within the zemindari and in the possession of Mahanth Hem Narayan Gir, Gadinashin of the Astan Math at Budh-Gaya, and I, under orders of the King of Burma, want to make repairs. So I, also under the orders of the King of Burma, asked (permission) from the aforesaid Mahanth of Budh-Gaya, is iqrar ke ijazat dia ke :—Tum bamujib rai hamare iane jis jaga se jis jaga aur jis chiz ko jis tara se ham maramat karne ko ijazat dain, us tara se maramat karo, kis waste ke us mandil ko nazdik bahut sa deota mazhab-i-Hind aur qudeem hamare guru ka mandil aur ghar ra-aiya ka hai, ke jismen uska kisi tara se be dharmi wo nuqsani na pahunche ; aur us Budh Deota ka aur pipli ka aur pipli ke niche jo Deota wagairah hain, uski puja hamare shudamad-i-qadeem se chali ati hai, aur jatri log wahan darshan ko ate hain aur puja karte hain, aur waste hifazat us puja aur mandil ke hamare chela log wahan par rahte hain aur hifazat rakhte hain ; tumko us mandil ke hifazat karne se kuchh zarur nahin rahiga, aur bâd hojane maramat wo hata wo darwaza wo bhi koi mandil ya makanat wagairah ke tumhara kuchh dâvi nahin rahiga, aur bhi Shah Burma ke taraf se waste parastish ke jo mulazim hain aur rahangain unko bhi chahiye ke badastur zamindari-i-zamindar ke raha karain. Chunanchi manmuqir ne bhi bamujib ijazat Shah Burma Maha Dharam Raja ke amurat mutzakrai bala ko qabul karke iqrar karte hain aur likh dete hain, ke ham ya Shah Burma ya mulaziman Shah Burma jo hain aur rahangain bar khilaf iqrar mundarjai sadar koi amur nakarain; agar karain to bar waqt hakim-i-adalat na jaiz aur batil matasuwar hoi. Is waste eh chand kalima batariq iqrarnama ke likh dia ke sanialhal ke kam ave.

to make the repairs to the shrine. The said Mahanth of Bodh-Gaya, understanding that the work of antiquity would be saved (from being ruined), gave permission to make the repairs to the shrine, subject to the conditions in the words as follows :—" You (the executant of this deed) should make the repairs according to my (Mahanth's) directions, that is, from such place to such place and such things in such manner as will be permitted by me (Mahanth); because close to the said shrine there are many Gods of the Hindu religion and old shrines of my *gurus* and houses of tenants, which should not in any way be molested in point of religion, and no injury should be done to them. It has been the long standing practice with me (the Mahanth) to offer *puja* to the said Budh *deota* (god) and the pipal as well as to the gods, etc., placed at the foot of the pipal, and *jatris* (pilgrims) gather there for *darshan* and for offering *puja*, and my disciples are posted there to look after the offering of such *puja* and to take care of the shrine, and they have the charge. So you (the executant of this deed) shall not have the necessity to take care of the shrine. After the repairs have been done, you (the executant) shall have no claim to the compound and the doors, nor to any of the shrines or buildings, etc., and the servants that have been and that hereafter may be on behalf of the King of Burma for the purpose of worship, should stay, subject to the zemindari rules of the zemindar." So I, the declarant, with the permission of the Maha Dharam Raja King of Burma, accept the terms set forth above, and declare and give in writing to the effect as follows :—That I or the King of Burma, or the servants of the King of Burma, that have been or hereafter may be, will not do anything contrary to the conditions set forth above. Should I or he or they do so, it shall be held null and void before the Court for the time being. I therefore give in writing these few words in the shape of an *ikrarnama* (agreement) that it may be used, when required.

Number-i towzi.	Nam-i Mehal.	Jamma Sadar.	Nam-i Registry.	Nam-i Kalaktri.	Nam-i Thannah.
1636	Mehal Ladu.	Rs. As. 28,045 12	Gaya.	Gaya.	Gaya.

Towzi No.	Name of Mehal.	Sudder Jamma.	Name of Registry office.	Name of Collectorate.	Name of Thannah.
1636	Mehal Ladu.	Rs. As. 28,015 12	Gaya.	Gaya.	Gaya.

Tahrir fittarikh 11, Mah February, San 1877, mutabiq Mah Phagun, San 1284, Fusli.

Dated 11th February, 1877, corresponding with Phagun 1284, Fusli.

(In the margin.)

Signature in Burmese, which could not be read. Below it, in Hindi, Mahla Chowdin Saidu. Accepted.

By my own pen.

Witnessed by—

Rambakhsh Lal, at present residing at Bodh-Gaya, Pargana Maher, Zillah Gaya. On admission by the declarant.

By my own pen.

Witnessed by—

Mahadeva Misser, inhabitant of Pakror, Pargana Maher. On admission by the declarant.

By my own pen.

Witnessed by—

Baijnath Sahai, inhabitant of Pakror, Pargana Maher. On admission by the declarant.

By my own pen.

Witnessed by—

Narku Lal, inhabitant of Mouzah Pakror, Pargana Maher. On admission by the declarant aforesaid.

By my own pen.

Writer of this agreement—

Sheocharan Lal, Mukhtear of the Criminal and Revenue Courts of Zillah Gaya and inhabitant and part-proprietor of Mouzah Mahwanwan, Pargana Shaharghatty, Zillah Gaya.

ENDORSEMENTS.

Mahla Chowdin Saidu, son of Mahan Mahla Chowdin, resident of Mandalay.

(Signature of the Stamp-vendor and the date of sale and other things are written in mahajani character, and cannot be read).

(*English.*)

Presented for Registration between the hours of 1 and 2 P. M. on the 19th day of February, 1877, at the office of the Sub-Registrar of Gaya, by Mahla Chowdin Saidu, son of Mahla Maha Chowdin, executant.

W. RATTRAY,
Sub-Registrar.

19th February, 1877.

Signature of Mahla Chowdin Saidu in Burmese, and cannot be read.

Execution was admitted by Mahla Chowdin Saidu, Mandalay, Burma, Secretary to the King of Burma.

Signature of Mahla Chowdin Saidu in Burmese, and cannot be read.

Identified by Jagman Kahar, son of Kanchan Kahar, Taradih, Pargana Maher, Zillah Gaya, servant, who was identified by Bakhori Lal, Mukhtear.

I know the executant. Jagman Kahar.

By my own pen.

I know Jagman Kahar, who identified the executant. Bakhori Lal, Mukhtear.

W. RATTRAY,
Sub-Registrar.

19th February, 1877.

Registered in B. I. Vol. 8, Pages 86 to 87, being No. 344 in that Register for 1877.

W. RATTRAY,
Sub-Registrar.

20th February, 1877.

Certified to be a true copy.

SIVNATH ROY,

21st July, 1895. *Head Clerk, Gaya Magistracy.*

Authorised under Section 76 of Act I of 1872.

Certified that it is a true translation of the agreement, dated the 11th February, 1877, a transliteration whereof is given opposite.

ABDUL MALIK,

30th July, 1895. *Translator, High Court, Appellate Side.*

PETITIONS.

In the Court of the District Magistrate of Gaya.

COMPLAINT.

Description of the Complainant.	Description of the accused.	Name of the Witnesses.	Sections of the Indian Penal Code, the date of occurrence, and the Police Station.
H. Dharmapala, General Secretary, Maha-Bodhi Society.	(1.) Mahanth Krishna Dayal Gir of Buddha-Gaya Math. (2.) Gosain Jaipal Gir of Buddha-Gaya Math. (3.) Gosain Mahendra Gir of Buddha-Gaya Math. (4.) Gosain Shivanandan Gir of Buddha-Gaya Math. (5.) Hussain Baksh, servant of the Mahanth of Buddha-Gaya. (6.) Vijayananda, mukhtear of the Mahanth of Buddha-Gaya and some thirty others.	(1.) Moulvi Mahomed Fazalullah, Sub-Registrar, Gaya. (2.) Moulvi Mahomed Habibullah, Khan Bahadur, Deputy Magistrate, Gaya. (3.) Babu Bepin Behary Banerjee, Government Custodian of Buddha-Gaya Temple. (4.) M. Sumangala, } Priests, Gaya. (5.) N. Devananda, } Priests, Gaya. (6.) N. P. deSilva, Gaya.	Sections 147, 295, 296, 506 and 109, Indian Penal Code. Date of occurrence, 25th February, 1895. Mofussil Gaya.

Petition of Complaint.

The humble petition of H. Dharmapala, General Secretary to the Maha-Bodhi Society.

Respectfully Sheweth,

The Maha-Bodhi Temple at Buddha-Gaya is the most sacred of all Buddhist sites, and for 24 centuries it has been a place of pilgrimage to the Buddhists of China, Japan, Tibet, Corea, Siam, Ceylon, Burma, Arakan, Nepal and Chittagong.

2. Following the time immemorial Buddhistic custom of placing images of Buddha in this temple, the Buddhists of Japan, in a spirit of deep loyalty and devotion to their sacred shrine, entrusted your petitioner with a historical sandal-wood image of Buddha of great antiquity and of unrivalled artistic beauty to be placed on the altar of the second storey of the same.

3. That several alabaster images of Buddha have been enshrined on the altar of the lower storey of the temple by Burmese and other Buddhists; and hitherto nobody interfered with the performance of this highly cherished religious duty.

4. Considering it to be a religious duty incumbent on your petitioner and following the precedent of pilgrims, who on many previous occasions had placed images of Buddha and other ecclesiastical objects of veneration and decoration in the temple, your petitioner undertook the work of enshrining the image of Buddha above referred to.

5. That on the morning of the 25th of February, 1895, your petitioner visited the temple, taking the said sacred image and accompanied by two Buddhist priests and one Singalese layman.

6. That at the time that your petitioner and his companions were fixing this historic image, there were present watching the religious proceedings two Muhammadan gentlemen, named Maulvi Mahomed Fazalullah, Sub-Registrar, and Maulvi Mahomed Habibullah, Khan Bahadur, Deputy Magistrate, both of Gaya, and also Hussain Baksh, the Muhammadan mukhtear or servant of the Mahanth of Bodh-Gaya (though possibly the last-named person may not admit the fact).

7. That after having duly installed the image in a suitable place on the altar of the second storey of the temple, your petitioner sent for the Government custodian of the temple, Babu Bipin Behari Banerjee, and when he arrived, your petitioner asked him to be a witness to the ceremony of installation of the image, and the fulfilment of the duty entrusted to your petitioner by the Japanese Buddhists.

8. That some time after, as the priests were going to light the candles on the altar, several Sannyasis and several Hindu and Muhammadan retainers of the Mahanth came up and offered resistance to your petitioner and his companions by interfering with their devotions, insulting them and threatening to endanger their lives, if the image was not removed from the altar. A few of the Sannyasis remained standing on the altar in a defiant attitude. But, notwithstanding that your petitioner and his companions claimed their right to freedom of worship and begged them to leave them alone, and not desecrate the altar, they would not listen, but continued to threaten and molest them and wound their religious feelings, whilst the Muhammadan mukhtear, Hussain Baksh, told your petitioner to take away the image, and, in fact, assaulted him by pushing and thrusting him with his hands. Almost immediately the Hindu mukhtear, named Vijayananda, came up, and when your petitioner protested against the above described act, he retired for a short time, taking almost all the assistants with him. Thereupon your petitioner sat before the sacred image in

silent contemplation, considering his party safe at the time. But after the lapse of a short time, the same men with some others again rushed to the upper storey, and some of them, getting over the altar, dislodged the sacred image, carried it away downstairs, and placed it on the bare ground outside the temple in the open courtyard.

9. That your petitioner and his companion Buddhists were naturally shocked, grieved and hurt at this wrongful act of outrage and desecration. They were, however, helpless to do anything, as the people of Bodh-Gaya after the occurrence would not even draw water for them to drink through the fear of the Mahanth, who, though not personally present, your petitioner charges with instigating the occurrence.

10. That your petitioner has come to know that Maulvi Mahomed Fazalullah and Maulvi Mahomed Habibullah, Khan Bahadur, saw Mahanth Krishna Dayal Gir, after the installation of the image, and found him much enraged and excited; and coupling this fact with the retiring of Vijayananda with all the assistants and their second and renewed attack, your petitioner comes to the conclusion that the whole occurrence took place at the instigation and abetment of the Mahanth himself, who has always been antagonistic to your petitioner.

11. That amongst the persons who appeared on the first occasion of molestation and assault, your petitioner recognises—(1) Hussain Baksh, mukhtear of the Mahanth; (2) Jaipal Gir; (3) Shivanandan Gir; (4) Mahendra Gir and other Gossains, whom your petitioner can identify, but cannot name, also other Hindus and Muhammadans, whom your petitioner can identify, but cannot name, and Vijayananda, who came only for a few minutes. On the second occasion, when the sacred image was carried away, your petitioner recognised all the above persons and besides one stout Gossain whom he noticed particularly and can recognise, but not name. The total number of men on each occasion was thirty to forty, of whom some seven got on the altar.

12. That your petitioner knew the names of none of those now named by him till he learned them during the police enquiry. His witnesses are Maulvi Mahomed Fazalullah and Maulvi Mahomed Habibullah, Khan Bahadur, Babu Bipin Behari Banerjee, M. Sumangala and N. Devananda, priests, and N. P. deSilva.

13. That your petitioner also complains that during the past few months the Mahanth has caused the principal image of Buddha in the lower storey, which was placed by Mr. Beglar after the restoration of the temple, to be disfigured by putting paint on its forehead and covering the figure with colored cloth, thereby depriving the Buddhists from seeing it. This painting and disfiguring of the image is to the Buddhists most objectionable and painful, and they consider it a contamination of the image.

14. This aggressive innovation has been introduced, your petitioner believes, simply with the motive of desecrating the image and wounding and insulting the feelings of the Buddhists.

15. Your petitioner, therefore, prays that your worship will be graciously pleased to issue a warrant against the accused and decide this case.

And your petitioner, as in duty bound, shall ever pray.

GAYA;
Dated 28th February, 1895.

NAND KISHORE LALL,
Vakil.

To District Magistrate for orders.

28th February, 1895.

H. G. W. HERRON,
Joint-Magistrate.

Hevavitarna Dharmapala, on solemn affirmation, states :—

I COMPLAIN against the Mahanth of Bodh-Gaya, Jaipal Gir, Shivanandan Gir, Mahendra Gir, Hussain Baksh, Vijayananda and several other retainers of the Mahanth whom I cannot name but can identify. On the 25th instant, about a quarter to 9 A. M., I visited the Temple of Maha-Bodhi at Bodh-Gaya, the most sacred of all Temples in the eyes of Buddhists, accompanied by two Buddhist priests and a Singalese lay Buddhist, to make offerings to the temple. It is an immemorial custom for Buddhists to place images in the temple, and the Japanese Buddhists, in loyalty to the place and showing their utmost devotion, entrusted me with an image of Buddha of great antiquity and of unrivalled artistic beauty to be enshrined on the altar of the second storey of the sacred shrine. I had the image taken up to the second storey, and I myself enshrined the image on the altar there with the help of the priests accompanying me. When I was doing so there were present two Muhammadan gentlemen, whose names I have since learned to be Maulvi Mahomed Fazalullah, Sub-Registrar of Gaya, and Maulvi Mahomed Habibullah, a Deputy-Magistrate of Gaya. There was also with them the Muhammadan mukhtear of the Mahanth, whose name I have since learned is Hussain Baksh. I sent the Government chaprasi of the temple to call the custodian of the temple, Babu Bipin Behari Banerjee, to witness the enshrinement, and he came after it had been enshrined, whereupon I told him that the image was now under his control, and that I had freed myself from responsibility for taking care of it, and that my duty to the Japanese ceased from now. At his own request I placed the Japanese certificate on one side of the image. The two Muhammadan gentlemen and the mukhtear had by this time left the place. I am not sure if they left before the custodian came or not. I then began with the priests to make the necessary offerings, and was going to light the candles that had been placed in the candlesticks which were on the altar. The candlesticks and also two lotus flowers and an incense-burner had been brought with the image from Japan. At that stage we heard a great rush, and several of the Sannyasis came there. Several got up on to the altar, and one stood before me and the image and prevented me from lighting the candles. The Muhammadan mukhtear came back with these men there, and there came also several of the Muhammadan and Hindu retainers of the Mahanth. I did not at that time know the names of any Sannyasis who were there, but I noticed them at the time, and during the police investigation subsequently I identified them and ascertained their names. I have stayed at Bodh-Gaya on several occasions, and I know a good many people by sight, though not by name. I recognised Jaipal and Mahendra and Shivanandan Gir among those whose names I ascertained. These men in loud and vehement language threatened and insulted me, and some of them pushed me. In particular, I noticed that the Muhammadan mukhtear Hussain Baksh pushed me and assaulted me by thrusting his fists behind my shoulder. I understood only some of the words they used. I understood the mukhtear saying, "Take away the image, you have no right here." Jaipal Gir also said, "Remove the image, we have come to destroy it if you do not." I tried to make them understand, speaking in English, that I had perfect right to be there doing what I did, and the Government custodian tried to appease them, speaking in Hindustani. They could not understand me, and so they went and brought Vijayananda, the Hindu mukhtear of the Mahanth, who knows English. I myself am a Singalese, and know only a few words of Hindi. When Vijayananda came, I appealed to him, saying that this was desecration of the image, and that I hoped that they, as Hindus, would not interfere with our devotions. Then he retired, and all those who were assailing me left with him. I then thought I was no longer to be molested and felt glad, and I sat down before the image in silent contemplation. This forms part of Buddhist worship. Then about ten minutes or a quarter of an hour afterwards, as far as I remember, the party again came rushing in, about thirty or forty of them entering the upper storey, including all those whom I have named before, Hussain Baksh and Vijayananda, mukhtears, with them, and, in addition, one very stout fair-complexioned Gossain, whose name I have been unable to learn. About seven of them ascended on to the altar, and swooped down on the image and carried it away. I recognised among those seven Mahendra Gir. I could recognise others of the seven, I think all of them, if I saw them. The stout man did not get on to the altar, but he stood a fathom to my right. When they did this and carried the image away, I remained still seated. I did not notice whether the Government custodian was present or not when the image was taken from the altar. They took the image away downstairs. I remained, however, seated before the altar for about an hour and a half, and then came down. Before I came down, one of the Bodh-Gaya outpost police came and called me downstairs. I told him to send the jemadar up, and then the jemadar came up, and sat down before me. Then the Government custodian and Vijayananda came and sat near him, and all the Sannyasis then came and sat down too. The jemadar then asked me through an interpreter what had happened, and I there and then wrote down an account in English and gave it to him. He also put me several questions which I answered, and then told me to get up and go and take my food, as it was then about half past twelve. I had my watch and saw that. He also ordered the removal of the boxes, in which I had brought the image, &c., which were there. When I came downstairs, I saw the jemadar standing in a crowd in the open courtyard, and he called me to show me the image. I said, "It is not my business, you can do anything with it." Then I went on to the Burmese rest-house. I did not see the image until after five o'clock that evening, when the Collector came and called me. The image was then in the verandah of the Panchpandava Temple.

I charge the Mahanth with instigating the various acts, because I came to know that the two Muhammadan gentlemen, after witnessing the enshrinement of the image, did go to the Mahanth, and found him excited in consequence. I learnt this as I asked my pleader to enquire from them. I also charge the Mahanth on account of Vijayananda having retired for a little and come back.

I also lay a charge about the disfigurement of the central image on the ground floor by paint having been put on the forehead and coloured cloth having been put over it. I noticed this for the first time when I came there about a month ago. I had been on several previous occasions to the temple since 1891, and this had not been done before. On the contrary, it was so repellent to the Hindus to visit the place that I have seen eminent Hindus go there with their shoes on and making no bow. I reported the disfigurement to the Commissioner of Patna. The disfigurement referred to causes great pain to every Buddhist, and constitutes an insult to our religion. I have seen a Brahmin priest now putting flowers on the head of the image. The first time I noticed this was on the 25th instant. Putting flowers thus is also an insult to our religion.

The image was entrusted to me when I was in Japan in the end of 1893, with the intention that it should be presented as an offering to the temple, and placed on the altar of the second floor. It is one of the recognised customs all over the Buddhist world to present offerings consisting of images of Buddha to Buddhist temples, and specially so to the Maha-Bodhi Temple; and the Burmese have similarly presented alabaster images to the temple, several of which are still enshrined on the altar of the ground floor. No greater insult can be offered to a Buddhist than to forcibly remove such images from the altar. Every Buddhist regards it as the greatest desecration. A special significance attached to the enshrinement of the Japanese image, as it was their greatest and most venerable relic of Buddha, as set out in the certificate accompanying it, and they wished it enshrined in their most sacred temple to show their feelings of devotion. It is made of sandal wood and gilded over. I was told it was 700 years old and carved by the greatest Japanese artist by order of the Emperor. Last year I wished to put it in the temple, but I abstained from doing so, as I obeyed the instructions of the Collector issued in consequence of an apprehended breach of the peace.

H. DHARMAPALA.

D. J. MACPHERSON,

Magistrate of Gaya.

28th February, 1895.

H. Dharmapala recalled by Magistrate.

I DID not notice if any of the other three Buddhists with me were engaged in devotion, when my devotion was interrupted by the people coming to take away the image.

D. J. MACPHERSON,
Magistrate.

28th February, 1895.

Order on the Complaint laid by H. Dharmapala against the Mahanth of Bodh-Gaya and others, under Sections 147, 295, 296, and 506, Penal Code.

I RECORDED this complaint on the 28th February, and next day heard Counsel for the complainant on the subject of the offences under the Penal Code which the facts deposed to would constitute. Having taken time to consider the matter, I direct that summonses do now issue against the following persons, namely :—

(1.) Jaipal Gir,
(2.) Mahendra Gir,
(3.) Shivanandan Gir,
(4.) Bhimal Deo Gir, } All of Bodh-Gaya *Math*.
(5.) Hussain Baksh, karpardaz or mukhtear of the Mahanth.
(6.) Vijayananda Barma, mukhtear of the Mahanth,

calling on them to appear before me on the 13th instant to answer charges under the following sections of the Penal Code :—Sections 143, 295, 296, 352, 380, and 506.

I intimated on the 1st instant my intention of issuing process returnable on the 13th instant, and also stated that I did not think that on the face of the complaint itself there was sufficient ground to justify the issue of process against the Mahanth himself as an abettor. Counsel for the complainant thereupon stated that he did not press for this, and, in fact, that the prosecution was not prompted by vindictive feelings at all, and in the event of a conviction, would be content with a moderate sentence, the main object of the prosecution being to obtain a decision which would suffice to prevent a repetition of offences of the nature alleged, that interfere with the freedom of Buddhist worship in the Maha-Bodhi Temple at Bodh-Gaya.

As regards the charge of defilement of the great image on the ground floor of the temple, I direct process to issue, returnable on the same date, against the priest in charge, whose name seems to be Rami Panre, under Section 295 of the Penal Code.

CAMP, BODH-GAYA,
4th March, 1895.

D. J. MACPHERSON,
Magistrate of Gaya.

In the Court of the District Magistrate of Gaya.

QUEEN EMPRESS (THROUGH H. DHARMAPALA) ... *Complainant,*

Versus

HUSSAIN BAKSH AND OTHERS ... *Accused.*

PETITION OF H. DHARMAPALA.

RESPECTFULLY SHEWETH,

THAT in the aforesaid case important questions are likely to arise touching the religious rites and ceremonies of the Buddhists, and the mode of worship prevailing among them.

That the evidence of His Excellency Kin Woon Mengu, C. S. I., Prime Minister of the late King Thebaw, Mandalay, Burma, and Mr. U. Mra U., A.T.M., Extra Assistant Commissioner, Akyab, Arakan, who are considered to be eminent authorities on religious questions among the Buddhists, and who had come to Bodh-Gaya and performed there similar ceremonies to those which your petitioner alleges, is extremely necessary.

That the attendance of the gentlemen mentioned in the two preceding paras. of this humble petition cannot, by reason of the distance of their residence from this place and the eminence of their position, be procured without considerable delay, great inconvenience to them, and prohibitive expense to your petitioner. Your petitioner, therefore, submits that in the interests of justice a commission ought to be issued for their examination, interrogatories for which are herewith filed.

Under these circumstances, your petitioner prays that your Honor may be graciously pleased to issue commission for the examination of the said witnesses.

And your petitioner, in duty bound, shall ever pray.

KEDAR NATH,
Pleader.

Interrogatories.—

1. State your name, residence and position in life.

2. Are you a Buddhist?

3. Did you ever visit the Maha-Bodhi Temple at Bodh-Gaya in the District of Gaya, India?

4. Did you present any offerings? If so, give a description of their nature and value.

5. Did any one obstruct you or claim the right of inspecting your offerings before you were permitted to place them in the Temple or at the Bodhi Tree, or did you place them as a matter of right?

6. Did you present your offerings openly and publicly, so that every one concerned could know that you were presenting them, or did you offer them in a secret and surreptitious manner?

7. To the best of your knowledge and belief, have the Buddhists generally the right to place images of Buddha in the Maha-Bodhi Temple?

8. Besides yourself, were there any other Buddhist pilgrims at Bodh-Gaya during your visit?

9. Did any other Buddhist besides yourself make any offerings to the temple in your presence? Name the persons who made the offerings, and the nature of the offerings each person made, as far as you can now remember.

10. Is the making of offerings in temple dedicated to Buddha a meritorious and necessary act of religious worship among Buddhists?

11. Would the deprivation of the right to place images of Buddha in the Temple of Maha-Bodhi constitute a serious infringement of the principles of Buddhism?

KEDAR NATH,
Pleader.

ORDER.

THIS petition was sent to me when I was busy with preparations for the visit of His Excellency the Viceroy, and work requiring to be done before the close of the financial year, and I overlooked it till it was too late to have the commissions issued and returned before the date fixed for the hearing of the case, *i. e.*, yesterday.

I now direct the commissions to issue, on the grounds stated, to the Deputy Commissioners of Mandalay and Akyab in Burma. The date for their return will be fixed, when the hearing going on at present is adjourned. The other side may file interrogatories.

Dated 9th April, 1895.

D. J. MACPHERSON,
Magistrate.

In the Court of the District Magistrate of Gaya.

H. DHARMAPALA, ... *Complainant,*

Versus

JAIPAL GIR AND OTHERS, ... *Accused.*

List of Witnesses to be summoned on behalf of the said H. Dharmapala in the aforesaid case:—

1. Babu Harihar Nath, No. 1, Senior Government Pleader, Gaya.
2. Rai Baijnath Singh Bahadur, Zemindar, Sahibganj, Gaya.
3. Munshi Lachman Prosad, Pleader, Gaya.
4. Dr. Haridas Chatterjee, Gaya.
5. Babu Behari Lal Barik, Gayawal, Honorary Magistrate, Gaya.
6. Babu Tirbhowan Singh, late Teacher, Gaya, Zilla Gaya.
7. Pandit Gangadhar Shastri, Gaya Zilla School.
8. Babu Durga Shankar Bhattacharjya, Honorary Magistrate, Gaya.
9. Moulvi Mohiuddin Ahmed, Deputy Magistrate and Assistant Settlement Officer, Tikari Raj Estate.
10. Mr. James Keddie, District Engineer, Gaya.
11. Mr. C. L. S. Russell, Assistant Magistrate, Gaya.
12. Moulvi Tassadduq Hossein, Assistant Manager, Tikari Ward's Estate, Gaya.
13. Kazi Farzand Ahmed, Zemindar and Honorary Magistrate, Gaya.
14. Dr. R. Macrae, Civil Surgeon of Gaya.

H. DHARMAPALA.

DATED GAYA,
The 6th April, 1895.

M. A. GHANI,
Mukhtear.

ORDER.

The hearing of this case was fixed for the 8th instant, two days after this petition was filed (Sunday intervening). It is presumed these witnesses are not called to depose to the actual occurrence of the 25th February, 1895, but to depose to matters affecting possession and right, in regard to which it was arranged at the beginning a further opportunity would be given for citing evidence, it being thought evidence on this aspect of the case would be postponed. I have already intimated to the prosecution that they must file the list of witnesses by Thursday, the 11th instant, when the case would be adjourned in any case owing to the intervention of Easter holidays. Summonses will issue for these witnesses returnable on a date to be fixed when the hearing now going on is adjourned.

D. J. MACPHERSON,
Magistrate.

Dated 9th April, 1895.

In the Court of the District Magistrate of Gaya.

H. DHARMAPALA *versus* JAIPAL GIR AND OTHERS.

THE PETITION OF JAIPAL GIR AND OTHERS,
ACCUSED PERSONS.

SHEWETH,

1. THAT yesterday during the examination-in-chief of Bepin Bihari Banerjee, 1st witness for prosecution, certain questions were put to him with regard to the religious ceremonies in the temple, to which objection was taken by Mr. Cotton, your petitioner's Counsel.

2. That the propriety of allowing such evidence was to be discussed to-day.

3. That your petitioners are advised that all evidence relating to the religious worship at the temple is a matter distinct and foreign to this trial, and it is outside the jurisdiction of this Court.

4. That such questions can only be tried and determined by a competent Civil Court.

5. That it will be impossible at this early stage of the trial to discuss the question further without giving out and disclosing the case for the defence.

6. That your petitioners submit that right of possession of the temple by the Mahanth is wholly distinct and separate from any questions regarding the religious ceremonies and worship observed in the temple, and that this question of possession is essential and closely connected with the facts in issue in this case.

7. That your petitioners claim the right to adduce evidence of possession of the temple by the Mahanth, while objecting to the admission of any ecclesiastical evidence as being wholly irrelevant in the present case.

Under the circumstances and for the reasons hereinbefore stated, your petitioners protest against the reception of any such ecclesiastical evidence in this case.

MATILAL DAS,
Pleader.

9th April, 1895.

ORDER.

THE questions referred to in this petition were argued, and it was decided to admit the evidence tendered by the prosecution subject to further objection as to its relevancy, when the defence are in a position to enter on their case. A separate note on the subject will be recorded.

D. J. MACPHERSON,
Magistrate.

9th April, 1895.

In the Court of the District Magistrate of Gaya.

EMPRESS (THROUGH H. DHARMAPALA), ... *Complainant*,

Versus

GOSAIN JAIPAL GIR AND OTHERS, ... *Accused.*

THE PETITION OF JAIPAL GIR AND OTHERS,
ACCUSED PERSONS.

YOUR PETITIONERS PRAY—

THAT your Honor may be pleased to cause a notice to be served on Bepin Bihari Banerjee, witness for the prosecution, whereby he may be subpœnaed to produce in your Honor's Court without delay and before the time of his presenting himself for cross-examination, the following documents which are in his custody or possession :—

The order of the Executive Engineer or any and all other superior authorities, communicating to the said Bepin Bihari Banerjee his appointment as custodian of the relics at the Maha Bodhi Temple, and defining his duties and position as such, together with any other correspondence in his custody or possession on the subject either with the Magistrate of Gaya, or the Public Works Department of the Government of Bengal.

A. LAKSHMI NARAYAN,
Pleader.

6th April, 1895.

ORDER.

ISSUE summons to the witness to bring the documents in question in his custody to the Court to-morrow morning.

D. J. MACPHERSON,
Magistrate.

6th May, 1895.

In the Court of the District Magistrate of Gaya.

H. DHARMAPALA, ... *Complainant*,

Versus

JAIPAL GIR AND OTHERS, ... *Accused.*

BIJAYANANDA BARMA, *Petitioner.*

Your petitioner prays to be furnished with certified copies of the following official and public documents, which are now in your Honor's Court as Magistrate and Collector of Gaya, and which documents are urgently wanted for the purposes of your petitioner's defence :—

1. Reply of Mahanth Hem Narayan Gir, dated 18th January, 1875. to a letter of the Magistrate, dated 15th January, 1875.

2. Replies by the Mahanth of Bodh-Gaya to the following letters of the Magistrate, *viz.* :—

(*a*) Dated 23rd May, 1877.

(*b*) Dated 25th April, 1878.

(*c*) No. 1077, dated 3rd April, 1889.

3. Letter from G. A. Grierson, Esq., C.S., to the Commissioner of the Patna Division, No. 1134, dated 6th May, 1891, reporting on the subject of the Bodh-Gaya Temple, and the rights of the Mahanth thereto.

4. Letter of the Government of Bengal, Public Works Department, No. 1836, dated 7th July, 1891, forwarded to the Magistrate of Gaya by the Commissioner of the Patna Division with a covering Memorandum No. 333G., being a reply to the above.

5. Letter No. 240G., dated 23rd July, 1894. from the Commissioner of the Patna Division, to the Magistrate of Gaya, a copy of which was forwarded to H. Dharmapala by the Magistrate of Gaya, with a covering Memorandum No. 2297, dated 27th September, 1894.

6. Letter No. 7E., from Mahanth Krishna Dayal Gir, to the Magistrate of Gaya, dated $\frac{13}{18}$th June, 1894.

7. Order under Section 144, Criminal Procedure Code, dated 19th May, 1894, by the Magistrate, addressed to the Mahanth of Bodh-Gaya.

8. Order under Section 144, Criminal Procedure Code, dated 19th May, 1894, by the Magistrate, addressed to H. Dharmapala.

9. All correspondence in the office between the Mahanth of Bodh-Gaya, the Magistrate, the Executive Engineer, the Superintending Engineer, the Divisional Commissioner and the Government of Bengal, relating to the repairs of the Maha-Bodhi Temple, the position of Babu Bipin Bihari Banerjee as the custodian of the Temple and the orders and instructions furnished to the said Babu Bipin Bihari Banerjee on or after his appointment as custodian.

2nd May, 1895. BIJAYANANDA BARMA.

ORDER.

THE only public document here that there is a right of inspection of, is the notice under Section 144, Criminal Procedure Code, to the Mahanth, dated 19th May, 1895. Give a certified copy of that.

No such notice was served on H. Dharmapala, but I remember I sent him, in the urgency of the case, an instruction demi-officially that I could not let him place the image, as there was a fear of a breach of the peace.

D. J. MACPHERSON,

6th May, 1895. *Magistrate.*

In the Court of the District Magistrate of Gaya.

THE EMPRESS ON THE PROSECUTION OF H. DHARMAPALA,

versus

JAIPAL GIR AND OTHERS, ... *Accused.*

THE HUMBLE PETITION OF THE ACCUSED.

HUMBLY SHEWETH—

WITH reference to the application for copies of certain documents presented by your petitioners on the 2nd instant, and your Honor's directions to indicate the nature and substance of the documents, your petitioners beg hereby to furnish the information called for, and they humbly pray that either attested copies of those documents be granted to them forthwith on receipt of the usual fees, or that the Record-keepers of the Magistrate as well as of the Collector, or any officer or officers, who may have the custody of any or all of the documents, may be summoned to produce them in Court without delay and before the cross-examination of the complainant is concluded.

And your petitioners shall ever pray.

Document of which Copies are applied for.	*Information.*
1. Reply of Mahanth Hem Narayan Gir to a letter of the Magistrate, dated 15th January, 1875.	1. Original in Urdu. Subject—Proposed repair of the Maha-Bodhi Tree compound by the Burmese and the deputation of two men for worshipping daily. In this reply, Mahanth objects to any infringement of his rights or any practices contrary to Hindu ideas, otherwise has no objection to repairs and to deputation.
2. Replies of Mahanth Hem Narayan Gir to the following letters of the Magistrate :—	
(a) Dated 26th May, 1877.	*(a)* Probably in vernacular. Subject—To prevent the Burmese from doing any repairs to the temple.
(b) Dated 25th April, 1878.	*(b)* Probably in vernacular. Subject—To prevent the Burmese from doing any repairs to the temple.
(c) Dated 3rd April, 1889.	*(c)* Can't give any information.
3. Letter of Mr. Grierson, dated 1st May, 1891.	3. Copy annexed. Production of original draft or certified copy solicited.
4. Letter of Government of Bengal forwarded to the Magistrate of Gaya, No. 1836, dated 7th July, 1891.	4. Copy annexed.
5. Letter of the Commissioner of Patna, dated 23rd July, 1894.	5. Attested copy already in the possession of accused. Original draft solicited.
6. Letter No. 7E. from the Mahanth to the Collector of Gaya, dated $\frac{1}{8}$th June, 1894.	6. Copy annexed. Original to be produced.
7. Order under Section 144, Criminal Procedure Code, on H. Dharmapala, dated 19th May, 1894, by the District Magistrate.	7. Original order, dated 19th May, 1894, whereby the Mahanth was directed to abstain from preventing Buddhist pilgrims from worshipping according to custom, and Mr. Dharmapala directed not to set up or try to set up any image, without the Mahanth's consent.
8. All other correspondence in the office regarding the repairs of the temple and other portion of Babu Bipin Bihari Banerjee.	

A. LAKSHMI NARAYAN,
Pleader.

6th May, 1895.

ORDER.

None of the documents are public ones, that the parties have a right to inspect, and so, as I have said on the general application, certified copies cannot be granted.

But the Magistrate's and Collector's Head Clerks will cause a thorough search to be made for them to-day, and be ready to produce them in Court, though not necessarily for inspection or in evidence, when called on.

6th May, 1895.

D. J. MACPHERSON,
Magistrate.

In the Court of the District Magistrate of Gaya

Empress on the Complaint of H. Dharmapala,

versus

Jaipal Gir and others.

The Petition of Jaipal Gir and others, Accused persons.

Your Petitioners Pray—

1. That the District Magistrate and Collector of Gaya or his Record-keeper be forthwith subpœnaed to produce the undermentioned documents, which are of the utmost importance to your petitioners' defence :—

(a). Draft letter No. 1134, dated 6th May, 1891, from G. A. Grierson, Esq., C.S., to the Commissioner of the Patna Division.

(b). Copy of the letter No. 1836 A. Y., dated Calcutta, 7th July, 1891, of the Government of Bengal, Public Works Department, to the Commissioner of the Patna Division, being a reply to the Commissioner's letter No. 297 G., dated 21st May, and forwarded by the Commissioner to the District Magistrate of Gaya, with a covering Memo. No. 333 G., dated 14th July, 1891

2. Further, that the Commissioner of Patna Division or his Record-keeper be subpœnaed by telegraph, your petitioners paying the costs, to produce the original letter No. 1134, dated 6th May, 1891, of Mr. G. A. Grierson, C. S., to the Commissioner of the Patna Division, and also the original letter No. 1836 A. Y., dated Calcutta, 7th July, 1891, addressed by the Government of Bengal, Public Works Department, to the Commissioner of the Patna Division, being a reply to the Commissioner's letter No. 297 G., dated 21st May, 1891.

And your petitioners shall ever pray.

MATILAL DAS,
Pleader.

7th May, 1895.

ORDER.

The documents in question form part of a correspondence between the Magistrate or Collector and the Commissioner, and I have already, as Magistrate and Collector of the District, made a reference to the Commissioner as to whether he grants his permission for the production of the documents. His reply is expected to-day; so I defer passing further orders.

D. J. MACPHERSON,
Magistrate.

7th May, 1895.

In the Court of the District Magistrate of Gaya.

H. DHARMAPALA

versus

JAIPAL GIR AND OTHERS.

PETITION ON BEHALF OF JAIPAL GIR AND OTHERS, ACCUSED.

SHEWETH,

1. THAT from the examination of the complainant, Dharmapala, it is apparent that Mr. J. D. M. Beglar is a most material witness, and ought to have been called by the prosecutor, who has been unable to give any satisfactory reason for not examining him.

2. That in order to avoid delay likely to be caused by the fact of Mr. Beglar's residence at Chogdah in the District of Nuddea, your petitioners' Counsel requested the Court to summon Mr. Beglar by telegraph, in case his evidence should be necessary for the defence, expressly stating at the same time that such a request on their part must not be taken as implying an intention to call him, unless they seemed it to be absolutely necessary for the purposes of their case.

3. That the said Mr. Beglar is now in Gaya, in obedience to the telegraphic summons of the Court, but your petitioners are advised that the evidence already elicited in cross-examination rendering the calling of any witnesses for the defence wholly unnecessary, they ought not to be compelled to call Mr. Beglar, who is an important witness, as a witness for the defence.

Your petitioners, therefore, pray that in the interests of truth and justice, and having regard to the importance of the evidence of Mr. Beglar, as foreshadowed in the examination of the complainant, the Court will be pleased to take his evidence under Section 540 of the Code of Criminal Procedure.

And your petitioners, &c.

A. LAKSHMI NARAYAN,
Pleader.

9th May, 1895.

ORDER.

AT the close of the cross-examination of the witnesses for the prosecution today, the defence put in a petition, stating that Mr. Beglar is a most material witness in this case, and ought to have been called by the prosecution, but that as they (defence) consider the evidence elicited in cross-examination renders it wholly unnecessary to call any evidence, they ought not to be compelled to call Mr. Beglar, who is an important witness as a witness for the defence. But as he is in Gaya, in obedience to a telegraphic summons sent to him at the request of the defence, so that he might be at hand should the defence think it necessary to call him, the defence pray that " in the interests of truth and justice, and having regard to the importance of the evidence of Mr. Beglar, as foreshadowed in the examination of the complainant, the Court will call him as a witness under Section 540, Criminal Procedure Code."

Being asked by the Court to state why, if his evidence is important and material and necessary in the interests of truth and justice, the defence refuse to call him. Mr. Ghose, for the defence, says that looking to the charges drawn up and for the purposes of a criminal trial, the defence consider that that they have already elicited sufficient evidence to enable them to give a full legal defence to the charges. But that nevertheless Mr. Beglar is a very important witness for the purpose of proving under what circumstances the temple was repaired and the position of the Mahanth with reference to it, in view of an assurance stated by the defence to have been given by Sir Ashley Eden, Lieutenant-Governor of Bengal, to the Mahanth. At the same time, Mr. Ghose continues, the defence contend that that question cannot be gone into in this criminal trial, as it would be relevant only if Dharmapala were prosecuted for similar offences and were to raise the plea that he in good faith entered the temple; and consequently the defence do not consider it necessary to take Mr. Beglar's evidence on these points. Still, as the Court appeared anxious to sift the whole matter, the defence hope that in the interest of justice, Mr. Beglar's evidence should be taken by the Court in the case.

Mr. Sutherland, on behalf of the prosecution, says that Mr. Beglar was not a necessary witness for the prosecution, having regard to the offences with which the accused are charged, inasmuch as the case depends exclusively on matters other than who is the proprietor of the temple, whether Government or the Mahanth, or anybody else. Further, that the defence have given themselves the most excellent reason for his not being called by the Court, namely, that the evidence already elicited is quite sufficient to answer the criminal charges. Hence anything that Mr. Beglar might now state, would not be necessary or, as Section 540, Criminal Procedure Code, phrases it, essential to the just decision of the case.

The defence, in reply, say that one reason for not calling the witness is, that they undertook to finish the case as soon as possible, and that if he is called by the defence and be cross-examined at length, Counsel for the defence, not having the last word in that case, would have to anticipate in argument all that Mr. Sutherland might say, and would therefore have to address the Court at much greater length than would otherwise be necessary. Further, that the question whether it is essential to a just decision of the case to call him is one that the Court alone can have anything to say to.

It appears to me quite clear that the present application is a device of the defence to avoid calling any witnesses at all, so as not to have to address the Court until the prosecution have done with their say. It is perfectly clear that the defence is anxious to have Mr. Beglar's evidence taken in this case, and Mr. Ghose indeed admits that if he is called by the Court, his examination by it and cross-examination by each side would take up the best part of another day. The cross-examination of the witness for the prosecution has, it appears, been prolonged in endeavours to get on the record all the evidence possible without having to call direct witnesses to the matters on which they have been cross-examined; and it has been apparent from the proceedings that the defence have been aiming at freeing themselves from the necessity of calling witnesses, the object of course being not to have to state to the Court what the defence is. more than can be inferred from the line taken in cross-examination, until the mouth of the prosecution is shut. I do not think it would be fair for the Court to lend itself to a device of this kind which, it is obvious, could, if once admitted, be indefinitely extended in respect of a witness who, it appears, would be cross-examined, at great length, and the Court therefore considers that it ought to leave with the defence the responsibility of determining whether the evidence of Mr. Beglar is more material to a just decision of this case than the right of the defence to defer addressing the Court until the prosecution will have no right of reply.

D. J. MACPHERSON,

Magistrate.

11th May, 1895.

On the above being read out, Mr. Ghose asked the Court to note his most respectful protest against the use of the word "device," and stated that he had known the course to be adopted by eminent Counsel, and that no secret object was aimed at, as he had made no secret from the beginning of the case that he did not wish to lose the right of reply.

D. J. MACPHERSON,
Magistrate.

11th May, 1895.

THE defence say that they will not call Mr. Beglar, unless they will save thereby their right of reply.

D. J. MACPHERSON,
Magistrate.

11th May, 1895.

MEMORANDA.

WHEN the prosecution tendered as a witness Sumangala, the Singhalese priest, they stated that he knew neither English nor Hindustani, but there was in Court a Mr. Harrison who would be able to interpret the evidence. This Mr. Harrison had come up from Ceylon, being sent by the Singhalese to watch the case and help Mr. Dharmapala in it, and was himself a Buddhist.

There is no one else in the District so far as is known capable of interpreting the evidence; and so the above gentleman was sworn as an interpreter. The defence merely wish it recorded what he is, and under what circumstances he comes here. When he was called up to be sworn the defence stated that they objected to his being allowed to interpret in this case, owing to his being a Buddhist, and having come here to help the prosecution. There would be no other alternative than to postpone the evidence of these witnesses until an interpreter is obtained from Calcutta or elsewhere. The prosecution stated Mr. Dharmapala, of course, could also interpret, but this, of course, is still more objected to.

It was decided that an interpreter should be telegraphed for from Calcutta, the evidence of the Singhalese witnesses being therefore postponed.

The prosecution stated they considered it unnecessary to multiply evidence by calling Nirghin Ram, the Government custodian's chaprasi, and the *gariwân*, who had been summoned by the Court, though not cited by the prosecution.

D. J. MACPHERSON,
Magistrate.

17th April, 1895.

11TH APRIL, 1895.

A. R. LEWIS, a Singhalese interpreter, sent up at my request by the Commissioner of Police, Calcutta, took the oath as an interpreter in this case. He says he is a native of Ceylon, and a Christian by religion, but has for the last seven years been in Calcutta, as an assistant in shops and the like. He seems to know English sufficiently well. He has travelled all night from Calcutta, and arrived here 1½ hours ago.

D. J. MACPHERSON,
Magistrate.

Memorandum of discussion as to the admissibility of evidence as to whether the Maha-Bodhi Temple at Bodh-Gaya is a Buddhist or a Hindu one, that took place on 9th April, 1895.

I HAVE already, in recording the beginning of the deposition of witness Bepin Bihari Banerjee, No. II., for the prosecution, and also at the commencement of the proceedings on the 9th instant, noted that when the prosecution desired to put question bearing on the question of whether the Maha-Bodhi Temple was a Buddhist or a Hindu one, the defence objected to the admission of any evidence at all on this phase of the case, but that the Court had admitted such evidence subject to further discussion as to its relevance, when the defence were prepared to disclose their defence, that is, on beginning of cross-examination of the witness for the prosecution. I postponed recording a memorandum of the arguments used.

Mr. Sutherland for the prosecution, contended that, as a matter of history, the temple is a Buddhist one, and the Buddhists have always enjoyed a right to go there and worship. There has always been an image of Buddha there, and they can show that there was once one on the upper storey, and at any rate that they have always had the right to place one there. If the defence contends that the Mahanth has a right to the possession of the temple, the prosecution are entitled to show on the other hand that the Buddhists have a right to go to the temple, whenever they like, and worship in it in any form they like and place images there, and that they have done so, from time immemorial, that they have a right to go there and do all they wish there, and that the Hindus do not go and worship there, or do anything that can possibly be construed as limiting the right of the Buddhists to do what they like in the temple.

Mr. Cotton, for the defence, referred the Court to a written petition just put in to the effect that the evidence should be excluded, although the defence could not now state the grounds for claiming this, as it would be a disclosure of their case, but at the same time the evidence of the Mahanth's possession of the Temple should be admitted. The defence contended that if they can prove that the Mahanth has exercised rights of possession in this temple, that ends the question, and no question of ritual, &c., could possibly arise or could be tried in this case in a Magisterial Court, as it is not an ecclesiastical Court, and it would be preposterous for it to go into questions which only a Civil Court could discuss. They do not dispute the right of the Buddhists to go there and set up, without the Mahanth's consent, any image in the sense of an image to be worshipped.

In reply, Mr. Sutherland represented that the sections under which process was issued related to religion, and that rights of possession are subject also to all prescriptive rights; and that for the Court to go into these matters could not possibly be construed as establishing itself as an ecclesiastical Court.

In answer to a question by the Court as to how the question of whether Hindus worship there or not would be relevant, Mr. Sutherland stated that it is apparently contended by the defence that because Hindus worship there, they have a right to prevent the Buddhists from doing what they claim to do there, the Mahanth apparently claiming to dictate to them that the Buddhists are not to place an image there that does not conform to his ideas as to what kinds of images can be placed in the temple.

As regards the second count charged in the complaint—namely, defiling the great image of Buddha on the ground floor—Mr. Sutherland admitted that that could not be *fully* gone into, as the wrong accused person had been summoned by the Court to answer it; but evidence on that point would, nevertheless, be relevant as showing the state of mind on the part of the Mahanth and his party antecedent to what culminated on the 25th February, that is, as showing the intention which prompted their acts on that day.

So far as I can see, in the absence of the grounds on which the relevance of the evidence in question is disputed, on behalf of the defence, the evidence proposed to be given by the prosecution is relevant, and I therefore allow the question bearing on it to be put. When, however, the defence are prepared to disclose their case, which will, I understand, be before entering on the cross-examination of the witnesses for the prosecution, which I have allowed to be reserved, a further opportunity will be given for arguing out the question of the relevance of the evidence, and if it is held to be irrelevant, the cross-examination of the witness will, I understand, be materially shortened. In that case, the evidence that may be recorded meanwhile would be excluded in deciding the case.

D. J. MACPHERSON,

12th April, 1895. *Magistrate.*

Memorandum on certain facts elicited in Cross-examination.

In this case the defence cross-examined certain witnesses, namely, H. Dharmapala (complainant), Babu Durga Shankar Bhattacharjya, and Pandit Gangadhar Shastri, with regard to certain matters on which they had communication with me in my capacity as Executive Head of the District, and I mentioned in Court briefly how these matters stood, and suggested that I might perhaps place on the record a note in regard to them, whereupon Counsel for the defence stated he would be much obliged, if I would. The observations have no material bearing on the facts of the case, and are merely explanatory of certain remarks made in the depositions of these witnesses.

I.

Dharmapala states (*vide* pp. 37, 52, 53, of his deposition) that he intimated to me a few days before he placed the image in the temple that he intended doing so. I was away in camp, with the exception of a day occasionally, from the beginning of January until about the 20th of February, and Dharmapala wrote me from Calcutta in the first half of that month, asking when I should be at headquarters, that he might see me (he had not seen me since June, 1894, owing to my absence in Europe and his in Ceylon). I replied that I should be in Gaya about the 20th or 21st. In the same letter (or possibly in his reply saying he would endeavour to be in Gaya to see me then) he mentioned that he intended to place the Japanese image in the temple, as he could no longer be responsible to the Japanese for not doing so, and he was tired of waiting, and nothing had come of his petition asking for Government aid in the matter. I took no notice of this portion of his letter, as I expected he would see me before he actually carried out this purpose, and in any case the Commissioner had said it was not a matter in which the local authorities should interfere. His letter was of a private nature, and I have not been able to find it; but as the image was actually placed on 25th February, I had occasion to recall its purport when it was fresh in my mind, and to remember it since. No other communication passed between him and me on the subject of the image, and I did not know Dharmapala had actually returned to Gaya until I heard of what he had done from the Mahanth himself.

Then a telegram from him, published in the *Statesman* of 28th February, has been put in by the defence in his cross-examination (Exhibit D. 38), to the effect that I had expressed indignation at the occurrence. I stated at the earliest opportunity in Court (on 1st March) that this was not a fact. I stated that Dharmapala must have referred to a remark I made, on hearing the sudden clanging of bells inside the temple for the first time, that it gave me a shock to hear that. That occurred when I was sitting outside the temple recording statements on the evening of the 25th February, and my remark was made in presence of the Mahanth, who was seated at my table, and of every one. So far from expressing indignation, I said to Dharmapala, on seeing him that evening, by way of rebuke, that he had ventured to do a thing involving risk.

II.

THE defence have put in, as Exhibit D. 26, an announcement in the Maha-Bodhi Journal for May, 1894, to the effect that I would be present at the enshrinement of the image on the 19th of that month (*see* page 35 of Dharmapala's deposition). Dharmapala had asked me if I would be present at the enshrinement of so historical an image. Before assenting, I mentioned to the Mahanth that Dharmapala intended to place the image, as knowing the relations between them, I did not wish to be present, if he had any objection. As the Mahanth said he would have none, so long as it was not made of precious metal, which might tempt dacoits to steal it and lead to Government holding him, as custodian of the temple, responsible for its loss, and as I thereafter ascertained that this image was of wood, I gave Dharmapala to understand that I might probably go to Bodh-Gaya on the occasion, but could not absolutely promise to do so.

III.

THEN evidence has been given about my having consulted two of the witnesses (Durga Shankar Bhattacharjya and the Pandit) about the question of whether the Buddha of the Buddhists was an incarnation of Vishnu. As the Mahanth in May, 1894, mentioned to me that Buddha was also a Hindu deity, being an incarnation of Vishnu, and the temple therefore was a Hindu one, and this was a novel idea to me, I called together some of the more highly educated among the leading representatives of the people and also two or three Pandits, to ask them whether the Maha-Bodhi Temple was regarded by Hindus as a Hindu one, and whether there could be any objection to Dharmapala's placing a Japanese image in it. Those who attended the meeting came in response to a circular invitation I sent round, and I got the names of the Pandits from one of my Deputy Magistrates, and, as I stated in Court, one of the latter mentioned that Buddha, son of Suddhodhan, was an incarnation of Vishnu. As no public record of this meeting has been made, and the matter has been introduced into this case by the defence, I take the opportunity of recording that I should not have concerned myself with the matter—otherwise than as taking a *dilettante* interest in it—were it not that I considered it my duty to do so, on the ground that the temple is under the guardianship of the Collector. and I understood that the Government had fully as much right in it as the Mahanth. This also applies to my action directing the Mahanth to replace the Buddhist marble images removed by Jaipal Gir from the temple in May, 1894, which gave rise to a correspondence, in the course of which the Mahanth wrote the letter of $\frac{13}{18}$th June, 1894, that has been filed as part of the written statement in this case.

D. J. MACPHERSON,

Magistrate.

13th July, 1895.

Memorandum as to Documents admitted in evidence.

On the 10th and 11th May (*vide* pp. 59 and 65 of the deposition of witness Bipin Bihari Banerjee), it was decided to accept the official letters tendered by the defence as admissible without proof of the signature of the writers under Clause (7), Section 57 of the Evidence Act. They were marked for identification as Exhibits D. 54, D. 55, D. 57, D. 58, D. 59 and D. 60; but the question of their relevance was not discussed until the 11th May (*vide* order sheet). On the 9th May (*vide* order sheet), the prosecution had tendered a notice issued by Mr. Boxwell, Magistrate of the District, and the question of its relevance was also discussed on the 11th. The defence had besides called for the whole correspondence of the Magistrate's and Collector's offices relating to Bodh-Gaya affairs, and this was all produced and placed at the disposal of the parties on the 8th May. The defence had the whole of it in their custody from the forenoon of that day till the close of the Court on the 10th. The prosecution then got it and had it till the evening of the 11th, when the question of which portions of it should be put in evidence was discussed.

The prosecution objected to any correspondence at all going in, but claimed that if the Court admitted any that might be tendered by the defence, the whole correspondence should be put in in order to explain it. They argued that anything stated in it bearing on the question of who was proprietor of the temple, could not be evidence, unless it was shown that it was done with the knowledge of the Mahanth, so as to influence his belief, and, with reference to the Mahanth's letter No. 7E., dated 13/18th June, 1894, which the defence sought to put in, cited Section 13 of the Evidence Act, as showing that if it was relevant, the whole correspondence, showing the right claimed was disputed, would also be evidence. The defence said there could be no objection to the letter to which it was a reply being put in. As to the documents D. 57 to D. 60, the prosecution had no objection to their going in so long as the whole correspondence on the subject, including particularly the Commissioner's letter of 23rd July, 1894, is put in with it, and the whole is taken merely as an expression of individual opinion.

The defence contended that the documents D. 57 to D. 60 were relevant as the defence were aware of their purport, having copies of them in possession, and their belief as to the Mahanth's rights, which they were simply maintaining, had been influenced by it.

With reference to the order of Mr. Boxwell's tendered by the prosecution in order to show that the Buddhist referred to therein had a right to go into the Temple and worship there, the defence objected that it could not be evidence against those who were accused in this case, and that the order was in any case illegal.

The defence being asked by the Court if they wished to put in the correspondence relating to the repairs, stated that the only document from it they would put in was letter No. 1177, dated 8th December, 1875, from the Collector to the Commissioner. The prosecution claimed to put in the whole correspondence about that, and particularly that covered by the Commissioner's Memo. No. 343R., dated 20th November, 1875, as the Collector's letter No. 1177, of 8th December, 1875, was a reply to it and unintelligible without it. The defence objected that letter No. 343R. was irrelevant, as it, contained no reference to the only point on which Mr. Halliday's reply was of importance, namely, the fact that the Mahanth's consent was taken to the repairs being executed. The defence added that the Court, of course, could put in any of the correspondence it pleased.

The prosecution stated that they would, of course, refer to books, as allowed under Section 57 of the Evidence Act.

The defence stated that they would call no evidence in proof of the Mahanth's letter No. 7E., dated $\frac{13}{18}$th June, 1894, or of a registered document executed by the Burmese King's delegate in favor of the Mahanth, as they would thereby lose the right of reply to the arguments of Counsel for the prosecution, but had made them part of the written statement they were going to file.

I intimated on the 13th May what portions of the correspondence I held to be relevant (*see* order sheet).

As the prosecution refused to allow the Mahanth's letter No. 7E., dated $\frac{13}{18}$th June, 1894, to be put in without proof of signature, I declined to allow the correspondence explanatory of it to be put in.

I decided that Mr. Boxwell's order tendered by the prosecution was irrelevant to this case, though it might have been in disproof of the plea of *bonâ fide* belief set by the defence, could it be shown it had been brought to the defendant's knowledge.

The whole of the discoverable correspondence in the office relating to the Maha-Bodhi Temple, from the very earliest letter that could be traced till the time when Mr. Beglar left in 1884, after completing the repairs, was put in (*vide* evidence of Head Clerk called by the Court, page 96), as in view of the defence putting in Mr. Halliday's letter No. 1177, of 8th December, 1875, and raising the plea that the Mahanth's consent was taken before the Government repaired the temple, it was relevant to know what there was on the official records of the time to show this, and for what purposes he was consulted on the occasion. The correspondence extends from 1875 down to 1884, and is now marked Exhibits C. 1 to C. 22.

I decided that the claim of the prosecution that all correspondence leading up to and explanatory of letters put in by the defence was relevant, and accordingly admitted the Assistant Superintendent of Police's report of 2nd April, 1889, marked Exhibit F. 1 as explanatory of, and the occasion for, Mr. Grierson's letter No. 1077, dated 3rd idem to the Mahanth (Exhibit D. 54), and also my own letter No. 1588, dated 12th July, 1894, and the Commissioner's reply, dated the 23rd idem, marked Exhibits E. 1 and E. 2, completing the correspondence as regards the statement made in the Superintending Engineer's letter filed by the defence as part of Exhibit D. 57 as to the Mahanth's position with reference to the temple, for what the Commissioner's expression of opinion might be worth.

Exhibits D. 54, D. 55, and D. 57 to D. 60, that had been tendered by the defence and marked for identification, were formally admitted in evidence, and marked as Exhibits, on the ground that they were relevant to the question of the *bonâ fides* of the belief of the defendants that the Mahanth was in possession of the temple. Of these Exhibits D. 54 and D. 55, and copies of D. 57 and 59 were produced by the defence, so it appeared they were aware of them; but the copies of D. 57 and D. 59 were evidently obtained unauthorisedly from the office of the Government custodian, as appears from the endorsement on the copies filed with their petition of 6th May, 1895.

D. J. MACPHERSON,
Magistrate.

13th July, 1895.

JUDGMENT.

In the Court of the District Magistrate of Gaya.

H. DHARMAPALA *vs.* JAIPAL GIR AND OTHERS.

(Sections 295, 296, 297, 143 *and* 352, *Indian Penal Code).*

In this case the defendants, who are Hindu Sannyasis or monks of the monastery of Bodh-Gaya, are charged with disturbing the worship of the complainants and other Buddhists of Ceylon in the Temple of Maha-Bodhi at Bodh-Gaya on the 25th February last. The case is one of importance, as the disturbance in question is sought to be justified by the defendants on the ground that their superior, the Mahanth or Abbot of Bodh-Gaya, claims the right, though a Hindu, of regulating what worship shall be performed in this famous shrine, known as the Great Temple of Mahabodhi, and regarded by the Buddhists, that is, by about one-third of the human race, as the most sacred spot on earth.

The facts connected with the actual occurrence of the 25th February are practically undisputed.

Between 8 and 9 o'clock on the morning of that day, the complainant, who is a Buddhist gentleman from Ceylon and Honorary General Secretary of the Maha-Bodhi Society, arrived at Bodh-Gaya with two Singhalese Buddhist priests, Sumangala and Devananda, and a layman, Silva, of the same race and religion, and proceeded to enshrine a highly artistic, and, it is said, historical image of Buddha, sent from Japan for the purpose, on the altar in the chamber of the upper floor of the Maha-Bodhi Temple. While they were setting up the image, two Muhammadan gentlemen, namely, the Special Sub-Registrar and a Deputy Magistrate of Gaya, happened to come to see the place, and were accompanied by a Muhammadan mukhtear of the Mahanth of Bodh-Gaya, named Hussain Baksh, and by one Jagannath Singh, a Hindu doorkeeper, whom the Mahanth keeps at the Temple. After they entered the chamber Hussain Baksh said something to the latter, who thereupon left. The three Muhammadans also went away before all the paraphernalia of the image were set up. The image with censer, candlesticks and lotus flowers and also a Japanese dedicatory certificate, describing its history, was duly set up, and Dharmapala then sent word to the Government custodian of the Temple, and, on his coming six or seven minutes after, put the image in his charge, saying it had been sent by the Japanese. This done, Sumangala took one of the candles to light it, but at that moment about thirty or forty of the Mahanth's Sannyasis and other Hindus, and also the mukhtear, Hussain Baksh, came rushing into the place in a very rowdy fashion. Some got on to the altar, a couple of them placed themselves between Dharmapala and it, one snatched the candle out of Sumangala's hand to prevent its being lit, and most spoke in a vehement and imperative tone, commanding Dharmapala to take away the image and using such threats as "*budmash*, we will beat you, there are five hundred of us" The Muhammadan in particular kept pushing him on the shoulder vehemently, telling him to remove the image. The Government custodian, finding them much enraged, kept imploring them with folded hands not to act hastily. Dharmapala refused to remove the image, and, as he knows little of the language, a number of them went and fetched the Mahanth's Hindu mukhtear, Vijayananda, who happened to be at the monastery in connection with a document of the Mahanth's the Sub-Registrar had come to get registered. Dharmapala pointed out to Vijayananda what desecration it was for people to be on the altar, and the latter got one or two to come down. Thereupon this mukhtear and all but a few, who remained quietly looking on, left the temple, and Dharmapala and the two priests, thinking all opposition had ended, sat down to their devotion in front of the image in the characteristic Buddhist attitude of religious contemplation, the highest form of Buddhist worship. They were absorbed in this form of devotion for about a quarter of an hour, when the Hindus again came to the Temple and, heedless of their attitude, made a rush into the place and tumultuously carried off the image of Buddha and set it down in the open courtyard below. This tumult, and indeed the mere removal of the image itself, put an end to the devotional contemplation of the Buddhists. Dharmapala and one of the priests continued, however, to sit there, and in a few minutes a constable came up to call him down to the head constable, who had been sent for by the Government custodian, and to whom also the mukhtear, Hussain Baksh, had made a statement praying him to interfere. Dharmapala refused to go down, so the head constable had to come up where he was, and began questioning him in Hindi; but Dharmapala, not understanding this, wrote down there and then, at his request, a summary statement of the occurrence. I may add that shortly after noon that day the Mahanth himself came to me at Gaya, seven miles off, and I recorded his statement as a basis of the action he wished me to take; and as I was going down to the place with some visitors in any case in the evening, I there took down briefly the statements of some of the witnesses, and directed the inspector of police to make a full inquiry into the facts as to the removal of the image from inside the temple. Dharmapala remained at Bodh-Gaya while the police inquiry was going on until the evening of the next day, and on the 28th February he filed in Court the complaint which is the foundation of the present proceedings. The subsequent proceedings are set out on the order sheet of this case. The examination-in-chief of the witnesses was taken on the 8th, 9th, 11th and 12th of April, and their cross-examination and the other proceedings lasted from the 1st to the 15th of May. The charges on which the defendants have been tried, were framed before the cross-examination of the witnesses for the prosecution, and the defence have called no witnesses. At first I had suggested that the evidence for the prosecution should be taken in two separate stages, the first being confined to the actual facts of the occurrence of the 25th February, and the other extending to the various other questions involved, such as the Buddhist right of worship in the temple and the Mahanth's position with reference thereto; but it was soon found that this was impracticable. I ought to record that the reason I had suggested this was that, from the statements made by the Mahanth and by those examined on his behalf by the police, it appeared that the defence intended to deny the taking of the image inside the temple at all, and if this part of the complainant's case were not therefore proved, it would be unnecessary to go into the other large questions involved.

On the facts described above, the defendants, who are four of the Mahanth's disciples or monks, named, Jaipal Gir, Mahendra Gir, Bhimal Deo Gir, and Shivanandan Gir and the Muhammadan and Hindu mukhtears, have been charged under Section 296 of the Indian Penal Code with voluntarily disturbing an assembly lawfully engaged in the performance of religious ceremonies connected with the enshrinement of the image, and subsequently one engaged in religious worship; under Section 295, with defiling the image, and also a place of worship, with the knowledge that the Buddhists would likely consider such defilement an insult to their religion; under Section 297, with trespassing into a place of worship with the knowledge that the religion of the Buddhists who were there, would likely be insulted, and their feelings wounded thereby; and under Section 143, with being members of an unlawful assembly, having as its common object either the commission of the above offences or the enforcement by show of criminal force of the right or supposed right of preventing the Buddhists from accomplishing the enshrinement of the image. Certain of the defendants, namely, Jaipal Gir, Mahendra Gir and Bhimal Deo Gir and Hussain Baksh, mukhtear, who are expressly identified as having committed specific acts, namely, getting on to the altar, preventing the candle being lit, and removing the image in the course of the above proceedings, are further charged under Sections 295 and 296 with doing them with the knowledge described above, and Hussain Baksh is in addition charged under Section 352 with using criminal force to the complainant.

The defendants pleaded not guilty, and declined under the advice of Counsel to answer any questions the Court might put, but filed a written statement, the purport of which will be given presently.

As the defence in the case is a purely legal one, and the relevancy of many of the matters it will be necessary to discuss in this judgment might not be apparent without it, it is desirable to record here as concisely as may be the general line of argument presented to the Court by Counsel on each side. To avoid repetition in endeavouring to convey its general effect, I shall have to depart in some instances from the sequence in which the arguments were addressed.

The following is a summary of the main points urged by Counsel for the prosecution (Mr. Sutherland) :—

The question who is proprietor of the Temple is, he observed, quite irrelevant to this case, but the prosecution must incidentally challenge the assertion of the defence that the Mahanth is sole and absolute proprietor, and looking to all the facts connected with its repair and guardianship by Government, Dharmapala had good reason for considering Government to be the proprietor, and Government, in taking over the guardianship, undoubtedly continued freedom of worship to the Buddhists. Assuming, however, for the sake of argument, that the Mahanth was in some sort of possession, and was allowed to enjoy a certain usufruct in taking offerings, such possession was nevertheless subject to the long standing right of every Buddhist to worship and perform any ceremonies in accordance with the tenets of his religion in the temple, and neither Government nor the Mahanth is entitled to prevent the full exercise of that right. Even if the Mahanth were the proprietor, his property is subject to easements. The temple is, as a matter of common history, a Buddhist one. Witnesses have sworn that no Hindu has ever (unless possibly within the last few months) worshipped or could worship there, and have not been cross-examined on this point, and the defendants' written statement apparently does not deny the fact of the temple being a Buddhist one. The Mahanth's claim to regulate the worship, advanced in the written statement, has been put forward only at the very end of the case, and is one not cross-examined on, and not a question was put to the witnesses who depose to having put images, &c., in the temple, as to their having taking the Mahanth's permission before doing so. The defence, as disclosed in the written statement, is really one of the right of private defence of property or, as it is called in England, abating a nuisance, and under Section 105, Evidence Act, the onus lies on the defence. (Counsel then examined in detail the facts and the law bearing on each of the charges and the validity of the defence raised to them). The defendants cannot plead the right of private defence of property, as Dharmapala committed no offence, and they did not adopt the advice given by the Deputy Magistrate or take him to witness a protest on their part or wait till the police came. It was not necessary for more than one or two to go for the purpose alleged in the defence, and there is no evidence to show that they acted under or in accordance with the orders of the Mahanth. The complainant's party were in peaceable occupation of the upper chamber, into which it is not denied that every Buddhist has a right to enter, and the defendants therefore did not come to maintain existing possession and right of the Mahanth, but to assert a right against the actual enjoyment by the complainant of his rights. The defendants must have known of the respect paid to an image of Buddha, and must have often seen Buddhists seated in the attitude of religious contemplation before it, and there was no cross-examination as to its being a sham, as alleged by the defence now, and in any case there was no reason for their not waiting till it was over. The agreement filed as part of the written statement supports the case for the prosecution as to the temple itself being a Buddhist one, and its repairs being undertaken by the Burmese for the purpose of Buddhist worship. In support of various arguments, Counsel cited the following cases:—I. L. R. 3 Cal. 573 (*Empress vs. Rajkumar Singh*) ; I. L. R. 16 Cal. 206 (*Ganauri Lal Das vs. Empress*) ; I. L. R. 7 All. 461 (*Empress vs. Ramjan*), read with I. L. R. 12 All. 503 (*Ataullah vs. Azmullah*), to show that the case ultimately ended in a conviction ; and 23 W. R. p. 25, Cr. R. (*Pachgachia Amba case*).

The written statement filed by the defendants contains in a succinct form the nature of the case for the defence. Counsel stated that it was confined to what was considered a sufficient legal defence to the charges framed. The facts of the occurrence of the 25th February, as described by the witnesses for the prosecution, are either virtually admitted in it or not denied, but the defendants repudiate all guilty knowledge and claim to justify their action on the ground that they had every reason to believe, on grounds stated, that the Mahanth was the sole proprietor of the temple, and, as such, entitled to appropriate all offerings made by pilgrims, whether Hindus or Buddhists, whom he permitted to worship according to rules and directions which he alone was competent to frame and give; that the Mahanth had last year forbidden the Buddhists doing anything that might infringe his rights as regards worship by pilgrims in any part of the temple, in consequence of which an attempt by Dharmapala to place this very image in May, 1894, without his consent, had failed, the Magistrate, as they believed, having directed him to desist; and that all they did on the 25th February was done in good faith, under the general orders of the Mahanth, to maintain his existing possession and rights, and to prevent the enshrining of the image without his consent and without the requisite Hindu ceremony of *pranpratishta*, as they believed that this was merely an attempt on the part of Dharmapala to create evidence of some right adversely to the Mahanth, and that he and his comrades were not *bonâ fide* engaged in any worship or religious ceremony. They therefore disdain all intention or knowledge forming an ingredient in the offences charged, and allege that they were not aware that sitting in silent contemplation was a form of Buddhist worship, and say they are not even now prepared to believe the evidence in this respect. They protest ignorance of the rites of Buddhism prevailing in other countries, but allage that, believing Buddha according to the *Shastras* to be a Hindu deity, they treated the image with all respect, though it had come from a *mlechha* country. As part of this written statement, they set out certain documents which they allege confirmed the belief that the Mahanth was proprieter of the temple.

The arguments addressed to the Court by Counsel for the defence (Mr. Manomohan Ghose) were in effect an amplification of these, and the following is a summary of the main points he took in urging them :—

There is very little dispute, he remarked, as regards the occurrence of the 25th February, though there is a good deal as to the prior facts, and the matters bearing on the knowledge and intention of the accused. The main points are that the Mahanth really believed himself to be proprietor of the temple on the 25th February, and that he also believed that Dharmapala was on that occasion attempting to infringe on his rights. That being so, the defendants, who are his servants, were acting *bonâ fide* under his orders, and cannot therefore be held to have had the *mens rea* which is a requisite ingredient of all offences, except certain ones, such as fiscal and municipal offences. Still more is it incumbent on the prosecution to show that the accused had the intention or guilty knowledge expressly mentioned in the Penal Code, as requisite to constitute offences against religion. (In regards to this Counsel quoted Maxwell on the interpretation of Statutes, 2nd Edition, pp. 115, 116; Mayne's Penal Code, Section 298; Macpherson's Penal Code, Sections 295 and 296, and the second report of the Indian Law Commissioners on offences under Chapter XV., Madras Edition, 1888, page 409.) The documents which form part of the written statement show that, since 1877, the Mahanth believed himself, rightly or wrongly, to be proprietor and in possession, and that no one had a right to worship in the temple without his permission, and on the 19th May, 1894, he had already asserted that right. Further, the complainant's own admissions in the Journal of the Maha-Bodhi Society, of which he is editor, are ample proof of the Mahanth's ownership and possession for the purposes of this case. But it is sufficient that, on the 25th February last, the Mahanth was actually in possession, and that the defendants were acting in a *bonâ fide* assertion of his claim. The appointment of a custodian by Government was not an assertion of claim by the Government with the knowledge and acquiescence of the Mahanth, nor was it intended as such. As the Mahanth is the proprietor, the Buddhists would have to show that they have acquired a right of easement by having uninterruptedly for at least twenty years as a matter of right and to the knowledge of the Mahanth, exercised the right not only of general worship, but also of placing an unsanctified image in the upper chamber without his consent, and the burden of proving that must rest on the prosecution. Indeed, the Mahanth has, if he chooses to exercise it, a right to obstruct even the worship of the great image on the ground floor. Even if they should prove their right to set up this image, they would still have to show that the defendants did not *bonâ fide* believe Dharmapala had no such right. It is a matter of history that the Buddhists were swept out of the country by the Brahmans. Counsel then enlarged on the value of the legal defence put in to the charges under each section in detail. As regards defilement of the image, he contended that on the *ejusdem generis* principle of construction (Maxwell, pp. 398, 410), defilement in Section 295 of the Penal Code, must be taken to mean "physical defilement by throwing something on the object." Dharmapala's character, as revealed in cross-examination, and the history of his actions with reference to this image, and all the circumstances of the case, show that the setting up of the image and the ceremonies and alleged worship were all a sham and merely a *ruse* for creating evidence infringing on the Mahanth's rights; but it is sufficient that the defendants believed that he was not engaged in *bonâ fide* worship, and that they believed him to be in a place where he had no right to be without the Mahanth's permission, the onus of showing right lying on the prosecution, otherwise he could not be said to be "lawfully" engaged in worship. The defendants had a right to go where they did, so there was no trespass within the meaning of

Section 297 (see I. L. R. 3 Mad. 178, *in re Khaja Mahomed Hanim Khan*, and an unreported case of this year relating to the Gaya Church*), nor did they ever know that the upper chamber was a place of worship or the altar a sacred place. It is open to question whether Dharmapala could be convicted of criminal trespass, but see I. L. R. 6 Cal. 579, (*Empress vs. Panjab Singh*) and 24 W. R. p. 58 Cr. R. (*in re Sibnath Banerjee*); but the defence do not rest the case on the exercise of the right of private defence at all, and even if they did, they did no "harm" (section 99, clause (4) Penal Code) to Dharmapala. The defendants, however, rightly or wrongly, did regard him as committing criminal trespass, and are therefore protected by Section 98, Penal Code (see Macpherson's Penal Code) As regards the charge of unlawful assembly, it is admitted that, if the charges under Chapter XV of the Code are made out, the defendants are guilty under Section 143, Penal Code, but not as regards the alternative common object alleged, which must be proved by the defence (11 Cal. L. R. 232 *in re Kalicharan Mukerjee*). Counsel reviewed the case-law on the subject of the criminality of enforcing a right under Section 141, Penal Code, and maintained that it was Dharmapala who was seeking to enforce a right, and that all that the defendants were doing, was maintaining an existing right they had being going on, at least, since May, 1894 The rulings reviewed were those reported in 3 W. R., p. 41, Cr. R. (*Queen vs. Mitto Singh*); I. L. R 3 Cal. 573 (*Empress vs. Rajkumar Singh*); 4 Mad. H. C. Reports, App. 65; 19 W. R. p. 66, Cr. R. (*Birju Singh vs. Khub Lal*); 23 W. R., p. 25, Cr. R. (*Pachgachia Amba case*); I L. R. 16 Cal. 206 (*Ganauri Lal Das vs. Empress*); and I. L R 14 Bom 441 (*Empress vs. Nursing Pathabhai*). As regards Hindu worship of Buddha, it is sufficient that for some time prior to the 25th February Buddha has been regarded by Hindus as a deity to be worshipped, whether the Shastras actually justify such worship or not, and the Mahanth has a right to paint and clothe the images, as has been done to the great image on the ground floor, as they are his property, so long as he does not do this with the intent to injure any one else's religious feelings, for the purposes of his own worship. Though the defendants themselves, no doubt, would not say so, Counsel pointed out that when the Brahmans were endeavouring to expel Buddhism from India, they found it a matter of policy to convert all images of Buddha into an incarnation of Vishnu, and their worshippers therefore into Hindus; but that when they acquired full dominion over the Buddhists, it became unnecessary to continue such worship of Buddha, which would account for Hindu worship not having been carried on in the temple on the same scale as it has been within the last few months.

* *Hafiz Abdur Rahman vs. Empress*: February 26, 1895. Norris and Beverley, J.J.

In view of the defence put forward and the line taken in the prolonged cross-examination to which the complainant was subjected, it becomes necessary to consider the nature and objects of the Maha-Bodhi Society, of which the complainant is Honorary General Secretary, and the circumstances under which he resolved to enshrine the image in the Temple.

The Maha-Bodhi Society was founded in Colombo, in Ceylon, on the 31st May, 1891, with the object of establishing a Buddhist monastery, founding a Buddhist College and maintaining a staff of Buddhist *bhikshus*, or priests representing all Buddhist countries, at Buddha-Gaya, and carrying on the publication of Buddhist literature. Office-bearers were appointed, representing each Buddhist country, with the High Priest of Ceylon, H. Sumangala, as President, Colonel H. S. Olcott as Director and Chief Adviser, and H. Dharmapala, the complainant in the present case, General Secretary, all the offices being purely honorary (Exhibit III and witness I, pp. 48-49 *ante*). Dharmapala describes himself as being a religious student ever since he left College in 1883 (I. 7), and is supported by a wealthy father with an income of seventy or eighty thousand rupees a year, and a leading business in Ceylon (I. 48). Within the last three years he has visited most Buddhist countries in connection with the Society, and was also the special delegate of the Buddhists at the Parliament of Religions held at Chicago in 1893 (I. 49). In May, 1892, the Society started a monthly Journal for the interchange of news between the Buddhist countries and Bodh-Gaya, which was to be the Society's head-quarters. The head-quarters so far, however, have been in Calcutta, where the Journal is published (I. 49). It is edited by Dharmapala, when he is there; but he is often away for long periods in Ceylon or on his travels, and then it is edited by whoever may be the acting manager (I 49, 53). These details are mentioned as the defence have put in numerous passages from the Journal, which they seek to make out to be admissions by the complainant of the Mahanth's proprietorship and possession of the Temple.

Dharmapala, first visited Bodh-Gaya in January, 1891, and stayed there a couple of months worshipping in the temple. It was not till after his return to Ceylon in that year that the Society was founded. He has since visited the temple on many occasions and worshipped there (I. 1). The passages from the Journal put in by the defence show that since March, 1893, at any rate, it has been one of the main objects of the Society to obtain for the Buddhists fuller control over the temple than they possessed or yet possess, and for this purpose a proposal was mooted for the amicable purchase from the Mahanth of any rights he might be found lawfully to possess in the place. Dharmapala explains that this was because the place was neglected, having no priests, no offerings, no festivals, no celebrations—everything required for the central shrine of the Buddhists was wanting (I. 54). The idea indeed appears to have originated with Sir Edwin Arnold, apparently in 1886, on which point reference may be made to the article reprinted in the Journal for July, 1893, from the *Daily Telegraph*, and put in by the defence as Exhibit D. 7; but Dharmapala had no communication with him, until as Secretary he wrote to inform him of the founding of the Society some few years later (I. 7, 19). There can, however, be no doubt that the Maha-Bodhi Society is a genuine one, representing real Buddhist feeling in respect to the Maha-Bodhi Temple, and that Dharmapala is an accredited agent of it; and there is absolutely no ground for regarding him, as seems to be suggested, as carrying on a spurious agitation for the sake of personal notoriety or gain. Any one who has witnessed the splendour of Buddhist temples in various countries, as I have done, can well understand the feelings with which the bare aspect of the central shrine has inspired Buddhists who have visited Maha-Bodhi.

It appears that the idea of enshrining an image of Buddha in the chamber on the upper floor of the temple suggested itself to Dharmapala when he was in Japan in November, 1893, on his way back from attending the Parliament of Religions in America, and happened to read a passage in *Vinaya Pashpamala* to the effect that at the time of the Muhammadan invasion of Behar, *i.e.*, 1201 A. D., the Buddhist priests took away the image of Buddha that was in the temple and hid it in the forests of Rajgir (I. 34, 50, 51, 53). The *sanctum sanctorum* in a Buddhist Temple was always an upper chamber (I. 53, and Dr. Rajendra Lala Mitra's *Buddha Gaya*, 1878, p. 85); and the image that was there could not have been a large one like that which is now on the ground floor of the temple. There was no image of Buddha in the upper *sanctum* at all, and Dharmapala accordingly suggested to some Buddhists in Japan, and their High Priest in Tokyo, that a proper image should be sent for it (I. 34 and Exhibit D. 25), and they accordingly made over to him for enshrinement in the upper chamber, one which, according to the dedicatory certificate accompanying it (Exhibit A. and see I, 54, and top of p. 7), had been carved by order of the famous Shogun Yoritomo, who ruled at the end of the 12th century, and had undergone some vicissitudes of fortune thereafter. It is carved in wood, artistically lacquered in gold, and is undoubtedly a beautiful work of art.

Dharmapala got back to India on the 31st March, 1894, and brought the image to Gaya on the 17th May, with the intention of enshrining it on the 19th, the full-moon day, marking the anniversary of the birth of Buddha's enlightenment. He felt sure there would be no opposition to his doing so, and indeed announced his intention in his Journal, stating I would be present (I. 35 and Exhibit D. 26. The reason for this assurance is indicated in a proceeding recorded by me on the 9th June, 1894, on a complaint made by Nirghin Ram, P. W. D. chaprasi, against Jaipal Gir, which has not, however, been made evidence in this case,* although one letter of the Mahanth out of the correspondence to which the complaint gave rise has been reproduced as part of the defendant's written statement. In a separate note will be found a statement explaining the announcement in Exhibit D. 26 that I would be present at the ceremony.

* NOTE — *See post.* Part II, page 25.

At the last moment, however, the Mahanth objected to the image being placed in the temple, unless it was entrusted to him to do so and underwent the *prânpratishta* (life-giving) ceremony constituting it a Hindu deity (I. 35). Dharmapala desisted from placing the image on receiving a demi-official letter from me not to persist in the attempt on that occasion (I. 35). In para. 13 of the written statement it is said that the defendants believed I had directed him to desist from any further attempt, but I may mention that, as a matter of fact, he received no instructions to this effect beyond being advised to appeal to Government before proceeding further. Thereupon he filed a petition about this matter (I. 36), which I undertook to forward to the higher authorities, and early in August he went back to Ceylon, leaving the image in a rented house in Gaya (I. 36 and IX. 88-9). Before he went away, however, he wrote a letter to the Private Secretary to the Lieutenant-Governor, complaining of the grievance about the image (I. 32) and received a reply (Exhibit D. 23) that Government declined to exercise any influence with the Mahanth or to pass any other orders than those already communicated to him in a letter dated the 5th May of that year (Exhibit D. 22), in which it was said that there was perfect freedom of worship for all Buddhists at Bodh-Gaya, and that any well-grounded complaint about difficulties being imposed by the Sannyasis, who had hitherto given all reasonable facilities, would meet with ready attention and redress at the hands of Government. The Commissioner of the Division did not forward Dharmapala's petition to Government, but on the 28th July, 1894, intimated that if he wished to pursue the subject further, he should be referred for orders to Government [Exhibit D. 28 (*a*).]

I was then absent on leave in Europe, and this was not communicated to Dharmapala until, on my return, I ordered it on the 27th September (Exhibit 28 (*b*) and I 36). Dharmapala did not return from Ceylon until January of this year, when he accompanied his mother and over forty other Singhalese pilgrims to the Temple (I. 1, 4.) After his return to Calcutta he wrote to me in February, asking when I should be in from camp and able to see him, and I replied that I should be in Gaya about the 20th or 21st (I. 53.) He also wrote me, in a different letter, according to him (I. 52.), but in that one according to my memory (see note separately recorded), to the effect that he would place the image in the Temple, as he had a duty to perform to the Japanese. I took no notice of this as I had expected to see him about the date fixed above, but he did not come to Gaya until noon on the 24th, and did not come to see me, as he did not suppose I was still at headquarters (I. 53.) Next morning, as already related, he and his three companions proceeded to Bodh-Gaya with the express purpose of placing the image in the temple, arriving there between 8 and 9 A.M., and they appear to have gone about the matter quite openly. Several people would be required to carry an image and paraphernalia of the size, as the image itself, without, as I have seen, its pedestal or canopy, is about 18 inches high (I. 1), and two or three boxes were required for bringing it in from Gaya and into the temple (III. 68).

On these facts I do not think there is any ground for believing that Dharmapala was animated by any other motive than a genuine one to discharge the trust he had undertaken in Japan to enshrine a suitable image of Buddha in the *sanctum sanctorum*, where one was needed instead of the image of Mayadevi, Buddha's mother, that had been placed there at the restoration of the temple by Government. He had been informed by Government, whom he regarded as the custodian of the temple (I. 15, 51), that there was perfect freedom of worship in it to all Buddhists, and that any well-grounded complaint of difficulties being imposed would meet with ready attention and redress at its hands; and, when he did make a grievance of not being allowed to place the image in the temple, Government declined to exercise any influence with the Mahanth. It is not to be wondered at therefore that, when he was told later on by the Commissioner that the local authorities could not deal with the matter, and that he should address Government if he wished to pursue it, he felt there was nothing for it but to take his stand upon the freedom of worship Government had declared to exist, and which he knew existed, and free himself from the responsibility he had undertaken in bringing this historical image all the way from Japan by proceeding to place it in the Temple without seeking further orders on the subject. It is true he professed himself indifferent to its fate thereafter (I. 37), but the responsibility would not then be his, and as a matter of fact he entrusted the enshrined image to the Government custodian (I. 2, and II. 57). His position undoubtedly was an awkward one, as it was at his suggestion the Japanese had parted with the image, and to return it might seem an insult. I do not think he can in any way be blamed for taking the course he did in discharging the duty he had undertaken in an absolutely peaceable manner.

The case for the prosecution rests upon the fact of the Maha-Bodhi Temple being a Buddhist shrine with a right of Buddhists to worship in it and actual enjoyment of such right. The case for the defence rests on the existence of a *bonâ fide* belief on the part of the defendants that the Mahanth had proprietary rights and possession over the Temple, that gave him the right to prevent images being placed in it without his consent and without being sanctified by ceremonies enjoined in the Hindu religion It becomes necessary therefore to go into the question of the history and religious character of the temple, and the grounds on which the Mahanth bases his belief as to ownership and possession, and consider how far the patent facts support or negative the allegation of *bonâ fides* in the beliefs put forward by the defendants as justification for their conduct.

The history and religious character of this famous shrine are matters of "public history," and under Section 57 of the Evidence Act, "the Court may resort for its aid to appropriate books or documents of reference." The books I have principally consulted on this subject are the following:—Cunningham's *Mahabodhi* (1892); Rajendra Lala Mitra's *Buddha Gaya* (1878); Martin's Edition of Buchanan Hamilton's *Eastern India*, Vol. I (1838); *Archæological Survey of India*, Vol. I (Cunningham's Reports for 1862-65) and Vol. VIII (Beglar's Report for 1872-73,; Beal's translation of the Travels of Fa-Hien and Sung-yun, Buddhist pilgrims from China to India in 400 and 518 A. D. (1869); Stanislas Julien's French translation of the memoirs of Hiouen Thsang, a Chinese pilgrim who visited Maha-Bodhi in 637 A. D. (1857): and Fergusson's *History of Indian and Eastern Architecture* (1876). On the authority of these works and the inscriptions found at the Temple, the fact that it was originally a Buddhist shrine is unquestioned. It was a place of Buddhist pilgrimage and worship from at least the time of Asoka, who built the Temple on the exact site of the present one in the middle of the third century before the Christian Era (Cunningham, p. 4 and preface p. vii). Fa-Hien in 409 A. D. visited the temple here on pilgrimage (Beal, p. 126), but about 600 A.D. Raja Sasangka, who opposed Buddhism, destroyed the Bodhi tree (Hiouen Thsang II. 463). Raja Purnavarma however replanted it very soon afterwards and surrounded it with a stone wall (Hiouen Thsang II. 463-4). When the Chinese traveller Hiouen Thsang visited the place in 637 A.D. the very Temple still standing was there (Cunningham, p. 18). Many other Chinese pilgrims visited the place during that century. After the death of Harshavardhana in 648 A.D., however, the country was for some time left in the power of the Brahmans (Cunningham, pp. 31 and 68). Under the flourishing Buddhist dynasty of Pala Kings, who ruled the country from 813 A.D., to the time of the Muhammadan invasion in 1201 A.D., the place received much attention, and in the eleventh century many Chinese pilgrims visited it (Cunningham, pp. 31, 68, 80, 25, 29 and preface viii.) Twice in that century also, namely, in 1035 and 1079-1086 A.D., the Temple was repaired by the Burmese (Cunningham, pp. 27-28). The monastery alongside was probably destroyed during the Mahomedan invasion, but inscriptions on the granite pavement show that Buddhist pilgrims visited it in 1298, 1302, 1328 and 1331 A.D. (Cunningham, p. 56). Cunningham believes that the place was thereafter appropriated by the Brahmans, but gives no reason for this conjecture, except that a round stone with the feet of Vishnu carved on it was found in front of the Temple, bearing the date 1308 A. D. (p. 57). The stone was, however, lying loose (Martin's *Eastern India*, p. 74). It is said that the spiritual ancestor of the present Mahanth settled in the neighbourhood in 1590 A.D., attracted by the sylvan solitude of the place, and founded a small monastery which has developed into the present large one. This is about 400 yards from the temple. The Mahanth represents the sect of *Girs*, one of the ten Saivite orders founded by Sankara Acharya, a bitter opponent of Buddhism, who lived in the 8th or 9th century (witness X. pp. 5 and 22, and Hunter's *Indian Empire*, Ed. 1893, pp. 203 and 259). The traces of Hindu worship found about the place will be discussed presently. Whatever they may have been, it appears that at the time when Buchanan Hamilton was studying the antiquities of the District in 1811 A.D., there was no Hindu worship *inside* the temple. At that time the celebrated *pipal* or Bodhi tree stood on the back of the upper floor terrace, and was an object of worship by Hindu pilgrims to Gaya, as will be presently described, but a stair had recently been built on the *outside*, "so that the orthodox may pass up without entering the porch, and thus seeing the hateful image of Buddha" (Martin, p. 75). He regarded the Buddhists, it may be noted, as merely a heterodox sect of Hindus. Rajendra Lala Mitra formed the same conjecture as to its use (p. 64). An illustration of the stair will be found in Plate XV of his book and also on page 70 of Fergusson's *Eastern Architecture*, where the position of the tree, unlike anything now existing, is shewn. There were, as still, two stairs leading up to the terrace from *inside* the vestibule that could have been used (Martin, page 75). Two parties of Burmese appear to have visited the shrine about Buchanan Hamilton's time (Martin, pp. 71 and 77), and there was another Burmese Mission in 1833 (Archæological Survey Reports, Vol. I., page 8). The "hateful image of Buddha" referred to by Buchanan Hamilton was a "monstrous mis-shapen daub of clay" (Martin, p. 76). This appears to have been replaced by the Burmese who came in 1831 by a gilt stucco image which Rajendra Lala Mitra saw in 1863, and this in turn was replaced by the Burmese who came in 1876 by another of the same description, but "hideously ugly" (Rajendra Lala Mitra, p. 85). The Burmese who came on the last occasion commenced an extensive restoration of the whole Temple in the beginning of 1877, but, as the work was being done without any regard to the requirements of archæology, Dr. Rajendra Lala Mitra was deputed by Government to visit the place in the autumn of that year, and, in consequence of his report, Government in the following year took the work of restoration into its own hands and completed it, at what is known to have been an enormous expense, in the middle of 1884, the work being carried out under the supervision of Mr. Beglar (see Rajendra Lala Mitra's preface, p. iii, and the file of office correspondence marked Exhibits C 1 to C 22). Since then the temple has been kept in repair by Government (II. 38, 42). There is ample oral evidence on the record, which has not been questioned at all in cross-examination, that the Temple has continually and regularly been used of late years as a Buddhist place of worship by Buddhist pilgrims. Dr. Hari Das Chatterjee (witness VIII) has frequently visited it since 1873, and seen Buddhist pilgrims, Burmese and Tibetants, worshipping inside, and Babu Durga Shankar Bhattacharyya (witness IX) has also many times been to it, both before its restoration and since, and seen Buddhist pilgrims worshipping in it, though neither was asked specifically for how long they have seen such worship. The Government custodian, Babu Bipin Bihari Banerjee, (witness II), has seen the same regularly since he joined his post in July, 1890, and deposes to hearing the Brahman priests accompanying Hindu pilgrims to a *pipal* tree in the compound, forbid them entering the temple because of its being "a Jain one" (II. 23). The Buddhist witnesses, Dharmapala (witness I) since January, 1891, Sumangala (witness V) since July, 1891, and Devananda (witness VI) since May, 1894, have themselves regularly worshipped in it, and no attempt has been made to shake their testimony in this respect in cross-examination. The Hindu Pandit of the Government Zilla School, Gangadhar Shastri, (witness X), though he has been to it on three or four occasions, has abstained from entering it, as it is a Buddhist temple, and Hindus are forbidden to enter such. Finally, there is not one word in the written statement filed by the defence as to its not being a Buddhist temple. On the contrary, the fact that Buddhist pilgrims worshipped and made offerings at it is admitted, although it is now alleged that such worship has been with the permission of the Mahanth as proprietor of the Temple, and according to rules and directions he alone was competent to frame and give. The agreement, moreover, purporting to have been executed by the Burmese King's delegate on 11th February, 1877, and filed as part of the written statement, clearly contemplates the repair of the Temple by Buddhists for the purpose of Buddhist worship. Except as regards the placing in the Temple of the Japanese image, the claim set up by the Mahanth to regulate the worship in it has been advanced for the first time at the very close of the case, and is one in regard to which the defence did not cross-examine the witnesses. It is a mere assertion made for the purpose of supplying a defence to the present case, and is not only absolutely devoid of proof, but negatived by the positive testimony of the Buddhist witnesses who performed their worship and depose to making specific offerings without even thinking of obtaining the Mahanth's permission (I. 22 and V. 3).

I now proceed to discuss the evidence as to Hindu worship ever having been carried on in the Temple. I have consulted the authorities quoted above as to the existence of objects indicating any former or existing worship by Hindus in or near the temple. The defence have put in as Exhibits D. 41 and D. 61, two works published by Government entitled "A List of Objects of Antiquarian Interest in the Lower Provinces of Bengal," 1879, and "Revised List of Ancient Monuments in Bengal," 1886, the latter being a later edition of the former. At p. 125 of the former and 120 of the latter, it is stated that "one of the four sacred places in the annals of Buddhism" (the reference being apparently to Buddha-Gaya) "has been appropriated to Hindu worship." The whole passage in question is quoted nearly word for word from the first paragraph of Rajendra Lala Mitra's "Buddha-Gaya," which is quoted in the introduction as one of the works from which the List has been compiled. The passage, however, appears to have been written for epigrammatic effect, for it is materially contradicted in other parts of the work. For instance, on p. 20, Dr. Rajendra Lala Mitra says that "Uruvilva, which was never entirely converted into Hindu worship, was appropriately named the Gaya of the Buddhists, or Buddha-Gaya," and on p. 138, that "the place was never thoroughly converted into Hindu usage, and none thought of dedicating Hindu images there;" and it is clear from the passage on p. 64, already referred to, in which he gives his opinion as to the use of the outside stair, that he did not intend this description to apply to the shrine itself, for he regards it as having been built "to provide an easy passage for the Hindu pilgrims wishing to visit the Bodhi tree without subjecting them to enter the porch of a heterodox shrine." No weight whatever can be attached to the repetition of the remark in the edition of 1886 (Exhibit D. 61), as apparently it was desired to retain the description applicable to the state of things before the repairs (see paragraph on p. 121 and the remark made in the last column against it). Now Rajendra Lala Mitra's book seems to enumerate carefully all the objects about, which showed signs of appropriation to Hindu worship, namely, the temple of Tara Devi and Vagesvari Devi (pp. 60-61), the image of Savitri Devi (p. 65), the images in the Panch Pandava temple (p. 71), the Buddhapad, apparently never anything but a Vishnupad (pp. 100 and 201), four images of Hindu divinities at the base of the Bodhi tree (p. 99), a few Hindu or quasi-Hindu images enumerated at p. 139 (none of them in the temple itself), and a votive *stupa* made to do duty as a *lingam* set up in the shrine on the ground floor (p. 84). This last is the only one that was inside the Temple, but images at the base of the Bodhi tree were at that time on the upper terrace outside at the back. Indeed, from the passage on p. 201, it would appear that with the conjectural exception of the front courtyard, the terrace with the tree was the only portion of the structure appropriated for purposes of Hindu worship. As regards the only evidence on which the exception relating to the courtyard is based, it may be remarked that Rajendra Lala Mitra notes that the pavilion that had been over it near the Punch Pandava Temple had been removed by the Burmese repairers (p. 101). There may possibly be other traces of Hindu objects mentioned in the book, but these are all I have noticed.

Now it is quite in keeping with what we know of the receptive character of Hinduism and the expedients to which the Brahmans resorted as a matter of policy to extend its influence, that the Bodhi tree, a *pipal*, should be selected on the establishment of Gaya as a place of Hindu pilgrimage, as one of the 45 places in and around the city at which the Hindu should offer oblations for the purpose of freeing the souls of his ancestors from purgatory. It is not, it may be remarked, one of the places to which it is obligatory to go (witness VIII. 82). But the Bodhi tree in question was dead, and had been knocked down by a storm by the time Rajendra Lala Mitra visited the place in 1887; and the tree which the Hindus have substituted for it is one about 80 feet away to the north of the temple, as deposed to by the custodian (II. 43). This they, no doubt, did at the very time, as the whole place was then undergoing repair. The Buddhists on the other hand have been worshipping as the Bodhi tree, one planted close to the west wall of the temple, that is, on the supposed site of the original Bodhi tree (Cunningham, page 31). Hindus, the custodian says (II. 68), do not perform any kind of worship at the latter, but he has seen Hindus go and bow before it. All this Hindu worship is conducted under the auspices of the Gayawal priests of Gaya itself, who are Vaishnavites, and not of the Mahanth of Bodh-Gaya, who is a Saivite (II. 66 and X. 96). It was suggested in cross-examination of the custodian that there were disputes between them in regard to the Hindu offerings at the tree, but so far from such being the case, he deposed that the Mahanth's men appropriate the pice, while the Gayawals' men take all the other offerings (II. 66). It is established therefore that the Bodhi tree at the Temple itself has been abandoned as an object of Hindu worship, and that the Mahanth has acquiesced in that arrangement.

I now turn to the question of the existence of Hindu worship inside the Temple. It has been mentioned that a votive *stupa* did duty as a *lingam* in the *sanctum*. As it existed in 1872-73, when Mr. Beglar visited it, the place was oblong instead of square, as is the all but universal custom in Hindu temple building (Archæological Reports, Vol. VIII., p. 67). There was evidence, however, in the thickness of the side walls that an attempt had been made to make it square, and he attributed this to the time of Sasangka (600 A. D.), when, according to Hiouen Thsang (Julien II., p. 469), a wall was built in front of the image of Buddha so as to hide it, and an image of Maheshwar was placed in front of it (Archæological Reports, Vol. VIII., pages 67-73). The *lingam* is in the centre of the *sanctum*, as it would have then been reduced (*idem*, p. 71), and Mr. Beglar attributes it therefore to Sasangka also. All this is, of course, mere conjecture, but it is mentioned to illustrate the force of the observation that the *sanctum*, if it ever was made square, was again made oblong against the rule in Hindu temples. See also Rajendra Lala Mitra, page 84, which was quoted by the prosecution. Dr. Rajendra Lala Mitra, it is observed, mentions at page 84, that the *lingam* was worshipped by the Mahanth, but, of course, a remark of that kind is not regular proof, and it is utterly opposed to all the evidence given in this case. There has been some spurious worship of the image of Buddha, as will be presently noted: but otherwise all the witnesses, who were in a position to give evidence on this point, positively deny having ever seen any Hindus worshipping or performing ceremonies in the temple (see I. 5; II. 57; V. 72-73; VIII. 81; IX. 83). The evidence of the custodian on this point is particularly valuable, as he has been in the place for nearly five years now, during which period he has gone inside the temple on 20 to 22 days out of every month and round it daily, and on days when there is a crush of pilgrims, he sometimes has to remain inside all day (II. 62). He never saw any Hindu performing any religious worship in it, though a few would bow before the image (II. 57), which, I dare say, is of no more significance than my taking off my hat, as I always do, when I enter the *sanctum*. And he never saw either the late or the present Mahanth or any of their disciples worshipping or ever bowing the head before the image (II. 57), as Sumangala likewise deposes (V. 73), although he has had ample opportunities of observing, having stayed, for instance, in the Burmese rest-house, which is beside the temple, for seven months in 1891 (V. 71). Babu Durga Shankar Bhattacharjya deposes that no Hindu could worship an image made of brick and mortar, such as he saw in the shrine before the restoration, though one of unburnt clay can be worshipped (IX. 83, 86). Nor did he himself ever take off his shoes in the temple, except when he noticed Buddhist pilgrims at their worship (IX. 83). He never saw anything on either the old or the present image to indicate that it was ever worshipped by Hindus (IX. 88), and no Hindu would ever believe that it was a Hindu deity (IX. 83). The defence have sought to discredit this witness in cross-examination, as he is a friend of Dharmapala, but he is a highly respectable witness, occupying a prominent public position in Gaya (IX), and frankly acknowledged that he was in favour of Dharmapala succeeding in this case, as he considers his cause the right one (IX. 88). The witness, Dr. Hari Das Chatterji (VIII), is his brother-in-law. The latter, whom Counsel for the defence characterised as probably the most truthful witness of all, has deposed to witnessing facts which are quite incompatible with the existence of genuine Hindu worship in the Temple, such as the offering by Burmese pilgrims of Huntley and Palmer's biscuits and the burning of lard candles (VIII. 81). So also Durga Shankar Babu deposed to seeing European essences, such as lavender water, being used in the Buddhist ceremonies there, which would be desecration to a Hindu (IX. 83). The custodian deposes to Europeans entering the shrine with their shoes on, though he leaves his own outside (II. 58). And Muhammadans as well as Europeans, including the Mahanth's own mukhtear, Hussain Baksh, freely enter the temple, as the fact of three of them happening to be present when the image was enshrined, shows.

All the correspondence forthcoming in the office of the Magistrate and Collector in connection with the repair of the temple by the Burmese and Government has been put in from the beginning of 1875 down to 1884 for the purpose of showing how far the Mahanth was consulted in the matter (Exhibits C. 1 to C 22.) The Mahanth was communicated with in November, 1875, on the subject of the proposals made by the King of Burma for the repair and future management of the Temple, but his reply is not forthcoming. Being apparently in the vernacular, it would ordinarily have been destroyed after a time. Its purport is, however, given in letter No. 1177, dated the 8th December, 1875, from the Collector, Mr. Halliday, to the Commissioner of Patna (Exhibit C.3). In agreeing to the proposals, the Mahanth made the reservation that the sacred enclosure of the Bodhi tree should not be pulled down and a new one erected, as there were several Hindu images on it where the pilgrims performed their religious rites; that the Hindu idols near the Bodhi tree should not be destroyed in repairing the temple; that in propping up the branch of the tree, the Hindu idols under the branch should not be injured or concealed by masonry; that similar care should be taken of Hindu idols placed near the Temple many years before, in repairing the various structures in the enclosure; and that the people of the monastery that was to be established should not interfere with the religious rites of the pilgrims who go round the tree. It will be observed that there is not a word here that would imply that there were any Hindu objects inside the temple or that the Mahanth made any reservation with respect to that part of the building.

So also the agreement purporting to be executed in favor of the Mahanth by the Burmese delegate on the 11th February, 1877, which has been filed as part of the written statement, recites that the Mahanth, in permitting the repairs to be done, stipulated that it should be within certain limits to be prescribed by him, for the reason, that near the Temple were many Hindu images and a temple of a former Mahanth and the houses of tenants that were not to be defiled or injured, and reserved his right, arising from immemorial usage, to appropriate the offerings of the Budh *deota*, *i.e.*, Buddha, and of the *pipal* tree and of the deities below the *pipal* tree, saying pilgrims came there to pay reverence and make offerings; but at the same time there is an acknowledgment by the Mahanth that people would remain on behalf of the King of Burma to perform devotions, who would have to conduct themselves as is customary in zamindaris. Not a word is there about Hindu worship or images inside the Temple.

An attempt was made by the defence to show by extracts from the Maha-Bodhi Journal that the complainant has made admissions of the fact of Hirdu worship in the shrine. The passages referred to are Exhibits D. 9, D. 16, D. 29, and D. 31, (Gaya in the last named means Gaya proper). It is unnecessary to discuss their significance as such here, nor was any of them referred to in the address of Counsel. The cross-examination on the subject (I. 22, 26, 40, 41,) and the articles themselves will show, I think, that no probative effect can be given to them as against the case for the prosecution or the general evidence in the case. On a full review of the evidence, I find it established that, at any rate in recent times, no form of Hindu worship has been carried on inside the Maha-Bodhi Temple, and there is nothing to show that any such has actually been carried on in it for many centuries, if ever since Sasangka's attempt about 600 A. D.

But since July of last year there has undoubtedly been an attempt, at the instance of the Mahanth and his disciples, to carry on a semblance of Hindu worship of the great image of Buddha which is on the altar of the *sanctum* on the ground floor of the temple. Since then, as deposed to by the custodian, a Brahman priest, named Bishum Misser, has been employed, who passes a light in front of the image, sounds bells and laves the image and altar (II. 68), and a *tilak*, or Hindu caste-mark, has been painted on the forehead, and the image clothed with a regular vestment, and the head decked with flowers (I. 4, II. 57, V. 72, 75, 76 and VI. 79). The custodian, who is a Kulin Brahman of the highest caste, deposes that, nevertheless, what is done does not constitute complete Hindu worship (II. 68); and it must be remembered that, in spite of all this, neither the Mahanth nor any of his disciples nor any Hindu has ever been seen by him worshipping inside the temple. The defendants' written statement is silent on the subject of Hindu worship ever having gone on in it, but they do not take their stand on the ground that what they did on the 25th February was for the purpose of preventing prejudice to the Hindu character of the shrine, but solely on their belief in the right of the Mahanth as its proprietor to do what he likes with his property. Prior to July, 1894, there had never been any Hindu priest or Brahman at all employed in the temple. The only person who looked after it on behalf of the Mahanth, was a Kshattri, named Jagannath Singh, who acted as doorkeeper and swept the inside, while a Dosadhin woman swept the courtyard (II. 57, 63, 67). A question was put by the defence implying the suggestion that this might be because the Bodh-Gaya Sannyasis do not recognise caste distinction among themselves (II. 67), but the *durwan* was produced in Court, and one could see by his dress he was not a Sannyasi He used sometimes to place two or three flowers on the altar, but this was not by way of *puja*, but merely on behalf of pilgrims to get paid by them for the attention (II. 62, 66). The custodian first saw the form of worship described above, on his return from three months' leave in July last, but it had not apparently begun by the end of May, as Devananda worshipped the great image on the last day of that month. It is immaterial for the purposes of the case against the present defendants to discuss what effect all this had on the religion of the Buddhists, but it is in evidence that Sumangala and Devananda had to confine their worship in consequence to the Bodhi tree, as it was gross defilement of the image, and that when Dharmapala and a party of pilgrims came in January, they removed the vestment and obliterated the *tilak* mark on the forehead before they could perform their worship—an act, by the bye, which was not presumably objected to by those who represented the Mahanth at the temple (V. 72, VI. 79 and I. 54). Since November last, even the votive marble images placed on the altar by the Buddhist pilgrims from foreign countries have been clothed (V. 75, 76). Dharmapala was cross-examined with reference to a passage in the Journal for December, 1892 (Exhibit D. 32), in which he stated that images of Buddha and Boddhisatvas in the Mahanth's *baradari* (reception-house) had been transformed by having clothes put on them, but explained this by saying he merely assumed they were originally Buddhistic images (I. 42). He admitted having seen in an outer enclosure of the monastery, so far back as January, 1891, some Buddhistic images painted red so as to obliterate their Buddhistic aspect (I. 41), and that the Temple of Annapurna Devi in the compound of the Maha-Bodhi Temple is regularly worshipped by Hindus (I. 41). All the Hindu worship started last year in the temple was begun, it will be observed, shortly after Dharmapala endeavoured to place the Japanese image in the temple, and on a review of the evidence there is no room for reasonable doubts that it is of a spurious kind, started as a mere strategem for giving the Mahanth a pretext for interfering with the dealings of the Buddhists with the temple and strengthening whatever prescriptive rights he may possess to the usufruct of the offerings made at it.

This conclusion is not weakened by the evidence put in to the effect that the worship of Buddha as one of the ten *avatars* or incarnations of Vishnu is justified by the Hindu *Shastras*. It is not necessary for me to discuss whether this is strictly justifiable or not. The authorities quoted are the following:—

(1.) *Bhagwat*, Part I. Chapter III. sloka 1 to sloka 2 (Exhibit VI).
(2.) *Do.* Part II. Chapter VII. sloka 37 (Exhibit VII).
(3.) *Vishnu Puran*, Part III. Chapter XVIII. sloka 2 (Exhibit VIII).
(4.) *Vayu Puran*, Chapter 49, sloka 26, page 637 (Exhibit D. 42).
(5.) *Bhavishya Puran*, page 433 (Exhibit D. 43 *a*.)
(6.) *Do.* *do.* *do.* (Exhibit D. 43 *b*.)
(7.) *Do.* *do.* page 399 (Exhibit D. 44).

(These last three in a Hindi translation.)

(8.) *Nirnaya Sindhu*, page 3 (Exhibit D. 45*a*.)
(9.) *Do.* *do.* *do.* (Exhibit D. 45*b*.)
(10.) *Agni Puran*, page 13 (Exhibit D. 46*a*.)
(11.) *Do.* *do.* *do.* (Exhibit D. 46*b*.)
(12.) *Do.* *do.* *do.* 44 (Exhibit D. 47).
(13.) *Lingam Puran*, *do.* 268 (Exhibit D. 48).
(14.) *Varaha Puran*, *do.* 47 (Exhibit D. 49).
(15.) *Do.* *do.* *do.* 250 (Exhibit D. 50).
(16.) *Srimat Bhagwat*, *do.* 118 (Exhibit D. 51).
(17.) *Brihannardi Puran* *do.* 49 (Exhibit D. 52). (Bengali transliteration.)

One of the incarnations of Vishnu was admittedly Buddha, but the Zilla School Pandit (Witness X), who was examined in regard to all these passages, maintained, in opposition to the defence, that this was not the same as the Buddha of the Buddhists, son of Suddhodan. The passages quoted from the *Agni Puran* (Exhibit D. 46) indicate, however, that, no doubt in pursuance of the politic device already referred to, an attempt was made by the Brahmans to establish an identity between the two Buddhas; and the passage from the *Vayu Puran* (Exhibit D. 42) enjoins bowing down at the Maha-Bodhi tree. The device referred to may account for the form of the legend attaching to this incarnation of Vishnu with regard to his spreading of false doctrine to befool the enemies of the gods (*see* Exhibits VII., D. 46 (*b*), and D. 51). Such devices were not unknown in uneducated Christendom, as Mr. Elworthy, for instance, endeavours to show in his recent book on " The Evil Eye," in regard to the identity of the Madonna in Naples and elsewhere with Diana. But, justifiable though the worship of Buddha by Hindus may be, it is impossible to believe that the Mahanth or any other Hindu *bonâ fide* believe that genuine worship of the kind could be performed by orthodox Hindus inside the Temple of Maha-Bodhi, which has, as I have shown, all along been a temple for Buddhists. One of the passages put in by the defence, that from the *Brihannardi Puran* (Exhibit D. 52), indeed lays down the following injunction:—" Should a twice-born go to a *Bauddhalay*," (temple of Buddhists or temple of Buddha, it is not certain which), " even when in great distress, he cannot be freed from sin even by performing a hundred *praschits* (atonements). Buddhists are heretics and deceitful because they speak ill of the Vedas. Therefore the twice-born-one who loves the Vedas should not look at them. No twice-born one who knowingly or unknowingly goes to a *Bauddhalay* can be freed from sin. This has been determined by the Shastras." In any case, if it was felt expedient to endeavour to establish Vaishnavite worship, it was an anomaly for the Mahanth, a Saivite, to set himself up as its founder. All this serves to cast a doubt on the good faith pleaded for him and his followers.

I have dwelt at length on the question of the essentially Buddhistic character of the temple, because the position established by the evidence in regard to it appears to me to have an important bearing on the question of the *bonâ fides* of the belief the defendants profess to entertain that the Mahanth had a right to dictate to the Buddhists what images should be placed inside the Temple and to prevent the enshrinement of any that were unsanctified according to the requirements of the Hindu Shastras, and that they were justified in enforcing or maintaining that right in the manner they admit having done on the 25th of February. The history of the practice of Buddhist worship in the temple has an important bearing also on another aspect of the case—namely, on the contention on the part of the defence that Dharmapala had no right to go to the Temple to enshrine the Japanese image without the Mahanth's consent, unless he could show that the Buddhists had enjoyed such an easement as of right for at least twenty years. But before discussing this point I proceed to deal with another matter in respect of which the defence pleaded good faith, namely, that they *bonâ fide* believed the Mahanth to be proprietor and possessor of the Temple to the extent of having the right to do what he pleased in it. To this point a vast amount of cross-examination of the complainant and Government custodian has been directed, and voluminous documentary evidence has been filed in explanation of it ; but I do not think it will be necessary to discuss much of this evidence in detail, as there can be no reasonable doubt that the defendants did *bonâ fide* believe that the Mahanth did enjoy possessory right of a certain kind over the Temple and its precincts. But it is not so easy to accept the plea that they *bonâ fide* believed this possession to be of so complete a character as to connote full proprietorship or carry with it the right claimed by the Mahanth to do what he liked inside the Temple.

In the first place there is nothing to show that the Mahanth has ever really been proprietor of the Temple. That he is proprietor of the revenue-free village of Mastipur Taradih is, of course, established by the Mogul Emperor's *farman* of 1727 A.D., conferring the grant, which is filed in original (Exhibit D. 19) ; but the complainant is not prepared to admit that the Temple is situated within the limits of the grant. The Survey map filed by the defence (Exhibit D 36) shows a "temple" near the margin of it, which very likely means the Maha-Bodhi Temple. But the complainant appears to have been led to believe that the Maha-Bodhi Temple is really in the village of Bodh-Gaya, or Mahabodh (as I usually hear it called), which belongs to one branch of the Tikari Raj, so much so that the idea appears to have been entertained of purchasing that property from it (I. 23, 27, 30, 45, 50 and Exhibit D. 11). It is a confusion in respect of this that appears to have given rise to the exception taken by Dharmapala to the *kabuliyat* he executed in favor of the Mahanth on the 24th August, 1891, for a piece of land on what is known as the "Fort" in the village of Mahabodh (Exhibit D. 21 and I. 30). I mention all this, however, as merely explanatory of some portion of his cross-examination. But there is no mention at all of the Temple in the *farman*, and of course no weight can be attached to any statements in regard to the Mahanth's proprietary rights in it, made in the History of the Bodh-Gaya *Math* compiled in 1891 by a Deputy Magistrate of Gaya, apparently from information supplied by the Mahanth, which has been put in by the defence as Exhibit D. 18. However, we are justified in assuming for the purposes of this case that the Temple is really on land which is the property of the Mahanth, but this does not make the building itself his property ; compare the case of *Thakur Chandra Paramanik*, B. L. R. Sup. Vol. 595 and 6 W. R. 228, and *Safru Shaikh Darzi vs. Fath Shaikh Darzi*, 15 W. R. 505, the latter of which deals with the right of the proprietor of the ground to a building used as a house of prayer ; and there is absolutely no evidence that he ever exercised any proprietary rights in the Temple. But the defence consider that it is sufficient for the purpose of this case that they *bonâ fide* believed the Mahanth to be owner of the place, and that he had every reason to entertain this belief in consequence of admissions to this effect made by Government. For instance, in the List of Ancient Monuments published by Government in 1879 and 1886, the Mahanth is spoken of as a person "who owns the place," though this does not necessarily mean the temple building (Exhibit D. 41, page 127, and Exhibit D. 61, page 121), and on page 120 of the latter, the Temple is described as being in his "custody." Again the defence allege in paragraphs 7 and 8 of their written statement that since 1891 they have been in possession of certain correspondence which passed between the then Collector, (Mr. Grierson,) the Commissioner and Government in that year, in which Mr. Grierson enquired whether he might give the Mahanth a copy of the instructions issued by the Superintending Engineer for the guidance of the Government custodian, in which that officer stated that "the building is not the property of Government, and is only taken charge of with the consent of the Mahanth." Mr. Grierson, as the letter shows, could find no correspondence in his office as to the arrangement come to when the repair of the temple was undertaken, and it appears from Exhibit C. (see evidence of the Head Clerk called by the Court) that the correspondence put up to him went back no further than 1884. The correspondence itself proves nothing, as it ended in a decision by Government not to take any action at present in the matter to disturb existing arrangements, whatever these were (see also Exhibit E. 2 completing this correspondence); and if the custodian has not been under a misapprehension in this respect, Mr. Grierson's personal opinion, elicited in cross-examination by the defence, appears to have been adverse to the Mahanth's proprietorship (II. 59, 60, 64, 67). The point however which the defence make is that as the Mahanth had had the letters in his possession since 1891, they were justified in the belief they entertained as to his proprietorship. It is apparent from the copies of the correspondence filed with their petition of the 6th May, that it was obtained in some unauthorised manner from the custodian's office. But how can I believe that the Mahanth had the letters mentioned in paras. 7 and 8 of the written statement until after the case arose, when a misleading statement has been made in the next para. as to his possession of Mr. Grierson's letter of 11th November, 1891, which the defence never got till I handed it to them within a couple of days of the written statement being filed, it not being one that had ever gone to the custodian at all? In the latter para. the words "has been since the year 1891," which occur in the previous paras., have been scored through under the initials of defendant's pleader, but this does not alter my utter disbelief that a copy of that letter was ever in the possession of the Mahanth at all.

The correspondence showing the terms on which the repair of the Temple was undertaken by the Burmese and subsequently by Government, has now been obtained and filed in this case (*vide* Exhibit D. 20 filed by defence and Exhibits C. 1 & C. 22). From this it appears that when the King of Burmah asked the good offices of the Government of India in connection with a deputation he was sending to see about repairing "the compound of the Bodhi Tree," (*i.e.*, the premises of the Maha-Bodhi Temple), and locating two priests near it for the purpose of daily worship at the Tree, the Collector of Gaya, Mr. Palmer, wrote to the Mahanth on the 15th January, 1875, enquiring whether he approved of and agreed to this. The Mahanth's answer has been searched for, but is not forthcoming. Then in November, 1875, the specific proposals of the King were communicated to him, and the letter No. 1177, dated 3rd December, 1875, from the Collector, Mr. Halliday (Exhibit C. 3), gives the purport of his reply, the material portions of which I have already set out in discussing the existence of Hindu images on the premises. The Mahanth apparently asserted no claim to the Temple, but was merely anxious to preserve the Hindu images lying about from injury. He agreed to give land free of cost for a monastery and treasure-house the King wished to erect, on an agreement being executed for the land. Then the agreement of 11th February, 1877, executed by the Burmese delegate in favor of the Mahanth, which is put in as part of the written statement of the defendants, contains an acknowledgment that the Temple is in the zamindari and possession of the Mahanth, and that the limits, within which the repairs were to be carried on, were to be prescribed by him so as not to injure the Hindu images and Mahanth's temple (really mausoleum) that were near, or the houses of his tenants. It does not appear from the subsequent correspondence that the Mahanth was consulted in any way when Government took the repairs out of the hands of the Burmese, so that there seems no foundation for the statement made in para. 3 of the written statement as to his consent having been obtained to the repairs being executed by Government. On the whole, there is nothing in the correspondeuce from first to last that can be held to imply any recognition of the Mahanth as proprietor of the Temple building, though it must, no doubt, be taken as acknowledging certain undefined rights in the vicinity, which rendered it desirable to consult him. The Temple has ever since been kept in repair at the expense of Government, and the custodian who carries out the repairs and is in charge of the building with its enclosure and the relics lying about, always performs his duties without reference to the Mahanth, (II. 66-7). The letters of Mr. Grierson to the Mahanth, dated 3rd April and 8th July, 1889, put in by the defence (Exhibits D. 54 and D. 55) do not help the case in any way. Exhibit F. 1 on which the former was based, shows that the land spoken of as being in the Mahanth's possession was away outside the Temple enclosure altogether, and the correspondence marked C 1 to C 22 shows that the Burmese bungalow, the propriety of repairing which Mr. Grierson suggested to the Mahanth, was built at the expense of the Burmese, and the custodian deposes that it is being kept in repairs at the expense of Government (II. 66).

Notwithstanding all this, there is a door to the Temple of which the Mahanth has the key (II. 63), and it cannot therefore be held that the defendants did not *bonâ fide* believe him to be in possession. But it is clear from the long standing practice of Buddhist worship in the Temple and the dual custodianship which has existed ever since its restoration was undertaken, that that possession is of a modified description and can in any case form no legal justification for the absolute right claimed by the Mahanth to do what he likes with the Temple, as if nobody else had any rights in it at all, and to dictate to the Buddhists what images they are to place and how their worship should be regulated. It seems now unnecessary to refer in detail to the prolonged cross-examination to which the complainant was subjected with the view of eliciting from him acknowledgments of admissions made by him in the Society's Journal as to the Temple being in the hands of the Mahanth and as to his having certain rights in it, which it was proposed to buy up so as to secure full control to the Buddhists themselves. He struggled much to avoid endorsing those admissions, distinguishing rather finely in some cases between personal knowledge and belief, with the result of creating a somewhat unfavorable impression, but much allowance must be made for his position and for the fact of this being his first appearance in a Court of law (I. 48). The defence must have felt that they had realised the wish of the worthy who exclaimed "Oh that mine enemy would write a book!" It would certainly be going too far to draw an inference adverse to the truthfulness of Dharmapala. The Exhibits which bear on this point are the following, but only Exhibits D. 11, D. 12 and D. 13 were quoted by Counsel in his address ; D. 1, D. 2, D. 3, D. 4, D. 5, D. 6, D. 7, D. 8, D. 9, D. 10, D. 11, D. 12, D. 13, D. 14, D. 16, D. 30, D. 33, and D. 37.

The general effect of those, for which Dharmapala is responsible, may be taken, in the light of what he had said in cross-examination, to be that the Maha-Bodhi Society have been desirous of extinguishing by purchase on equitable terms any legal rights the Mahanth might be found to have in the place, without at the same time expressly admitting that he has any lawful right. Be that as it may, there does seem ground for believing that the Mahanth has been in the habit of appropriating, by some sort of prescriptive right, offerings made by pilgrims at the Tree and Temple, though it may be a question whether his right to take them is other than that of a trustee, and it may be observed that he agreed to the proposals made in 1875 for the erection by the King of Burmah of a *paribhoga* or building for the deposit of the royal offerings (Exhibit C. 3). But it is difficult to give him or the defendants credit for a *bonâ fide* belief that this right to take offerings included the right to remove images from the Temple, as alleged in para. 12 of the written statement, and, in particular, to remove the Japanese image the complainant had enshrined in the upper *sanctum*.

Counsel for the defence contended that it was for the prosecution to make out a right to go to the Temple and enshrine the Japanese image without the Mahanth's consent, by proving that they had enjoyed such an easement as of right for at least twenty years. This contention is based on the provisions of Section 26 of the Limitation Act XV of 1877. But there is a long course of rulings to show that this Act is merely a remedial one, and neither prohibitory nor exhaustive, and that while its provisions would enable a person to acquire a right who had no other right at all, they do not exclude or interfere with the acquirement of rights otherwise than under them, so that proof of long enjoyment may justify the presumption of a grant or other legal origin of the easement independently of the provisions of the Act. See the Privy Council case of *Raj Rup Koer vs. Abdul Husain* (I. L. R. 6 Cal. 394), and also the following:—I. L. R. 6 Cal. 812; I. L. R. 8 Cal. 956; I. L. R. 5 Mad. 226, and I. L. R. 6 Bom. 20. Similar presumption of a grant was made in a series of rulings prior to the passing of the earlier Limitation Act of 1871, but it is unnecessary to quote any but the latest of these already cited, namely, *Safru Shaikh Darzi vs Fateh Shaikh Darzi*, 15 W. R. 505, which is in some respects analogous to the present case, and is to the following effect:—"A thatched house which had been used by the proprietor of the land whereon it stood as a house of prayer for himself, family, neighbours, and the public, having been blown down, a brick-built one was erected in its stead by public subscription and maintained for the same purpose. After the proprietor's demise, his heirs claimed the right and title to the house. Held that the consent of the proprietor, added to the long use of the house by the public, entitled the public, by way of implied grant, to the occupation of the same as a house for prayer, and the plaintiffs could not succeed."

Now in the present case there is historical proof that the Temple was used as a Buddhist one for ages before the Mahanth's organisation ever settled in Bodh-Gaya (about three centuries ago) or became the proprietors of Mastipur Taradih (in 1727 A.D.,) and no evidence that the Mahanth's permission has ever been required for the worship by Buddhists, which is proved to have gone on regularly in it in recent times; and I have already found it established that "at any rate in recent times no form of Hindu worship has been carried on inside the Maha-Bodhi Temple, and that there is nothing to show that any such has actually been carried on in it for many centuries, if ever since Sasangka's attempt about 600 A.D," until after the Mahanth attempted to exclude the Japanese image a year ago. I consider, therefore, that there is in the present case sufficient proof of the existence of a Buddhist right of worship and placing of images in the Temple, absolutely free from regulation by the Mahanth, to throw on the Mahanth the burden of proving that it should not be presumed to have had a legal origin, whether with his consent or otherwise. I hold that it is not the case that either on the 19th May, 1894, or on the 25th February, 1895, there was any subsisting possession or right on the part of the Mahanth which the defendants were justified in maintaining as against Dharmapala's right to place the Japanese image in the Temple.

I do not think, however, that it is necessary in this case to determine what the real legal civil rights in the matter are. Be that as it may, I think that the defendants *bonâ fide* believed that Dharmapala had been prevented on the 19th May, 1894, from placing the image in the Temple until he received the Mahanth's consent, and that, that prohibition subsisted, and that the common object in going to the Temple on the 25th February was to remove it, and not to commit the offences described in Chapter XV of the Code. Their conduct, however, indicates that though two mukhtears happened to be present, they entertained doubt as to their right to remove the image, once it had been placed on the altar, for they did not venture to attempt to do this themselves, though demanding of the complainant that he should do so, until at least one reference to the Mahanth had been made. At the same time, having regard to the current of judicial rulings on the subject, I find it difficult to hold that what they did amounts to enforcement of a right by show of criminal force under circumstances legally constituting an offence under section 143, Indian Penal Code.

Having regard also to the position of the Mahanth with reference to the Temple and the object with which the defendants made their actual entry into it, I do not think that there is sufficient proof of the "trespass" and knowledge at the time entry was made that such entry would be likely to wound the feelings of the Buddhists, which are essential ingredients of an offence under Section 297, as expounded in the unreported case relating to the Gaya Church.*

* *Hafiz Abdur Rahman vs. Empress*: see Appendix to Judgment, *post*, p. 159.

There remain the offences under Sections 295 and 296 with regard to the defilement of the image and of the altar and *sanctum* where it was placed, and the voluntary disturbance of an assembly lawfully engaged in worship and ceremonies.

The image of Buddha is a very sacred object to his worshippers. To enshrine one in a temple is one of the highest forms of Buddhist worship, and its subsequent removal from the altar would be a gross insult and injury to the feelings of its worshippers (I. 4, 5; V. 73), and the defendants admit that they regarded it as one to be treated with a certain amount of respect (para. 22 of written statement). But I entertain a certain amount of doubt as to whether, under all the circumstances of this case, as described fully in the present judgment, the defendants knew that the removal of the Japanese image on the occasion of its being enshrined for the purpose, as they no doubt did believe, of creating evidence of a right adverse to the Mahanth, would likely be considered by Buddhists as a class as an insult to their religion. The defence to this section must rest on the provisions of Section 79 of the Penal Code and the burden of proving actual justification in law, or *bonâ fide* belief owing to misconception of fact, rests, under Section 105 of the Evidence Act, on the accused. In this case no justification in law has been made out for the removal of the image, even although it may have been *bonâ fide* believed that it was placed in the temple solely for the purpose of creating evidence of a right adverse to the Mahanth; but there is some ground for believing that the accused were under a misconception of fact as to enshrinement of the image having been accomplished, so as to make its removal an actual defilement of it. It is undoubtedly not easy to understand how any misconception of fact in regard to the matter should have arisen, but having regard to all the circumstances of the case, there does exist a doubt in my mind on the subject, more especially as regards the knowledge that Buddhists *as a class* would be likely to consider themselves insulted, and I think the benefit of that doubt may reasonably be accorded to the accused. Still less do I feel myself justified in holding that there was criminal defilement of the altar and *sanctum* under the circumstances, with the above knowledge. This must not be understood to imply that I for one moment accept the presumptuous claim advanced in paragraph 24 of the written statement that, because the defendants are Hindu Sannyasis and holy men, and the Buddhists are *mlechhas*, touching or removing a Buddhist image could not amount to defilement or insult! An acquittal of the charge under Section 295, Penal Code, in respect to the image, precludes the issue of any order under Section 517, Criminal Procedure Code, for its disposal, but it is of course open to the complainant to go to the Civil Court, the proper tribunal to decide such a question, and seek an injunction to restrain the Mahanth and his Sannyasis from interfering with its replacement in the temple or continuance therein.

With regard to the charge under Section 296, Penal Code, however, of voluntarily disturbing an assembly engaged in devotional contemplation constituting a recognised form of Buddhist worship, I cannot possibly entertain the slightest doubt as to the guilt of the accused who entered the *sanctum* on the occasion of the actual removal of the image. The facts are beyond dispute. The defence indeed allege that the worship was not *bonâ fide* (para. 21 of written statement) and say that they are "not prepared to believe" the evidence of Dharmapala and his witnesses that the mere sitting in silence constituted worship according to the Buddhist religion, or that it was improper to disturb it (para. 25); but there is no attempt made in cross-examination to destroy the effect of the evidence given as to this being indeed the chief form of Buddhist worship (I. 3 and V. 72), or as to Dharmapala and his companion priests being actually engaged in the performance of this form of worship, when the defendants rushed in and disturbed it by their tumultuous conduct and the removal of the image. It may be said, though it has not been actually urged in this case, that Dharmapala did not specifically mention the disturbance of religious contemplation in the statement he wrote down when the police came up to the place (Exhibit I), but he distinctly mentions, quite apart from the other acts he complained of, that they were insulted when they were at their *devotions*, and that he kept perfectly still at the removal. It cannot be held that this in any way contradicts the evidence in this case as to their having been disturbed when they were in devotional contemplation, as he was not cross-examined on the point after drawing his attention to the matter. The statement to the police was not intended as a full account or as a complaint, as an angry mob was around and his mind was not calm (I. 44), and the introduction of the reference to the Government letter about freedom of worship shows how his narrative was interrupted. Besides the statements of the Buddhist witnesses themselves, there is the evidence of the custodian that he witnessed their contemplation (II. 67). The demeanour of the complainant's companion priests and of the custodian under examination unmistakeably proclaim them to be witnesses of truth; and no attempt has been made in cross-examination to show that their narrative of the occurrence has been embellished in one single detail.

It has not been contended for the defence that the three Buddhists who were engaged in worship, did not constitute an assembly within the meaning of Section 296. In the Christian scriptures, there is warrant for holding merely "two or three persons" to be a gathering for worship, if animated by the necessary spirit, and if a conviction under Section 29 could be had for disturbing two or three Christians under such circumstances, it could also be had in the case of Buddhists.

That their worship on that occasion and in that place was lawful, is beyond dispute, in view of all that has already been held as established in this judgment. Dharmapala had worshipped in that *sanctum* before whenever he went to the upper storey (I. 39). It is of no avail for the defendants to plead that they had never witnessed any such worship in that particular *sanctum* before, nor do I understand that any such contention has been advanced in this case, nor can it be any defence to this charge that they thought the worship to be a sham. That it was genuine cannot for a moment be doubted. Dharmapala had every reason to feel assured that, when the people had almost all retired after the Hindu mukhtear had made some of them get off the altar, he was secure from further interruption and may well have felt some ecstacy which would add unusual earnestness to his devotions (I. 38). The defendants gave themselves no time to assure themselves that the sitting in silence on that occasion was mere sham. They did not pause when they observed it or act with due care and attention, in other words with "good faith," in proceeding to do what they knew must necessarily disturb it. There were there already apparently some few of their number who had been quietly watching the whole time about a quarter of an hour (I. 38), and they never thought of asking them about it (I. 38). When they saw this, what was the occasion for the hurry to remove the image, merely to prevent the creation of evidence adverse to some supposed right of the Mahanth? Why could they not have waited for the police to whom Hussain Baksh had gone to give information and who came up in six or seven minutes after this, the outpost being outside the Mahanth's gate about 400 or 450 yards from the temple? It would have been sufficient for the purpose they had in view to await their arrival and make formal protest before them. Why would they not at any rate have gone back and consulted the Mahanth when they found worship going on? He had already been advised by the Deputy Magistrate not to do any thing, but to inform the Magistrate or the Police, as the mere placing of the image could not create any possession (IV. 70, *see* also III. 69), and it must be remembered that Hussain Baksh, whom the Mahanth originally told to go and see what was going on, was present when the Deputy Magistrate and Special Sub-registrar went to the Mahanth and also the other mukhtear Vijayananda Barma (III. 69 and IV. 70 and latter's written statement). There is indeed nothing to show that these two mukhtears came to the temple on the final occasion and very likely they did not: but this should have made the rest all the more cautious in acting as they did without them to advise them. The history of this case shows that it was not Dharmapala who was practising sham religion, but the Mahanth himself for the sake of temporal advantage.

Apart from the tumult, the mere removal of the image constituted a disturbance of the worship. It must have been manifest that the Buddhists were contemplating before it, and Dharmapala deposes that the presence of the image was necessary for the performance of this form of worship, and that its removal disturbed it (I. 3, 37, 51, 52). This is the chief and most characteristic form of Buddhist worship which the defendants must have constantly seen performed at the Temple and the Tree (where there is also an image of Buddha on the wall), as I myself have on many occasions; and evidence as to this having been practised before seemed apparently so unnecessary that I find specific questions were not asked by the prosecution on the subject (but *see* VI. 78 and V. 71). Above all the tumultuous manner in which the removal of the image was carried out by a crowd of thirty or forty people, must effectually have disturbed the worship of the Buddhists, and no amount of argument on the subject of *mens rea* will get over the patent fact that the accused, when they did this, knew, or at any rate had good reason to believe, that this would be likely to cause such disturbance. Under Section 39 of the Penal Code, therefore, they caused it "voluntarily," and if that state of mind existed, as it unquestionably did, an offence under Section 296 is made out. I have carefully read the remarks of the Indian Law Commissioners, quoted to me by Counsel for the defence, on the chapter relating to offences against religion, and I find nothing in them to militate against the view of the law on the subject of guilty knowledge which I take here. Much of what is there stated refers rather to offensive remarks made in the course of religious discussions or preaching than to disturbance of religious worship. In this matter there could have been no possible misconception of fact which could have led them in good faith to entertain the belief that they were justified by law in disturbing the complainant and his companions when obviously engaged in silent devotion. The burden of proving that there was such, under Section 79 of the Penal Code, would in any case rest upon them. It is unnecessary to discuss the effect of the passages and rulings quoted by Counsel for the defence from Maxwell on the Interpretation of Statutes in regard to the English doctrine of *mens rea*. I have carefully read them all, and the conclusion I have come to is, that in a comprehensive code of general offences like the Indian Penal Code all this has been provided for in the general explanations and exceptions contained in Chapters II and IV, and by the introduction of such words as "voluntarily" into the sections defining the offences themselves. I cannot conceive how this doctrine can seriously be applied to warrant the disturbance of worship that took place on this occasion on the ground that the defendants believed they were justified by law in endeavouring to prevent what they believed to be an attempt to create evidence of some right infringing on those of the Mahanth.

Let me put forward two hypothetical cases which might meet the circumstances of this case. Suppose I owned an estate in Scotland containing an old abbey which fell into neglect and disuse on the supplanting of the Anglican by the Presbyterian form of worship, and that I considered myself owner of the building, or at any rate was in possession. Suppose that fifteen years ago I repaired it at my own cost and permitted Anglican worship to be resumed in it without imposing any restriction as to particular forms of ritual to be observed. Would I have a right to come into the place and disturb a few worshippers assembled and engaged in worship, in order to prevent candles being lit on the altar? Surely it would be held that I voluntarily disturbed their worship. I might believe I had a right to remove the candles afterwards, but I could not help being aware that my act must necessarily disturb worship, if I did it at the time.

Again suppose I lent a portable organ for the service in the church, but, finding it was getting injured, I prohibited its being used, and said I should remove it if it were opened. If afterwards I heard it being played on and sent a number of my retainers, who were aware of my rights and the above prohibition, to remove it, would they if, on entering the church, they found silent prayer going on, be excused if they went up to where the organ was and began to remove it out of the church? I had evidently a right to remove the instrument, but could I do so while service was going on? Even though I believed it was being played on solely to assert a right to continue to do so, I should not be justified in attempting to remove it until the service was quite over.

In every view of the case I find that an offence under Section 296 of the Penal Code has been established in respect of the worship that was going on. It only remains now to consider who were concerned in causing that disturbance. There is abundance of testimony that Mahendra Gir was there, and indeed, took a personal part in moving the image (I. 2, 3, 4, 38; II. 57; V. 72; VI. 77). Not only the Buddhists but the custodian speak to this. The custodian also saw Jaipal Gir take part in removing, though he did not actually touch it (II. 57). Both these persons took a leading part in the affairs of that day from first to last, and there could be no mistake as to their identity. Their appearance is of a marked character. The witness, Sumangala, also deposes to Bhimal Deo Gir having taken a personal part in lifting the image (V. 72). He says three persons altogether actually removed it, and two of them were Mahendra and Bhimal Deo (V. 72), and in para. 19 of the written statement the defendants admit that two of their number removed the image from the altar. Mahendra, Bhimal Deo and Jaipal were specifically charged with removing it (head V. of charge), and these three also have been specifically charged with disturbing the worship (head IV. of the charge). All of the defendants have, however, also been included in a general charge of disturbing the worship by their tumultuous entry along with others (head III. of charge). There is no specific evidence, however, that Shivanandan or the two mukhtears were among those who did so. It must be assumed, as Palis Silva (witness VII) was not cross-examined, though it was not thought necessary to examine him in chief, that he would not have contradicted the evidence of the rest on the above points. No attempt whatever has been made in cross-examination to shake the evidence of the witnesses as to the identification of the persons who took part in the several stages of the proceedings, and the written statement contains admissions implying that all of the Sannyasi defendants went into the *sanctum* for the purpose of removing the image, and there is no qualification limiting this only to the first visit to the place. I find it proved that the accused Jaipal Gir, Mahendra Gir and Bhimal Deo Gir took part in committing the various offences charged under Section 296 of disturbing the worship.

I have anxiously considered what sentence I should impose upon them. It is apparent that no mere sentence of fine would be any punishment to the accused themselves, as pecuniary penalties would no doubt be at once paid by the Mahanth, and it is necessary to bring home to each of them individually the responsibility for acting with due care and attention irrespectively of the instructions they may actually receive from the Mahanth to enforce the altogether unproved right he claims to interfere with what the Buddhists may do in the Temple, in the exercise of their free right of worship in it, and to remove images that have been enshrined by way of devotion on the altars. But the acts of the accused on this occasion were altogether unjustifiable in the disturbance they caused to the Buddhist worship, and had those whose feelings were wounded on this occasion belonged to a less peaceable religion than the Buddhist, the consequences might have been most serious. Jaipal Gir and Mahendra Gir took a leading part throughout the whole affair, and it seems necessary to impose some restriction on their impetuous spirit and deter them in future from acts such as they were guilty of on this occasion. I have, therefore, after full consideration of the matter, come to the conclusion that it is expedient for the ends of justice to impose a sentence of imprisonment, but in consideration of the order to which they belong, I think that it may appropriately be simple. The justice of the case might possibly be met by such a sentence without carrying the right of appeal, but in view of the attention which the case has received at the hands of both parties, I think it desirable to afford them an opportunity of filing a regular appeal. I accordingly add a sentence of fine. I find the accused Jaipal Gir, Mahendra Gir and Bhimal Deo Gir guilty of an offence under Section 296 of the Indian Penal Code of voluntarily causing disturbance to an assembly lawfully engaged in the performance of religious worship, as set out in heads I. III. and IV. of the charges framed in this case, I acquit them on the other charges drawn up. I acquit the rest of the accused on all the charges.

The order of the Court is that the said Jaipal Gir, Mahendra Gir, and Bhimal Deo Gir, be each sentenced to undergo simple imprisonment for a term of one month, and to pay a fine of one hundred (100) rupees, or in default of payment to undergo fifteen days' additional simple imprisonment.

I make no order as regards the disposal of the image, which has formed the subject of this prosecution.

GAYA,
19th July, 1895.

D. J. MACPHERSON,
District Magistrate.

P.S.—With regard to the question as to whether the acquisition by the Mahanth of the proprietory right in the land on which the Maha-Bodhi Temple stood, could carry with it the right to regulate worship in the temple itself, I had intended to add the remark that, supposing a Hindu purchased all proprietory rights of a Muhammadan *malik* in a certain village which contained a mosque owned by the Muhammadan as *malik* of such village, no one would surely say that this would give the new Hindu proprietor a right to dictate to the Muhammadans how they should worship in it—supposing, to complete the analogy, he had consented to their continuing to worship there—or that the new proprietor could ever in good faith believe he could exercise such a right. This, of course, is merely by way of illustration and argument, and as it was not incorporated in the judgment, it cannot be taken as part of it, but should be included as a postscript in the copies to be issued of it.

GAYA,
20th July, 1895.

D. J. MACPHERSON,
District Magistrate.

In the Court of District Magistrate of Gaya.

No. 280 of 1895.

H. DHARMAPALA *versus* JAIPAL GIR and others.

ORDER SHEET.

1. This is an important complaint, and I wish to consider what offences are disclosed in it before passing further orders. Adjourned in the meantime till to-morrow.

28th February, 1895. D. J. MACPHERSON, *Magistrate.*

2. Heard Counsel on the subject. Orders will be issued after I have considered a report, which the police have submitted on the occurrence.

D. J. MACPHERSON,
1st March, 1895. *Magistrate.*

3. Summonses ordered to issue under sections 143, 295, 296, 352, 380 and 506, I. P. C., against Jaipal Gir, Mahendra Gir, Shivanandan Gir, Bhimal Deo Gir, Hussain Baksh and Vijayananda Barma, mukhtear, and under Section 295 against Rami Panre for the 13th March.

D. J. MACPHERSON,
4th March, 1895. *Magistrate.*

4. In this case an application is made on behalf of Mr. John, who appears for the defence (and I have, since coming to Court, received a similar application by telegram from Calcutta from Mr. Cotton, who says he is also engaged for the defence), praying for a postponement of this case until Monday, the 18th instant, on the ground that the defence wish Counsel from Calcutta who cannot come to-day. I intimated that, while prepared to hear the examination-in-chief of the witnesses for the prosecution to-day and part of to-morrow, I could not fix any other day for hearing the case until after the visit to Gaya of His Excellency the Viceroy, as the defence stated that the cross-examination would be somewhat prolonged, that of one witness being likely to last a couple of days. Defence Counsel stated that he was instructed in any case to press for postponement of the cross-examination of witnesses until the 18th; but I remarked that in view of its being likely to be lengthy, I should postpone that. Counsel for the prosecution, while prepared to go on with the examination-in-chief of witnesses for prosecution to-day, consented to the adjournment of the whole case, and it was thereupon, with consent of parties, adjourned to Monday, the 8th April. It was understood that possibly a convenient arrangement would be to hear first the case so far as it depended on the facts of the actual occurrence, and to postpone going into the evidence affecting the questions of possession and right, but this was left an open matter.

The accused are all present, and are hereby ordered to give each bail in Rs. 150 and recognizances in Rs. 500 to appear on the 8th proximo and on all further dates fixed for hearing until finally discharged. The witnesses present will give Rs. 25 recognizance to appear on that date and until further orders.

D. J. MACPHERSON,
13th March, 1895. *Magistrate.*

5. Examination-in-chief of complainant and part of that of second witness taken. Case adjourned till to-morrow for reasons recorded on deposition of latter.

D. J. MACPHERSON,

8th April, 1895. *Magistrate.*

6. Examination-in-chief of witnesses for prosecution, who are present, taken, except Singhalese witnesses, for whom an interpreter is required. Two witnesses present, one of whom was not cited by the prosecution, but was called by the Court, are discharged as not being needed. Case adjourned till to-morrow for evidence of Singhalese witnesses, in the hope that an interpreter may be here by then.

D. J. MACPHERSON,

9th April, 1895. *Magistrate.*

7. The interpreter not having come, the case is adjourned to to-morrow.

D. J. MACPHERSON,

11th April, 1895. *Magistrate.*

8. To complete the record, it is here recorded, with the consent of parties, that all the accused are represented by Messrs. John, Cotton and Halim, Barristers-at-Law, and that the accused have authorised them to appear on their behalf. The same is said on behalf of the accused as regards Babu Moti Lal Das, who appears as pleader for them all. It was agreed that it would suffice if depositions were read over to witnesses in the presence of one of these on behalf of the accused.

Evidence of remaining witnesses present recorded. Case adjourned to to-morrow morning, at request of both parties, for remaining witnesses for prosecution not yet present. All witnesses, except complainant, will give Rs. 25 recognizances each (but Palis Silva Rs. 100) to appear on the morning of 2nd May for cross-examination, and Mr. Dharmapala to appear on 1st May for cross-examination, dates being arranged to suit convenience of Counsel.

D. J. MACPHERSON,

12th April, 1895. *Magistrate.*

9. Examined three more witnesses for prosecution. The prosecution say they do not propose to examine more witnesses or ask now for the commissions previously applied for, in order that the case may not be prolonged, and it seems unnecessary to call more evidence. But they may file some documentary evidence between now and the next date.

The case is now adjourned until the 1st of May for cross-examination of the witnesses for the prosecution. The defence intimated that it might be convenient to them to go on with the evidence for the defence immediately thereafter, and the Court stated that it would probably find this convenient also.

The accused Rami Panre is discharged under section 253, Criminal Procedure Code, as no evidence has been offered against him specifically (see separate judgment).

The other accused will be on the same bail and recognizances as before to appear on 1st May. The witnesses examined to-day have been ordered to appear on the 4th May.

D. J. MACPHERSON,

13th April, 1895. *Magistrate.*

10. After complainant was recalled to prove two documents, the defence claimed the right to have charges framed before commencing cross-examination of the witnesses for the prosecution. The prosecution objected to this, as after the cross-examination, it might be necessary to modify the charges, which would give the defence a right to recall the witnesses for still further cross-examination, and besides, if the framing of charges be postponed till cross-examination is over, the case might possibly be shortened, as it might not be found necessary to frame any charges at all. The defence stated that by knowing beforehand the charges to be met, they would be able to curtail cross-examination, as it was never anticipated that a claim would be made to frame charges at this time, and the Court had not looked at the evidence since last hearing nearly three weeks ago. So as to be able to judge what charges should be framed, while the prosecution also were probably unprepared to specify precise charges, it was decided to adjourn the case till to-morrow for the purpose of framing charges, the defence declining to begin cross-examination to-day even though charges would be drawn up to-morrow morning before going on further. It was arranged that the prosecution should, at the close of cross-examination, have a right to apply to modify or add to the charges. The defence intimated that they expected to be able to finish the cross-examination by Saturday next, the 4th instant, and would call their evidence, so far as procurable in time, immediately after such was finished, and undertook to do everything possible to assist in bringing their witnesses to Court in the beginning of next week so as to enable the case to go on to an end *de die in diem*.

D. J. MACPHERSON,

1st May, 1895. *Magistrate.*

11. The accused were examined to-day, but refused to answer any question. The framing of the charges was then discussed and charges drawn up, read and explained to the accused who pleaded not guilty. They were then called on to enter on their defence, and Counsel said he would do so by recalling and cross-examining the witnesses for the prosecution. On the application of Counsel for the defence, as it was getting late, the cross-examination was postponed till to-morrow.

D. J. MACPHERSON,

2nd May, 1895. *Magistrate.*

12. Complainant was recalled and cross-examined the whole day, and case was then adjourned till to-morrow.

D. J. MACPHERSON,

3rd May, 1895. *Magistrate.*

13. Complainant under cross-examination the whole day. Case adjourned over Sunday to the 6th instant.

Counsel for the defence applied to be allowed until Monday to mention the names of their witnesses, as there was only one who was not living in Gaya, and it might not even be necessary to examine him.

D. J. MACPHERSON,

4th May, 1895. *Magistrate.*

14. Complainant under cross-examination the whole day. Case adjourned to complete it till to-morrow.

D. J. MACPHERSON,

6th May, 1895. *Magistrate.*

15. Complainant under cross-examination and re-examination the whole day. Case adjourned till to-morrow.

D. J. MACPHERSON,

7th May, 1895. *Magistrate.*

16. Cross-examination and re-examination of other witnesses for the prosecution taken, and case adjourned till to-morrow for cross-examination of remaining witnesses for prosecution.

The correspondence of the Magistrate's and Collector's office that had been called for by the defence, was produced, and arrangements made for its inspection, the Commissioner of the Division having intimated that there was no objection to its production.

D. J. MACPHERSON,

8th May, 1895. *Magistrate.*

17. At the commencement of proceedings to-day, prosecution gave notice they would put in a notice, that had been issued by Mr. Boxwell, as Magistrate, declaring the right of one Dharamraj to worship and remain in the Temple, and had only just been found. (It is referred to in the correspondence produced.) Defence said they would object. This matter was postponed.

Cross-examination and re-examination of other witnesses for the prosecution was continued, and case adjourned till to-morrow for cross-examination of remaining witnesses for prosecution, &c.

D. J. MACPHERSON,

9th May, 1895. *Magistrate.*

18. Cross-examination of remaining witness gone on with, and case adjourned to to-morrow to finish that of one.

D. J. MACPHERSON,

10th May, 1895. *Magistrate.*

19. Cross-examination of remaining witness finished. After other proceedings case adjourned to later on to-day for completing case and filing of written statements.

D. J. MACPHERSON,

11th May, 1895. *Magistrate.*

20. The Court met again in the afternoon and put some questions to complainant and the witness for the prosecution, and defence then stated what documents forming part of the official correspondence produced they wished to put in, and discussed the relevancy and irrelevancy of it respectively on the questions of its admissibility as relevant. The Court reserved its decision. The defence then put in three written statements which are hereby ordered to be filed with the record. The case is now adjourned to Monday morning (to-morrow being Sunday) the 13th instant, for arguments of Counsel, and filing of the Sanskrit passages recited by the Pandit called for the prosecution and his translation in Hindi of these and also of those he was cross-examined on.

D. J. MACPHERSON,

11th May, 1895. *Magistrate.*

21. Complainant examined further by Court, one witness recalled to file passages from Sanskrit works, one witness (Head Clerk) called and examined by Court as to correspondence exhibits. Court intimated what correspondence would be admitted, but reserved record of formal order of it and marking of it as exhibit. Case was then closed, and Mr. Sutherland for the prosecution addressed the Court on the case. Case adjourned till to-morrow without his completing his address.

D. J. MACPHERSON,

13th May, 1895. *Magistrate.*

22. Counsel for prosecution (Mr. Sutherland) concluded his address, and Mr. Howard for prosecution also addressed Court on one matter, namely, the registered document forming part of the written statement. Mr. Monomohan Ghose, Counsel for defence, then addressed the Court and had not concluded when the Court rose for the day. Adjourned till to-morrow.

D. J. MACPHERSON,

14th May, 1895. *Magistrate.*

23. Mr. Ghose addressed the Court during the whole sitting to-day. On the conclusion of his address, the Court intimated that it would take time, probably till after the end of this month, to deliver judgment, and would give notice in due course. Defence asked for a week's notice of the date. Case therefore adjourned *sine die*. Accused told to appear again when called on.

D. J. MACPHERSON,

15th May, 1895. *Magistrate.*

23. I have been unable, owing to pressure of other duties arising from congestion of work consequent on the time which had to be given up to this case during the month of May, and a succession of annual reports to write in various departments, to obtain leisure to devote myself entirely to a study of this case for some days in succession until the other day. Consequently, I have been unable to deliver judgment in the case until to-day.

Judgment has been delivered convicting the accused Jaipal Gir, Mahendra Gir and Bhimal Deo Gir of an offence under section 296 of the Indian Penal Code, and sentencing them each to one month's simple imprisonment and to a fine of rupees 100, or in default, to fifteen days' additional simple imprisonment, and acquitting them of the remaining charges, and the rest of the accused of all the charges. No order made as to the disposal of the image.

D. J. MACPHERSON,

19th July 1895. *Magistrate.*

H. DHARMAPALA *versus* RAMI PANRE.

(*Section 295, Penal Code.*)

ORDER OF DISCHARGE.

In paragraph 13 of his written petition of complaint, and in the penultimate paragraph of his complaint as recorded in this Court, the complainant laid a charge of defilement of the great image of Buddha on the ground floor of the Maha-Bodhi Temple by Hindu *tilak* marks being put on the forehead and a coloured vestment on the figure and flowers on the head. In issuing process against a number of persons who were charged with having removed an image of Buddha from the upper floor of the Temple and disturbing the worship before it, I accordingly directed process to issue under Section 295 of the Penal Code against the priest in charge of the shrine on the ground floor, adding that his name seemed to be Rami Panre. Summons was accordingly issued for Rami Panre, and he has appeared and been present while the evidence for the prosecution has been given in this case. No evidence has, however, been produced to show that Rami Panre is the person who defiled the image in the manner alleged, and the prosecution intimate that they are not proceeding against Rami Panre. I assumed that that was the name of the priest who caused the defilement because in a cross proceeding he was named as the priest in charge, though it was there stated that he was appointed only on the 1st of Phagun. As no evidence is offered against him specifically, I discharge Rami Panre under section 253, Criminal Procedure Code; but it will, of course, be open to the complainant to apply for similar process against whoever he may have evidence of having caused the defilement complained of. As the evidence in chief for the prosecution in the general case has now been completed, that charge, if renewed, would now be tried separately, for it is presumed that some of the witnesses for the prosecution would be those already examined and would in any case therefore have to be examined *de novo*.

D. J. MACPHERSON,

12th April, 1895. *Magistrate.*

APPENDIX.

JUDGMENT IN THE GAYA CHURCH CASE.

In the High Court of Judicature at Fort William in Bengal.

The 26th February, 1895.

CRIMINAL JURISDICTION.

Present:

THE HON'BLE MR. JUSTICE NORRIS,

AND

THE HON'BLE MR. JUSTICE BEVERLEY,

(Two of the Judges of the Court.)

IN THE MATTER OF HAFIZ ABDUR OR ABDUL RAHMAN ... ... *Petitioner,*

versus

THE QUEEN EMPRESS ... ... *Opposite party.*

THE petitioner in this case, Hafiz Abdur Rahman, and seven others were convicted by the Deputy Magistrate of Gaya under Section 297 of the Indian Penal Code. The petitioner and six of the accused, all Mahomedans, were sentenced to six months' rigorous imprisonment, and one of the accused, Sukhi Christian, was sentenced to nine months' rigorous imprisonment. The convictions and sentences were upheld on appeal by the Sessions Judge.

The facts of the case are as follows :—

On the 19th October last, Mr. McLeod, an Engineer in Burma, who was spending his furlough in Gaya and living just opposite the Church of England Church there, observed a light in the Church, and on looking through one of the windows, saw some fifteen or sixteen men gambling with pice and cowrie. He reported what he had seen to Mr. Holmwood, the District and Sessions Judge, not in his official capacity, but as a person interested in the Church. Mr. Holmwood requested Mr. McLeod to make a sworn statement to the Joint Magistrate. This was done, and the Joint Magistrate ordered a police enquiry to be made, the result of which was that the petitioners and seven others were sent up for trial under Section 297 of the Indian Penal Code.

The accused, Sukhi Christian, who is the Church bearer, made a statement to the Deputy Magistrate as follows :—"I am in charge of the Church buildings. Last evening at about candlelight I was inside the Church. Bakor, Budhu, Abdul Rahman, Lall Mahomed, Mohamdu, Toran, Kalal, all of Gayalwal bigha, all these men were at the Church. Bakor, Budhu, Abdur Rahman, Toran were gambling inside with shells (6-cowries play). They were playing for coppers. The men were of my Mohulla, so they came in. I did not call them, I was not playing or gambling. I stood there."

This statement, which was subsequently withdrawn, the Deputy Magistrate calls "a confession;" and the Sessions Judge speaks of it as "a full confession." It is in no sense of the word a confession.

The Deputy Magistrate examined five witnesses in support of the charge against the accused persons and seventeen witnesses for the defence. Two of the witnesses for the prosecution, Bisu Kahar and Buddesur, deposed to "seeing Sukhi Christian leading the rest of the accused to the Church." Mr. McLeod swore to having seen some fifteen or sixteen men gambling in the Church, but he was unable to identify any one but Sukhi. Sukhi's so-called confession was, under Section 30 of the Evidence Act, "taken into consideration" as against the other accused persons. As the statement was not a confession, this was clearly an error on the part of the Deputy Magistrate.

We think that in law the conviction cannot stand.

Section 297 of the Indian Penal Code provides that "whoever with the intention of wounding the feelings of any person, or of insulting the religion of any person, or with the knowledge that the feelings of any person are likely to be wounded, or that the religion of any person is likely to be insulted thereby, commits any trespass in any place of worship or in any place of sepulchre or any place set apart for the performance of funeral rites or as a depository for the remains of the dead, or offers any indignity to any human corpse, or causes disturbance to any persons assembled for the performance of funeral ceremonies, shall be punished with imprisonment of either description for a term which may extend to one year, or with fine, or with both."

To sustain a conviction under this section, it must be proved that the accused persons trespassed into the Church with the intention or knowledge mentioned in the section. Being in the Church and doing an act with the intention or knowledge mentioned in the section is not sufficient. There must be trespass, an unlawful entry, into the Church Now the evidence for the prosecution shows that the accused, other than Sukhi, were led into the Church by him. He was the Church bearer, and the accused may well have believed that he had authority to let them into the Church ; but however that may be, if they were let into the Church by him, they cannot be said to have trespassed therein. Then as regards Sukhi himself, he clearly cannot be said to have trespassed.

In the result, the rule must be made absolute, the conviction and sentence of the petition set aside, and he must be discharged from his bail bond.

Having the records before us in the exercise of our revisional jurisdiction, we set aside the convictions and sentences of the other seven accused persons and direct that they be released and discharged.

We feel bound to add that even if the convictions could be upheld, the sentences passed were out of all proportion to the offence committed.

The Courts below do not find that the accused persons had any such intention as it is mentioned in the section. They find only that they had knowledge that the Christian religion would be insulted. Even if the accused persons had this knowledge, looking at the fact that the extreme penalty provided for a trespass into a place of worship with the deliberate intention of insulting the religion of any person, is one year's rigorous imprisonment with or without a fine, and considering that, in all probability, the accused had the knowledge which has been imputed to them, and that their object in going into the Church was to gamble in security from the interference of the police, a far lighter sentence would have met the justice of the case.

JOHN F. NORRIS.

The 26th February, 1895.

H. BEVERLEY.

True Copy.

J. LOUIS,

Assistant Registrar, High Court.

Certified to be a true copy.

BIRESWAR BOSE,

14th May, 1895.

Head Clerk, Gaya Magistracy.

PART II.

PROCEEDINGS IN THE APPELLATE COURTS.

PART II.

INDEX.

PROCEEDING.

HAVING heard Mr. Cotton, Counsel for the appellants, on the question of bail, I find that the sole ground of conviction is that the Magistrate holds that the defendants acted with *mens rea* within the meaning of Section 296 of the Indian Penal Code. As the Buddhists were apparently sitting motionless, as no force or violence appears to have been used, and as the Mahanth of Bodh-Gaya disputes the *bonâ fides* of the worship, I think that this is a question for argument *prima facie;* and as there is no chance of the case being argued before me until Wednesday next, I consider it advisable to admit the accused to bail each in his own recognisances in Rs. 500, together with one surety each in Rs. 500.

H. HOLMWOOD,

19th July, 1895. *Sessions Judge.*

Appeal admitted subject to amendment, and, as far as I know at present, Wednesday next, the 25th instant, will be fixed for hearing. I shall be obliged if Mr. Macpherson could let me have the judgment this evening for an hour or two. I will return it the first thing to-morrow morning. The Magistrate will kindly see the bail order carried out.

The Judge has informed me he means Wednesday, the 24th. Intimate and take fresh bonds.
D. J. M.
20th July, 1895.

H. HOLMWOOD,

19th July, 1895. *Sessions Judge.*

Release at once, to appear on 25th.

19th July, 1895. D. J. MACPHERSON,

Magistrate.

COURT OF SESSIONS, APPELLATE JURISDICTION.

The 30th July, 1895.

CRIMINAL APPEAL NO. 13 OF 1895, FOR 3RD QUARTER, 1895.

Appeal from the order of D. J. Macpherson, Esquire, District Magistrate of Gaya, dated the 19th July, 1895.

1. JAIPAL GIR .... }
2. MAHENDRA GIR ... ... } *Appellants.*
3. BHIMAL DEO GIR .... }

For the Appellants.—Mr. M. Ghose, Mr. Cotton, and Mr. Stevens, Barristers-at-Law, and Akhori Lakshmi Narayan, Pleader.

For the Crown.—No appearance.

For the Prosecutor.—Sir Griffith Evans, Advocate-General, Mr. Sutherland, and Mr. Howard, Barristers-at-Law, and Babu Nand Kishore Lall, Pleader.

JUDGMENT.

THIS is an appeal from a judgment of Mr. D. J. Macpherson, District Magistrate of Gaya, convicting the three appellants under Section 296 of the Indian Penal Code of voluntarily disturbing an assembly of Buddhists on the upper storey of the great Pagoda of Maha-Bodhi at Bodh-Gaya on the 25th

February, 1895, and sentencing them to simple imprisonment for one month each and a fine of Rs. 100 each, in default 15 days' further simple imprisonment. The accused were originally charged with other accused under several other sections of the Penal Code, including Sections 295, 297 and 143, and one Hussain Baksh was charged in addition under Section 352. It is argued that the net is cast thus wide in order to catch the accused somewhere, and that in the event of a conviction under Section 295 an order under Section 517 of the Criminal Procedure Code was contemplated, restoring the image to the place in the temple whence it was removed by the accused. The charges were settled in Court by the learned Counsel on either side and the Magistrate, and I do not think that in any case any inference of fact as to the intentions of the prosecutor, who is a Singhalese, absolutely ignorant of the Indian law, can be drawn from a purely legal discussion. The consideration upon which Mr. Macpherson has acquitted the accused could not arise until the judgment came to be written, and there was evidence on the record which *prima facie* rendered it necessary to consider the charges framed. I do not think that in any case an order under Section 517, prejudicial to the proprietary rights of the Mahanth, could have been passed. The second clause of Ssection 517, Criminal Procedure Code, obviously implies that the order for disposal of property must be by consigning it to one or other of the parties, or by destroying or confiscating it. Nothing in the nature of a perpetual injunction restraining the Mahanth from removing the image could be passed under that section. An order to restore the image to the prosecutor at the spot where it was taken away from him would have been futile, as if he chose to leave it there, and the Mahanth has the right to remove it, a right which can only be determined in a Civil Court, no order under Section 517 could prevent the Mahanth from disposing of the image as he chose.

Mr. Macpherson, in a long and exhaustive judgment, extending to 102 pages, has fully set out all the facts and circumstances nearly and remotely connected with the case, and his full review of the history of the temple and the ancient authorities on Hindu and Buddhistic lore, which render his judgment a most valuable State paper and a contribution to the polemic literature on the much vexed question of the respective rights of Buddhists and Hindus, (which will no doubt be read with interest long after those questions are settled, either by judicious compromise or by the only judicial tribunal which can settle them, *viz.*, the Civil Courts of this country, and Her Majesty's Privy Council,) has opened the door to considerable discussion in my Court as to the limits to which this criminal case must necessarily be confined, and I think to a good deal of unnecessary animadversion on Mr. Macpherson's assumed unconscious bias in the matter.

It will clear the ground for my decision in this appeal if I at once lay down that I fully accept the last proposition that Mr. Manomohan Ghose, the learned Counsel for the appellants, laid before me in his general reply on the case, that if the proved facts do not bring the accused strictly within the four corners of Section 296 of the Indian Penal Code, this conviction cannot stand. It is necessary, therefore, to set out what are the ingredients required to bring an accused within the penalties prescribed by that section, and to see that facts that have been proved in this case bear on those ingredients, and how far they establish them or fall short of doing so.

According to the defence those ingredients are :—

1. That the disturbance must be caused "voluntarily," and in this connection Mr. Ghose dwells at great length on the doctrine of *mens rea*.

2. That the Buddhists were lawfully engaged in worship.

3. That the religious worship must be real worship, and not a sham.

It may be conceded that the worship must be real worship in the sense that it must be the worship proper to the sect and to the occasion, and that so much is included in the word "lawful" and the word "religious." But that every member of the assembly must be perfectly sincere and single-minded in his worship, as the cross-examination of Dharmapala and the violent attacks on his good faith would seem to suggest, is, of course, a matter with which the law can have nothing to do, and the addition of the words "religious ceremonies," as differentiated from "religious worship" in Section 296, would seem to strengthen the contention of the prosecution that no immunity from this section can be claimed by a person, because he believes, however honestly, that the assembly is not worshipping in reality. The very argument put forward by the defence shows how impossible it would be for the law to take any account of the sincerity of the worshippers.

It is argued that before the Court can hold that there was any intention voluntarily to disturb the assembly, there must be evidence that the accused knew that the Buddhists were engaged in lawful contemplation. Mr. Ghose argues that Dharmapala himself says (p. 3 of the paper book printed by the defence, to the pages of which I shall always refer as P. B. for the sake of convenience and ready reference) that after the removal of the image he remained sitting as before, but not in religious contemplation. How are the accused to know what was going on inside Dharmapala's mind, and at what particular moment he was in religious contemplation, and therefore engaged in worship? Obviously the law can take no cognizance of such distinctions. Either the posture of contemplation is the outward and visible sign of Buddhist worship and the accused knew this, or it is not such a sign, or the accused did not know it. The knowledge that it is not religious worship may absolve a man, as in the illustration given by Mr. Ghose of a number of dacoits suddenly falling down when they are going to be arrested, and saying, "now we are in religious contemplation, you cannot touch us." The fallacy in this illustration lies in the fact that unless the assembly is engaged in an honest act, showing that they are intending dacoity, (*sic*) no body has any right to arrest or molest them. Once a man has a knowledge that they are dacoits, the right to arrest or eject is established, and their sitting down in religious contemplation in order to escape arrest or ejectment would no more affect that right than their attempting to run away. I find as a fact that it is the well-known outward and visible sign of Buddhistic worship to sit in contemplation in the attitude in which the sitting Buddha is often depicted, and that the accused had the best possible means of knowing this. A great deal is made of the fact that the enshrinement of an image is said to be the highest form of Buddhistic worship, but this had seldom if ever been practised before, and how could the accused be aware of it?

It is, however, in evidence that on every occasion of Buddhistic worship specially referred to in the record, before the Bo Tree (p. 79, P. B.), before any statue of Buddha selected by the pious from among those in the niches round the Temple (p. 79, P. B.), before the great image on the lower floor when cleansed of its Hindu trappings (p. 72, P. B), before the marble images placed in November, 1891, by the Burmese in front of the great image (p. 75, P. B.), this outward and visible sign of Buddhistic worship was invariably employed, and the Sannyasis are surrounded whenever they go in the Temple, all over the courtyard and even in their own monastery, with representations of Buddha, many in this exact attitude and many with this only difference (as in the case of the Japanese image in dispute) that the hand of Buddha is uplifted to teach or to bless. It is, as the Magistrate finds (p. 85 of his Judgment), and the learned Advocate-General very forcibly argues before me, impossible to believe that the defendants did not know this. But Mr. Ghose argues that even if they did know this they had good and valid grounds for believing that the assumption of this attitude on this particular occasion was a sham and a fraud merely intended to create evidence of a right. He also argues that their state of mind, being absolutely known, the Court cannot go into the question of "reason to believe." The limitation which the learned Advocate-General places on the word "voluntarily" by referring to its definition in Section 39 of the Penal Code cannot apply to a case where the state of mind of the accused is certain. The only idea in their mind was that Dharmapala had come to set up evidence of a right opposed to the proprietary rights of their master the Mahanth, and there is no reason to suppose that they noticed Dharmapala's attitude or that of his priests, or attached any significance to it. In this connection he reads passages from Maxwell on Statutes, pp. 115, 116, and the Report of the Indian Law Commissioners. He also cites *Reg. vs. Tolson*, 16 Cox, 629. I must hold, as the Advocate-General very properly pointed out, that the passages in Maxwell and the principles laid down in *Reg. vs. Tolson* merely apply the limitation of the Penal Code contained in the words, "voluntarily," &c., to the old incomplete and uncodified statutes of the English Law, whereby a man could be hanged for any felony irrespective of his intention, as far as the wording of the Law was concerned, and the Report of the Indian Law Commissioners is of little worth as a commentary on the chapter of the Indian Penal Code on offences against religion, inasmuch as the present sections of the Code, which are only four in number, do not appear to have been in any way based on the eleven sections drafted by the Law Commissioners, nor upon their commentaries thereon. For instance, the Law Commissioners wished to give license to missionaries to deliver religious addresses to large bodies of Hindus assembled at fairs and other open-air gatherings of a semi-religious character, as all Hindu gatherings are. No offence could be maintained, unless the missionaries actually assaulted the Hindus. The Penal Code has abolished this distinction. Missionaries can now preach in Hindu assemblies only at their own risk, and it will be for them to show that they have not used language offensive to Hindu religion, if there is a disturbance.

The findings of the Magistrate on which the defence rely for the proposition that the "state of mind" of the accused is absolutely known, are as follows:—First, on page 59 (Judgment, see p. 145, P.B.) the finding amounts to this, that the accused *bonâ fide* believed the Mahanth to be proprietor, and his rights were undefined [p. 66 J., see p. 146, P.B.; *vide* also page 70, (p. 147, P.B.], a passage on which Mr. Ghose also greatly relies, although it appears to me that the Magistrate who had before spoken of the Mahanth's right as "undefined," goes a long way in this passage towards defining them. Secondly, on page 74, (p. 148, P.B.) the Magistrate finds the defendants *bonâ fide* believed that Dharmapala had been prevented on the 19th May, 1894, from placing the image in the Temple until he received the Mahanth's consent, and that that prohibition subsisted. Thirdly, he finds (p. 76, see p. 149, P.B.) that their intention was to prevent Dharmapala from creating evidence of a right adverse to the Mahanth. We have, therefore, say the defence, in these three findings, a complete account of the state of mind of the accused at the time of the occurrence. This I cannot admit. A thousand thoughts and many motives may be present together in the human mind, and the learned Counsel for the defence had made a precisely similar logical omission in dealing with Dharmapala's motives. There is also another flaw in the argument. I am asked to find that the defendants had a right to act on any civil rights which they *bonâ fide* believed the Mahanth to possess, and it is rightly argued in the same breath that the civil rights of the parties cannot be touched on in this case.

How this affects the case can be seen by a consideration of the one purely civil question, which the defence have endeavoured to raise, *viz.*, the absence of any evidence of an easement extending over twenty years in favor of the Buddhists, and the consequent contention that the Buddhists' worship in the Temple is permissive and not as of right. Now there can be no doubt that this is a question purely of civil law, and therefore must be rigidly excluded from this case. By what criterion, then, are we to judge the claim of the Buddhists to have lawfully entered the Temple on the 25th of February and the claim of the Mahanth to forcibly eject their image? The Buddhists may or may not have a twenty years' easement in the Temple. They cannot set it up in this case. It has never been declared by a Civil Court, and the Criminal Courts are precluded from entering into it. The Mahanth is undoubtedly owner of the place, as far as the present knowledge of any body in the world goes. There have been allusions to some theory that the great Temple is really situated in the seven annas Raj of Tikari, but such a theory has never yet assumed the form of a legal allegation supported by evidence, and is really quite in the clouds. For this reason I do not think it necessary to refer to the survey map, which was exhibited in this connection. I use the expression "owner of the place" advisedly, as it is the strongest expression of the Mahanth's proprietary right on the record. It is to be found at page 121 of the Government List of Ancient Monuments in Bengal, 1886. (Exhibit D. 61.) The passage runs thus:— "Thirty-two pillars of this railing (the Asoka railing) were also traced in the veranda of the private residence of the Mahanth or Abbot who owns the place." It is true, Mr. Macpherson shows, that the account of Bodh-Gaya, given in this publication, is very inaccurate, and requires altogether revising at the present day. But Mr. Ghose argues, and I think rightly, that this was the unauthoritative declaration of Government in 1886, and the Mahanth can rely on it as such. But what is connoted by the words, "the Mahanth or Abbot who owns the place"? The use of the expression "Abbot" as explanatory of "Mahanth" implies a trust and not an absolute proprietary right, while the wrod "place" in its literal sense, which is all the law can look at, means the "site" or "mahal" in which monastery, Temple and precincts are alike situated. It is argued that the Magistrate's finding of proprietorship with limitations prejudges certain civil rights. No limitation to the Mahanth's proprietorship can be considered until he puts it to the test, and his right to do any act or any order with the property is questioned. In this connection I threw out the doubt whether the Mahanth could be considered to have the right to pull down the great Pagoda and turn it into a vegetable garden. Mr. Ghose contended that the Mahanth's predecessor had undoubtedly had the right to remove the ruins from his grounds, and he thought it was arguable whether the gratuitous act of the Bengal Government in restoring the Temple could not have made any difference to his civil right. Such a question could, however, only be decided when it arose, and the Mahanth was not likely to be so foolish as to destroy a shrine which brings him Rs. 80,000 a year.

I may here mention that it is exceedingly doubtful whether the great Pagoda itself brings the Mahanth and his college even Rs. 1,000 a year. The agreement between the King of Burma and the Mahanth, dated February 11th, 1877, clearly shows that at that time the income of the shrine itself was almost *nil*. It was in absolute ruins, and Burmese pilgrims only came at odd times. It cannot be pretended that any Hindu gave the Mahanth one pice for the mere antiquarian pleasure of looking at it. The object of pilgrimage in the vicinity, which the King of Burma agreed not to interfere with, is enumerated in the agreement (annexure A., p. 107, P. B.), and for the purpose of this argument the printed translation, which is said to have been made by a translator of the High Court,* may be accepted. There is no direct mention, however, in this document of the principal source of income to the Mahanth for the precincts of this great Temple, *viz.*, the Hindu Bo Tree with its great platform covered with Hindu images and emblems, which stands well away from the shrine at a distance of some forty to eighty yards to the north, where the Vaishnava pilgrims, who are of course the great source of income to Gaya, and the Gayawals come in their hundreds to offer *pindas* to their ancestors. Of course the Mahanth as a Saivite has nothing to do with this worship, but in his character of proprietor he reaps liberal toll from the devout. This is indicated in the evidence of Bipin Bihari Banerjee, the Government custodian, at pages 61, 62, 66, and more specially page 68, of his evidence (P. B.) It is true he says (p. 67) that he does not know whether the Brahmans, who came with pilgrims on behalf of the Gayawals, are Vaishnavas or Saivites, but this extraordinary ignorance is self-convicted by its own terms. The fact that they come on behalf of the Gayawals and offer *pindas* proclaim them Vaishnavas beyond all doubt, though the point is immaterial. Indeed it establishes, if any thing, the fact that the Mahanth exercises the right of collecting toll from pilgrims of all sects. It will be seen from pages 196 to 198 of Martin's *Eastern India*, Vol. I, a book relied on by the defence, that the *Dasnam* Sannyasis, to which order the Mahanth belongs, are not themselves visited by outside pilgrims. They have many followers or disciples of three castes only, but these all join the order and give up distinction of caste. The principal income of the Mahanth from pilgrims, therefore, must be derived from the

* NOTE.—A copy of the translation put in by the defence during the hearing of the appeal, will be found at page 18, post.

Vaishnava Hindus who come with Brahmans deputed by the Gayawals. But in addition, he has an enormous zemindari endowment, and his Sannyasis, who travel all over the neighbouring districts, are assiduous beggars (Martin's *Eastern India)*, and collect much from the villages.

Before leaving the document, annexure A. (P. 107 P. B.), I wish to make a short digression for the purpose of pointing out that for. three out of four of the statements for which it was relied on by the defence, the translation is wrong, and exceedingly misleading. As this document may be looked upon as the Magna Charta of the Buddhists, an accurate translation of it is essential.

The four passages are :—

1. "Budha Bhagwan" (God), line 6.
2. "And in the possession of," line 10.
3. "That he offers his worship and idols," (lines 21, 22).
4. "And to assist in the worship" (lines 25, 26).

Now, with the exception of No. 2, which is correct, I have no hesitation in finding that these passages, as translated in the printed book, are grossly misleading.

The translation of Bhagwan, as used by the King of Burma, by the word God, is not only wholly without authority, but is quite contrary to ordinary usage. "Bhag" means (*vide* Forbes' Dictionary) prosperity, or supreme power ; "wan" is an affix, denoting the holder of Bhagwan, and in its ordinary sense is translated "adorable," "divine." It is also applied by Hindus to the Deity, the Supreme Being, just as Bhagwat, "divine," "glorious," is. But to translate it as God here is begging the whole question, misleading a Court into thinking that the King of Burma speaks of Buddha as "The God Buddha." Now, "the Lord Buddha" is the invariable translation of this and similar expressions in Buddhistic writings, and there can be no possible suggestion that the King of Burma in the year 1877 meant to admit that Buddha was an *avatar* deity of the Hindus or indeed that he was a deity at all.

The third passage runs thus in the original : "*Aur us Budh Deota ka aur pipal ka nichhe jo deota oghairah hain us ka puja hamare shudamad-i-kadim se chali ati hai, aur jatri log wahan darshan ko ate hain aur puja karte hain.*" These are, it will be observed, the words of the Mahanth, and may be literally translated as follows: "And of that Budh Divinity and of the Divinities and other objects that are beneath the *pipal* tree, the worship (*puja*, including both offerings, and spiritual worship) of those is going on according to ancient custom, and the pilgrims come to worship (*darshan*, confined to spiritual worship) there, and do *puja* (as before) there." Not a word about a long-standing practice of the Mahanth's that he offers his worship to the god Budh and idol. The *deota oghairah* under the *pipal* tree are of course the Hindu Deities and emblems referred to by Bipin Bihari Banerjee, and with these we have nothing to do. The Budh Deota may be conceded to be some image of Budh, which the pilgrims may have worshipped as an *avatar* or incarnation of Vishnu, but does not necessarily or probably refer to the hideously ugly image mentioned by Dr. Rajendra Lala Mitra as newly set up in the great Temple by the King of Burma in 1877, nor would it in any case have been worshipped by the Saivite Mahanth. It much more probably refers to the present great image on the ground floor, which was there on the same authority (Dr. Rajendra Lala Mitra, pp. 84, 85) in a little Hindu Temple within the precincts of the Math. While engaged on pp. 84 and 85 of Dr. R. L. Mitra's book, on which Mr. Ghose greatly relies, I would point out that this great authority goes on to say (on p. 85), speaking of the upper or second storey room (the place of occurrence in this case) :—"There was unquestionably a highly-prized statue in it, for it was the *sanctum sanctorum* to which only the select few, who feed the priests heavily, were allowed to enter." He is here of course speaking of ancient Buddhist times. I mention this here, though it is not relevant to this part of my judgment, to save the necessity for referring to these pages again when I come to consider the *bonâ fides* of Dharmapala.

I now come to the fourth passage, which runs in the original :—" *Aur waste hifazat us puja aur mandil ke hamare chela log wahan par rahte hain aur hifazat rakhte hain,*" which may be translated "and for the protection of that worship and of the Temple our disciples live on the spot and take care of them." This, read with the further provision that the care of the shrine will not devolve on the King of Burma's servants, but his servants shall only remain there for the purpose of conducting worship on behalf of the King of Burma, obviously can only bear the interpretation put upon it by the learned Advocate-General, namely, that the King of Burma has no occasion to look after the preservation of the place, as that is the Mahanth's business, but his priests, Buddhists of course, can remain and do Buddhistic worship there as long as they conform to " the zemindari rules of the zemindar." What then, I again ask, is the criterion by which the conduct of the Mahanth and his disciples must be judged in a Criminal Court? He rigidly and very properly excludes all civil questions and relies only on that assertion of possession which is always relevant in criminal cases. What possible criterion can there be but his own acts and declarations? Dharmapala's acts and motives are, as Mr. Ghose points out, only a secondary consideration. He claims to have shown that they are all sham from beginning to end, but if as a fact, his motives were mixed, and he and his priests were really engaged in an act of lawful worship, the existence of mixed motives in his mind is immaterial. The accused have no right to assume that his motives are necessarily bad. The leading element in the defence is that the Mahanth had the right to prevent the enshrining of an image in his Temple and that his disciples did not know that they were doing anything beyond enforcing that right. To follow strictly Mr. Ghose's doctrine as to the limitations of the Mahanth's proprietorship, what rights has he claimed before this occurrence and what acts has he done to constitute Bodh-Gaya a place of public worship for Buddhists and possibly also for Hindus? Has he done anything to derogate from the right claimed since 1877 by Buddhists to freedom of worship and from the expressed declaration of the Bengal Government that there is perfect freedom of worship for Buddhists in the Temple, and that the Government considers (wrongly, as it turns out) that the Mahanth and his disciples are ever ready to meet all reasonable requirements of worshippers?

It is perfectly open to the defence to argue, as they do, that the declaration of the Bengal Government does not in any way bind the Mahanth, but when he says "you can't limit my proprietary rights until I assert something which the Civil Courts declare invalid," it is time to ask what limitations he has voluntarily imposed on himself. That the most despotic of Emperors, as well as the humblest proprietors, can impose limitations on himself, is, I presume, undisputed.

The illustration of the Duke of Devonshire and Bolton Abbey is put before me by the defence. Bolton Abbey is an old ruined shrine, formerly worshipped in by Roman Catholics. The Duke of Devonshire is the proprietor, and it stands on his private grounds. Everybody may come and visit the place and pray in it, if he likes, in his own manner. But, asks Mr. Ghose, if a number of Roman Catholics came with an image or crucifix and tried to set up Roman Catholic worship there, could not the Duke of Devonshire, if he objected to their proceedings, stop their doing so? Could they claim, as of right, to worship in the ancient manner, because the Abbey was last used as a Roman Catholic place of worship centuries ago? The illustration exposes the whole strength of the Mahanth's position, and its extreme weakness as a defence to this case.

It is obvious that the illustration does not touch the crucial point of this case at all, nor has Mr. Ghose, as far as I have been able to discover in all the ten hours of his first argument, or in his exceedingly brilliant and able address in reply to the Advocate-General, in which in a little more than an hour he said more to the purpose than in the whole of the two previous days, offered any argument on the point.

Granted that the Mahanth as proprietor has the right to lock the door of the Temple and prevent people going inside, granted that he has the disposal of all images,—has he the right to interfere with Buddhist worship, which he by his own acts and concessions resuscitated, when it is actually going on, even though an image may have surreptitiously been carried into the Temple without his consent and in derogation of rights which he avers are part of his proprietary right, but which I shall show are rather based on a certain spiritual claim which he has newly asserted only of late and since the controversy about this Japanese image began?

To make the above illustration complete, we must imagine that the Duke of Devonshire entered into a registered and valid agreement with the Roman Catholic King of the Belgians to restore Bolton Abbey as a place of Roman Catholic worship. That the Duke of Devonshire reserved the rights of certain Protestants, who had been in the habit of holding prayer meetings on a platform from 40 to 80 yards off the abbey, and who had also made use of certain small chapels within the precincts for the purposes of Protestant worship. That he also laid it down that the priests must conform to the ordinary rules that governed his tenants, which in this particular case would include non-interference with the Protestants and payment of a toll on every pilgrim who might visit the shrine. That after this agreement was signed, sealed and delivered, the British Government stepped in and said: "Bolton Abbey is a historical monument, and although we have no objection to the restoration of Roman Catholic worship in it, we insist on preserving its distinctive character as an ancient English Abbey and restoring it correctly from an archæological point of view, and we cannot allow the King of the Belgians to repair it after the style of modern Belgian Churches or in any other way he may think fit." That the Duke of Devonshire acceded to this position and Government spent ten or fifteen thousand pounds on the restoration, to which the Duke contributed five or six hundred. That in the meantime the Duke never resiled from his agreement with the King of the Belgians as far as the Belgian priests were concerned, and that, during and after the restoration, not only Belgian but French and Italian priests were allowed to come with pilgrims and conduct worship in the Abbey. That during the restoration, an image was found lying in the tool house of the Duke of Devonshire's garden, and with the Duke's consent set up by the architect in the central shrine of the Abbey. That thereafter Roman Catholics fully adopted the image as a holy relic, and came freely and worshipped before it, no man making them afraid, and the Duke who had retained the key of the Abbey as being still his private property, opened the Abbey to the public every morning and locked it up at night. That the French priests had offered the Duke to buy the place outright or to lease it from him, because the Protestant worship was offensive to them, and the Duke had finally refused to have anything to say to their offers, because the Protestants looked upon the platform as a very sacred place, and the Duke derived a large income from it. That the French priests had appealed to the British Government, who had altogether declined to interfere. That the French priests, finding this image to be an object of mockery and derision to the Protestants, and having no hope of excluding them, went off to Rome and persuaded the Pope to sanctify and present another ancient and valuable Roman image of the same character, but the Duke of Devonshire, under the impression that the Roman Catholics wanted to obtain possession or complete control of the Abbey, refused to allow it to be set up. That certain officious Protestants, remarking that the original image was unclothed and knowing that the Roman Catholics would not worship before an image so travestied, persuaded the Duke to dress it up as a Protestant clergyman, and to print something on its face symbolical of that character. That on the next occasion when the French priests took pilgrims there to worship, they took off the dress thus put on, and having cleansed the image, performed their usual worship before it. That, apprehending that the Duke would repeat the outrage, the French priests resolved to set up the Roman image without the Duke's consent on a platform above the high altar, to which there had always been free access by steps, and which was the place designated for its reception by the Pope, known to the French priests to be a specially sacred place and mentioned in the English records of the Abbey as the *Sanctum Sanctorum.* That this surreptitious placing of the image was further rendered necessary by a claim set up by the Duke for the first time when the Roman image was first presented to have every image that the Roman Catholics might bring to the Abbey, consecrated by a Protestant clergyman and set up by the Duke with his own hands. That on arrival at the Abbey at 9 A. M. on the day after his arrival in England from a prolonged visit to France, the principal French priest and his companions found the Abbey as usual fully open to the public, and in the presence of the Duke's solicitor (a Deist), a neighbouring justice of the peace (also a Deist), and the Government custodian deputed by the Archæological Department (a rigid Protestant), went up-stairs, set up the image and began to light candles before it. That thereupon the Deist solicitor, whose religion was alike abhorrent to both Protestants and Roman Catholics, rushed in with a number of the Duke's Protestant servants, and among them three of his cousins, and snatched away the candles, saying "Go down and worship the dressed-up image below," (for in the meantime the Duke had again had the original image dressed up), "we will not allow you to worship any image up here." That another Protestant solicitor of the Duke happening to come in, was persuaded by the French priests to remove many of the Duke's followers and relatives (for the Sannyasis are all brethren) from the platform, and that while two or three remained to watch, the French priests fell down in adoration before the newly set up image. That, while thus engaged, a number of the Duke's servants headed by his relatives, rushed tumultuously in and carried off the image bodily out of the Abbey, the French priests remaining in adoration, as, like the Buddhists, they do not of course worship the image itself.

These are the exact facts of the Budh-Gaya case as set out in the evidence, and, dropping the illustration, can any body conceive that the Mahanth's disciples are not amenable to the criminal law? That they may be amenable to many of the sections on which the Magistrate has acquitted them is, as was argued by the learned Advocate-General, perfectly possible. With that I have now nothing to do. The facts must be applied to Section 296 of the Indian Penal Code, and the defence on each specific act examined. Is there a particle of evidence that the Mahanth ever resiled from the grant of freedom of religious worship for Burmese Buddhists which he made to the King of Burmah? Can the interference of Government in the interests of Archæology, pure and simple, as the defence themselves maintain, be said to have in any way rescinded his avowed intentions as regards Buddhistic worship? Did he not rather leave the Bengal Government to suppose that they were right in declaring that there was perfect freedom of religious worship for Buddhists, and that he was honestly affording every facility in his power to pilgrims for their worship? Is there a particle of evidence that the Buddhists ever interfered with Hindu interests in the locality, or is there the faintest trace of a connection established between the known and published desire of the Buddhists and the Mahabodhi Society to purchase on lease the Temple, and the setting up of this image as an object of temporary or permanent worship? The connection is pure conjecture. A man's motives must be judged from the reasonable and probable consequences of his acts. Is it possible to conceive that the Mahanth's possession of the Temple could be disturbed by the existence of an un-Hinduized image of Buddha in the Temple, which the Buddhists could worship in peace and comfort? Had the Mahanth or his disciples any possible reason to believe that this could be an attempt to assert possession? Had any Buddhist, either in past Mahantships or within the knowledge of this Mahanth, ever been guilty of violence in word or deed within the precincts of the Mahabodhi shrine? What is the proved history of the Mahanth's objection to this image? In para. 10 of the accused's written statement (p. 103, P.B.) it is averred that "in the year 1894, the present Mahanth of Budh-Gaya, suspecting and believing that the real object of Dharmapala and the Mahabodhi Society was to deprive him of the possession and control of the Mahabodhi Temple, declined to permit Dharmapala or the Buddhists to do any act without his permission, which was likely to infringe upon the rights which he possessed from time immemorial as regards worship by pilgrims in any part of the Temple, and its premises." This is the phraseology of a lawyer, and there is not a particle of evidence to show that any such notice was issued to Dharmapala or to the Mahabodhi Society. The letter to Mr. Macpherson, No. 7 E., dated 12/18th June, 1894, and cited by the defendants in paragraph 12 of their written statement, refers to the Mahanth's right to remove images and votive offerings of any kind, and there is not a particle of evidence to connect it with any act of worship of the Buddhists, or the faintest suggestion that it carried with it any such claim to regulate the worship of the Buddhists as is arrogated to the Mahanth in paragraph 10. No question of the Mahanth's right to remove image or votive offerings of any kind is now before me. The removal there contemplated is, of course, that appropriation by the Mahanth, as part of his perquisites, which the Buddhists had learnt to fully expect in every instance (*vide* page 37, P.B.)

To get at the real facts, we must turn to the cross-examination of the witnesses for the prosecution, which is the only evidential basis of the defendants' case. The origin of the dispute as to the Japanese image will be found in Dharmapala's letter, Exhibit D. 15, at page 25 of the printed book, put in as an exhibit by the defence. There it is averred that the Mahanth originally consented to the placing of the image on the 19th of May. Whether he did so or not is not very material. There is at least no denial of the statement, for the paras. 10 to 13 of the written statement do not deny the original consent, though they assert the final refusal of the Mahanth to allow it. The cross-examination of Dharmapala, however, at page 35 (P.B.) would lead me to suppose that the Mahanth never really consented, except conditionally on the *pránpratishta* ceremony being performed. But it is this *pránpratishta* ceremony, and this alone which caused the trouble, and when we come to consider what it was, its immense significance is at once apparent. The Mahanth claimed the right to turn the statues of Buddha into living Hindu Gods. This would have utterly destroyed their value as Buddhist images. Dharmapala is cross-examined at p. 33 (P.B.) with a view to showing that the Mahanth performed the *pránpratishta* ceremony on the great image when it was originally set up by Mr. Beglar, and that he knew this. But there is not a particle of evidence to show that this was ever done, far less that Dharmapala had ever heard of it. It was not a point which the prosecution had in any way to establish, and it is absurd on the part of the defence to contend that they summoned Mr. Beglar up from Calcutta, and yet the prosecution were bound to examine him. All the Buddhists wanted was an image to worship. They did not object to worshipping their old image when divested of Hindu trappings, although they had no reason to suppose the *pránpratishta* ceremony had ever been performed on them, but they mutually preferred an altogether unsullied image. From a careful perusal of the cross-examination of Dharmapala and his remarks about this *pránpratishta* ceremony, I very much doubt whether to this day he realises the full significance of it. Buddhists as a class do not, as Mr. Macpherson has found, seem to regard any act of an alien, short of mutilation to their images, an act of defilement. This shows that they do not and cannot worship them as Gods, but sit before them in contemplation only. On page 35 (P.B.) Dharmapala speaks of the Mahanth's proposal as "a Hindu ceremony called, I believe, the *pránpratishta*." Evidently he does not know or has not cared to enquire what is its significance. But the point I desire to bring out is the manifest *mala fides* of the Mahanth. He is a Hindu chosen as Abbot for his great learning and piety (see Babu Ram Anugrah's Book, Exhibit D. 18, at p. 3, and Rajendra Lala Mitra, p. 5). He may be as ignorant as he likes of Buddhist worship and doctrines, but he cannot but know that Buddhism is a religion to which his own predecessors were bitterly opposed, and that all the ceremonies of Buddhism are absolutely abhorrent to Hindus. Huntley and Palmer's biscuits, candles of lard, and cheap English scent would be profanation to a Hindu deity. When the Mahanth therefore insisted on turning this Buddha into a Hindu deity, whatever his own theories may be as to Buddha being an *avatar* of Vishnu, he must thereby have intended to prevent Buddhists from ever offering impure articles of food, candles, scent, etc., to the image, and as he allowed this to be done to the great image and other images, it is clear he did not perform *pránpratishta* on them, or regard them as his Gods, as he would be unclean and an outcaste if he ever touched them. It cannot be said that Sannyasis do not know what tins of biscuits, composite candles and English scent are. No orthodox Hindu would ever run the slightest risk of being contaminated. I think there can be no doubt that he made this impossible proposal to Dharmapala, simply to bring things to an *impasse*, or deliberately to interfere with the freedom of worship of the Buddhists. It was a purely ecclesiastical question, nothing to do with his proprietary or possessory rights over the Temple. The above simple principles of Hinduism must, I hold, be equally well-known to his disciples, the accused, all of whom are Sannyasis of his own order, eligible by learning or piety, or even, as Dr. R. L. Mitra avers, by good looks or by personal resemblance to the Mahanth, to succeed him or to be appointed *karpardaz* with the title of Mahanth at any one of the numerous subordinate *maths* of the foundation. What therefore I find the Mahanth and his *chelas* were fighting for was not a proprietary right at all, but a spiritual right with which the Courts have nothing to do, and which could not be put forward as a defence to this charge.

As regards Dharmapala's shuffling about the proprietorship of the Mahanth, I find that, according to our ideas, he undoubtedly did shuffle, but the Magistrate, who saw his demeanour in the witness-box, is convinced he is a witness of truth. It is not alleged that he has lied as to the events of the 25th of February. His religious sincerity and scrupulous truthfulness as to what is connected with that is strikingly brought out in his examination-in-chief (p.3, P.B.), a passage I have already quoted as relied on by Mr. Ghose to show defendant's want of guilty knowledge. Why should he make this admission as to his sitting in the same posture as before, but not in religious contemplation? If he was a witness of untruth, what was to prevent him averring he was in religious contemplation all the time? He does not say this to account for his noticing the removal of the image, for he says he noticed that while he was in religious contemplation, nor, as far as I can make out, from any other sinister motive. Even Mr. Ghose, violently as he attacked his credibility, does not impugn his veracity here. Such a statement would easily have been credited in a country where the capacity of *jogis'* far absorbed contemplation is so well known. But no such advantage is taken by him to make his case a better one. I am not concerned to defend his prevarication as to the proprietorship. If any part of his case in the Criminal Court depended on the Mahanth's rights as proprietor, he has lost it. He was evidently misled as a foreigner and student singularly ignorant of the world, into the belief that it was a matter of supreme importance to deny the Mahanth's proprietary right. Having once embarked on the troubled sea of prevarication, he was an easy tool in the practised hands of the Counsel for the defence. Oriental standards of truth are not the same as ours, and Mr. Justice Field, in his admirable introduction to the Evidence Act, has shown that the maxim *falsus in uno falsus in omnibus* cannot be applied to the East. All his prevarication, however, centres round this one point, and as I hold that the proprietorship of the Mahanth has nothing to do with this case, and his evidence as to the facts of the 25th February, 1895, is unshaken and is corroborated by the witnesses who do not pretend to take up the same position as Dharmapala does with regard to the civil rights in dispute, I do not see how his prevarication affects the case, except as regards the sections where the Mahanth's proprietary right may have been in issue, on which I have nothing to say, as the Magistrate has already acquitted.

It is true Mr. Ghose violently attacks his credibility on another point also, that of the relic of Buddha carried in his writing case, together with the two Government letters; but as the Advocate-General pointed out, it is usual in all countries for religious devotees to carry relics and charms about with them, not for any special purpose, but as a protection from evil. It is his inability to invent any excuse for carrying about a useless relic which seems to have unfavourably impressed Mr. Ghose. It would be much more extraordinary to my mind if a person possessing such a relic, which Europeans would carry on their persons, but Orientals having no pockets and being liable on ceremonial occasions to have to remove their clothes, cannot, should produce it and leave it lying about, while he himself became absorbed in religious contemplation. Its conjunction with the two Government letters is very significant. He set particular store on those letters, though we know, and the English-knowing mukhtear, to whom he showed them, knew, they were of no possible value to him, and he kept them and the relic in his writing case. He expected opposition, and it is characteristic of the peaceful nature of the man that he relied for his protection on the sacred splinter of Buddha's bone and on two Government letters. For a person possessed so strongly with the *cacoethes scribendi* as Dharmapala, there is nothing surprising in his taking writing materials to describe his great adventure as soon as possible after it was over. There is really no reason, as the learned Advocate-General very temperately pointed out, for making this evidence a ground for a violent attack upon the man's veracity.

We find then the Mahanth on and after the 17th May, 1894, deliberately interfering with the freedom of worship of the Buddhists, which he had himself granted, and this in a characteristically ecclesiastical manner, which neither the British Government nor the local authorities would be likely to see any occasion to interfere with. This rankled in Dharmapala's mind, and he determined at whatever risk to secure one spiritual triumph for Buddhism. He is credited with the one sole desire to annex the Temple and revenues of Buddha-Gaya, but—apart from the fact that there is nothing to show what the Buddhistic revenue would be and that in any case he could never touch the endowment of the monastery nor the Mahanth's income from Hindu pilgrims, and would have to pay a large subsidy to the Mahanth for Buddhist pilgrims even if he established all his claims and reached the height of his ambition—the desire to further the ends of Buddhism as a religion is apparent throughout the man's writings and conduct. Another great point in his favor is his extreme peaceableness. Never has he attempted to take a crowd of followers with him, nor has such a thing as a stick or a stone in the hands of a Buddhist been alluded to throughout the trial. What is here said as to Dharmapala applies with equal or greater force to his two companions, the Buddhist priests, who are assumed to be mere creatures of his, and are not deemed worthy of attack either as regards their veracity or their singleness of motive.

Dharmapala's essential insincerity is argued from his not worshipping at Buddha-Gaya more often, and this argument is also specially applied to his priests. The centre of this attack is directed to his having failed to go to the great festival of Buddha's enlightenment on the 19th May, 1894, solely, it is argued, because he could not have his way as regards his wordly purpose of enshrining the image. It is perfectly clear that he did not go because he was afraid of a riot (p. 36 P. B.). Those pilgrims who did venture to go that night went under police escort. The occurrences of that night are only so far important in that they furnish the only instance in which the Mahanth can be said to have made that proprietary use of the key which he claims as the chief symbol of his power to control the worship. When the pilgrims got out there, they found the Temple locked, and it is inferred that the Mahanth opened it only in deference to the Magistrate's order under Section 144 of the Criminal Procedure Code, which being of doubtful validity could not create a precedent for the future. I see no reason to suppose this. It is the usual practice to lock up the Temple at night, and the Mahanth opened it again on this special occasion for the convenience of the pilgrims. He would probably have done the same, if he had only received a demi-official request from the Collector, or even on the application of the pilgrims themselves.

There is this further consideration as regards Dharmapala and his companion priests not coming to worship frequently at the Temple, and that is, that they are enlightened Buddhists, and it must be pain and grief to see what they consider desecration of the sacred shrine daily going on. They know they have no right to complain. They have done what they can for the rank and file of Buddhists, who are presumably not so particular, and they are now waiting for better times. This suggests a far stronger motive for the act of the 25th February than the impossible idea that it could conceivably be any evidence of the establishment of a right. Dharmapala tells us that he experienced an ecstacy of delight at the partial success of his religious adventure, and I can have no reasonable doubt, bound as I am as a Judge to take into consideration the immense power of religious enthusiasm over devout minds, that this was so. And such devotion is by no means incompatible with what Mr. Ghose aptly calls "a little venal perjury," in minds which have succeeded in absorbing the old sophistical axiom "the end justifies the means"; and minds which are devoted to the exclusive consideration of religious dogmas are far more apt to absorb this, the most practically pernicious dogma of them all, than those who, being occupied in the storm and stress of daily life, recognise the fact that for the preservation of society such a doctrine, if carried to excess, can only land its holder in the Criminal Courts.

So much for Dharmapala and his companions. They are fully corroborated by Bipin Behari Banerjee, the Government custodian, a Kulin Brahmin of the highest class, on whose orthodoxy no suspicion of any kind is cast. He also has special instructions to refer to the Mahanth in all things and not to give him reasonable cause of offence, on pain of losing his appointment. He is not, therefore, likely to be a witness deliberately hostile to the Mahanth.

He is only impugned because he is supposed to have shown bias in scratching out certain words which he had entered in the Revised List of Antiquities he was preparing for Government in September, 1893. The circumstances under which he did so do not clearly appear in his cross-examination on p. 63 (P. B.), but he was, in my opinion, perfectly justified in considering that he had no right to impose a purely speculative opinion, which he admits he himself held, on the Bengal Government. His evidence is very important (pp. 57 and 58, P. B.), as showing that the accused clearly understood what they were doing, namely, interrupting an act of worship. They came with the deliberate intention of stopping worship, and the witness saw Dharmapala arguing the matter with Vijayananda, the mukhtear.

I pass over the disgraceful incident of a Musalman mukhtear being employed to interfere in religious question between Hindus and Buddhists, because the Magistrate has for some reason absolved him from guilt, probably because, as he holds, the worship had not begun when the candles were being lighted, and this man Hussain Baksh interfered.

Neither Bipin Behari nor the special Sub-Registrar nor the Deputy Magistrate saw the interference of Vijayananda, but Bipin Behari shows that there was an interval while parleying went on, and I see no reason to suppose that the evidence of the Buddhists that they were left undisturbed for some minutes in worship is not the strict truth. Bipin Behari does not pretend to have been inside all along. He was going in and out, trying to pacify the Sannyasis. Obviously therefore some of them had been persuaded to go outside. The fact is established that the accused came with the first batch (p. 57, P. B.), that they were also actively concerned in the removal of the image, which constituted the interruption (p. 58), after distinct warning that worship was going on, and having ample time and opportunity to see that worship was in the ordinary form of the Buddhists, which they themselves, according to the agreement with the King of Burma, were specially appointed to protect.

I will pass over in a few words the other evidence, which is that of Hindu gentlemen, as to the impossibility of Hindus worshipping in a Buddhist Temple, for it is unimportant except as regards the Huntley and Palmer's biscuits, lard candles and scents which Dr. Hari Das Chatterjee saw. A great deal has been said of his want of orthodoxy, but if he was unorthodox, that is all the less reason for his noticing these things, and there is no possible doubt as to his veracity. As a matter of fact, stray sheep who have been received back into the fold are always more strictly looked after than those that have never erred.

His brother-in-law Babu Durga Shankar Bhattacharjya, Honorary Magistrate and Chairman of the Local Board,—whose evidence I believe for the same reason as the High Court and the Privy Council refused to disbelieve Babu Dirgopal Singh, a brother zemindar, and Mr. Abul Hassan, Small Cause Court Registrar of Calcutta and brother of Maulvi Khoda Baksh, Chief Justice of Hyderabad, in the great Tikari Will case, *Choley Narain Singh* vs. *Ratan Koer*, I. L. R. 22 Cal. 519, namely, his unblemished character and high respectability,—has been the subject of a remarkable attack by Mr. Ghose on account of his answers in cross-examination at the bottom of page 85 (P. B.) and top of p. 86. The central question, the answer to which Mr. Ghose says must be false, is " Did you hear from Dharmapala that he wished to have control and possession of the Mahabodhi Temple on behalf of the Buddhists ?" and the answer is, " I never heard that." Why should this be false? I have never heard it, and I have had before me an immense mass of Dharmapala's writings and an extraordinary long cross-examination. He nowhere says he (personally) wished to have control and possession of the Mahabodhi Temple.

The next answer is certainly more difficult to believe. " I never heard from him or any one else that it was his wish that the Buddhists should have control and possession of the Temple." As he says he first knew Dharmapala in 1891 or 1892, it is probable that he would have heard of the negotiations to purchase or lease the Temple. It will be, however, observed on p. 85 (P. B.) that he only speaks of having had two conversations with Dharmapala, first on the occasion of his coming to put up the Japanese image, and, secondly, on the occasion of his coming to bring this case. On neither of these occasions is it at all necessary that Dharmapala should have expressed the wish alluded to, and the fact that he did not, as deposed to by this most reliable witness, greatly supports the finding I have already come to that there is no proved connection between Dharmapala's previous negotiations to get possession of the Temple by open bargaining and his later conduct in trying to secure freedom of worship in their own way for the Buddhists. The quibble about the word "help" is explained by the fact that Mr. Ghose is a far better English scholar than Babu Durga Shankar Bhattacharjya. In any case there is no proof of any underhand *mala fide* attempt on the part of the Mahabodhi Society to obtain physical possession of the Temple.

The last witness, the Pandit, is only as regards the immaterial but much vexed question of the ninth or tenth *avatar* of Vishnu. The astute Vishnu appears from the Puranas to have purposely assumed a lying form to deceive the Brahmins into Buddhism. There is no evidence that there is any sect or any temple in the whole length and breadth of India devoted to the worship of this *avatar*. It is a deity which Vaishavas would probably feel shy of. The astute Mahanth, who is a Saivite, may stultify himself by trying to set up such a worship, but it obviously could not amalgamate with or be anything but abhorrent to the religion of the real Buddha, whose personality the Hindus believed Vishnu assumed. The only other evidence is that Hindus in past ages have made the Buddhistic images into Gods, and also that the pious predecessor of the present Mahanth consecrated and worshipped a half-buried stupa in the great shrine, which he thought represented a *lingam* or emblem of Siva. This, however, appears to have been dug up and thrown away by Mr. Beglar without objection, and it in any case has nothing to do with Buddha Bhagwan, or any other Buddha.

There is one other point in the case which, having dealt with the evidence and other arguments, I ought not to pass over. The Magistrate has found that the disturbance took place to ceremonies connected with the enshrinement of the Japanese image. Surely, say the defence, the enshrinement of an image is an act derogatory to our proprietary rights? There is nothing to show what particular significance is attached by the Magistrate to the word 'enshrinement.' What the Buddhist witnesses tell us is the highest form of worship, is simply placing an image of Buddha on an altar, lighting candles, etc., before it, and then sitting in contemplation. I have avoided using the word as much as possible, as I do not consider that there is any evidence that the Buddhists intended to permanently enshrine the Japanese image that day. The nature of the ceremony precludes any idea of permanency, for, if it was permanent, it could never be repeated without bringing a new image. The bitter words of Dharmapala, when he is cross-questioned as to the meaning of his exclamation, "now the Mahanth can do what he likes" (p. 37, P. B.), show that he had no hope of the image being allowed to remain in its position, and no intention of avenging it. I do not, therefore, think that there was any enshrinement of the image with a view to subsequently make a claim for damages for its removal. But even if there had been, I do not think the act of the accused could be justified, if the Buddhists can show that they were engaged in lawful worship, and this I think Dharmapala has amply succeeded in establishing. His only immediate objects appear to have been to gain a spiritual triumph for Buddhism and to get rid of a responsibility which, although he had sought it himself in the greatest hope and confidence, he now felt was an intolerable burden.

I have incidentally remarked that the act of the disciples of the *math* is the act of the Mahanth and his followers. The accused, being Sannyasis and brother monks of the Mahanth must have as much knowledge as he has, as regards the freedom of worship actually given to Buddhists by the Mahanth's agreement and by his subsequent conduct. They could not, therefore, in any case plead the orders of the Mahanth. It is true Dharmapala directly charged the Mahanth with instigating this occurrence, and the defence claim this as an absolute admission in their favour. The reason Dharmapala gave for his assumption, for it was nothing more than an assumption, was that the Mahanth became very excited as messengers arrived relating what was occurring. It, however, at once appeared that the Deputy Magistrate had been sitting with the Mahanth throughout the time when there was any evidence as to his conduct, and he therefore could not give any directions calculated to cause an illegal disturbance. That being so, the Magistrate declined to act on Dharmapala's information against the Mahanth, and the latter was in no way on the record during the trial of this case. The case as against the Mahanth was practically dismissed under Section 203, Criminal Procedure Code, and the information, which did not amount to a criminal information at all, being utterly insufficient, cannot be used as an admission of what it never asserted, namely, that the accused acted under orders of the Mahanth.

I therefore find that the accused acted independently on their own responsibility. Nothing remains but to give my findings on the evidence as applied to Section 296, Indian Penal Code. They are as follows :—

That the three accused persons who have been convicted, caused a disturbance to the assembly "voluntarily," because they caused it by means whereby they intended to cause it, having announced their intention to stop all worship except that to a dressed up Hinduized image on the ground floor which, as instructed Hindu monks, they knew was impossible for the Buddhists to worship at that moment. It is enough for this that they knew, as they must have known, that the Buddhists had removed these trappings and cleansed the image in November before worshipping it, and that under the direction of the Mahanth and the members of the order who assert the right to assist at the worship in the Temple (*vide* their own translation of the agreement with the King of Burma), it was dressed up again in a Hindu fashion on or before the day of occurrence. I have found, however, as a fact that they had many independent means of knowing what they were about.

Secondly, I find on this word "voluntarily," that they employed means which they knew, or had reason to believe, to be likely to cause disturbance to religious worship. This I have shown by their knowledge that sitting in contemplation in a Buddhistic posture was the most common universal form of Buddhist worship, which they must have seen almost every day of their lives. Believing, as they say they did, that these Buddhists' minds were filled with the idea of enshrining the image against the wishes of the Mahanth, they cannot have imagined that the removal of the image would not disturb their contemplation, and how far that contemplation was sincere it was not for them to judge.

Thirdly, I find that the Buddhists were lawfully engaged in religious worship, and that, as they had assumed the well-known outward and visible sign of that worship, the defendants cannot plead that they thought their worship was a sham. The words "lawful worship" do not apply to whoever voluntarily disturbs, but to the worshippers engaged under Section 296.

Fourthly, I find, as I have fully set out, that the Buddhist worship was by no means a sham, but a very grave reality.

This being so, the findings of the Magistrate on which Mr. Ghose so largely relies can at most only amount to extenuating circumstances. The accused may have believed that the Mahanth was proprietor and his rights "undefined," but he is not Nebuchadnezzar, and they perfectly well knew that his proprietary rights could not justify him in arbitrarily interfering with the purely religious side of Buddhist worship. I hold that the Buddhists were as much entitled to use this Japanese image in their worship as I am to use a particularly large and gorgeous prayer book if I like.

The image appears to be used for a precisely similar purpose as the prayer book, namely, to direct the thoughts. What the Mahanth could do with my prayer book afterwards, if I chose to leave it behind, is an altogether different matter and does not come in in this case, nor whether I should have any right, if I found the Mahanth had locked the door of the place, to force it open. These are civil questions; but the one question I have to deal with, the disturbance of religious worship, permissive if you like, seems to me perfectly clear and free from doubt.

Secondly, as to his finding that they *bonâ fide* believed that Dharmapala had been prevented on the 19th May, 1894, from placing the image in the Temple until he received the Mahanth's consent, and that prohibition subsisted.

Their belief appears to have been grounded on the prohibitory order under Section 144, Criminal Procedure Code, served on the Mahanth on an assumption that a similar order must have been served on Dharmapala. The learned Advocate-General has very rightly argued that there is no possible reason for the contention of Mr. Ghose that Mr. Macpherson was guilty of a quasi-irregular act in sending Dharmapala a demi-official letter instead of a notice under Section 144. The property was in the possession of the Mahanth, and the Mahanth was urgently directed to take such order with it as should prevent a breach of the peace. The information was that he had collected a body of armed men. Nobody complained to Mr. Macpherson that Dharmapala was likely to commit a breach of the peace. The section specially provides that such a order may be passed *ex parte*.

If, as they now say, they thought an order under Section 144 must have been passed, they must have known that it could only remain in force two months, as ignorance of the law cannot be pleaded, and I observe that the learned Counsel, on whose sole responsibility the written statement of the accused must have been filed, since he refused to allow his clients even to give their names to the Magistrate (p. 100, P. B.), has carefully avoided making any such assertion in para. 13 of the written statement. He merely says they believed that Dharmapala would not make a second attempt.

The third finding of the Magistrate, that their intention was to prevent Dharmapala from creating evidence of a right, I find simply incredible, since, as

I have shown, no possible evidence of any civil right whatever could be established by Dharmapala's conduct, and the very same thing had been done before in the installation of the small Burmese marble images (p. 75, P. B.), and the Mahanth, so far from objecting, has since had them dressed up as Hindu deities, and there is nothing to show that he would have objected to the Buddhists undressing them again just as they did the great image in November, 1894.

But while I find that these are not extenuating circumstances in law, I do not see that any good purpose can be served by imprisoning these three men, who after all are only imbued with the same spirit of religious animosity as the whole of the rest of their order, an animosity which no doubt had its origin in a fear of being deprived of the pice of the pilgrim, but which in this case has assumed a purely personal and religious aspect. The great point in their favour is that they refrained from personal violence. In this respect the Mahanth appears to be as peaceable a man as Dharmapala. Though I would not answer for all his three hundred disciples being the same, the fact remains that these three men did not use personal violence, and although they took upon themselves in the name of their Abbot and of their order to do a wholly unauthorized act, their Abbot and their order would appear to endorse their conduct, and a general punishment, such as a fine, which will serve as a warning to the whole order, is, I think, more suitable than imprisonment.

In a long series of years, under circumstances of considerable delicacy and difficulty, owing to the absence of a proper understanding between Government and the Mahanth when the Temple was restored, and owing also, I think, to a mistaken impression on the part of Government that the Mahanth could and would afford every facility in his power to Buddhists to worship in "perfect freedom," Hindus and Buddhists have managed to get along peaceably together, and at this first breach of the public peace, a breach which was inevitable sooner or later, it is, I think, the duty of the Criminal Courts only to give a distinct and certain warning to the parties what their liabilities under criminal law are in cases of this nature. In the hope and belief that both parties will seek to settle their unhappy differences either by arbitration or by recourse to the Civil Courts, and that after this warning there will be no further breach of the Criminal Law, I direct that, while the conviction of all three accused under Section 296 is upheld, the sentences will be modified by reversing the sentences of one month's simple imprisonment in each case.

The result is that, Jaipal Gir, Mahendra Gir and Bhimal Deo Gir, will have to pay the fine of Rs. 100 each as ordered by the Magistrate, or in default undergo fifteen days' simple imprisonment.

GAYA, H. HOLMWOOD,
30th July, 1895. *Sessions Judge.*

Translation of Agreement, dated 11th February, 1877.

Copy put in by the defence during the hearing of the Appeal.

Stamp correct under Article 37, Section II, Act XVIII of 1869.

Admissible under Sections 21, 23, 28 and 32, Act VIII of 1871.

I am Mahalia Chowdin Sadir, son of Mahalia Chowdin, inhabitant of Mandalay, in the kingdom of Burma and Wazir (minister) of the King of Burma.

Whereas the King of Burma is a Buddhist, and there is a shrine of Buddha Bhagwan (God) at Bodh-Gaya, that is in Mouzah Taradih, which was constructed from time immemorial. At present it is in a dilapidated state and wants repairs. Therefore the King of Burma desires that he, for his spiritual benefits and for perpetuation of his name, should repair the shrine. But the said shrine stands within the zemindari and in the possession of Mahanth Hem Narayan Gir, Gadinashin of Asthan Math at Bodh-Gaya, and I, under orders of the King of Burma, want to make repairs. So I, according to the orders of the King of Burma, spoke to the said Mahanth regarding the repairs of the shrine. The said Mahanth, understanding the work of antiquity will be saved from being ruined, gave permission to make the repairs, subject to the conditions herein set forth :—That I shall cause the repairs to such portions of the shrine as will be shown by the Mahanth and in such manner as will be directed by him, because close to the said shrine there are many Gods of the Hindus and old temples of the Gods of his *gurus* as well as houses occupied by tenants, and he wanted that they should not in any way be molested in point of religion or any injury done to them. That it has been a long standing practice that he offers his worship to the God Budh and idols, as well to the idols which are placed beneath them, and such worship is allowable, and people gather there for *darshan* and worship. His disciples are posted there to take care of the said shrines and to assist in the worship. So I shall have nothing to do with the taking care of the shrine. That after the repairs have been done, I shall not be competent to claim either the compound, or the doors, or any of the shrines or any of the buildings, &c., and that the servants that have been and may hereafter be there for the purpose of worship on behalf of the King of Burma, should stay there, observing the zamindari rules of the zamindar. I also with permission of the Maha Dharan Raja King of Burma have accepted the said conditions and hereby declare and give in writing that I or the King of Burma or his servants, that have now been or that may hereafter be shall never transgress any of the conditions set forth above. Should it be so, it shall be held null and void before the Court for the time being. I therefore give in writing these few words in the shape of an agreement that it may be used, when required.

In the High Court of Judicature at Fort William in Bengal.

CRIMINAL REVISIONAL JURISDICTION.

The Empress on the Prosecution of H. Dharmapala,

versus

Jaipal Gir and Two others.

The humble petition of Jaipal Gir, Mahendra Gir and Bhimal Deo Gir of Bodh-Gaya.

Humbly Sheweth,

That your petitioners, who are Sannyasis and disciples of Mahanth Krishna Dayal Gir of Bodh-Gaya, were on the 19th July last convicted by the District Magistrate of Gaya (Mr. D. J. Macpherson) of an offence under Section 296 of the Penal Code, and sentenced each to one month's simple imprisonment and to pay a fine of Rs. 100 each, or in default to undergo fifteen days' additional simple imprisonment.

Your petitioners appealed against the said conviction and sentence to the Sessions Judge of Gaya, who on the 30th July affirmed the said conviction, but reduced the sentence as regards each of your petitioners to one of a fine of Rs. 100 only.

Your petitioners submit that the said conviction and sentence should be revised and set aside on the following grounds :—

1. For that, on the facts as admitted by the prosecutor and his witnesses, and on some of the findings arrived at by the District Magistrate, your petitioners ought to have been acquitted.

2. For that the Courts below ought to have held that the prosecution had failed to establish any one of the three necessary ingredients required for a conviction under Section 296, Penal Code.

3. For that the Sessions Judge is entirely in error in holding that, although Dharmapala and the Buddhists have not proved an easement regarding their right to worship in the Temple, of which the Mahanth has now been found to be "undoubtedly the owner," Dharmapala was entitled as of right and against the expressed directions and wishes of the Mahanth, to worship or to place an image in the Temple on the 25th February. On the findings of the Sessions

Judge himself, Dharmapala could not have been *lawfully* engaged in worship on the 25th February, 1895.

4. For that the Sessions Judge is in error in supposing that the question of easement or the right to worship, claimed by Dharmapala, must be rigidly excluded. Such a question, though ordinarily determinable by a Civil Court, must be considered incidentally in this trial, as the whole case for the prosecution fails, if Dharmapala had not the right to enshrine or place the image against the wishes of the proprietor of the Temple.

5. For that the Sessions Judge is entirely wrong in holding, without any evidence whatever, that the Mahanth had in any way at any time himself imposed limitations on his rights as absolute owner of the Temple.

6. For that the District Magistrate having found that your petitioners "*bonâ fide* believed that Dharmapala had been prevented on the 19th May, 1894, from placing the image in the Temple until he received the Mahanth's consent, and that that prohibition subsisted," the Courts below ought to have held that your petitioners did not commit any criminal offence by removing the image on the 25th February, 1895.

7. For that on the finding of the District Magistrate that your petitioners "did *bonâ fide* believe that the Mahanth enjoyed possessory rights of a certain kind over the Temple," and on the clear finding of the Sessions Judge that the Mahanth was "undoubtedly the owner," the Sessions Judge ought to have held that your petitioners as agents of the Mahanth committed no offence in removing the image under the circumstances alleged.

8. For that on the finding of Mr. Macpherson that your petitioners' intention was "to prevent Dharmapala from creating evidence of a right adverse to the Mahanth"—a finding which is fully warranted by all the circumstances of the case, and which is the only finding which can be arrived at—the Sessions Judge ought to have held that your petitioners had not "voluntarily" disturbed any worship within the true meaning of the section.

9. For that the Sessions Judge has wholly misunderstood the argument of your petitioners' Counsel, who had drawn a clear distinction between the sincerity or otherwise as regards the faith of the worshippers, and the question as to whether the worship was real and *bonâ fide* and not colorable and brought about for ulterior purposes. It is submitted that what the section contemplates is real worship for religious purposes only, and not worship got up (even though it be by sincere votaries) for the purpose of asserting a claim or a right.

10. For that the Sessions Judge ought to have held that the so called worship or religious ceremonies on the 25th February, 1895, were not real, but simply colorable, and held solely for the purpose of asserting a claim which Dharmapala had been wishing to assert.

11. For that the Courts below ought to have held that Dharmapala and his comrades were not lawfully engaged in worship in the upper chamber of the Temple on the 25th February last.

12. For that the Sessions Judge is entirely in error in holding that "even an honest belief" on the part of your petitioners that the worship was a sham would be no defence in the case.

13. For that both the Courts below have misread and misconstrued the Burmese agreement, dated 11th February, 1877, which the Sessions Judge calls "the Magna Charta of the Buddhists." That agreement, if correctly read and interpreted, furnishes very strong evidence in favour of the position taken up by your petitioners.

14. For that the misconstruction of the said agreement has so seriously prejudiced your petitioners as to vitiate all the material findings of fact arrived at by both the Courts below against your petitioners.

15. For that the Sessions Judge is wholly wrong in falling back at the last moment in appeal, upon an untenable distinction between the Mahanth's claim as proprietor and what the Judge calls "his spiritual claim." Such a distinction was never suggested at any time in the first Court, and is not warranted by the evidence in the case.

16. For that the Sessions Judge is entirely in error in holding that the Mahanth, though full proprietor of the Temple, and not having a limited right, as was first suggested by the learned Judge in argument, had not the right to claim that he alone was competent to enshrine any new image.

17. For that the Sessions Judge is entirely wrong in supposing that Dharmapala did not intend enshrining the image "permanently," or that any image had ever before been enshrined or placed in the Temple without the Mahanth's permission and consent.

18. For that there is no analogy between the placing of the marble images referred to by the Sessions Judge and the placing of the Japanese image, as the former were so placed with the consent of the Mahanth, and there is nothing to show that they were placed as of right and without his permission.

19. For that there being no evidence in support of any of the following facts, the conviction cannot be sustained :—

(a) That any image within the knowledge of your petitioners had been enshrined or placed without the Mahanth's consent prior to the 25th February, 1895.
(b) That there was, to your petitioners' knowledge, any worship by Buddhists in the upper chamber prior to the 25th February.
(c) That your petitioners knew that sitting in contemplation was any form of Buddhist worship, or that any one had a right to sit in contemplation in the upper chamber.
(d) That your petitioners knew, or had reason to believe, that Dharmapala was really sitting in contemplation when the image was removed on the 25th February.
(e) That the claim set up by the Mahanth, whether spiritual or as proprietor, was not *bonâ fide* on his part.

20. For that on a consideration of the whole evidence, this Honorable Court ought to hold :—

(a) That the so-called worship by Dharmapala was not real, but that it was colorable, and intended for the assertion of a right.
(b) That your petitioners had no guilty mind, and therefore not punishable criminally.
(c) That your petitioners acted *bonâ-fide* and under a claim of right.

21. For that, there being no evidence on the record that the Buddhists had worshipped as of right for more than 20 years in the Temple, the prosecution had failed to establish any case of easement on which they had relied in the first Court, and therefore the Courts below ought to have held that Dharmapala had no right to place the image on the 25th February without the permission of the Mahanth, assuming, for the sake of argument, that a right to worship would necessarily include a right to enshrine a new image.

22. For that, in the absence of any evidence to establish an easement by the Buddhists, the Sessions Judge ought to have held that, without the Mahanth's permission, Dharmapala was not entitled to do what he was doing on the 24th February, and that your petitioners were therefore not guilty of any offence, especially as the Sessions Judge himself remarks:—"If any part of Dharmapala's case depended upon the Mahanth's rights as proprietor, he has lost it."

23. For that the Sessions Judge is entirely wrong in holding that the Burmese agreement, dated 11th February, 1877, shows that any right was claimed by the Buddhists or asserted by them as against the Mahanth.

24. For that there is no evidence to show that the Mahanth's claim to perform the *Prânpratishta* ceremony was not *bonâ fide*, or even that he knew that such ceremony would be objected to by the Buddhists as a class.

25. For that there is no evidence to show that the Mahanth or his disciples knew that the light in which Buddhists regarded Buddha, differed from his ideas, or of those Hindus who worship Buddha as an *Avatar*.

26. For that there is ample evidence to show that Buddha had been regarded from ancient times as a Hindu deity, and that his image had been worshipped by Hindus inside as well as outside the Temple for centuries.

27. For that the Sessions Judge's judgment contains various assumptions and statements which are not borne out by the evidence, and he has dealt with the case in a manner which has materially prejudiced your petitioners.

28. For that both the Courts below have taken an erroneous view of the evidence of Dharmapala and his witnesses in important particulars.

29. For that the Sessions Judge's finding that your petitioners acted independently and not under the orders of the Mahanth, is entirely opposed to the evidence and the probabilities of the case.

30. For that the District Magistrate, having long before the 24th February, 1895, formed, as the evidence shows, and as appears from the facts set out in the annexed affidavit, a strong opinion against the rights of the Mahanth and in favor of Dharmapala's claim, and having expressed that opinion repeatedly in his executive capacity, as well as in an *ex parte* judgment in the absence of the Mahanth or his men, ought not to have tried the case, involving, as it did, the determination of important questions on which he had already expressed a strong opinion. This has seriously prejudiced your petitioners, who have been practically deprived, at any rate so far as the first Court is concerned, of a trial by a Judge, who had previously formed no opinion on the subject.

31. For that Mr. Macpherson was greatly influenced in his decision by many documents, a good many of which, though inadmissible, were marked as Exhibits long after the trial had concluded, and that the Sessions Judge, although he has not relied upon those documents in his judgment, has unconsciously been led to attach great weight to the findings of the Magistrate based upon those documents.

32. For that having regard to the importance of the questions involved in this case, this Honorable Court ought, if necessary, to find the facts for itself, and hold that the case for the prosecution is not made out, and that the judgments of the Courts below should be set aside.

33. For that the Courts below ought to have referred Dharmapala to the Civil Court, and held that the object of the prosecution was not the vindication of public justice, but to get from the Criminal Courts a decision on important questions affecting civil rights.

Your petitioners therefore pray that your Lordships will be pleased to set aside the conviction and sentence, or to pass such other order as to your Lordships may seem just and proper.

And your petitioners as in duty bound shall ever pray.

JAIPAL GIR, MAHENDRA GIR, & BHIMAL DEO GIR,

By

SARAT CHANDRA ROY & HARAPRASAD CHATTERJEE,

5th August, 1895. *Vakils.*

ORDER.

On the motion of Mr. M. Ghose, let a rule issue calling upon the Magistrate and on the complainant to show cause why the conviction and sentence should not be set aside on the ground that, on the facts as found by the Courts, and upon the facts disclosed by the evidence, no offence under Section 296 of Indian Penal Code has been committed, and the ground that the agreement dated the 11th of February, 1877, between the Secretary to the King of Burma on the one part and the Mahanth of Budh-Gaya on the other, has been misconstrued and misunderstood by the Courts, and that this misconstruction has led them to form a wrong conclusion as to the right of this parties.

Let the rule on the complainant be served on Babu Saligram Singh, who undertakes to put in a *vakalatnama* on behalf of the complainant.

Send for the record.

W. MACPHERSON,
GOOROO DAS BANERJEE.

The 5th August, 1895.

In the High Court of Judicature at Fort William in Bengal.

CRIMINAL REVISIONAL JURISDICTION.

QUEEN-EMPRESS (ON THE PROSECUTION OF H. DHARMAPALA)

Versus

JAIPAL GIR AND OTHERS.

IN THE MATTER OF THE PETITION OF JAIPAL GIR AND OTHERS.

I, Bijayananda Barma, son of Nageswar Prosad, a resident of Gaya, do hereby solemnly affirm and declare as follows:—

1. THAT I am a mukhtear duly enrolled under the legal Practitioners' Act, and practise as such in the Revenue and Criminal Courts of Gaya.

2. That I hold a general power of attorney or am-mukhtearnama from Mahanth Krishna Dayal Gir, the present Mahanth of Bodh-Gaya.

3. That I was also an accused person in the abovenamed case in which H. Dharmapala is the prosecutor, but I have been acquitted by the District Magistrate, Mr. Macpherson, in whose Court I was present throughout the trial.

4. That it was only during the trial of the said case and after the cross-examination of the complainant had commenced, that we came to know for certain that Mr. Macpherson, the presiding Magistrate, had, prior to the 25th February, 1895, expressed himself against the position taken up in the case by the said Mahanth, not only as regards his proprietary rights, but also as regards the character of the Temple and the worship of Buddha by Hindus as a Hindu deity.

5. That I declare that neither the Mahanth nor any one of the accused was aware, until Mr. Macpherson, towards the close of the case, handed over to the Counsel for the defence certain papers which had been called for by the defence, that he, Mr. Macpherson, on the 9th June, 1894, in an *ex parte* case, has expressed his views strongly on some of the points which he was called on to decide in the trial then going on.

6. That similarly none of us was aware before the commencement of the said trial that, in a note written by Mr. Macpherson in Bombay on the 28th June, 1894, and sent by him to the officer then acting for him, he had similarly expressed himself strongly on many of the points which had to be judicially determined by him in connection with the occurrence of the 25th February, 1895.

7. I have now obtained a certified copy of the *ex parte* order of Mr. Macpherson, dated the 9th June, 1894, referred to in para. 5 of this affidavit, which copy is herewith annexed and Marked A.

8. As regards Mr. Macpherson's note from Bombay, dated 28th June, 1894, of which I do not possess a certified copy, I give the following extracts from it, which I believe to contain the exact words used by Mr. Macpherson, in the said note, showing the views he had then expressed on some of the important questions he had subsequently to try judicially:—

"The removal of these images was probably intended to further the novel idea, started by the Mahanth since this image question has arisen, that the Mahabodhi Temple is a Hindu one, and that the image of Buddha in the shrine is an incarnation of Vishnu. This, he fancies, may increase his hold on the Temple, and give him an advantage he does not possess, in the negotiations with the Buddhists as regards its future control. But the theory is as foolish from the point of view of the Mahanth's own interest, as it is preposterous. No Hindus have ever worshipped at the Temple, except perhaps that some ignorant pilgrims may have gone to see it out of curiosity, and done reverence to the image inside."

* * * * * * * * *

"It will be found that the Mahanth has never had any control over the Temple itself, except since its restoration by the British Government."

* * * * * * *

"The great Temple is also apparently in the village of Mastipur Taradih, which was settled revenue free with the Mahanth's, but I believe that in none of the grants is any mention whatever made of the Temple itself. There is nothing to show that the Mahanths ever concerned themselves with it, and even when the Burmese King proposed to do something for its restoration, no question appears to have arisen as to the Mahanth's having any right in the Temple itself. A perusal of the correspondence forwarded to the Commissioner of Patna with the Bengal Government's Memo. dated the 16th October, 1875, and of the reply of Mr. Halliday, the Collector of Gaya, dated 8th December, 1875, will show that the only matters on which the Mahanth was consulted, or with regard to which he made any representations, were as to care being taken not to interfere with certain Hindu idols in the vicinity of the Temple, and to a proper agreement being executed for the land the Burmese wished for the erection of a monastery and of a *paribhoga* or the magazine for the deposit of offerings made at the Bodhi Tree."

* * * * * * *

"But I do not think that it can be fairly said that he has any right of ownership, as against the Crown, in a Temple that was an abandoned building until it was restored at the expense of the Crown."

* * * * * * *

"I am of opinion that the right of free worship in the Mahabodhi Temple to which the Buddhists are undoubtedly entitled, may fairly be held to include the rights claimed in the present petition. These are in effect the following:—

(1). The right to set up images and present other votive offerings in the shrine.

(2). The right to enter and remain in the Temple at all times, irrespective of the consent of the Mahanth—in other words, to possess the key of the door."

* * * * * * * *

9. I declare that, when we discovered the documents above referred to, we were advised that it would then be too late to apply for a transfer of the case from the file of Mr. Macpherson, and that, having regard to the fairness, impartiality and care with which he had been recording the evidence, we need not apprehend that, although he had prejudged some of the issues in the case, he would not be able to divest his mind of all preconceived ideas at the time of coming to a judicial decision.

10. That, besides the documents already referred to, evidence was elicited in the course of the cross-examination of the witnesses for the prosecution, and certain official correspondence was placed by Mr. Macpherson himself before the Counsel of both sides, all of which tend to show that Mr. Macpherson had formed so strong an opinion against the Mahanth before the commencement of the case, that he ought not to have taken the responsibility of trying it himself.

11. That I was present during the argument of this case on appeal in the Sessions Court, and I say that Mr. M. Ghose, Counsel for the appellants, urged as a ground of appeal that Mr. Macpherson had prejudged the case by expressing himself strongly in his letters and notes and in the *ex parte* case, referred to above.

12. I further declare that the Counsel for the appellants contended before the Sessions Judge that a large mass of correspondence put in by Mr. Macpherson and marked by him long after the arguments were over in his Court, were inadmissible, and that thereupon the learned Judge said they ought to be excluded.

13. That I verily believe that the accused by reason of the strong opinion which Mr. Macpherson had formed against the Mahanth's claims prior to the 24th February, 1895, have been seriously prejudiced, although Mr. Macpherson himself during the trial maintained an attitude of strict impartiality and showed every desire to do justice.

BIJAYANANDA BARMA.

No. 252.

SOLEMNLY affirmed before me, this 5th day of August, 1895.

H. H. ARDWISE,

Commissioner.

The deponent is known to me.

AGHORE NATH ROY,

Clerk to Babu Haraprasad Chatterjee,

Vakil.

Prepared in my office.

HARAPRASAD CHATTERJEE,

Vakil.

EXHIBIT A.

REFERRED TO IN THE AFFIDAVIT.

Complaint regarding the removal of Buddhist Images from the Temple of Mahabodhi on the 17th May, 1894.

Statement of Nirghin Ram, son of Sahay Ram, Kahar of Telpamalla, Gaya Town, on solemn affirmation:—

I COMPLAINED to my superior officer, the Overseer at Gaya, that seven images, which we call Buddha images, had been removed from the Temple by Jaipal Gir, the *Kothari* of the Mahanth of Buddha-Gaya. I am chaprasi of the Public Works Department appointed to look after the Temple. The Overseer of the Public Works Department in charge of the Temple, went on three months' leave on the 8th April, and the Overseer, Kali Babu, at Gaya, is in charge in his absence. The images were taken away on Friday about a fortnight ago at 9 or a quarter past 9 o'clock at night. Jaipal Gir came with a number of the villagers and took away the images. I tried to stop him. I said, "Don't take away the images; why are you taking them?" He replied, "They are my property, I will take them." I said, "I would go and inform my master." He said, "By the time you have gone and informed him, they can be replaced, and then you will be found to have told a falsehood and will be dismissed." I could say no more. They took away the images. I was at my lodging, when they arrived, and went to the Temple on hearing their voices and the noise of their shoes. Then in the morning I gave information to the Police at Buddha-Gaya. The Munshi asked me if I wanted to prosecute a case. I said I would go first and complain to the Babu. Then I came to Gaya that day to report the matter to the Overseer Babu Kali Babu. The Babu was away elsewhere, I did not see him that day. So I got a report written and left it at his office. The head-constable was on his rounds when I gave information to the Police. I saw the Temple yesterday, and the images had not been replaced by them. People told me they were taken and put inside the Mahanth's *math*, and I saw them myself being taken off in that direction. The images were in the Temple since before my employment there. I have been employed there for over two years. During these two years they were never removed from the Temple. Two of them used to be on one side of the great image of Buddha and five on the other side.

That was in the shrine on the ground floor. I did not see the Mahanth on the day they were taken or next day.

I complained about the matter to the Overseer, because the Temple and things were under my charge, but the Mahanth's people keep the key of the Temple.

D. J. MACPHERSON,

31*st May*, 1894. *Magistrate.*

I sent for the above chaprasi on receiving his complaint through the Executive Engineer, and have formally recorded his complaint above. I shall pass orders on it to-morrow.

D. J. MACPHERSON,

31*st May*, 1894. *Magistrate.*

The above complaint discloses an offence on the part of Jaipal Gir, the steward of the Mahanth of Bodh-Gaya. The apparent claim of right to remove Buddhist images from a Buddhist Temple—from the most sacred shrine in the eyes of Buddhist of the whole world—is an entirely novel one. From facts within my own knowledge as to what was going on at the time, I have no doubt as to what was the motive for this act. The Buddhists are seeking to come to an arrangement with the Mahanth, whereby they may have greater control over the

Temple than at present, and in order to obtain a greater advantage over them in the negotiations and ground for extracting from them a heavier pecuniary compensation than he could otherwise reasonably claim, the Mahanth has, within the last two or three weeks, suddenly conceived the novel idea, that the Temple is really a Hindu one, and the great image of Buddha therein, an incarnation of Vishnu. I can vouch for the fact that this is a perfectly novel idea. It was manifest, however, that the fact of Buddhist worshippers having placed images of Buddha alongside the great image in the shrine would militate against that idea. Two days after the removal of these images, moreover, it had been arranged that an historical image of Buddha received from Japan should be set up in the Temple. I had mentioned this intention on the part of those who had brought the image, to the Mahanth about a month before, and he had no objection then to this, so long as it was not made of metal (*dhatú*) such as gold or silver, as if it were of intrinsic value, dacoits might be tempted to steal it, and he, as custodian of the Temple, might be held responsible. This image, however, was not of metal at all. Nothing more occurred until the 17th, the day on which the images were removed from the Temple. On the morning of that day one of the Mahanth's disciples, Ramkaran Gir, and a Muhammadan agent of the Mahanth's, came to my house with a copy of the *Indian Mirror*, announcing that the image was to be set up on the 19th, and with a verbal complaint to the effect that they were much perturbed (*ghabrao*) over this. I told them that if they had any representation to make, they must do so through the Mahanth, with whom the matter had already been arranged. The Mahanth came to me at 8 o'clock the same evening, *i. e.*, about the time when his steward was removing the images, and stated that if he allowed the image from Japan to be placed in the Temple, his *chelas* might turn him out. There was no time to discuss the matter with him at that hour, and I told him to come next morning, which he did. I then told him that he and Dharmapala, who had arrived with the image, should meet and arrange matters. They met, but no arrangement was come to, owing to the attitude the Mahanth took up as to the necessity for the *pránpratishta* ceremony, which would be equivalent to making the image a Brahmanic deity. As a breach of the peace was apprehended after the withdrawal by the Mahanth of his consent, the image was not placed in the Temple. The right of the Buddhist pilgrims who had come to worship in the Temple on the night of the 19th May, the anniversary of the birth of Buddha, and the holiest night in the year in the eyes of Buddhists, was, however, enforced.

This recital of what was going on at the time, illustrates the motive with which the images were removed. I did not learn of their removal until I received the chaprasi's complaint through the Executive Engineer, Bankipur, on the 30th May.

The object with which the images placed by Buddhist pilgrims were removed was, in view of all the circumstances, to cause wrongful gain to the Mahanth in connection with the negotiations contemplated by the Buddhists for obtaining greater control over the Temple. The removal was, therefore "dishonest" in the eye of the criminal law. It was also misappropriation, as there was no meaning in their being anywhere else, than in the shrine where the Buddhist worshippers had put them. Jaipal Gir could, therefore, be charged with criminal misappropriation under Section 403, and with theft from a building under Section 380, of the Penal Code. More than this, the removal of these Buddhist images from a Buddhist place of worship constituted a defilement of that place of worship, with the knowledge that it would likely be considered by Buddhists an insult to their religion, an offence under Section 295 of the Penal Code.

I had contemplated issuing process against Jaipal Gir under those sections, but I thought it advisable to give the Mahanth an opportunity of receding from the position he apparently sought to take up. I therefore wrote to him a letter, informing him of what had come to my notice, and requesting him to cause the images to be replaced at once. He has complied with this request, but seeks to justify the removal by alleging that he has always been in the habit of taking such images placed there recently as offerings by pilgrims, together with presents and fees. I have informed him that he has no authority to remove images or other votive offerings of any kind, not being of a perishable description, that may be placed by Buddhist worshippers in the Temple.

Under the circumstances, I do not think it necessary to proceed further with this complaint, and I dismiss it under Section 203 of the Criminal Procedure Code.

D. J. MACPHERSON,

9th June, 1894. *Magistrate of Gaya.*

APPENDIX.

[The following is the full text of Mr. Macpherson's Note from Bombay, to which reference is made in para. 8 of Bijayananda Barma's affidavit (*ante*, p. 23,) and of Dharmapala's petition to the Magistrate, dated June 12th, 1894, on which the Note is based. The documents are those referred to in Exhibit D 28 (*a*), for which see Part I, p. 36.]

Petition of H. Dharmapala to the Magistrate of Gaya, dated 12th June, 1894.

To His Worship D. J. Macpherson, Esq., District Magistrate, Gaya.

The humble petition of H. Dharmapala, General Secretary of the Maha-Bodhi Society.

SHEWETH,—That the Maha-Bodhi Temple at Buddha-Gaya is the central shrine most sacred to the four hundred and seventy-five millions of Buddhists throughout China, Japan, Siam, Burma, Ceylon, Arakan, Tibet, Chittagong, Nepal and other places. To them, your petitioner submits, the site is as sacred as Jerusalem is to the Christians, Mecca to the Musalmans, and Benares to the Hindus.

2. That the Maha-Bodhi Temple was in utter ruins till 1876, when the Government of King Mindoon Min of Burma commenced to repair it, but, in the interest of archæology, the then Lieutenant-Governor of Bengal, His Honor Sir Ashley Eden, interfered, and had the restoration completed at great cost to the British Government. The place has ever since risen to eminence, owing to the great facility of travelling caused by the opening of the Patna-Gaya State Railway, attracting great many visitors from different parts of the world, as well as pilgrims from all Buddhist countries, who are actuated with the religious devotion and fervour of paying their respect to that most hallowed spot where Prince Sakya Singha sat in meditation, and at last founded the religion which now sways the destiny of one-third of the whole human population.

3. That ever since the temple has been restored, the Buddhists have been freely worshipping in the temple, setting up images, bells, flag-staffs, and performing other rites in accordance with their religion, and the former Mahanth of Budh-Gaya never interfered and objected to the same being done.

4. That Krishna Dayal Gir, the present Mahanth of Budh-Gaya, ascended the *Mahanthi Gadi* of the Budh-Gaya Sannyási Math in February, 1892, and unfortunately he has ever since taken an antagonistic attitude towards the Buddhists in general and your humble petitioner in particular.

Notes on a petition, dated the 12th June, 1894, filed before the Magistrate of Gaya by H. Dharmapala, General Secretary of the Maha Bodhi Society.

THIS petition was filed before me on the 12th instant by H. Dharmapala, General Secretary of the Maha Bodhi Society, with the main object of being accorded permission to set up in the Temple of Maha-Bodhi at Bodh-Gaya an historical image of Buddha, which had been entrusted to him for the purpose on the occasion of his passing through Japan recently on his return from attending the "Parliament of Religions" at Chicago. It had been arranged, with the consent of the Mahanth of Bodh-Gaya, that this image was to be placed in the Temple on the 19th of May last, but in consequence of a very threatening attitude of opposition adopted by the Mahanth and his followers at the last moment, I found it expedient in the interest of the peace to inform Mr. Dharmapala that he should postpone doing this, unless in the meantime he was able to convince the Mahanth that it in no way infringed on any supposed rights that the latter claimed in connection with the temple, and obtained a renewal of his consent. Not having succeeded in this, he has now filed the present petition with a view to its being declared that the Buddhists have an absolute right of worship, irrespective of the Mahanth's consent, to set up the image in the temple. This is claimed as involved in the right of freedom of worship in the temple which the Bengal Government have recently declared that the Buddhists possess (*vide* the Government letter of the 5th May, 1894, quoted in para. 12 of the petition). The opportunity is taken of pressing one or two other matters which are held to be implied in the right of free worship, namely, to establish and set up images, &c., in the temple, and to attach Buddhist priests to the shrine who would have access to it at all times, without having to go at all to the Mahanth, who keeps a lock on the door of the temple.

2. The following is a statement of the circumstances, which give rise to the present petition.

3. About the middle of April last, Mr. Dharmapala visited Gaya on his return to India, and informed me that when passing through Japan, he had been entrusted with an historical image of Buddha, which he was commissioned to have set up in the Temple of

5. That shortly before the temple was restored under orders of the benign British Government, King Mindoon Min of Burma (King Thibaw's father) purchased a piece of land, west of the temple compound, from Mahanth Hem Narayan Gir, the preceptor and predecessor of the present Mahanth, and built a small building (now called the Burmese rest-house) for the permanent residence of Buddhist priests, who were sent out here to officiate at the daily worship which was carried on three times a day; and the Burmese priests resided in the house and officiated at the religious service, till one of them died there and was buried at Budh-Gaya, his tomb or *stupa* being just south of the Burmese rest-house, and the others left the country on account of political unrest caused in Burma by the death of the old King and the accession of King Thibaw. That your petitioner also stayed with a Japanese priest at the Burmese rest-house for nearly three months from January to March 1891: and that there were other Buddhist priests who permanently resided there, and regularly officiated at the daily services from July 1891, to January 1893, when some of them were brutally assaulted by the retainers and servants of the present Mahanth.

6. That the late Mahanth Hem Narayan Gir, who was himself a learned man and Sanskrit scholar, was always friendly to your petitioner and the Buddhists, and had leased out to your petitioner one bigha of land west of the Burmese rest-house for its extension, and your petitioner had built a kitchen and a latrine for the use of the priests, but the present Mahanth, who is bent upon cancelling the lease by refusing to accept the rent, has pulled down the additions made on the land after the priests had left the place after the assault.

7. That the Buddhists of Japan having come to know that the original image of Buddha in the second storey in the Buddha-Gaya Temple was removed to the forest of Rajgir by the Buddhist priests in the temple in the 12th century A. D., through fear that it might be destroyed by the conquering Mussalmans, and also having come to know that the image that is placed there at present is not the original image, but one set up by Mr. J. D. Beglar after the temple was repaired, and of course, without any ceremony prescribed by the Buddhist code of religion, they, on behalf of the whole Japanese nation, presented to the Maha-Bodhi Temple a very historic image of Lord Buddha, carved by the great artist Sadatomo of Nanto, by command of the ruling Shogun Minamoto Yoritomo, 700 years old, and entrusted your petitioner with it to have it placed with due religious rites and ceremonies on the second floor of the temple in your Worship's presence. They also entrusted him with a letter to your address, requesting your Worship to take charge of the image and have it placed in the temple, and your petitioner has already presented to your Worship the original letter in Japanese character.

8. That in the month of April last, Mahanth Krishna Dayal Gir himself admitted before your Worship that he had no objection to the image in question being placed in the temple, provided that it was not a metal one, on the ground that it might be stolen, and he may be held responsible for the loss or theft; and consequently your petitioner, with your Worship's permission and consent, made all preparations, and underwent some expense to take the image in procession from Gaya to Budh-Gaya with fitting pomp and grandeur, and fixed the full-moon day of Baisak (19th May, 1894,) which is the holiest day in the Buddhist calendar, this being the anniversary of Lord Buddha's birth as well as of his attaining supreme enlightenment under the Bodhi-tree at Budh-Gaya, and also of His entering Nirvana, and your Worship was informed of the date. That on the 17th of May last, when all the arrangements were nearly completed, and when the High Priest of Japan, who had come out to India on a pilgrimage, had consented to officiate at the enshrining of the image in the temple, and had arranged to arrive there on that date, the Mahanth refused to allow your petitioner to set up the image in the temple, and

Maha-Bodhi in my presence. He stated that a Japanese letter to my address accompanied the image, in which I was requested to take charge of it, and see it placed in the second storey of the temple. I requested Mr. Dharmapala to obtain for me an English translation of the letter, but this has not yet been got, and the letter is still with him. The Mahanth came to see me at the same time, and I informed him of the image that had been sent from Japan to be placed in the second storey of the temple, and enquired if he had anything to say about the matter. The Mahanth informed me that he would have no objection so long as the image was not of metal (*dhatu*). When I asked him what was the objection to a metal image, he replied, that one of gold or silver might be stolen by dacoits, and that he might be held responsible for it. I did not at the time know what material the image was composed of. However, this was the only objection of any kind the Mahanth hinted at, and I took it as implying that he consented to the placing of any other image in the temple and informed Mr. Dharmapala of this. As the image is one of sandalwood, Mr. Dharmapala assured me that everything was all right, and arranged to set up the image on the full-moon day in May, *i.e.*, the 19th of May, as being the anniversary of the birth of Buddha and also of the day on which he obtained enlightenment under the Bodhi-tree at Maha-Bodhi.

4. Mr. Dharmapala, who was away from Gaya from the time when I saw the Mahanth, returned on the 17th of May, bringing the image with him. The Mahanth himself was away in the east of the district for about ten days until that date also. On the morning of the 17th of May, one of his disciples and a Muhammadan mukhtear of a very inferior status came to me with a copy of the *Indian Mirror*, and said they were alarmed about a paragraph in it, to the effect that the Buddhists were going to set up a great image in the temple with some ceremony on the 19th. I declined to discuss matters with them, and said that any representation on the subject must come from the Mahanth personally, with whom I said the matter had, however, already been arranged. The Mahanth himself came to me at 8 P. M. that evening; and it was evident from his tone and conversation that his disciples had been working upon him, and that he and they were afraid from the importance that was apparently being attached to the setting up of the image, that it was part of a surreptitions attempt on the part of the Buddhists to oust him from the temple altogether.

I learned, a day or two after, that one or two Bengalis in the town of Gaya had put the Mahanth up to this, in order to make capital out of it. I assured the Mahanth that as regards the question of general control over the temple, the Buddhists had no intention of doing anything that would be prejudicial to his interests, if only he would discuss matters with them in a reasonable spirit, with a view to an amicable arrangement; and I reminded him that he had had no objection to the image being set up, so long as it was not made of metal, which it was not. He replied that his disciples were agitated and dissatisfied at this. But I said he ought to explain matters to them. I had no time to discuss things further with him at that inconvenient hour and directed him to come back in the morning. When he returned, he said it was Mr. Dharmapala's duty to have gone personally to him to obtain his consent to the setting up of the image; and I told him I would instruct Mr. Dharmapala to go and discuss the matter with him, and that, until matters were cleared up between them, the image would not be allowed to be put up.

5. Mr. Dharmapala, as requested by me, went to the Mahanth, but the latter insisted on the unreasonable condition that the *pranpratishtha* ceremony must be undergone before the image could be placed in the shrine, which would be equivalent to constituting it a Brahminical deity. As no arrangement could consequently be come to, the image could not be taken to Budh-Gaya on the 19th. Indeed, considerable preparations were made by the

collected a large band of armed men to resist the procession; that when the matter was brought to your notice, your Worship immediately ordered your petitioner to postpone the ceremony, and the enshrining there was accordingly suspended, and the image, which is a mastepiece of Japanese work of art, is still lying in your petitioner's hands in great danger of being damaged.

9. That the said Mahanth on the full-moon day of Baisak last actually locked the doors of the Maha-Bodhi Temple, and the gate was barred against all Buddhist pilgrims; and that some pilgrims, who had come from Ceylon, had to proceed from here to Budh-Gaya under a special police escort, ordered by your Worship, and that instructions from your Worship to the Budh-Gaya Police were necessary to procure safety for the High Priest of Japan, who had gone to worship at Budh-Gaya, and that, notwithstanding the above arrangements, your petitioner was, on account of the personal animosity that the Mahanth shewed towards him, constrained to forego the right of worship in the Budh-Gaya Temple, on the holiest day of the year.

10. That it is evident from what is stated above that the attitude taken by the present Mahanth of Budh-Gaya Math is becoming more inimical and aggressive day by day, and unless your Worship kindly intercedes in the matter, your petitioner is afraid that the Buddhists' right of free worship in the temple will practically, and to all intents and purposes, be taken away from them by the Mahanth.

11. That in his letter No. 6 P. D., Political Branch, dated Darjeeling, the 5th May, 1894, the Chief Secretary to the Government of Bengal assured your petitioner "that there is perfect freedom of worship for all Buddhists at Budh-Gaya, and the Hindu *Sannyásis* who have held the place for over five centuries are ever ready to meet all reasonable requirements of worshippers. Any well-grounded complaint that difficulties were imposed will meet ready attention and redress at the hands of the Bengal Government.

12. Your petitioner most humbly and respectfully begs to submit that there can be no "perfect freedom of worship for all Buddhists," until the Buddhists are allowed to keep their own priests to officiate and preside at the daily worship which is to be carried on three times every day, to go in and out of the temple freely at all hours and pass some special nights within the temple, chanting prayers and reading religious books, to burn incense, &c., at the altar, to embellish and decorate the place, to enshrine images, to hang bells, and to perform other rites in accordance with their own religion, and not to be dictated to by the Mahanth, who is a Hindu Saivite, at what time and in what way they are to conduct their religious worship there.

Your petitioner, therefore, most respectfully approaches your Worship, who is the representative of the Government in this district, with this petition, and humbly prays:—

(1). That the Mahanth of Budh-Gaya Math may be ordered not to interfere with your petitioner in setting up the aforesaid image of Lord Buddha, presented to the Maha-Bodhi Temple by the Japanese nation, with befitting rites and ceremonies;

(2). That the Buddhists' right of perfect freedom of worship in the shape of flowers, scents, &c., and in the suitable embellishment of the temple and its precincts by setting up images, bells, flagstaffs, &c., may be practically enforced;

(3). That the presence of Buddhist priests to officiate at the worship of Buddhist pilgrims being *absolutely* necessary according to the dictates of the Buddhist religion, their presence in the temple for this purpose and for the daily worship of Lord Buddha, which consists of the performance of certain ceremonies thrice a day, as is done in the Buddhist Temples of Ceylon, Burma, Siam, Japan and China, be permitted without let or hindrance on the part of the Mahanth and his people;

(4). That such other or further order or orders be passed as to your Worship may seem fit to meet the requirements of the case which may seem just and proper.

Mahanth's followers in order to oppose by force the taking of the image there, and Mr. Dharmapala received information as to an intention to assault him personally, which made him so apprehensive that he thought it prudent to abstain from worshipping at the Temple on the holy night. Some Buddhist pilgrims also, who arrived at Gaya on that day, appealed to me for protection, and I had to issue an order forbidding all interference with the worship of the Buddhists at the temple, and to send down the inspector of police to the temple to enforce it. The sub-inspector got there at 9-30 P.M., and found an assemblage of people, headed by some of the Mahanth's disciples, collected at the temple. They pretended they had come there to receive alms from the pilgrims that were expected that evening: but the inspector ordered them to open the door of the temple, which was locked. They made some demur, saying it was too late, and so on. The inspector, however, insisted, and the pilgrims were able to conduct their worship in peace. It is certain that, had I not sent down some police, the Buddhist pilgrims who had come from far, specially to worship at the temple on that most holy night, would not have been allowed by the Mahanth's men to enter it on that occasion.

6. I learned subsequently from a communication received from the Executive Engineer, Eastern Sone Division at Bankipore, in whose charge the temple is, that on the night of the 19th, just about the time when the Mahanth was at my house, his steward, Jaipai Gir, *kothari*, removed from the temple, under protest from the Public Works Department peon in charge, seven images that had been placed there by Buddhist pilgrims some years before.

As soon as I heard of this, I issued a peremptory order to the Mahanth to replace the images; and he did so, but at the same time he claimed the right to take any images that might be placed in the temple. In conversation with me since, he has explained that if he does not maintain his right to take even common images, such as those of clay, he would become a loser, if the Buddhists take to placing gold and silver images there. In other words, as he himself admitted to me, he would not be able to appropriate the precious metals in them. This brings me to the crux of the whole question connected with the control of the Mahanth over the temple, and I believe myself that, if an equivalent for images and votive offerings can be arranged, the whole matter can be amicably settled. It is preposterous, however, for the Mahanth to appropriate entirely to his own use any votive offerings placed in the temple by the Buddhist worshippers. He is not a Buddhist priest, and if he has actually taken such already, as there is no doubt he has, it can only have been in his capacity as a custodian of the temple, and he can have no right to do more than simply take charge of them in the absence of any others who could do so.

7. The removal of these images was probably intended to further the novel idea, started by the Mahanth since this image question has arisen, that the Maha-Bodhi Temple is a Hindu one, and that the image of Buddha in the shrine is an incarnation of Vishnu. This, he fancies, may increase his hold on the temple, and give him an advantage he does not possess, in the negotiations with the Buddhists as regards its future control. But the theory is as foolish from the point of view of the Mahanth's own interest as it is preposterous. No Hindus have ever worshipped at the temple, except perhaps that some ignorant pilgrims may have gone to see it out of curiosity, and done reverence to the image inside.

If the temple were a Hindu one, it would have been defiled by the Buddhists' offerings of biscuits and burning of tallow-candles at the shrine, nor would a *chamar* woman ever have been allowed to sweep it. Nor does it stand to reason that the temple of an incarnation of Vishnu would ever be the special charge of a Saivite priest like the Mahanth. The tree to the south of the temple is one of the places at which Hindu pilgrims to Gaya offer *pindas*, but they do so under the auspices of the Vaishnavite Gayawal priests, and have no concern with the Mahanth.

And your petitioner, as in duty bound, shall ever pray.

H. DHARMAPALA,
Genl. Secy., Maha-Bodhi Society.

NAND KISHORE LAL,
Vakil.

Dated Gaya, the 12th June, 1894.

I have not gone into the whole question of the Mahanth's right in the temple, nor have I by me, as I write, any of the authorities that might throw light on the subject ; but it will be found that the Mahanth has never had any control over the Temple itself, except since its restoration by the British Government.

When Gosain Ghamandi Gir, the founder of the monastery near by, settled here about 1590 A. D., it was not the temple, but the beauty of the spot, that attracted him. The temple was indeed in ruins and half burried, and he and his successors never made the slightest attempt to put it into order or to worship in it. The truth is that it is a sin for a Hindu to enter a Buddhist temple like this, and particularly so for a follower of Sankaracharyya, the bitter opponent of the Buddhists, like the Mahanth of Budh-Gaya. The Mahanths have, it is true, cleared a space in the vicinity of the temple where mausoleums have been erected to them, and they have converted a small temple in front of the larger one into a Hindu one, and called it that of Tara Devi, though the image in it is not that of a goddess at all.

The Great Temple is also apparently in the village of Mastipur Taradih, which was settled revenue free with the Mahanths, but I believe that in none of the grants is any mention whatever made of the temple itself. There is nothing to show that the Mahanths ever concerned themselves with it, and, even when the Burmese King proposed to do something for its restoration, no question appears to have arisen as to the Mahanth's having any right in the temple itself. A perusal of the correspondence forwarded to the Commissioner of Patna with the Bengal Government's memo., dated the 16th October, 1875, and of the reply of Mr. Halliday, the Collector of Gaya, dated the 8th December, 1875, will show that the only matters on which the Mahanth was consulted, or with regard to which he made any representations, were as to care being taken not to interfere with certain Hindu idols in the vicinity of the temple, and as to a proper agreement being executed for the land the Burmese wished for the erection of a monastery and of a *paribhaga*, or a magazine for the deposit of offerings made at the Bodhi-tree.

Practically all that the Buddhists now wish was conceded on that occasion, or would undoubtedly have been, had the idea occurred at the time that the Mahanth's consent was necessary for anything connected with the internal arrangements of the temple. Since its restoration, however, the Mahanth appears to have acquired certain prescriptive rights in connection with the shrine, principally because there was no Buddhist representative on the spot to prevent his appropriating votive offerings made at it ; and his possession of the key of the *sadar* gate, in the door-way of the temple, has served to enhance his control over it.

But I do not think that it can be fairly said that he has any right of ownership as against the Crown in a temple that was an abandoned building until it was restored at the expense of the Crown.

However, as I have said, I have not studied all the facts bearing on the question ; anyway, whatever prescriptive rights the Mahanth may have acquired, need not stand in the way of granting the Buddhists full control over the Temple, as they are prepared to buy up those rights, and there need be no fear that any action taken in furtherance of this object will in any way affect Hindu religious susceptibilities. All the Hindus to whom I have spoken, including the Vishnuvite Gayawal priests, say that there can be no possible objection to the temple being handed over entirely to the Buddhists, and that it would indeed be a sin for any Hindu to have anything to do with it. There was one Pandit, however, Chandrashekhar Bhatta, who sought to support the Mahanth's theory that the Buddha in the shrine was an incarnation ; but he showed his ignorance of everything connected with Buddhism, when he finally said that the only objection to the Buddhists having full control over the Temple, would be that they might sacrifice animals at it which would be offensive to the Hindus. What reverence for animal life is included in the Hindu religion is usually attributed to the influence of Buddhism itself, and one of the main principles of the Buddhist religion is that there is no efficacy in sacrifice.

8. I am of opinion that the right of free worship in the Maha-Bodhi Temple, to which the Buddhists are undoubtedly entitled, may fairly be held to include the rights claimed in the present petition. These are in effect the following :—

(1.) The right to set up images and present other votive offerings in the shrine ;

(2.) The right to enter and remain in the temple at all times, irrespective of the consent of the Mahanth—in other words, to possess the key of the door ;

(3.) The right to have Buddhist priests to assist in the worship at the shrine.

9. In my last conversation with the Mahanth, however, held the day before this petition was filed, he expressed a desire that no further steps should be taken in the matter until my return from leave, as he seems desirous now of coming to an amicable arrangement with the Buddhists, seeing that he has everything to lose by not doing so. He parted with me on the understanding that I would recommend this, and I stated the same to Mr. Dharmapala. I would strongly recommend, therefore, that no order might be passed on this petition on any matter connected with the temple in the meanwhile. I am prepared to go into the whole question patiently in the cold weather.

D. J. MACPHERSON,

Magistrate of Gaya, on leave

Bombay, 28th June 1894.

PART III.

JUDGMENT OF THE HIGH COURT.

In the High Court of Judicature at Fort William in Bengal.

The 22nd August, 1895.

CRIMINAL JURISDICTION.

Present:

THE HON'BLE MR. JUSTICE MACPHERSON,
AND
THE HON'BLE MR. JUSTICE BANERJEE.
(Two of the Judges of the Court.)

IN THE MATTER OF JAIPAL GIR, MOHENDRA GIR, AND BHIMAL DEO GIR ... ... *Petitioners*

versus

H. DHARMAPALA ... . *Opposite party.*

FOR PETITIONERS.—Mr. M. Ghose, Mr. Hill, and Mr. Cotton, Counsel, and Babus Sarat Chunder Roy and Hara Prasad Chatterjee, Vakils.

FOR OPPOSITE PARTY.—Sir Griffith Evans, Officiating Advocate-General, and Babus Saligram Singh and Mahabir Sahai, Vakils.

Macpherson, J.—The three petitioners, who are described as Hindu Sannyasis of the Monastery of Bodh-Gaya, have been convicted under Section 296 of the Penal Code of disturbing the worship of the complainant and other Buddhists of Ceylon in the Temple of Mahabodhi at Bodh-Gya on the 25th February last, and the conviction has been upheld by the Sessions Judge. They were tried and acquitted on other charges under Sections 295, 297 and 143.

The Magistrate says, "the case is one of importance, as the disturbance is sought to be justified by the defendants on the ground that their superior, the Mahanth of Bodh-Gya, claims the right, though a Hindu, of regulating what worship shall be performed in this famous shrine, known as the Great Temple of Mahabodhi, and regarded by the Buddhists, that is, by about one-third of the human race, as the most sacred spot on earth." That, I think, is rather misleading. No such broad question arises, and it is desirable to keep the case within its proper limits. It is for the complainant to prove that he and his co-religionists, when disturbed, were *lawfully engaged* in the performance of religious worship or religious ceremonies, a fact which the petitioners denied. The defence may have put their case higher than was necessary, but it is not right to say that it is the defence which gives the case its importance.

There is no doubt, however, that the case has attracted a good deal of attention from the prominence which has been given to it, and from the nature of the dispute and the position of the parties. It has been fought with a persistency and at a cost which would have been more appropriate, if it had been brought in a Court which could finally determine the rights of the parties, and not in a Criminal Court where the narrow issue is whether a criminal offence has been committed.

The trial has occupied a long time, leading Counsel have been retained, and very lengthy judgments, traversing the whole history of the Temple, have been recorded. It may well be doubted whether the object of the complainant was not to do something much more than to punish a crime. It has been contended throughout that no criminal offence was committed, and, in the Appellate Court, that on the facts found there was no criminal offence. As it seemed to us very questionable if the conviction was right, we gave a rule to show cause why it should not be set aside, and the case has now been fully argued by the learned Counsel who argued it before the Sessions Judge. It was suggested, when the rule was applied for, that the petitioners had not a perfectly fair trial, as the learned Magistrate had formed an opinion, before this dispute took place, of the rights of the parties, which necessarily, but perhaps unconsciously, influenced his decision. We did not give a rule on that ground, and I think it right to say that, both in the conduct of the trial and in his very long and careful judgment, the Magistrate seems to have been scrupulously fair.

The facts connected with the occurrence of the 25th February are thus stated by the District Magistrate and not disputed. He says :—

"Between 8 and 9 o'clock on the morning of that day, the complainant, who is a Buddhist gentleman from Ceylon and Honorary General Secretary of the Mahabodhi Society, arrived at Bodh-Gaya with two Singhalese Buddhist priests, Sumangala and Devananda, and a layman, Silva, of the same race and religion, and proceeded to enshrine a highly artistic, and, it is said, historical image of Buddha, sent from Japan for the purpose, on the altar in the chamber of the upper floor of the Mahabodhi Temple. While they were setting up the image, two Muhammadan gentlemen, namely, the Special Sub-Registrar and a Deputy Magistrate of Gaya, happened to come to see the place and were accompanied by a Muhammadan mukhtear of the Mahanth of Bodh-Gaya, named Hussain Baksh, and by one Jagannath Singh, a Hindu door-keeper, whom the Mahanth keeps at the Temple. After they entered the chamber, Hussain Baksh said something to the latter, who thereupon left. The three Muhammadans also went away before all the paraphernalia of the image were set up. The image with censer, candlesticks and lotus flowers and also a Japanese dedicatory certificate, describing its history, was duly set up, and Dharmapala then sent word to the Government custodian of the Temple, and, on his coming six or seven minutes after, put the image in his charge, saying, it had been sent by the Japanese. This done, Sumangala took one of the candles to light it, but at that moment about thirty or forty of the Mahanth's Sannyasis and other Hindus, and also the mukhtear, Hussain Baksh, came rushing into the place in a very rowdy fashion. Some got on to the altar, a couple of them placed themselves between Dharmapala and it, one snatched the candle out of Sumangala's hand to prevent its being lit, and most spoke in a vehement and imperative tone, commanding Dharmapala to take away the image and using such threats as "*budmash*, we will beat you, there are five hundred of us." The Muhammadan in particular kept pushing him on the shoulder vehemently, telling him to remove the image. The Government custodian, finding them much enraged, kept imploring them with folded hands not to act hastily. Dharmapala refused to remove the image, and as he knows little of the language, a number of them went and fetched the Mahanth's Hindu mukhtear, Vijayananda, who happended to be at the monastery in connection with a document of the Mahanth's the Sub-Registrar had come to get registered. Dharmapala pointed out to Vijayananda what desecration it was for people to be on the altar, and the latter got one or two to come down. Thereupon this mukhtear and all but a few, who remained quietly looking on, left the Temple, and Dharmapala and the two priests, thinking all opposition had ended, sat down to their devotion in front of the image in the characteristic Buddhist attitude of religious contemplation, the highest form of Buddhist worship. They were absorbed in this form of devotion for about a quarter of an hour, when the Hindus again came to the Temple and, heedless of their attitude, made a rush into the place and tumultuously carried off the image of Buddha and set it down in the open courtyard below. This tumult, and indeed the mere removal of the image itself, put an end to the devotional contemplation of the Buddhists. Dharmapala and one of the priests continued, however, to sit there, and in a few minutes a constable came up to call him down to the head constable, who had been sent for by the Government custodian, and to whom also the mukhtear, Hussain Baksh, had made a statement praying him to interfere. Dharmapala refused to go down, so the head constable had to come up where he was, and began questioning him in Hindi ; but Dharmapala, not understanding this, wrote down there and then, at his request, a summary statement of the occurrence."

I may add to them that the image and all its paraphernalia were conveyed in boxes to the chamber of the upper floor and opened there, that the door-keeper, who was apparently the only person encountered, made no opposition to the entry, and that neither the Mahanth nor any one else connected with the Temple, nor any Government official, had been informed of the complainant Dharmapala's intention to place the image there.

It may be conceded that the Mahabodhi Temple, which is very ancient and very sacred to Buddhists, was a Buddhist Temple, that, although it has been in the possession of Hindu Mahanths, it has never been converted into a Hindu Temple in the sense that Hindu idols have been enshrined or orthodox Hindu worship carried on there, and that Buddhist pilgrims have had free access and full liberty to worship in it. It does not appear that any hindrance was ever offered to them or that any complaints were ever made by them, and, before the occurrence in question, there is no instance of any disturbance between the Buddhist worshippers and the Hindu Mahanths or their subordinates in regard to their respective rights. This fact is of some importance in the present case, where each party charges the other with being the aggressor. The petitioners, no doubt, now say that the Buddhists worshiped by permission and not of right. That is a question which it is unnecessary to consider. I shall assume for the purpose of this case that the worship which they were in the habit of performing was of right. It will, however, be necessary to consider the nature of that worship and the nature of the act which gave rise to the disturbance complained of, in order to see whether a criminal offence has been committed.

A great part of the lengthy judgments of the Magistrate and of the Judge is devoted to a discussion of the Mahanth's position in regard to the Temple and the extent of his proprietary right and power of control. His possession is found, but the extent of his proprietary interest and power of control is questioned. It is quite unnecessary to discuss his proprietary interest. There is no doubt that he is in possession, that he is the sole superintendent of the Temple, and that he takes all the offerings both of Hindus and Buddhists, and the present state of things appears to have been in existence for many years, if not for centuries. It is not proved, I do not think it is even alleged, that any Buddhist priests have ever exercised any control or authority in the Temple within living memory. The Government has had no occasion to interfere in the internal management, even if it could do so, and that is not a question which need be considered in this case. If the control and superintendence of the Temple is not vested in the Mahanth, it does not appear to be vested in any one.

The Judge seems to think that the Mahanth placed some limitation on his own rights or powers by the agreement entered into in 1877 with the representative of the King of Burma. This agreement and the translation of it will be found at page 107 of the paper book, part I. The correctness of the translation of the third passage, referred to in the Judge's judgment, is a matter of dispute, but the Judge in his translation has omitted to give any effect to the word *hamare* in the passage *uski puja hamare shudamad-i-qadeem se chali ati hai.* It may or may not be that that agreement has some bearing on the question whether Buddhists worship by permission or of right, and which, as I have said, is now immaterial, but neither the agreement nor the subsequent appointment of a Government custodian, whose principal duty it apparently is to look after the building and relics generally, have, I consider, made any difference in the Mahanth's position for the purposes of this case. That position I find to be this, that he held possession of the Temple and had the control and superintendence over it, subject to that right of Buddhists to worship there in the customary manner, that is to say, in the manner in which they had been in the habit of worshipping. I see nothing in the judgments of the Lower Courts, which goes against this finding. The difficulty is to understand from those judgments where the freedom of worship ends and the right of control begins.

The question really is, whether the freedom of worship enjoyed by the Buddhists covered what Dharmapala and his associates did. It is for the latter to bring the case strictly within the four corners of Section 296, and prove that they were, when disturbed, lawfully engaged in the performance of religious worship or religious ceremonies.

The petitioners say, that they were not so engaged, that what they did was something which had never been done before, and that it was done, not for the purpose of religious worship, but for another object, in the assertion of a right and with the knowledge that they would be resisted. This renders it necessary to consider in some detail the nature of the act done and resisted, and the nature of the worship which the Buddhists were in the habit of doing.

Dharmapala was subjected to a very long cross-examination on his denial that the Mahanth was either the owner or the person in possession of the Temple. Whatever excuses may be made for him, he certainly came very badly out of it, and furnished the other side with good grounds for questioning his general veracity. It is amply shown from his own writings and from writings published with his knowledge and under his authority, that he always regarded the Mahanth, whatever the latter's strict rights may be, as the owner. Dharmapala was not in the position of an ordinary devotee, worshipping at the shrine. He was undoubtedly a religious enthusiast and an agitator. I use the word in no offensive sense, for I may freely concede that he was thoroughly sincere in his religious views and in promoting the work which he had undertaken. He was the Secretary of the Mahabodhi Society, which was started in Ceylon in May, 1891, and also the Editor of a monthly journal started to promote the objects of the Society. One of the objects of the Society was, he admits, to recover the possession of the Mahabodhi Temple from the Mahanth, and the prospectus moots the idea "of restoring the central shrine and transferring it from the hands of the usurping Saivite Mahanths to the custody of the Buddhist monks." Numerous extracts from the journal which were put in, show that the object was to establish Buddhist control in the Temple. In February, 1893, he and Colonel Olcott, an Honorary Director of the Society, interviewed the Mahanth with the view of acquiring the religious custody of the Temple for the Buddhists of all nations, but the Mahanth, as the correspondence shows, refused either to sell or give a lease on any terms. Dharmapala then, according to a letter addressed to the President of the Society and signed by himself and Colonel Olcott, began to enquire into the legality of the Mahanth's tenure. In 1893, when in Japan promoting the objects of the Society, he conceived the idea of enshrining a new image of Buddha in the Temple, as there was, he says, no image in the upper floor chamber, which he regarded as the *sanctum sanctorum*. The result was that the image in question was sent to him in March, 1894. It is described as a beautiful work of art and it was accompanied by a dedicatory certificate addressed to him by the High Priest of Tokio. It is there described as a very ancient and holy image, and it was presented "to be enshrined in the second storey of the Budh-Gya Temple."

Dharmapala announced in his journal that the image would be placed in the Temple on the 19th May, a very holy day with Buddhists, in the presence of the Collector. There was no authority for the latter part of the announcement, and the Mahanth had not been consulted. The latter, learning of the intended installation by Dharmapala, objected to it and closed the Temple door to prevent it. This he afterwards opened in compliance with an order of the District Magistrate made under Section 144, Criminal Procedure Code. It was mentioned in the order that no image would be set up in the Temple that night without the Mahanth's consent, and the Magistrate at the same time sent a demi-official letter to Dharmapala, in consequence of which he desisted from placing the image.

In April, 1894, Dharmapala invoked the assistance of the Bengal Government in aid of the Mahabodhi Society, and received, in reply, the letter, Exhibit D. 22, which he produced. This is dated the 5th May. In it he is informed that the Lieutenant-Governor can take no measures for the furtherance of the general objects of the Mahabodhi Society, that there is perfect freedom of worship for all Buddhists at Bodh-Gya, and that any well-grounded complaint that difficulties were imposed would meet with ready attention and redress at the hands of the Bengal Government.

In June, 1894, he again addressed the Lieutenant-Governor, complaining, as he says, of the refusal to allow the image to be placed in the Temple. He denies that he asked for help or Government influence. In reply, he received the letter, Exhibit D. 23, from the Chief Secretary, dated 22nd June. In it he is told that the Government must decline to exercise any influence with the Mahanth of the Bodh-Gya shrine, and he is referred to the letter, Exhibit D. 22.

In June, 1894, he also petitioned the Magistrate on the subject of the Japanese image and was informed in September (Exhibits D. 28*a* and D. 28*b*) that the local authorities could not deal with the matter.

Nothing more happened till the morning of the 25th February, 1895, when he went surreptitiously, as the Judge says, to set up the image in the upper chamber, and the occurrence took place of which he now complains. He says he did not anticipate opposition, but it is impossible to believe this. He had no reason to believe that the opposition had ceased, and he had every reason to believe that as his position and motives became better known, the opposition to his doing anything which might lead to give him a better foothold in the Temple would be more intense.

I have said that Dharmapala was not in the position of an ordinary devotee, but he is, of course, entitled to have the legality of his act judged as if he was one. He could do as much, but no more, and if his act was in itself lawful, his previous failure and his failure to get the assistance of the Bengal Government or of the local executive officers would not make it any the less so. But his position and his past conduct are of importance in judging of his motives and the motives which led to the opposition.

Now what Dharmapala wanted and attempted to do, was to enshrine this image in the upper room of the Temple against the will of the Mahanth, in whose possession and under whose superintendence the Temple was, and there is no doubt that it was the attempted enshrinement which led to the disturbance. The Judge, whose judgment I have felt some difficulty in following, takes exception to the word "enshrine" which the Magistrate uses, as he says there is no evidence that the Buddhists intended permanently to enshrine the image that day. It seems to me that no other conclusion is possible The image had been obtained for enshrinement in the upper chamber, and it was sent for that purpose, as the dedicatory certificate, which was placed alongside it, shews. Moreover, Dharmapala, when putting it up, sent for the custodian, Bepin Behary, and said, "this present from the Japanese Government is now placed on the shrine, and now it is under your control." This clearly shews that he intended it to remain there. If he merely intended to do an act of worship before it, and then remove it, why did he go surreptitiously to the upper chamber? Giving him credit also for the religious feeling which he claims to have, it is absurd to suppose that he was indifferent to the fate of this image, if the Mahanth afterwards removed it, although the course which he might have taken in such an event is a matter of conjecture. It does not appear that there is any special ceremony connected with the enshrinement of an image, but, however that may be, I have no doubt that Dharmapala's object was to make the altar of the upper room the permanent shrine of this image.

As regards motive, the Judge says, that the Mahanth has no ground for anticipating any injury to his interest from the act of Dharmapala, and that there was no ground for injuring any connection between the known and published desire of the Buddhists and the Mahabodhi Society, in connection with the Temple, and the setting up this image as an object of temporary or permanent worship. His final conclusion is that Dharmapala's immediate object was "to gain a spiritual triumph for Buddhism, and to get rid of a responsibility, which, although he had sought it himself in the greatest hope and confidence, he now felt was an intolerable burden." The spiritual triumph meant doing what he originally intended to do, and in the face of opposition, and as for the burden, a man cannot be allowed to relieve himself by doing a wrong, and then complaining that he has reasonable ground for inferring a connection. The Mahanth certainly seems to have thought so in 1894, probably much more in 1895. Dharmapala has no cause for surprise if his intentions and motives were misconstrued. Now I think Dharmapala has failed to shew that he had any right to do what he did against the known will of the Mahanth, or that he went to perform a religious worship or a religious ceremony of a kind which was customary with Buddhist worshippers at the Temple.

It is said, and, no doubt, with truth, that to enshrine an image of Buddha, or to place such an image in an altar and sit before it in contemplation, are high forms of Buddhist worship, but the image must be placed where there is a right to place it. There was no image of Buddha in the upper chamber, and, whatever may have been the case in remote ages, none can speak to ever having seen such an image there, and there is no evidence that Buddhist worshippers generally used to go to that chamber for worship. At the time of this disturbance, and both before and after the restoration of the Temple, there was a large image of Buddha in the shrine on the ground floor of the Temple, and before this Buddhist devotees used to worship and make offerings. They seem to have been content with this, and before Dharmapala came, no one wanted to do anything more. He himself has worshipped many times before the great image since 1891, without any opposition, and he says he had no reason to be dissatisfied with it as everything about it was right. He also says that he has no knowledge of any Buddhist having attempted to enshrine an image in the upper chamber. There is evidence upon which reliance is placed, that Burmese pilgrims in November and December, 1891, placed some marble images of Buddha by the big image on the altar downstairs without asking the Mahanth's permission. That may be so, and it is clear that the Mahanth did not object, but what was then done was in no way analogous to what was done here. The Mahanth, in whose possession the Temple is, objected to Dharmapala's enshrining this image in the upper floor of the Temple, and there is nothing on the evidence to justify the Court in holding that the right to place it there existed, or that the Mahanth's objection could be disregarded. Dharmapala may possibly be able to establish the right which he asserts, but that is a question for another tribunal. It is enough to say that he has not proved it in this case so as to justify his act.

The evidence shows, and the Magistrate finds, that since July, 1894, the Mahanth and his disciples have been carrying on a sort of spurious Hindu worship of the great image of Buddha on the altar of the ground floor, and that the image has been dressed in a way which renders it repugnant to Buddhist worshippers. The Magistrate regards this is as a stratagem on the Mahanth's part to strengthen his position against, I suppose, some threatened danger. This was extremely wrong, but it does not, I think, affect the present case. In January, 1895, Dharmapala and a party of pilgrims worshipped before the great image after removing the vestments and obliterating the *tilak* marks, and no objection was made to their doing this. The Mahanth's conduct does not seem to have been made the subject of any remonstrance to him or of complaint to any one else, and it cannot be said to have led to Dharmapala's action on the 25th February. That the Mahanth really believed that his position was threatened by Dharmapala, whose views with reference to the Temple must have been well known, I cannot doubt, and it is impossible to say that there was not some ground for the belief. The desire to enshrine the Japanese image in the upper floor of the Temple, where no image had been before, may have been very laudable from a purely religious point of view, but it is at least open to doubt whether his motive was purely religious and not to further his known desire to bring the Temple under Buddhist control. Any how, as he has not proved his right to put it there against the will of the Mahanth, he has not shown that, when putting it, he was lawfully engaged in the performance of religious worship or religious ceremonies. It is said, however, that there were two disturbances with an interval between them, and that, even if there was no disturbance of a lawful religious worship or ceremony on the first occasion, when Dharmapala was told to remove the image and was prevented from lighting the candles, there certainly was on the second, when the image was removed, as the Buddhists were then sitting on contemplation before the image and actually and to the knowledge of the disturbers engaged in religious worship. It is argued that the worship having commenced, they were lawfully engaged in it, and that even if the petitioners had the right to remove the image before worship commenced or after it ended, the removal of it during worship was a disturbance and an offence under Section 296. Several cases have been put by way of analogy, and I may concede that, if the petitioners, in effecting an object which they were legally entitled to effect, disturbed an assembly lawfully engaged in the performance of religious worship by means which they knew must disturb it, they would be guilty of an offence under Section 296, even if they had no intention of disturbing it. But it is quite clear that the worship referred to in Section 296 must be a real worship and not a cloak for doing something else, and that the assembly must be lawfully engaged in worship. It is quite true that if I see persons in a posture of worship, it is no excuse for disturbing them to say that I thought they were not worshipping and that they were thinking of something which they ought not to have been thinking about, but obviously much must depend upon the circumstances under which they were worshipping. Here I think it is quite open to the petitioners to say that there was no real worship, but I do not wish to decide the case on that ground, or to hold that the Buddhists were not really contemplating and that they merely fell into a posture of worship for appearance's sake. I prefer to hold, as I do, that they were not lawfully engaged in worship, that the disturbance must be regarded as continuous, and that if they were not lawfully engaged at first, they were not lawfully engaged afterwards. They went to enshrine an image in a place where they had no right to enshrine it. The enshrinement may have involved the performance of religious worship or religious ceremony, but their immediate object was to enshrine it and not simply to perform an act of worship. They were told, before the enshrinement was complete or before worship commenced, to remove the image, they were prevented from lighting the candles, and all the persons who went to interfere did not leave the room. Dharmapala says that sitting in contemplation before an image of Buddha is the highest form of Buddhist worship, but that there are other forms—the offering of flowers and the burning of candles being the preliminaries. He says they were not allowed to light the candles, and that "the prevention of the lighting of the candles was a disturbance of a part and parcel of our religious worship." If so, it was a disturbance from the first and a disturbance which continued, and the mere circumstance of their falling into a posture of worship in front of the image which they had been ordered to remove, but before it actually was removed, an act which nothing but the use of personal violence could have prevented, does not put them in any better position that they were at first.

To say that there was at first no disturbance of their religious worship or ceremony which amounted to an offence, but that there was such a disturbance afterwards, is to put the case on very narrow grounds, and the answer is, I think, clear. For these reasons I hold that no offence has been committed under Section 296, which was never intended to apply to a case like this, and that the conviction must be set aside and the fine refunded.

It is greatly to be regretted that this criminal case should have been brought and pressed in the way it has been. Dharmapala's motive in bringing it is, I think, very questionable, and a perusal of his evidence, which is open to severe criticism, shows that he is responsible for the great length to which the trial has been prolonged.

Banerjee, J:—I am of the same opinion.

The accused in this case were convicted by the District Magistrate of Gaya of the offence of voluntarily causing disturbance to the complainant and his associates, who were found to have been lawfully engaged in the performance of religious ceremonies and religious worship in the Mahabodhi Temple at Buddha-Gaya and were sentenced under Section 296 of the Indian Penal Code to one month's simple imprisonment and a fine of Rs. 100 each.

On appeal by them the learned Sessions Judge has affirmed the convictions and the sentences of fine, but set aside the sentences of imprisonment.

They now ask us in the exercise of our revisional powers to set aside the conviction and sentences, on the ground that upon the facts as found by the Courts below and upon the facts disclosed by the evidence, no offence under Section 296, Indian Penal Code, has been committed by them.

We have heard learned Counsel on both sides at some length and considered the evidence and the elaborate judgments of the Courts below, and the conclusion we have arrived at is that the contention of the petitioners is correct.

To constitute an offence under Section 296 Indian Penal Code,

(1) There must be a *voluntary* disturbance caused.

(2) The disturbance must be caused to an assembly engaged in *religious worship or religious ceremonies*, &c.

(3) The assembly must be *lawfully* engaged in such a worship or ceremonies.

These being the ingredients necessary to constitute the offence, let us see how far the evidence establishes their existence.

The evidence which has been fully discussed in the judgment of my learned colleague and which I need not therefore refer to at any length, taken along with certain books of public history such as Martin's edition of Buchanan Hamilton's "Eastern India" and Rajendra Lala Mitra's "Buddha-Gaya," which may be referred to under Section 57 of the Evidence Act, proves the following facts.—

(1) The great temple at Buddha-Gaya, said to occupy the site of Buddha's hermitage, was originally a Buddhist temple; but it has for a long time (how long it is neither easy nor necessary in this case exactly to determine, but certainly for more than a century) been in the possession and under the control of the Hindu Mahanth of that place.

(2) Buddhist pilgrims have, however, from time to time continued to visit the temple and perform their worship there; but there is no reliable evidence to show that the upper chamber had in recent times been ever resorted to by Buddhists. The Temple has however, not been shown to have been converted into a place of Hindu worship, though there is a spot in the Temple compound, which is resorted to by Hindus as a sacred place for offering *pindas* or oblations to ancestors.

(3) Early in 1893 an endeavour was made on behalf of the Maha-Bodhi Society of Ceylon (established in 1891), of which the complainant Dharmapala is the General Secretary, to obtain a conveyance or lease of the Temple from the Mahanth, and on the negotiations for the purchase or lease failing, the complainant, it seems, applied to the Government of Bengal in April 1894, requesting it to help the Maha-Bodhi Society in obtaining the transfer of the Buddha-Gaya Temple from the Mahanth, but was told in reply that the Government was not in a position to help him.

4. In the meantime, in November 1893, the complainant obtained from Japan an image of Buddha highly artistic in execution and said to be of historic importance, with a document purporting to be signed by the High Priest of Tokio, for the purpose of enshrinement in the second story of the Buddha-Gaya, Temple, and "as a good sign" (as the document puts it) "for the success of the restoration of the Buddha-Gaya Temple;" and he advertised in the Maha-Bodhi Society's journal that on the 19th of May 1894, in the presence of the Collector of

Gaya he would place that image in the Temple; but he had to desist from placing the image there upon the objection of the Mahanth and upon receipt of a prohibitory order from the Magistrate.

5. No further attempt was made to place the Japanese image in the Temple until the 25th of February 1895 (the day of the occurrence, which has given rise to this case), when between 8 and 9 in the morning the complainant with two other Singhalese priests and one Singhalese layman went with the image to the upper floor of the Temple, and after they had set up the image on the altar and were about to light one of the candles, as a preliminary to their worship, a number of retainers of the Mahanth came, snatched the candle away, and commanded the complainant to remove the image. After some expostulation all but a few left the Temple; and Dharmapala and the two priests sat down to their devotion in front of the image in the characteristic Buddhist attitude of religious contemplation, when in about a quarter of an hour, a number of men, including the accused, came and tumultuously carried off the image and set it down in the open court-yard below.

As regards the first of these facts, the complainant professes not to be aware of the Mahanth's right to, or possession of, the temple, but he is contradicted by his own writings in the journal of the Maha-Bodhi Society and by his own conduct in seeking to obtain a conveyance or a lease of the temple from the Mahanth. The shuffling nature of his evidence has been unfavourably commented upon in the judgments of both the Courts below, and the learned Sessions Judge, in order to reconcile his view of the general truthfulness of Dharmapala's evidence with the unreliable character of this part of it, has to rely upon the erroneous and somewhat mischievous theory of the oriental standard of truth being different from the normal standard, a theory, the application of which must often lead, as it has in this instance led, to incorrect estimation of evidence. I deem it right here to observe that the question what the exact nature and extent of the Mahanth's control over the Temple is, the evidence adduced in the case does not enable us to determine.

With reference to the second fact, it was urged on behalf of the petitioners that the Buddhists cannot claim it as a matter of right to worship in the Temple, and that they have hitherto done solely by the permission of the Mahanth; but I do not think it necessary to determine the point in this case.

Touching the remaining three facts, there was practically not much dispute.

These being the facts of the case, Mr. Ghose, for the petitioners, contended that they disprove the existence of the three ingredients necessary to constitute the offence of which the petitioners have been convicted.

He contended first of all, that it was evident from facts 1, 3 and 4, and from the finding of the District Magistrate, which was fully borne out by the evidence and had been erroneously set aside by the Judge, that the accused, in removing the image which had been placed in the Temple by the complainant in the assertion of a right he did not possess and in denial of the Mahanth's rights, acted under a *bonâ fide* belief that they were only defending the rights of the Mahanth without any intention of disturbing any one; and that they cannot therefore be said to have voluntarily caused any disturbance. Having regard to the definition of the word "voluntarily" as given in Section 39 of the Indian Penal Code, I do not think this contention is correct. Intention to cause a certain result is not an element necessary to constitute a voluntary causing of that result, but knowledge of, or belief in, the likelihood of the result following, though not intended, may supply the place of intentions. If, therefore, the accused knew or had reason to believe that their act in removing the image was likely to cause disturbance to any religious worship, then, though they might not have intended to cause such disturbance, yet the causing of the disturbance would be voluntary within the meaning of the Penal Code. There would no doubt still remain the question whether the accused knew or had reason to believe that the complainant and his companions were engaged in religious worship at the time, and that their act in removing the image was likely to cause disturbance of such worship. But, having regard to the position of the accused as members of a religious fraternity and to the means they enjoyed of observing Buddhist worship in the Temple, which lies close to their monastery, I am not prepared to dissent from the conclusion arrived at by the Courts below that this question should be answered in the affirmative.

The learned Counsel for the petitioners next contended that the religious worship and religious ceremonies which Section 296, Indian Penal Code, contemplates, must be real religious worship and real religious ceremonies, and not such as are colourable only, and that the worship and ceremonies which the complainant and his party were engaged in, were merely a pretext to cover their act of asserting their right against the claims of the Mahanth. Whilst admitting fully the correctness of the first branch of this contention, that the religious worship and ceremonies contemplated by the section must be such as are real, and conceding also that the previous acts and conduct of the complainant, as proved by his own writings in the journal of the Mahabodhi Society, tend to show that his action on the 25th of February, 1895, was more in the assertion of a right to worship than for the purpose of worshipping, I should still hesitate to hold that the worship was not real, when those engaged in it swear that it was so.

The last contention of Mr. Ghose was that, granting that the complainant and his companions were engaged in religious worship, and granting that they were voluntarily disturbed by the accused, it is not shewn that they were lawfully engaged in such worship, and that the disturbance does not therefore constitute an offence under Section 296, Indian Penal Code. I am clearly of opinion that this contention is sound. To sustain a charge under Section 296, it lies upon the prosecution to show that the persons who were disturbed in their religious worship or ceremonies were lawfully engaged in the performance of the same, that is, that they had the right to do what they were doing. But the prosecution has utterly failed to discharge the burden of proof that lay upon it. What the complainant and his associates were engaged in doing, was not simply to worship in the upper chamber of the Temple, but to enshrine a new image of Buddha on the alter of that chamber, and that after the refusal of the Mahanth, in whose possession and under whose control the Temple was, to allow such enshrinement, as shown by the events of May, 1894, and without any further intimation to him. It is evident, too, from the previous acts and conduct of the complainant himself, reluctantly admitted by him in his cross-examination, that his object on this occasion was not simply to worship in the Temple, but to assert his right to worship there in a particular way, that is, to enshrine the image there in disregard of the authority of the Mahanth, or, to put it in the mild language of the learned Sessions Judge, "to give a spiritual triumph for Buddhism, and to get rid of a responsibility which, although he had sought it himself in the greatest hope and confidence, he now felt was an intolerable burden." In other words, he wanted indirectly and in a covert way to do that which he had failed to do directly and openly, namely, to bring the Temple under the control of Buddhist priests.

Now, though the Buddhists may have the right to worship in the Temple, there is no evidence to show that they have any right to resort to the Temple to secure such an object as the one referred to above, or to enshrine a new image in the Temple against the wish, and in the face of, the express prohibition of the Mahanth. The learned Sessions Judge, in his judgment, takes exception to the word "enshrinement," but that is the word used in the charge to which the accused were called upon to answer, and that is the word used by the complainant himself with reference to the placing of the Japanese image in the Temple. His intention evidently was to place the image in the Temple as a permanent object of worship, and he has adduced no evidence to show that he had the right to do so. That being so, it cannot be said that in doing what he did, he was lawfully engaged in religious worship or religious ceremonies. The learned Adovocate-General, no doubt, felt the difficulty of the position, and the way in which he sought to get over the difficulty was by arguing that, even if the Mahanth had the right to prevent the setting up of the new image, his subordinates, the accused, were at best entitled to stop the placing of the image on the altar before the commencement of the worship or to remove it after the conclusion of the same, but they were not justified in disturbing the worship during its continuance. To this argument, there are two answers. In the first place, however desirable it may be that religious worship from its sacred character should, while it is going on, be secured against molestation, even though the worshipper be a wrong-doer and a trespasser, that is not provided for by our Criminal law, and the Legislature has thought it fit to make molestation of religious worship an offence only when people are lawfully engaged in their worship. And in the second place, upon the admitted facts of the case, the opposition effectually began before the worship had commenced and the lighting of the candles, which is regarded as a necessary preliminary, had taken place, and the subsequent removal of the image was only a continuation of the first opposition.

I, therefore, think that it is not established that the complainant and his associates were lawfully engaged in religious worship, when they were disturbed, and that the accused, therefore, in causing the disturbance have committed no offence under Section 296, Indian Penal Code, and I agree with my learned colleague in holding that this rule should be made absolute, the convictions and sentences set aside, and the fines, if realised, refunded.

(True Copy.)

J. LOUIS,

Assistant Registrar High Court.

PART IV.

DOCUMENTARY EVIDENCE.

DOCUMENTARY EVIDENCE.

EXHIBITS PUT IN BY PROSECUTION.

Exhibit I.

See Part I, page 43.

Exhibit II.

[NOTE.—This is a photograph of the Japanese image and is not reproduced.]

Exhibit III.

See Part I, page 49.

Exhibit IV.

See Part I, page 50.

Exhibit V.

See Part I, page 51.

Exhibit VI.

ततः कलौ प्रवृत्ते संमोहाय सुरद्विषाम् । बुद्धो नाम्नाजिनसुतः कीकटेषु भविष्यति ॥

(*Bhagwat*—Part I, Chapter 3, Sloka 24).

Translation.

"Then, at the commencement of the *kali-yuga* (iron age) the son of Jina, whose name is Buddha, will be born in Kikat (*Kikatdesh, i. e.*, Gaya) for the suppression of the enemies of the gods (*rakshasas*.)"

Exhibit VII.

देवद्विषां निगम वर्तनि निष्ठितानां पूर्भिर्मयेन विहिताभिरदृश्यतूर्भिः ।
लोकान् घ्नतां मतिविमोह मतिप्रलोभं वेषं विधाय बहुभाष्यत औपधर्म्यम् ॥

(*Bhagwat*—Part II, Chapter 7, Sloka 37).

Translation.

"When the enemies of the Devas (the Asurs or *rakshasas*) will forcibly begin to walk in the path prescribed by the Vedas, and to annoy the people, seated in the *puris* built by Maya Danava (*i. e.*, the heavens), with unseen force, the Lord will assume the garb of an infidel, a form which will deprive the Asurs of their senses and delude them, and preach to them various false doctrines of religion."

Exhibit VIII.

ततो दिगम्बरो मुण्डो बर्हिपत्रधरो द्विजः । मायामोहोऽसुरान् श्लक्ष्णमिदं वचनमब्रवीत् ॥

(*Vishnu Puran*—Part III, Chapter 18, Sloka 2).

Translation.

"O Dwija or Brahman! then Maya Moha (a character created by Vishnu) assumed a form, naked and shaven-headed, and with peacock's feathers in hand, addressed the Asurs in these sweet words."

[NOTE.—The object of Maya Moha was to drive the Asurs from the path of virtue which they were treading, by force.]

Exhibit IX.

न वदेद्यावनी भाषा न गच्छेज्जैन मन्दिरम् ॥ हस्तिना पौड्यमानोऽपि प्राणे कण्ठागतैरपि । १ ।

यावनी अर्थात् फारसी अर्बी भाषा न बोले जैनमन्दिर अर्थात् बौद्ध के मन्दिर में न जाय यदि हाथी भी उसको दांत से मारता हो और प्राण कण्ठ में भी आया होय तौभी बौद्ध मन्दिर में न जाय—

पण्डित गङ्गाधर शास्त्री हेडपण्डित गया जिला स्कूल—ता: १२ । ५ । ९५ ।

Translation.

"The language of the Yavans (Persian and Arabic) should not be uttered, and the Temple of the Jainas should not be entered, and this should not be done, even if one is tortured by an elephant, or if he be at the point of death."

[NOTE.—The original text given above was written out from memory by Witness No. X(see Part I, page 96) at the request of the Court. No reference to any *Puran* was given.]

EXHIBITS PUT IN BY THE DEFENCE.

Exhibit D 1.

See Part I, page 9.

Exhibit D 2.

See Part I, page 10.

Exhibit D 3.

See Part I, page 12.

Exhibit D 4.

See Part I, page 13.

Exhibit D 5.

See Part I, page 15.

Exhibit D 6.

See Part I, page 16.

Exhibit D 7.

See Part I, page 18.

Exhibit D 8.

See Part I, page 21.

Exhibit D 9.

See Part I, page 22.

Exhibit D 10.

See Part I, page 23.

Exhibit D 11.

See Part I, page 23.

Exhibit D 12.

See Part I; page 24.

Exhibit D 13.

See Part I, page 24.

Exhibit D 14.

See Part I, page 24.

Exhibit D 15.

See Part I, page 25.

Exhibit D 16.

See Part I, page 26.

Exhibit D 17.

See Part I, page 26.

Exhibit D 18.

See Part I, page 27.

Exhibit D 19.

See Part I, page 29.

Exhibit D 20.

See Part I, page 30.

Exhibit D 21.

See Part I, page 30.

Exhibit D 22.

See Part I, page 32.

Exhibit D 23.

See Part I, page 32.

Exhibit D 24.

See Part I, page 33.

Exhibit D 25.

See Part I, page 34.

Exhibit D 26.

See Part I, page 35.

Exhibit D 27.

See Part I, page 36.

Exhibit D 28 (*a*).

See Part I, page 36.

Exhibit D 28 (*b*).

See Part I, page 36.

Exhibit D 29.

Sec Part I, page 40.

Exhibit D 30.

Sec. Part I, page 40.

Exhibit D 31.

See Part I, page 40.

Exhibit D 32.

See Part I, page 41.

Exhibit D 33.

See Part I, page 42.

Exhibit D 34.

See Part I, page 45.

Exhibit D 35.

See Part I, page 45.

Exhibit D 36.

(Revenue Survey Map of Mauza Mastipur-Taradih, Pargana Maher, Season 1842-43 ; not reproduced.)

Exhibit D 37.

See Part I, page 46.

Exhibit D 38.

See Part I, page 47.

Exhibit D 39.

See Part I, page 47.

Exhibit D 40.

See Part I, page 48.

Exhibit D 41.

(*See* over.)

Exhibit D 41.

Extract from "A List of the Objects of Antiquarian Interest in the Lower Provinces of Bengal," edition of 1879, page 125 to page 139.

PATNA DIVISION.—(*Continued.*)

No.	District.	Locality.	Object.	Description and history of the object.	Remarks.
...	Gaya ...	Buddha-Gaya.	...	The four sacred places noticed in the annals of Buddhism are Kapilavastu, the birth-place of Buddha; Buddha-Gaya, his hermitage; Benares, where he first promulgated his doctrine; and Kusi, the place of his *nirvana*, to the attainment of which he had devoted his long and arduous life. They were all places of great sanctity, and for 1,500 years were held in the estimation of his followers as the holiest places of pilgrimage on earth. With the expulsion of Buddhism from India, three of them have fallen into oblivion, and one has been appropriated to Hindu worship. Buddha-Gaya is now a large thriving village on the west bank of the river Lilajan about six miles from Gaya. There are several small mounds and a large one on the east side of the village. They mark the sites of ancient buildings which have long since crumbled to dust. The largest mound covers an area of 1,500 by 1,400 feet, and is divided into two unequal parts by a village road. The southern portion is about one-third the size of the northern one, but it is most important, as in its centre stands the most ancient monument in the village, the Great Temple, which will be noticed below.	
16	Do.	Do.	The Great Temple of Buddha-Gaya.	The most important object of antiquity is the Great Temple there, which is also remarkable as being the finest brick structure still standing in India. The bricks are of large size, 15 × 9 inches, carefully made and dressed, so as to rest smoothly on each other without the use of cement. The cement used was clay, both for the walls and the arches; cement of *surki* and lime, however, was not unknown at the time, for it has been used on roofs, copings and other exposed places, and also for plastering the walls, and for the formation of mouldings and ornamental figures. The Temple was built in the first century B. C. on the site of a still older one built by the Emperor Asoka 150 years before that date. It was surrounded by a stone railing set up by that monarch, and within this enclosure, it would seem, originally no other building existed. A part of this railing was found *in situ* by Captain Mead in 1864, when he carried on, by order of Government, certain excavations round the Temple. Thirty-two pillars of this railing were also traced in the verandah of the private residence of the Mohunt or Abbot who owns the place. The only part of the building which remains at all entire is the Great Shrine. It is a slender quadrangular pyramid of great height. The spire is on three sides surrounded by a terrace about 25 or 30 feet high, the extreme dimensions of which are 78 feet wide by 98 long. One end of this terrace towards the east formerly covered the porch, which has now fallen, and brought down part of the terrace with it. A stair from each side of the porch led up to the terrace, on which there was a fine walk round the Temple, leading to the second storey of the Shrine in front, and to a large area behind, on which is planted the celebrated *peepul* tree. The interior of the Shrine consists of a chamber. At the far end is a throne of stone, on which is placed a misshapen daub of clay, representing the Deity. Above this chamber are two others, one on the level of the old terrace, and the other still higher; but the falling of the porch has cut off all communication with these chambers.	

Exhibit D 41.—(Continued.)

No.	District.	Locality.	Object.	Description and history of the object.	Remarks.
				The doorway of this Temple is placed on the east side, and measures $6\frac{1}{3}$ feet in breadth, forming, with the depth of the wall, a vestibule $6\frac{1}{3}$ feet by $13\frac{1}{3}$ feet. The door frame is formed of stone bars of a reddish grey colour, and over it there is a cross-bar of grey-coloured stone, forming a strong hyperthereon. Then follows a blocking course of considerable thickness, and the space over it was left open, the sides first rising upright, but at a greater distance from each other than the width of the doorway, and then approaching each other, so as to form a triangular slit of large dimensions. The opening was produced by the gradual corbelling of the walls from the two sides, which gave to the sides the appearance of reversed flights of steps, each step being three bricks deep. The two sides met at the top in a point. This shows the outline of the true Indian horizontal arch to perfection. It is said that this space was left open for the purpose of allowing the light at dawn to fall on the presiding divinity of the Temple. The Temple itselt is now in a very ruinous condition. It has lately undergone repairs by some Burmese gentlemen, in conection with which Dr. Rajendra Lala Mitra was deputed by Government to institute enquiries and to report— *1st.*—As to the operations already carried on by the Burmese excavators, and the manner in which their action should be controlled by Government ; *2nd.*—As to the sculptures and architectural stones exhumed by them ; and *3rd.*—As to the disposal of those remains. His report, dated 31st October. 1877, thus describes the condition of the different portions of the Temple:— *The Southern Façade.*—This side of the Temple is now in a fair state of preservation. Its brick mouldings are generally entire, and there is enough of plaster on them to show very clearly what the details on them originally were. In the course of the several repairs the Temple has undergone, most of the finer chunam mouldings, particularly on the bases and the capitals of the pilasters, have been covered over ; fine, bold, clear crolls and forms, which, with the first touch of the repairer, became coarse and rude and subsequently entirely hidden, changing well-formed ribbed myrobolan capitals into misshapen round balls, and floral bases into ugly plain toruses; but by peeling off the outer layers, the original moulding *in situ* has always been found. *The Northern and Western Façades.*—These faces have been seriously injured, and large portions of brickwork have peeled off and are completely destroyed. It is evident, however, that these sides were the counterparts of the southern façade, and originally had exactly the same mouldings and ornaments. *The Eastern Façade.*—This side is also in a condition which is fairly indicative of its original character, except as regards the porch, which has fallen down. The upper part of this façade corresponds with the other three sides, but the lower part is partly so dilapidated and partly so renewed that it is difficult to restore it with the same rigid confidence as in the case of the other three sides. The space immediately in front of the wall on this side is held sacred to Savitri, a	

Exhibit D 41.—(Continued.)

No.	District.	Locality.	Object.	Description and history of the object.	Remarks.
				Hindu goddess, and an image stands right against the wall to represent her. *Roof of Porch.*—The roof immediately over the porch was formed of a pointed radiating arch built of dressed bricks, having one end broader than the other, to provide for the difference in the span of the estrado and the intrado, and very neatly and closely put together. But the voussoirs, placed edge to edge and cemented with clay, could not but produce a very weak form of arch. *Pavilions on Staircases.*—Entering the porch, there is on either hand a flight of steps covered by a semi-circular vaulted arch and leading to the terrace round the temple. Round the upper end of this flight, at the south-east corner, there are remains of walls which formed a pavilion over the stairs. A similar pavilion most probably also existed at the north-east corner; but this corner having been rebuilt within the last 150 years, no trace of it could be found. The remains of the pavilion at the south-east corner consist only of a few inches of the base of the surrounding walls, and it is impossible to make out what the pavilions were like in their entirety. *Pinnacle of the Temple.*—The top of the Temple is broken. According to Hiouen Thsang, it had originally a gilt copper crown shaped like a ribbed melon (*amla sila*) surmounted by a pinnacle of the same metal. A part of the brick core of the melon-shaped structure still exists. There is nothing to show what was the exact form of the pinnacle over the melon, but as it was a conventional ornament, it is believed its shape must have been like that of the *kalasas* which surmount the miniature stupas, of which hundreds are scattered all over the place. *Terrace round the Temple.*—The Great Temple has a terrace round it which now measures 19 feet above the ground. With the portion now buried under ground, it was 24 feet high and 14 feet wide all round. The side walls of this terrace were elaborately niched and panelled in keeping with the shaft of the Temple; but at about the end of the last century, the wall on the northern side had been injured and rebuilt on the old foundation and not, as shown in General Cunningham's plan, in front of it. In 1864 the wall on the western side had been forced out of perpendicular by the roots of the sacred Bo Tree, and this has been now rebuilt, but at a distance of 10 feet from the foundation, so that the ground plan of the Temple, which was square before, has now been changed to an oblong shape. The new walls are perfectly plain and not at all in keeping with the east and the south sides. The height has also been raised, so that the terrace is now two feet six inches higher on the north and the west sides than on the east and the south sides.	
17	Gaya ...	Buddha-Gaya.	Monastery or math.	Next to the Great Temple, the largest building in the locality is a monastery or *math*. It is situated on the left bank of the Lilajan, in the midst of a garden extending over an area of about 20 acres, and surrounded by a high masonry wall. It is four-storied in some parts, but three-storied all round a small quadrangle. The ground floor round the quadrangle is faced by a one-storied verandah built on sculptured monolithic pillars on three sides, and on wooden pillars on the fourth side. The roofs are low, and the windows	

Exhibit D 41.—(Continued.)

No.	District.	Locality.	Object.	Description and history of the object.	Remarks.
				very small and few in number; but the building is very substantial, and in excellent repair. To the north of this there are three two-storied buildings of moderate size, and long ranges of out-offices and stables in front on the east. On the south there is a commodious three-storied building, called *báradári*, with a terrace in front of it. There are also four temples, one of which contains only a marble slab, originally designed for a chiffonier, but now bearing an inscription partly in Sanskrit and partly in Burmese; a second contains some Buddhist statues. Outside this monastery, towards the west, on a part of the large mound aforesaid, there is a two-storied building of good make and size. It belongs to the monastery, and around it are four Hindu temples, one of which is dedicated to Jagannátha, one to Ráma, built by Gángá Bäi, who died at the beginning of this century, and the rest to Sivá. Towards the south-west corner of the outer wall of the monastery there is a cemetery, also attached to the monastery. The dead bodies of the monks, unlike those of other Hindus, are buried, and the cemetery contains the graves of about two hundred persons. The body is buried in a sitting posture; and in the case of mere neophytes a small circular mound of solid brickwork from three to four feet high is all that is deemed necessary for a covering for the grave. For men of greater consequence a temple is held essential; and in it, immediately over the corpse, a lingam is invariably consecrated. For the mohunts the temple is large and elaborately ornamented. It would seem that even for neophytes a lingam was held essential; but in the majority of cases its place was supplied by a miniature votive stupa picked up from the Buddhist ruins in the neighbourhood. Half-buried on the top of the mound, it passes very well for a lingam. In the way from Gayá to Buddha Gayá there are several monasteries of Hindu Sannyasis; everywhere the graves are alike.	
18	Gaya ...	Buddha-Gaya.	The *Bodhi-drum* or the Tree of Knowledge.	This is to the west of the temple itself, and is famous throughout the Buddhist world as the tree under which Sakya Sinha sat for five years in mental abstraction until he obtained the perfection of wisdom. It is still visited by pilgrims from Burmah, Ceylon, and other Buddhist countries. It is believed by the Buddhists to have been planted by Dugdha Kamani, King of Ceylon, 2225 years before Christ. The Hindus say it was planted by Brahma himself. It is said to have been rooted out by a Brahmanist king, Sasángka, and renewed by his contemporary, the Buddhist king Purna Varmma. When the tree died or was cut down new seedlings or shoots were planted on the site, more generally in an axila or hole in the old trunk, and, in order to protect the new plant from being blown down, sufficient soil had to be supplied to its root, which gradually raised the level of the platform. The process by which this rising took place having been continued even after the platform had risen to the height of the terrace, recourse was had to circular steps round the stem, and a circular encasing wall has lately been built to the height of three feet six inches, raising the lower end of the trunk of the tree to the height of 11 feet above the terrace, or 35 feet from the ground.	
19	Do.	Do.	The stone seat of Buddha.	The *Vajrásana*, or the adamant seat on which Buddha was seated during his protracted meditation under the Buddha tree, is a circular slab of blue-coloured stone, five feet in diameter, carved on the upper face in an elaborate and ingenious design. It is now lying in the porch of an un-	

Exhibit D 41.—(Concluded.)

No.	District.	Locality.	Object.	Description and history of the object.	Remarks.
				finished and unroofed temple dedicated to Vágiswari Devi, and would seem to be the identical stone described by Fa Hien, a Chinese pilgrim, who visited the holy places at Buddha Gayá between A.D. 399 and 414.	
20	Gaya ...	Buddha-Gaya.	Temple of Tara Devi.	To the east of the Great Temple, and close to it, there is a smaller one dedicated to Tara Devi. In style it is a miniature representation of the Great Temple. It has been built with bricks of the same size and make as are found in the Great Temple, and cemented with clay. The portion now visible measures 36 feet 5 inches in height on a base of 15¾ feet by 15¾ feet. The chamber inside is 5 feet 8 inches by 5 feet 10 inches by 11 feet 2 inches, having a vaulted roofing formed of a pointed Gothic arch. It was probably plastered in the same way as the Great Temple. It was not provided with a porch.	
21	Do.	Do.	Mounds ...	There are some mounds now existing outside the new boundary wall of the temple, and, if dug into, traces might be brought to light of the site of some of the numerous stone temples and stone houses in the neighbourhood. Monolithic columns of six to eight feet in height, and of rich designs, are largely met with, and bases for these, of equally elaborate designs, are also abundant. Fragments of mouldings, friezes, architraves, and other architectural stones are to be met with in almost every hut, stuck in the mud wall, over an area of five miles around the sacred spot. These prove the former existence of a considerable number of stone temples or other buildings in the neighbourhood of the Great Temple. The stones used for these works of art are granite, grey sandstone, basalt, and the dark blue potstone for which Gayá is so famous. The works in granite are the oldest, and they are at the same time the roughest. The other stones came into use successively in the order named, and neatness and artistic excellence followed the same order. For boldness and freedom of execution, however, the carvings on the granite pillars of Asoka do not yield to the most finished work on the softest potstone. On the contrary, the latter is thoroughly conventional, whereas the former display a considerable amount of natural grace and freedom of action.	

Exhibit D 42.

पूर्व्वं हि ब्रह्मतीर्थे च कूपे श्राद्धादिकारयेत् । ततकूपयुपयोर्मध्ये सर्व्वांस्तारयते पितृन् ॥
धर्म्मं धर्म्मेश्वरं नत्वा महाबोधितरुं नमेत् ।

(*Vayu Puran*, Chapter 49, Sloka 26, page 637.)

Translation.

" After saluting Dharma, the god of all virtues, the Peepul Tree is to be saluted."

[NOTE.—This is in connection with *Sradh* for the salvation of the deceased ancestors. The *mantra* to be recited follows this couplet.]

Exhibit D 43 *(a).*

इन मंत्रों से पूजन कर कलश के ऊपर सुवर्ण की बुद्ध भगवान की प्रतिमा स्थापन कर पुजन करै और ब्राह्मण को देवै यह व्रत शुद्धोदन ने कीया जीससे बुद्ध भगवान उसके पुत्र बने औ शुद्धोदन भी बहुत काल राज्य सुख भोग परम गति को प्राप्त भया। इसी रीति से भाद्र शुक्लद्वादशी को स्नान आदि कर। कल्किने नमः पादयोः।

(*Bhavishya Puran*—page 433.)

Translation.

"This *mantra* is recited in worshipping a golden image of Buddha-Deva, placed on a jar. The image is then given away to a Brahman. This *vrata* or vow was observed by Suddhodana, and in consequence thereof Suddhodana obtained Buddha for his son, reigned in happiness for a long time and then obtained salvation in the end. Hence there has been a custom to bathe and perform similar ceremonies on the 12th day of the bright fortnight in the month of Bhadra."

[The *mantra* runs thus: 'Salutation to Kalki, at the feet' and so forth.]

Exhibit D 43 *(b).*

बुद्धाय नमः पादयोः। श्रीधराय नमः कट्याम्। पद्मोद्भवाय नमः उदरे संवत्सराय नमः उरसि। सुग्रीवाय नमः कंठ विश्वबाहवे नमः भुजयोः। शंखाय नमः शंखे। चक्राय नमः चक्रे।

(*Bhavishya Puran*—page 399.)

Translation.

"At the feet, salutation to Buddha; at the waist, salutation to Sridhar; at the belly, salutation to Padmodar; at the breast, salutation to Sangbatsara; at the neck, salutation to Sugriva; at the hands, salutation to Vishva Báhu; at the conch-shell, salutation to Sankha (which adorns the hand of Vishnu); and at the *chacra* (discus), salutation to Chacra (weapon which adorns the hand of Vishnu.)"

Exhibit D 44.

प्रथम गन्ध पुष्प धूप दीप आदि उपचारों करके—

(मत्स्यं कूर्म्मं वराहञ्च नारसिंहञ्च वामनम्। रामं रामञ्च कृष्णञ्च बुद्धञ्च कल्किनं तथा॥
गतोऽस्मि शरणं देवं हरिं नारायणं विभुम्। प्रणतोऽस्मि जगन्नाथं स मे विष्णुः प्रसीदतु॥
छिनत्तु वैष्णवीं मायां भक्त्या प्रीतो जनार्द्दनः। श्वेतद्वीपं नयत्वस्मान्ममात्मा सन्निवेशितः॥

इन मंत्रोंसे दश अवतार का पूजन करै इस प्रकार जो इस व्रत को करै वह भगवान के अनुग्रह से जन्म मरण से छुटै औ सर्व्वदा विष्णुलोक में निवास करै॥

(*Bhavishya Puran*—2nd Part, Chapter 73, page 399.)

Translation.

"Furnished with sandal, flowers, *dhup* (a kind of burning incense), burning lamp, &c., the Vishnu should be worshipped in his ten incarnations and prayed to in the following words:—

"I bow down to Matsya (fish), Kurma (tortorse), Baráha (boar), Narasinha (half-man and half-lion), Bamana (dwarf), Ram, Parus Ram, Krishna, Buddha, and Kalki (*i. e.*, the ten incarnations of Vishnu), and to the Protector and Lord Deva Hari, Narayan. I bow down to Jagannath, may that Vishnu be pleased (with me). Pleased with my devotion, may Janardan, &c., cut the ties of *Vaisnavi Maya* (the power or energy of divine Vishnu in the preservation of creation), which binds me to the world; seated in my *atma* or soul (may he) lead me to Svet Dwipa (white island, the seat of Vishnu.)"

Exhibit D 45 *(a).*

ज्येष्ठशुक्लद्वितीयायां बुद्धजन्म भविष्यति।

(*Nirnaya Sindhu*—2nd Chapter, page 3.)

Translation.

"Buddha will be born on the second lunar day, if the moon be in the asterism Jaishtha."

Exhibit D 45 *(b)*.

पौषशुक्लस्य सप्तम्यां कुर्य्यात् बुद्धस्य पूजनम् ॥

(*Nirnaya Sindhu*—page 3.)

Translation.

"The worship of the Buddha should be held on the seventh day of the bright fortnight in the month of Pous."

Exhibit D 46 *(a)*.

वक्ष्ये बुद्धावतारञ्च पठतः शृण्वतोऽर्थदम् ।
पुरा देवासुरे युद्धे दैत्यैर्देवाः पराजिताः । रक्ष रक्षेति शरणं वदन्तो जग्मुरीश्वरम् ॥

(*Agni Puran*—Chapter XVI, Slokas 1, 2, page 16.)

Translation.

"I now relate the incarnation of Buddha, the reading and hearing of which is interesting. Formerly in a war between the Devas and the Asurs, the Devas, being defeated by the Asurs, sought the protection of the Lord, saying—'save us, save us.'"

Exhibit D 46 *(b)*.

मायामोहस्वरूपोऽसौ शुद्धोदनसुतोऽभवत् ॥

(*Agni Puran*—Chapter XVI, Sloka 2, page 16.)

Translation.

"He, the very prototype of Maya Moha, became the son of Suddhodan."

Exhibit D 47.

शान्तात्मा लम्बकर्णश्च गौराङ्गश्चाम्बरावृतः । ऊर्द्ध्वपद्मस्थितो बुद्धो वरदाभयदायकः ॥

(*Agni Puran*—Chapter 49, Sloka 8, page 44.)

Translation.

"Buddha, who is of tranquil spirit, having long ears, of fair complexion, covered with cloth, seated on a raised lotus, giver of blessings and security from fear."

Exhibit D 48.

अथवा विष्णुमतुलं सूक्तेन पुरुषेण वा । विष्णुञ्चैव महाविष्णुं सदा विष्णुमनुक्रमात् ।
स्थापयेद्देवगायत्र्या परिकल्प्य विधानतः ॥
वासुदेवः प्रधानस्तु ततः सङ्कर्षणः स्वयम् । प्रद्युम्नो ह्यनिरुद्धस्तु मूर्त्तिभेदास्तु वै प्रभोः ॥
बहूनि विविधानीह तस्य शापोद्भवानि च । सर्ववर्त्मसु रूपाणि जगताञ्च हिताय वै ॥
मत्स्यः कूर्म्मोऽथ वाराहो नारसिंहोऽथ वामनः । रामो रामश्च कृष्णश्च बौद्धः कल्की तथैव च ॥
तथान्यानि च देवस्य हरेः शापोद्भवानि च । तेषामपि च गायत्रीं कृत्वा स्थाप्य च पूजयेत् ॥

(*Lingam Puran*—Chapter XLVIII, page 268.)

Translation.

"Or the Vishnu who has no second, that Vishnu, Moha-Vishnu, and Sadá Vishnu in succession, should be installed with the recitation of Dev-Gayatri composed duly according to the *Purus Sukta* (hymns) of the Rig Veda. Basu-deva, the chief of all, Sankarshan himself, Praddumna (son of Krishna or Cupid), and Anirúdha (grandson of Krishna), are all but distinct images of the Lord. Besides, various and many have been the forms sprung from his curse, created for the good of the universe, and these are:—Matsya (fish), Kurma (tortoise), Baráhi (boar), Narasingha (half-man and half-lion), Bamana (dwarf), Ram (son of Dasarath), Ram (Parusram), Krishna, Buddha, and Kalki, and there are like incarnations, sprung from the curse of Hari. For these, *Gayatris* ought to be composed (and their images) installed and worshipped."

Exhibit D 49.

उपोषितायां तस्यां तु राज्यं लब्धं त्वयानघ। सर्व्वापत्सु च सा देवी भवन्तं परिरक्षति॥
यथा विनिहताः क्रूरा म्लेच्छाः पापसमन्विताः। भवांश्च रक्षितो राजन् श्रावणद्वादशीति सा॥२३॥
एकैव पाति चापत्सु राज्यमेकैव यच्छति। किं पुनर्द्वादशी तास्तु याश्च ऐन्द्रस्य गच्छति॥२४॥
इति वराहपुराणे बुद्धद्वादशीव्रतं नाम सप्तचत्वारिंशोऽध्यायः।

(*Varaha Puran*—Chapter XLVII, Slokas 22-24, page 47.)

Translation.

"That Goddess who destroyed the sinful and wicked (envious) *mlecchas*, and through whose favour you have gained a kingdom, protects you from all dangers. That Goddess, who protected you, O King, was *Srávan Dwadashi* (twelfth day of the moon of the month of *Sraban*.) One part of such a day alone gives protection from all danger, one alone gives a kingdom, and what to say of the twelve such parts, which give *Indratya* (the monarchy of heaven)?"

Exhibit D 50.

रूपकामो यजेद्बुद्धं शत्रुघाताय कल्किनम्।
एवमुक्त्वा नरस्तस्य द्वमासेवाब्रवीन्मुनिः॥ ४८ अध्याय। २२।

(*Varaha Puran*—Chapter XLVIII, Sloka 22, page 250.)

Translation.

"One wishing beauty should worship Buddha, and one wishing the destruction of his enemies should worship Kalki."

Exhibit D 51.

नमो बुद्धाय शुद्धाय दैत्यदानवमोहिने। म्लेच्छप्रायक्षत्रहन्त्रे नमस्ते कल्किरूपिणे॥
भा० १० स्क०। ४० अ०। २२

(*Srimat Bhagwat*—page, 118.)

Translation.

"Salutation to Buddha, the pure, the deluder of the Daityas and Danavas; and to one who incarnated as Kalki, the destroyer of the Kshetries, who behaved like *mlecchas*."

Exhibit D 52.

बौद्धालयं विशेद् यस्तु महा-पद्यपि वै द्विजः। तस्य वै निष्कृतिर्नास्ति प्रायश्चित्त शतैरपि॥
बौद्धाः पाषण्डिनः प्रोक्ता यतो वै वेदनिन्दकाः। तस्माद्द्विजस्तान्नेक्षेत यदि वेदेषु भक्तिमान्॥
ज्ञानतोऽज्ञानतो वापि द्विजो बौद्धालयं विशेत्। ज्ञात्वा वै निष्कृति नास्ति शास्त्राणामेष निर्णयः॥
बृहन्नारदीयपुराण चतुर्दशोऽध्यायः ६९। ७०। ७१ श्लोकः।

(*Brihannardi Puran*—Chapter XIV, page 49.)

Translation.

"He who enters the abode of a follower of Buddha (*bauddhalaya*) is never saved even by hundreds of atonements, even if he be a Brahman fallen in great danger. The followers of Buddha are called atheists, because they hate the Vedas. So a Brahman, if he has faith in the Vedas, should not even look at their faces. Hence it has been held in the *Shastras* that if a Brahman enters the abode of a follower of Buddha (*bauddhalaya*), knowingly or unknowingly, he is never saved, if he does so knowingly."

Exhibit D 53.

See Part I, page 59.

Exhibit D 54.

See Part I, page 60.

Exhibit D 55.

See Part I, page 60.

Exhibit D 56.

See Part I, page 63.

Exhibit D 57.

See Part I, page 63.

Exhibit D 58.

See Part I, page 64.

Exhibit D 59.

See Part I, page 64.

Exhibit D 60.

See Part I, page 65.

Exhibit D 61.

(*See* over).

Exhibit D 61.

Extract from "A List of Objects of Antiquarian Interest in the Lower Provinces of Bengal," edition of 1886, *page* 119. *(Segg.)*

PATNA DIVISION.—*(Continued.)*

Number.	District.	Locality.	Name of object.	Any local history or tradition regarding it.	Custody or present use.	Present state of Preservation.	Whether restoration is desirable and possible.		Whether photographs, plans, or drawings of the building exist.	Remarks.
							Class.	Remarks.		
16	Gaya ...	Buddha Gaya	......	The four sacred places noticed in the annals of Buddhism are Kapilavastu, the birthplace of Buddha; Buddha Gaya, his hermitage; Benares, where he first promulgated his doctrine; and Kusi, the place of his *nirvana*, to the attainment of which he had devoted his long and arduous life. They were all places of great sanctity, and for 1,500 years were held in the estimation of his followers as the holiest places of pilgrimage on earth. With the expulsion of Buddhism from India, three of them have fallen into oblivion, and one has been appropriated to Hindu worship. Buddha Gaya is now a large thriving village on the west bank of the river Lilajan, about six miles from Gaya. There are several small mounds and a large one on the east side of the village. They mark the sites of ancient buildings which have long since crumbled to dust. The largest mound covers an area of 1,500 by 1,400 feet, and is divided into two unequal parts by a village road. The southern portion is about one-third the size of the northern one, but it is most important, as in its centre stands the most ancient monument in the village, the Great Temple, which will be noticed below.						
17	Ditto ...	Ditto	The Great Temple of Buddha Gaya.	The most important object of antiquity is the Great Temple there, which is also remarkable as being the finest brick structure still standing in India. The bricks are of large size, the largest being 18″ × 18″ × 4 nearly. These however are only found in the	Mahant	In good order ...	*ia.*	Already repaired.	Yes.	

Exhibit D 61.—(Continued).

Number.	District.	Locality.	Name of object.	Any local history or tradition regarding it.	Custody or present use.	Present state of Preservation.	Whether restoration is desirable and possible. — Class.	Whether restoration is desirable and possible. — Remarks.	Whether photographs, plans, or drawings of the building exist.	Remarks.
				very lowest courses; the rest vary from 18" × 12" × 2" to 12" × 8" × 2". The cement used was clay both for the walls and the arches. Cement of *surki* and lime, however, was not unknown at the time, for it has been used on roofs, copings and other exposed places, and also for plastering the walls and for the formation of mouldings and ornamental figures. The temple was built in the first century A. D., on the site of a still older one built by the Emperor Asoka 250 years before that date. It was surrounded by a stone railing set up by that monarch, and within this enclosure, it would seem, no other building originally existed. A part of this railing was found *in situ* by Captain Mead in 1864, when he carried on, by order of Government, certain excavations round the temple. Thirty-two pillars of this railing were also traced in the verandah of the private residence of the Mahant or Abbot who owns the place.						
				The only part of the building which remains at all entire is the Great Shrine.* It is a slender quadrangular pyramid of great height. The spire is on three sides surrounded by a terrace about 25 or 30 feet high, the extreme dimensions of which are 78 feet by 98 feet. One end of this terrace, towards the east, formerly covered the porch, which has now fallen and brought down part of the terrace with it. A stair from each side of the porch led up to the terrace, on which there was a fine walk round the temple, leading to the second story of the shrine in front, and to a large area behind, on which is planted the celebrated *pipal* tree. The interior of the shrine consists of a chamber. At the far end is a throne of stone, on which is placed a mis-shapen daub of clay representing the Deity. Above this chamber are two others, one on the level of the old						* The description refers to the temple before repair, the triangular slit referred to having been caused by the falling in of the triangular piece above the doorway below.

Exhibit D 61.—(Continued).

Number.	District.	Locality.	Name of object.	Any local history or tradition regarding it.	Custody or present use.	Present state of Preservation.	Whether restoration is desirable and possible. Class.	Whether restoration is desirable and possible. Remarks.	Whether photographs, plans, or drawings of the building exist.	Remarks.
				terrace, and the other still higher; but the falling of the porch has cut off communication with these chambers.						
				The doorway of this temple is placed on the east side, and measures 6⅓ feet in breadth, forming, with the depth of the wall, a vestibule 6⅓ feet by 13⅓ feet. The door frame is formed of stone bars of a reddish grey colour, and over it there is a cross bar of grey-coloured stone, forming a strong hypertherion. Then follows a blocking course of considerable thickness. The space over it was left open, the sides first rising upright, but at a greater distance from each other than the width of the doorway, and then approaching each other so as to form a triangular slit of large dimensions. The opening was produced by the gradual corbelling of the walls from the two sides, which gave to the sides the appearance of reversed flights of steps, each step being three bricks deep. The two sides met at the top in a point. This shows the outline of the true Indian horizontal arch to perfection. It is said that this space was left open for the purpose of allowing the light at dawn to fall on the presiding divinity of the temple.						The temple, necropolis, ghat, monasteries and stupas have been repaired and only need keeping up.
18	Gaya ...	Buddha Gaya	Monastery or *math.*	Next to the Great Temple, the largest building in the locality is a monastery or *math.* It is situated on the left bank of the Lilajan, in the midst of a garden extending over an area of about 20 acres, and surrounded by a high masonry wall. It is four-storied in some parts, but three-storied all round a small quardangle. The ground floor round the quadrangle is faced by a one-storied verandah built on sculptured monolithic pillars on three sides and on wooden pillars on the fourth side. To the north of this there are three two-storied buildings of moderate size, and long ranges of out-offices and	......	The roofs are low, and the windows very small and few in number, but the building is very subtantial and in excellent repair.	iii.	No.	Yes.	

Exhibit D 61.—(Continued).

Number.	District.	Locality.	Name of object.	Any local history or tradition regarding it.	Custody or present use.	Present state of Preservation.	Whether restoration is desirable and possible.		Whether photographs, plans, or drawings of the building exist.	Remarks.
							Class.	Remarks.		
				stables on the east front. On the south there is a commodious three-storied building called *bâraddri*, with a terrace in front of it. There are also four temples, one of which contains only a marble slab, originally designed for a chiffonier, but now bearing an inscription partly in Sanskrit and partly in Burmese; a second contains some Buddhist statues. Outside this monastery, towards the west, on a part of the large mound aforesaid, there is a two-storied building of good make and size. It belongs to the monastery, and around it are four Hindu temples, one of which is dedicated to Jagannatha, one, which was built by Ganga Bai, who died at the beginning of this century, is dedicated to Rama, and the rest to Siva. Towards the south-west corner of the outer wall of the monastery there is a cemetery, also attached to the monastery. The dead bodies of the monks, unlike those of other Hindus, are buried, and the cemetery contains the graves of about two hundred persons. The body is buried in a sitting posture, and, in the case of mere neophytes, a small circular mound of solid brickwork, from three to four feet high, is all that is deemed necessary for a covering for the grave. For men of greater consequence a temple is held essential, and in it, immediately over the corpse, a lingam is invariably consecrated. For Mahants the temple is large and elaborately ornamented. It would seem that even for neophytes a lingam was held essential, but in the majority of cases its place was supplied by a miniature votive stupa picked up from the Buddhist ruins in the neighbourhood. Half-buried on the top of the mound, it passes very well for a lingam. On the way from Gaya to Buddha Gaya there are several monasteries of Hindu Sannyasis; everywhere the graves are alike.						

Exhibit D 61.—(*Continued*).

Number.	District.	Locality.	Name of object.	Any local history or tradition regarding it.	Custody or present use.	Present state of Preservation.	Whether restoration is desirable and possible.		Whether photographs, plans, or drawings of the building exist.	Remarks.
							Class.	Remarks.		
19	Gaya ...	Buddha Gaya	The stone seat of Buddha.	The *Vajrasana*, or the adamant seat on which* Buddha was seated during his protracted meditation under the Buddha tree, is a circular slab of blue-coloured stone, five feet in diameter, carved on the upper face in an elaborate and ingenious design. It is now lying in the porch of an unfinished and unroofed temple dedicated to Vagiswari Devi, and would seem to be the identical stone described by Fa Hien, a Chinese pilgrim, who visited the holy places at Buddha Gaya before A. D. 399 and 414.	......	......	ii*b*,	Yes.	Yes.	* The stone was supposed to be the *Vajrasana*, and is so referred to in works hitherto published. Recent research proves it not to be the *Vajrasana*.
20	Do. ...	Ditto ...	Temple of Tara Devi.	To the east of the Great Temple, and close to it, there is a smaller one dedicated to Tara Devi. In style it is a miniature representation of the Great Temple. It has been built with bricks of the same size and make as are found in the Great Temple, and cemented with clay. The portion now visible measures 36 feet 5 inches in height on a base of 15¾ feet by 15¼ feet. The chamber inside is 5 feet 8 inches by 5 feet 10 inches by 11 feet 2 inches, having a vaulted roof in the form of a pointed Gothic arch. It was probably plastered in the same way as the Great Temple. It was provided with a porch.	......	In good order ...	ii*b*.	Already repaired.	Yes.	Already repaired.
21	Do. ...	Ditto ...	Mounds ...	There are some mounds now existing outside the new boundary wall of the temple, and, if dug into, traces might be brought to light of the sites of some of the numerous stone temples and stone houses in the neighbourhood. Monolithic columns of 6 to 8 feet in height and of rich designs are largely met with, and bases for these, of equally elaborate designs, are also abundant. Fragments of mouldings, friezes, architraves, and other architectural stones are to be met with, stuck in the mud walls of almost every hut, over an area of five miles around the sacred spot. These prove the former	......	......	ii*b*.	......	No.	They have been dug into as far as the Mahant would permit; but further exploration is desirable, as only recently the entire lower part of a monastery was exhumed by Mr. Beglar at the in-

Exhibit D 61.—(*Concluded*).

Number.	District.	Locality.	Name of object.	Any local history or tradition regarding it.	Custody or present use.	Present state of Preservation.	WHETHER RESTORATION IS DESIRABLE AND POSSIBLE.		Whether photographs, plans, or drawings of the building exist.	Remarks.
							Class.	Remarks.		
				existence of a considerable number of stone temples or other buildings in the neighbourhood of the Great Temple. The stones used for these works of art are granite, grey sandstone, basalt, and the dark blue potstone, for which Gaya is so famous. The works in granite are the oldest, and they are at the same time the roughest. The other stones came into use successively in the order named, and neatness and artistic excellence followed the same order. For boldness and freedom of execution, however, the carvings on the sandstone pillars of Asoka do not yield to the most finished work on the softest potstone. On the contrary, the latter is thoroughly conventional, whereas the former display a considerable amount of natural grace and freedom of action.						stance of General Cunningham and with the Mahant's consent.

EXHIBITS PUT IN BY COURT.

Exhibit A.

See Part I, page 54.

Exhibit B.

[This is merely a transcript made by witness No. X (see *ante*, Part I, page 95), at the request of the Court, of the original Sanskrit passages shown him in cross-examination, with his Hindi translation of them.]

Exhibit C.

(*Note on the docket of letter No.* 1006, *dated* 24*th March*, 1891, *from the Superintending Engineer, Sone Circle, to the Magistrate of Gaya, forwarding letter No.* 1005, *Ex. D* 53.)

Submitted with old correspondence 1884. Serial numbers 1 and 3 of the year will give some information on the point. Government order of 1890 transferring the Temple to the Public Works Department is herewith submitted.

HARAN CHUNDER BANERJI,
Head Clerk.

Dated 4*th May*, 1891.

[NOTE.—A number of letters were marked by the Magistrate on 13th July, 1895, as Exhibits C 1 to C 22, E 1, E 2, F 1, and F 2: but these documents were ruled on appeal to have been improperly admitted, as not having been marked as Exhibits when tendered on 13th May. They will be found printed in their proper chronological order, together with the rest of the correspondence relating to the Bodh-Gaya Temple, in Part V.]

PART V.

CORRESPONDENCE ON THE SUBJECT OF THE BODH-GAYA TEMPLE (IN CHRONOLOGICAL ORDER.)

Correspondence on the Subject of the Bodh-Gaya Temple (in Chronological Order.)

[*Exhibit D* 20.]

SEAL. By order of the Magistrate of Gaya.

MY DEAR MAHANTH OF BODH-GAYA,

MAY you live comfortably. In sending herewith an extract from the letter of the King of Burma to His Excellency the Viceroy in Council regarding the wishes of the King of Burma to have the compound of the Bodhi Tree repaired and the deputation of two men near the said Tree for the purpose of its daily worship, and also as regards the sending of articles of worship to be offered to the Tree once or twice a year, I request you to let me know whether you approve of and agree to the same. Be it known that an early reply to this is required.

A. V. PALMER,
Magistrate and Collector.

Dated 15*th January*, 1875.

Enclosure.

Extract from a translation of a letter from the Foreign Department, Mandalay, to the address of the Secretary to the Government of India, Foreign Department.

As in 1234, corresponding with 1872 A.D., His Excellency the Governor-General of India sent a delegate (envoy) with presents to the King of Burma, the King of Burma has now in return ordered a royal letter with presents to be sent by way of friendship, and also that his delegates do see the Bodhi Tree in Hindoostan. As under this Bodhi Tree, which has been very sacred and incomparable during three *yugas* (ages), the all-knowing Buddha had his Buddha dominion under it, the King therefore wishes that religious offerings to God be made before the sacred tree on the understanding as if Buddha is in existence. With this view the King has ordered that articles of offering be made over to the delegates. The following four persons have been appointed delegates :—

(1). Andok Mahe Manhila Zethoo.
(2). Tarini Dogi Nimboo Mandar Rithoo.
(3). Ajud Dogi Nimboo Mandar Kayoogong.
(4). Noorthe Diu Tisi Thod.

The articles of offering have been made over to the above named persons for offering to the Bodhi Tree and their being sent to Hindoostan. It is hoped that on arrival of the delegates, the Secretary by way of friendship will do his best towards the realization of their object, and after helping them in delivering the letter and the royal presents, will render every assistance in their visit to the Tree in Hindoostan, and also in making offering and worshipping the Tree on behalf of the King. The King further desires that the compound of the Tree, which may have been burnt on account of age, be repaired. It is also his wish that two persons be deputed near the Bodhi Tree for daily worship. He also wishes that once or twice a year his people may take offering to the Tree, as he may desire ; and it is hoped that the Secretary will lay before His Excellency the Viceroy the objects of the King and help in their fulfilment.

To

THE MAGISTRATE OF GAYA.

Dated Bodh-Gaya, 18th January, 1875.

HONORED SIR,

BEING informed as to the contents of your Honor's *parwana*, dated the 15th January, 1875, and of the translation of the letter sent therewith, I have the honor to submit as follows :—

I have no objection to carry out your Honor's order, but the real facts of the case are as follows :—

(1). As to the compound of the Bodhi Tree, which the King of Burma wishes to repair, His Majesty is at liberty to do so, if he so desires.

(2). Secondly, the King of Burma may at his pleasure depute two persons to officiate at the worship of the said Bodhi Tree.

But I have to submit that beneath the Bodhi Tree there are *vedis* and gods of the Hindus. These *vedis* are visited by the Rajas and Maharajas, who offer *pinda* there and worship the gods. There is now at present near the Bodhi Tree, and within its enclosure, a place of pilgrimage (*tirtha*) of the Hindus. Therefore the offering of such articles as are against the Hindu religion will be objected to by the Hindus. If His Majesty, however, wishes to offer such articles as are not against the Hindu religion, His Majesty is at liberty to do so, and to offer them to the said Tree : and the Hindus will have no objection to his doing so. Besides your Honor is *malik*. I am ready to obey whatever orders your Honor may pass.

HEM NARAYAN GIR,

Mahanth of Bodh-Gaya.

[*Exhibit C* 1.]

8175 and 1876.

Fly. leaf—Collector's Office, General Department.
Collection—XIII, Miscellaneous.
No. of File—93.
Subject—Repairs of Bodh-Gaya Temple.

Serial No. of Paper.	From whom received.	Subject.	No. and Date.	Class of Paper.
1	From Commissioner of Patna.	Forwards copies of the following correspondence regarding certain repairs to the enclosure of the Bodhi Tree by the King of Burma :— (1) India Government letter No. 2725 P. of October 8th, 1875, to Bengal Government. (2) Resident at Mandalay's No. 89 P., dated 23rd August, 1875, to Government of India. (3) Translation of a letter from the Minister of Foreign Affairs to the Agent of the Viceroy at Mandalay, dated 18th August, 1875. (4) Bengal Government letter No. 3340 T., dated 16th, forwarding above translation to Commissioner of Patna. (5) Bengal Government letter No. 3117, dated 5th November, 1875, to Commissioner of Patna.	No. 343 R, dated 20th November, 1875.	A.
2	To Commissioner, Patna.	Forwards Mahanth's opinion regarding the repairs to the Temple, &c.	No. 1177, dated 8th December, 1875.	A.
3	From Commissioner	Forwards India Government letter No. 156 P., dated 15th January, 1876, on the subject of repairs to the Temple.	No. 387 R., dated 27th January, 1876.	A.
4	......	Office-note showing contents of the file collection XIII, file 93, repairs to Bodh-Gaya Temple by the King of Burma.	18th May, 1876.	

BIRESWAR BOSE,
Head Clerk.

Dated 4th May 1895.

[*Exhibit C2* .]

No. 2725 P.

FROM

THE UNDER-SECRETARY TO THE GOVERNMENT OF INDIA,

TO

THE OFFG. SECRETARY TO THE GOVERNMENT OF BENGAL,

Political Department.

FOREIGN DEPARTMENT.
Political.

Dated Simla, 8th October, 1875

SIR,

WITH reference to the correspondence ending with the letter from the Officiating Under-Secretary to the Government of Bengal, No. 460, dated 2nd February, 1875, on the subject of the visit of certain Burmese officials to the great Bodhi Tree at Gaya, I am directed to forward copy of letter from the British Resident at Mandalay, with copy of a communication from the Burmese Minister of Foreign Affairs, respecting the several works which the King of Burma proposes to execute at Gaya.

No. 89 P. dated 23rd August 1875.

2. With regard to the request of the Burmese Government that assistance may be afforded to an official called the "Royal Scribe," now in Calcutta, in carrying out the projected works, I am to request that the Government of Bengal will ascertain whether there is any objection on the part of the Hindus, who also possess shrines near the Bodhi Tree, to the execution of the works specified, and that, should no such objection exist, His Honor will be good enough to cause every reasonable facility to be given to the scribe in carrying out His Majesty's wishes.

3. The result of the enquiry, and any orders which may be issued by the Government of Bengal in the matter, should be communicated for the information of the Government of India.

I have the honor to be,

SIR,

Your most obedient Servant,

F. HENVEY,

Under-Secretary to the Government of India.

Enclosures.

No. 89P.

FROM

LT.-COL. H. J. DUNCAN,

Resident at Mandalay,

TO

THE SECRETARY TO THE GOVERNMENT OF INDIA,

Foreign Department.

Dated British Residency, Mandalay,
23rd August, 1875.

SIR,

I HAVE the honor to inform you that on the occasion of my reception by His Majesty the King of Burma on the 14th instant, I told His Majesty, by the desire of the Viceroy, that it was His Excellency's wish to render His Majesty such assistance as was in his power in the arrangements necessary for the execution of certain works at the town of Gaya in connection with the Royal offering recently despatched by His Majesty to the Buddhist shrine at that locality.

I beg now to submit a free translation of a letter from the Minister of Foreign Affairs on the subject, giving in detail the various works which His Majesty proposes to execute, and asking that His Excellency the Viceroy will be good enough to aid the Royal Scribe (Ne Myoh Mendim Iseethoo), now in Calcutta, in carrying out the works.

His Majesty directed the Woondouk, who took the offerings to Calcutta in the beginning of the year, to call on me and say that, above all matters, His Majesty attached importance to executing these pious works: and he earnestly desired that the Viceroy would issue orders to enable the Royal Scribe to carry out the King's intentions. The Woondouk told me that, when he visited Gaya, the Brahmin priest in charge of the grounds near the Buddhist shrine (grounds apparently forming an endowment for the Temple) had granted permission for the construction of various buildings described in the Minister's letter. He further told me that, on the occasion of his visit he was very kindly received and assisted by Mr. Palmer, (apparently the Magistrate and Collector of the District), and that His Majesty is desirous of sending a small article as a present to Mr. Palmer. I reminded the Woondouk that English officials were debarred from receiving presents, and that it was most improbable that His Majesty's wish could be complied with. He said, however, that it was the King's particular desire that his wishes in this respect should be communicated to the Indian Government, as he was very grateful for the assistance rendered.

I have the honor to be,

SIR,

Your most obedient Servant,

H. J. DUNCAN, LT.-COL.,

Resident at Mandalay.

(Translation.)

FROM

HIS EXCELLENCY THE RIN WOON MEGYI,

Minister for Foreign Affairs,

TO

THE AGENT TO HIS EXCELLENCY THE VICEROY OF INDIA AND RESIDENT AT MANDALAY.

Dated Waning of Mohgoung, 1237 (18*th August,* 1875).

THE locality, where stands the Maha-Bodhi Tree of India, being the original spot where the Omniscient and Most Excellent Lord, on his blossoming to the dignity of Buddhahood, understood the four great truths—extraordinary reverence and homage should be paid to it. His Majesty the King accordingly intends to do that homage

(1). By repairing the Mahayan, or sacred enclosure, now in a state of decay, of the Maha-Bodhi Tree.

(2). By the repair of the ruined Chetiya, built by King Dhanna Asoka, over the site of the *aparajita* (conquering) throne.

(3). By firmly propping up with masonry the right branch of the Maha-Bodhi Tree.

(4). By repairing all ruined structures connected with the three treasures situated within the enclosure of the Maha-Bodhi Tree.

(5). By building near the Maha-Bodhi Tree a monastery capable of containing about twenty Royal Rahans, who will live there continually to perform the Bodhirangana duties, namely, those connected with the offering of food, those connected with the lighting of lamps, and those with the presentation of flowers and cold water.

(6). By enclosing the above Royal monastery with a solid wall of masonry.

(7). By hiring men to live on the spot to watch and to attend to the wants of the monastery.

(8). By erecting a *Paribhoga* for the depositing of the Royal offerings to the Maha-Bodhi Tree.

Orders have consequently been issued to the Royal Scribe, Ne Myoh Mendim Iseethoo, at Calcutta, to submit plans and estimate for the completion of the above-mentioned items.

You having communicated to His Majesty that His Excellency the Viceroy wished to give help in whatever His Majesty wished in connection with matters concerning the Maha-Bodhi Tree, I request you will communicate with His Excellency the Viceroy, asking him, in order that the Royal Scribe at Calcutta may effectuate matters, to associate with him one whom His Excellency the Viceroy considers trustworthy, and to give every help in the matter of the above-named items, which it is the Royal wish to complete.

No. 3340T.

Political.

Dated Darjeeling, 16th October, 1875.

FORWARDED to the Commissioner of Patna, with a request that he will be good enough to make an enquiry into the matter, and report the result for the information of the Lieutenant-Governor.

By order of the Lieutenant-Governor of Bengal,

J. CRAWFORD,

Offg. Under-Secretary to the Government of Bengal.

No. 3117.

FROM

THE OFFG. UNDER-SECRETARY TO THE GOVERNMENT OF BENGAL,
Political Department,

To

THE COMMISSIONER OF THE PATNA DIVISION.

Dated Calcutta, 5th November, 1875.

SIR,

I AM directed to acknowledge the receipt of your letter No. 146R. of the 19th ultimo, reporting the result of the enquiry made by you as regards the subject of the repairs of the Buddhist Temple at Bodh-Gaya, which the King of Burma proposes to execute.

2. In reply, I am to state that the Lieutenant-Governor approves of the proposal made by you, that, in order to give effect to the King of Burma's wish, a responsible person on His Majesty's part, acquainted with Hindi, should visit Bodh-Gaya, and point out the sites he may select for the monastery and the *Paribhoga* building. His Honor also approves of your proposal to instruct the Collector of Gaya to be present on the occasion, and to use his influence to obtain a gift of the necessary sites, after ascertaining and disposing, if possible, of any objection which may be raised by the Mahanth who resides at Bodh-Gaya.

3. I am to request accordingly that you will direct the Collector to communicate with the "Royal Scribe," deputed by the King of Burma, and who is now at Calcutta, with a view to his visiting the shrine, and such arrangements being made by the Collector as may be found feasible for giving effect to the proposals made by the King of Burma.

I have the honor to be,

SIR,

Your most obedient Servant,

J. CRAWFORD,

Offg. Under-Secretary to the Government of Bengal.

Memo No. 343R.

PATNA COMMISSIONER'S OFFICE,

Dated Bankipore, 20th November, 1875.

Revenue Department.

COPY of this letter and previous letter forwarded to the Collector of Gaya for information and early action.

By order of the Commissioner,

DURGA GATI BANERJEA,

Personal Assistant to Commissioner.

[*Exhibit C* 3.]

No. 1177.

FROM

F. M. HALLIDAY, ESQ.,

Magistrate and Collector, Gaya,

TO

THE COMMISSIONER OF THE PATNA DIVISION.

Dated Gaya, 8th December, 1875.

SIR,

WITH reference to your Memo. No. 343R., dated 20th ultimo, with enclosures relative to the temple at Bodh-Gaya, I have the honour to submit the following :—

2. On receipt of your instructions, I communicated with the Mahanth of Bodh-Gaya and have now received from him a reply, in which he raises no objections to the proposals of the King of Burmah. His communication is to the following effect :—With regard to proposal No. I, contained in the translation of the letter of the Burmese Minister of Foreign Affairs, appended to the enclosures of your memo. under reply, the Mahanth agrees to the sacred enclosures, now in state of decay, being repaired, but he would wish that it should not be pulled down and a new one erected, as there are several Hindu images on it, where the pilgrims perform their religious rites.

On proposal No. II, the Mahanth agrees to the repairs being executed in such a way as not to destroy the idols of the Hindus which are near the Bodhi Tree.

On proposal No. III, he has no objection to the branch of the Maha-Bodhi Tree being firmly propped up with masonry, but requests that regard may be paid to the Hindu idols under the branch, so that they may not be injured or concealed by the masomry.

On Proposal No. IV, he asks for the same care to be taken of the Hindu idols which have been placed near the Bodhi Temple many years ago.

On Proposal No. V, the Mahanth agrees to the building of the monastery at a distance of 15 *laggas* (equivalent to about 40 yards) on the west of the Maha-Bodhi Tree, with the understanding that His Majesty the King of Burma will execute an agreement for the land, which will be given by the Mahanth free of cost.

Proposal No. VI. He has no objection to the Royal Monastery being enclosed by a solid wall of masonry.

Proposal No. VII. The Mahanth asks that the men hired to live on the spot to watch and attend to the wants of the monastery may not be permitted to interfere in any way with the religious rites of the pilgrims, who go round the Tree.

Proposal No. VIII. The Mahanth agrees to the erection of the *Paribhaga* on the same understanding, as in Proposal No. V.

3. In the letter of the Government of Bengal to your address, I am directed to communicate with the "Royal Scribe," deputed by the King of Burma, and who is now in Calcutta, but as I do not know his address, I beg to submit the above information to you, and request you will be good enough to communicate with the "Royal Scribe." It will be more convenient for me, if the officer deputed on the part of the King of Burmah, could time his visit to Gaya about the 15th January, as my duties and the approaching visit of the Prince of Wales to Bankipore will prevent my personally assisting him and visiting Bodh-Gaya until that time.

I have the honour to be,
SIR,
Your most obedient Servant,

F. M. HALLIDAY,
Magistrate and Collector.

[*Exhibit C* 4.]

No. 156 P.

FROM

THE UNDER-SECRETARY TO THE GOVERNMENT OF INDIA,

To

THE SECRETARY TO THE GOVERNMENT OF BENGAL,
Political Department.

Dated Fort William, 15th January, 1876.

FOREIGN DEPARTMENT.
Political.

SIR,

WITH reference to the correspondence ending with Mr. Crawford's endorsement No. 3892, dated 21st December, 1875, I am directed to inform you that the Burmese Agent left Calcutta a few days ago to make arrangements for the reception of the envoys at Gaya. The envoys left Calcutta for Patna and Gaya on the 11th instant, and, as Mr. Halliday stated in his letter, No. 1177, of the 8th December last, that he would be at Gaya about the 25th instant, it is probable that the necessary arrangements for the repairs of the Temple will be concluded with the envoys and the Agent on the spot.

2. I am to add that the address of the Agent in Calcutta is 2, Hartford's Lane, near Sudder Street.

I have the honor to be,
SIR,
Your most obedient Servant,

F. HENVEY,
Under-Secretary to the Government of India.

No. 307.

Dated Calcutta, 22nd January, 1876.

Political.

COPY forwarded to the Commissioner of Patna for information with reference to his letter No. 207R., dated the 11th of December last.

By order of the Lieutenant-Governor of Bengal,

J. CRAWFORD,
Offg. Under-Secretary to the Government of Bengal.

MEMO. NO. 387R.

PATNA COMMISSIONER'S OFFICE,
Dated Bankipore, January 27th, 1876.

EVENUE.

COPY forwarded to the Collector of Gaya for information with reference to his No. 1177, dated 8th ultimo.

By order of the Commissioner,
DURGAGATI BANERJEA,
Personal Assistant to Commissioner.

OFFICE MEMO.

Dated Camp, February 22nd, 1876.

THIS letter has only reached me now to-day from the office, almost a month since the receipt of it. I wish to know the cause of the delay. Of the Burmese agent or envoy I have heard nothing. The Sherishtadar will prepare a *parwana* to the Mahanth of Bodh-Gaya, enquiring from him whether the Burmese agent or envoys have yet visited Bodh-Gaya, and, if so, what has been the result.

F. M. HALLIDAY,
Magistrate and Collector.

To

MAHANTH HEM NARAYAN GIR, OF BODH-GAYA.

Dated 11th October, 1877.

SIR,

AFTER paying due respect I have to submit and beg to inform you that you should not repair that old Temple, either the inner or the outer portion. Please let it remain in the state in which it is. You will carry out the orders of the Government thereto, which is expected within six weeks.

C. J. O'DONNELL,
Joint Magistrate.

To

MAHANTHJI SAHEB, THE FRIEND OF THE NEEDY, MAY GOD BLESS YOU.

AFTER paying my respects, and wishing an interview, I have the honor to inform you that General Cunningham is coming in this district in the coming cold weather to make a search and find out the old Temple, and he has been deputed for that purpose by the Government. That in Bodh-Gaya there are a good many stone pillars of the time of Buddha in the compound of your house, of which he wishes to take photos. The said General had also formerly got repaired the Temple of Buddha at Bodh-Gaya, which is now being repaired by the Burmese. The said General intends to remain there for some time to point out the manner in which it should be repaired, and he also wishes to dig out some land near it to find out old images. I therefore beg to inform you that as a favour you will give him all possible assistance in all matters, in the way you have been giving assistance in such matters heretofore, so that no difficulties beset him, and your rendering such assistance will give me and the General great pleasure. Good-bye.

F. M. HALLIDAY,
Magistrate and Collector.

Dated 8th December, 1877.

[*Exhibit C* (5.)]

1878-79.

Fly leaf—Collector's Office, General Department.
Collection—XIII. Miscellaneous.
No. of File—38.
Subject—Repairs of Bodh-Gaya Temple.

B and C papers destroyed.

1	2	3	4	5	6
Serial No. of Paper.	From whom received or to whom addressed.	Letter.		Enclosure.	Class of Paper.
		No.	Date.		
1	From Commissioner ...	20R	15th April, 1878	Forwards copies of the following correspondence relating to certain repairs to the Maha-Bodhi Temple at Bodh-Gaya :— (1) India Government Letter No. 599P, of 11th March, 1878, to Bengal Government. (2) India Government Letter No. 598P, of 11th March, 1878, to Resident at Mandalay. (3) Bengal Government Letter No. 1261, of 2nd April, 1878, forwarding above letters to Commissioner of Patna.	A.
2	Do. do. ...	23R	17th April, 1878	......	B.
3	To Station-master, E. I. Ry....	155	23rd April, 1878	......	B.
4	Do. do. ...	156	Do. do. ...	......	B.
5	From District Engineer, Gaya	37	Do. do. ...	......	B.
6	To Commissioner ...	172	Do. do. ...	......	B.
7	From Commissioner	68R	16th May, 1878	......	B.
8	Do. do. ...	121R	29th June, 1878	Forwards India Government letter No. 1132P, dated 4th June, 1878, and its enclosures on the subject of the restoration of the Temple at Bodh-Gaya.	A.
9	Do. do. ...	133R	11th July, 1878	......	C.
10	Do. do. ...	194R	17th August, 1878	Forwards Bengal Government letter No. 1726, dated 12th August, 1878.	A.

BIRESWAR BOSE,
Head Clerk.

4th May 1895.

[*Exhibit C.* (6.)]

No. 599P.

FROM

THE SECRETARY TO THE GOVERNMENT OF INDIA,

TO

THE SECRETARY TO THE GOVERNMENT OF BENGAL,
Political Department.

FOREIGN DEPARTMENT.
Political.

Dated Fort William, 11th March, 1878.

SIR,

I AM directed to acknowledge your letter No. 4405, dated 29th December, 1877, addressed to the Government of India in the Home Department, submitting a report by Dr. Rajendra Lala Mitra, upon the progress of the restoration and repairs of the old Temple at Buddha-Gaya, which are being executed by the Burmese, and bringing to notice that the work is being done upon no system, and that the so-called restorations are of a most indiscriminate character.

2. In reply, I am to refer you to the correspondence ending with this office letter No. 156P., dated 15th January, 1876, and to enclose a letter which has been this day addressed to the Resident at Mandalay on the subject. Pending a further communication from the Resident, I am to request that the Burmese workmen may be desired not to take any new work in hand, which is not included in the programme of operations in 1875. It would also be desirable that the Government of India should be informed whether the Burmese workmen have been working hitherto within the limits above sanctioned.

I have the honor to be,
SIR,
Your most obedient Servant,
C. U. AITCHISON,
Secretary to the Government of India.

Enclosure.

No. 598P.

FROM

THE SECRETARY TO THE GOVERNMENT OF INDIA,

To

THE RESIDENT AT MANDALAY.

Dated Fort William, 11th March, 1878.

FOREIGN DEPARTMENT.
Political.

SIR,

IN continuation of the correspondence forwarded to you under Foreign Department endorsement No. 2726P., dated 8th October, 1878, I am directed to send the further correspondence noted in the margin, and a copy of a letter and enclosures from the Government of Bengal, No. 4405, dated 29th December, 1877, bringing to notice that the Burmese workmen engaged in repairing the old Temple at Bodh-Gaya are conducting operations without any systematic plan, and in such a manner as to injure rather than improve the buildings.

From Government of Bengal; No. 3118P., dated 5th November, 1875.
To Government of Bengal; No. 3187P., dated 3rd December, 1875.
From Government of Bengal; No. 3892P, dated 21st December, 1875.
To Government of Bengal; No. 156P., dated 15th January, 1876.

2. I am to request you to be good enough to endeavour to impress upon His Majesty the King the desirability of carrying out these repairs and restorations on some fixed plan, in which the requirements of architecture and antiquarian research will be only considered. Perhaps the best course would be to obtain His Majesty's consent to his men being directed to work under the direction of our officers in completing the works they are engaged in. Pending your reply, no new work, which is not included in the programme of operations agreed to in 1875, will be sanctioned.

I have the honor to be,
SIR,
Your most obedient Servant,
C. U. AITCHISON,
Secretary to the Government of India

No. 1261.

Dated Calcutta, 2nd April, 1878.

FINANCIAL DEPARTMENT.
Miscellaneous.

COPY forwarded to the Commissioner of Patna with reference to the correspondence ending with this office endorsement No. 307, dated 22nd January, 1876, for issue of the necessary instructions with reference to paragraph 2, and also for the favour of the report called for by the Government of India.

By order of the Lieutenant-Governor of Bengal,
H. H. RISLEY,
Under-Secretary to the Government of Bengal.

MEMO. NO. 20R.

PATNA COMMISSIONER'S OFFICE,
Dated Bankipore, 15th April, 1878.

COPY forwarded to the Collector of Gaya, for information and guidance, in continuation of this office No. 387R. dated 21st January, 1876, with a request that the report on the point referred to may be duly submitted.

By order of the Commissioner,
DURGAGATI BANERJEA,
Personal Assistant to Commissioner.

Note by Magistrate.

SHERISHTADAR to ascertain whether the one Burmese is still at Bodh-Gaya and one only, where he lives, on what date the Wazir Saheb left, and whether anything has been done since in the way of alterations. A letter to the Mahanth may be sent by the Sherishtadar.

D. W. M. TESTRO,
Joint Magistrate.

21st April, 1878.

Office Note.

THE Mahanth says that there are two Burmese still at Bodh-Gaya. They live in the Mahanth's house. The Wazir Saheb has not yet come. He is still in Calcutta. One Burmese Pandit had come some time ago, but has returned. Nothing has been done in the way of alterations or repairs to the old Temple, but a new and small Temple has been built to keep stones &c., in. He further says that Burmese "Mooni" has left Calcutta for Bodh-Gaya, but has not yet arrived.

M. PRASAD.
Sherishtadar.

23rd April, 1878.

No. 15.

TO

MAHANTH, FRIEND OF THE NEEDY, MAY GOD BLESS YOU.

AFTER paying due respect, I beg to inform you that if the Burmese wish to repair the big Temple or the compound, you will prevent them from doing so up to the time you get permission from me.

This is the order of Government (*Sarkar*). You will keep me informed of the matter.

D. W. M. TESTRO,
Joint Magistrate.

Dated 25th April, 1878.

[*Exhibit C 7.*]

No. 1132P.

FROM

THE SECRETARY TO THE GOVERNMENT OF INDIA,

TO

THE SECRETARY TO THE GOVERNMENT OF BENGAL.

Dated Simla, 4th June, 1878.

FOREIGN DEPARTMENT,
Political.

SIR,

IN continuation of this office letter No. 599P., dated the 11th March, 1878, I am directed to forward copy of a letter from the Resident at Mandalay, No. 199-53, dated the 22nd April, 1878, regarding the restoration of the old Temple at Buddha-Gaya by the Burmese.

2. His Majesty the King has agreed to the proposal that his workmen should be placed under the direction of an officer appointed by Government. I am, therefore, to request that His Honor the Lieutenant-Governor will now be good enough to arrange for the proper supervision of the work, and that the Government of India may be informed of the name of the officer selected, for communication to the King.

I have the honor to be,

SIR,

Your most obedient Servant,

A. C. LYALL,

Secretary to the Government of India.

Enclosure.

No. 199-53

FROM

R. B. SHAW, ESQ., C. I. E.,
Resident at Mandalay,

TO

THE SECRETARY TO THE GOVERNMENT OF INDIA,
Foreign Department,

Dated Mandalay, 22nd April, 1878.

SIR,

I HAVE the honor to acknowledge receipt of your letter No. 598P., dated 11th March, 1878, and its enclosures, on the subject of the Burmese workmen engaged in repairing the old Temples at Buddha-Gaya conducting the operations without any systematic plan, and requesting me to obtain the consent of His Majesty the King to his men being directed to work under the direction of our officers in completing the works they are engaged in.

2. In reply, I have the honor to report that His Majesty the King agrees to the supervision being exercised over the operations of his workmen at Buddha-Gaya by an official appointed by the Government of India, but would at the same time be glad to be informed who that official is.

I have the honor to be,

SIR,

Your most obedient Servant,

R. B. SHAW,

Resident at Mandalay.

Office Memo. No. 596.

Dated Darjeeling, 20th June, 1878.

REVENUE DEPARTMENT
Miscellaneous.

THE accompanying copies of a letter from the Government of India, Foreign Department, No. 1132P., dated 4th June, 1878, and of its enclosure, regarding the restoration of the old temple at Bodh-Gaya, are forwarded to the Secretary to the Government of Bengal in the Public Works Department, with the request that the District Engineer, Mr. C. A. Mills, may be instructed to supervise, in communication with the Collector of Gaya and Dr. Rajendra Lala Mittra, Rai Bahadur, the work of repair and restoration carried on by certain Burmese workmen under the orders of the King of Burma.

By order of the Lieutenant-Governor of Bengal,

A. MACKENZIE,

Secretary to the Government of Bengal.

No. 597T.

REVENUE DEPARTMENT.
Miscellaneous.

Dated Darjeeling, 20th June, 1878.

COPY of the letter from the Government of India, No. 1132P., dated 4th June, 1878, and of its enclosure, forwarded to the Commissioner of Patna, in continuation of this office No. 1261, dated 2nd April, 1878, for information and guidance.

By order of the Lieutenant-Governor of Bengal,
A. MACKENZIE,
Secretary to the Government of Bengal.

No. 121R.

PATNA COMMISSIONER'S OFFICE,
Bankipur, 29th June, 1878.

COPY forwarded to the Collector of Gaya for information and guidance, in continuation of this office No. 20R., dated 15th April last.

The Government order should be communicated to Mr. Mills.

By Order of the Commissioner,
DURGA GATI BANERJEA,
Personal Assistant to Commissioner.

Dated Gaya, 2nd July, 1878.

COPY to Mr. Mills for information and guidance. I hope this additional duty will in no way interfere with his work in connection with the District Roads.

E. J. BARTON,
Magistrate and Collector.

[*Exhibit C* (8)].

No. 199.

FROM

C. A. MILLS, ESQ., C. E.,
District Engineer, Gaya.

TO

THE MAGISTRATE AND COLLECTOR OF GAYA.

Dated Gaya, 23rd July, 1878.

SIR,

WITH reference to your note dated 2nd instant on the Commissioner of Patna's No. 121R., dated 29th June, 1878, with enclosures as per margin, I have the honor to inform you that I visited Bodh-Gaya on the 21st instant, having heard that the Burmese Superintendent of the works to be carried out on the Temple had arrived.

From Secretary to Government of India to Secretary to Government of Bengal, No. 1132P, dated 4th June, 1878.
From Resident at Mandalay to Secretary to Government of India, No. 199-53. dated 22nd April, 1878.
From Secretary to Government of Bengal to Secretary to Government of Bengal Public Works Department, No. 596, dated 20th June, 1878.
India Government No. 597T to the Commissioner of Patna, dated 20th June, 1878.
Commissioner of Patna No. 121R, dated 29th June, 1878.

2. I informed this gentleman that it was the desire of Government that no work should be commenced on the Temple without your sanction as well as that of Dr. Rajendra Lala Mitra, Rai Bahadur, and that any such work would be supervised by myself. He fully understood this, and consented to delay operations until I had communicated with and received a reply from the Government and Dr. Rajendra Lala Mitra, Rai Bahadur.

3. Referring to my former letter on the subject, No. 37. dated 23rd April, 1878, I must again point out that it is most desirable that a specially-selected subordinate should be deputed for this work. At present I have not my full staff of subordinates, as the names of two are before

Government for approval, one of whom only has been temporarily appointed in anticipation of that approval. Also, when my staff is complete, it will be absolutely required for District works, the outlay on which this year is very large.

4. In view of the importance of such a work as the restoration of the Bodh-Gaya Temple, and considering the great antiquity and consequently ruinous state of the building, I beg to submit for your consideration that it is highly desirable that a man of first-rate qualifications should be appointed for this work alone; and I have the honor to request that you will apply to Government for the same. My letter above quoted will show you that the work, if thoroughly carried out, will cost about half a lakh of rupees, and this large cost will, I think, justify the application. I would further request that you would apply to Dr. Rajendra Lala Mitra, Rai Bahadur, for detailed drawings of the work to be done, with a full expression of his desires as to the manner in which it is to be carried out, especially with regard to the ornamentation. On receipt of answers to the above, I shall be glad to commence the work, and give it all the attention I can spare from my other duties.

I have, honour to be,

SIR,

Your most obedient Servant,

C. A. MILLS,

District Engineer.

[*Exhibit C* (9).]

No. 720.

FROM

E. J. BARTON, ESQ.,
Magistrate and Collector of Gaya,

TO

THE COMMISSIONER OF THE PATNA DIVISION.

Dated Gaya, 24th July, 1878.

SIR,

I HAVE to acknowledge the receipt of your letter No. 121R, dated the 29th ultimo, with its enclosures, and in reply thereto to forward therewith copy of a letter No. 199, dated 23rd July, 1878, from the District Engineer of Gaya. It would seem that the orders of Government and of Dr. Rajendra Lala Mitra are necessary before the Burmese Superintendent of Works can proceed with the repairs of the Temple at Bodh-Gaya. I would ask that these should be obtained. There can be no objection to the repairing of the Temple, and Mr. Mills will be informed to this effect.

2. With regard to Mr. Mills' application for a specially selected subordinate, I am myself not clear that such a person is necessary, although probably on this point the opinion of Mr. Mills is worth more than mine. I presume that if Mr. Mills were to visit the Temple, say, once a week, or once a fortnight, he would be able to give the work of repair as much supervision as the Government desires that it should receive from him. At the same time, if such a subordinate is necessary, I think it hardly fair that a subordinate of the road-cess should be specially deputed upon the duty at the cost of this District Committee, more especially as there is work enough for all our men on our District Roads. Probably Dr. Rajendra Lala Mitra will be able to form an opinion on this point. If such a subordinate is necessary, I certainly think he should be sent either from Calcutta or Burma, at the expense of the King of Burma, who, I believe, has undertaken the cost of repairs.

3. Mr. Mills wishes Dr. Rajendra Lala Mitra to send him detailed drawings of the works to be done, and also other instructions, which are described in his letter.

4. I certainly think Mr. Mills should be supplied with what he wants.

I have the honor to be,

SIR,

Your most obedient Servant,

E. J. BARTON,

Magistrate and Collector.

No. 721.

Dated Gaya, 24th July, 1878.

COPY to Mr. Mills for information with reference to his letter No. 199 of 23rd July, 1878.

E. J. BARTON,
Magistrate and Collector.

[*Exhibit C* (10).]

No. 1726.

FROM

H. H. RISLEY, ESQ.,
Under-Secretary to the Government of Bengal,
Revenue Department.

TO

THE COMMISSIONER OF THE PATNA DIVISION.

Miscellaneous.

Dated Calcutta, 12th August, 1878.

SIR,

I AM directed to acknowledge the receipt of your letter No. 80R., dated 31st July, 1878, and its enclosures, regarding the work of repair and restoration of the old Temple at Bodh-Gaya by Burmese workmen, and in reply to say that at present no special subordinate officer can be placed in charge of the works, as proposed by Mr. Mills. An extract from the correspondence, regarding detailed instructions required by Mr. Mills, will be forwarded to Dr. Rajendra Lala Mittra, who will be requested to communicate direct with the Collector of Gaya, as it is not necessary that, in future, this correspondence about details should pass through you and Government.

I have the honour to be,
SIR,
Your most obedient Servant,
H. H. RISLEY,
Under-Secretary to the Government of Bengal.

Memo. No. 194R.

PATNA COMMISSIONER'S OFFICE,
Dated Bankipore, 17th August, 1878.

COPY forwarded to the Collector of Gaya for information with reference to his No. 720, dated 24th ultimo.

By order of the Commissioner,
DURGA GATI BANERJEA,
Personal Assistant to Commissioner.

No. 851.

Dated Gaya, 19th August, 1878.

COPY to Mr. Mills for information.

E. J. BARTON,
Magistrate and Collector

[*Exhibit C* (11).]

No. 842.

FROM

E. J. BARTON, ESQ.,
Magistrate and Collector, Gaya,

TO

THE COMMISSIONER OF THE PATNA DIVISION.

Dated Gaya, 19th August, 1878.

SIR,

IN reply to your No. 194R., dated the 17th instant, received to-day, in which the Government have declined to allow Mr. Mills' special assistance in superintending the restoration of the Buddhist Temple at Bodh-Gaya, I have the honour to make the following representation, and to beg you will forward it with your approval to Government, or to Dr. R. L. Mittra.

2. Since I wrote to you on the subject of the Temple in July last, I have gone over to Bodh-Gaya and seen the ruins myself. The work of restoration will be not only an extensive one, but a delicate one, requiring special knowledge and much care, inasmuch as a good deal of scaffolding and moulding, in addition to masonry, will be required. Also, if the restoration is not carefully carried out with great attention and caution, there is danger of the ruins tumbling down bodily, judging from their present appearance. Originally they seem to have been built of bricks and mud, unmixed with lime or other cement. An experienced and careful subordinate must, therefore, constantly be on the spot, when the work of restoration is going on.

3. Mr. Mills informs me that he would prefer, for the purpose, an experienced subordinate of the rank of a Sub-Engineer in the Public Works Department, who has a practical knowledge of ornamentation, such as is carried out on most of the buildings in Calcutta. The whole of the restoration will certainly not cost less than half a lakh of rupees, and probably more. The work will also extend a period of nine months. The fact that Mr. Mills has recently been entrusted with the drainage survey of Gaya, renders it the more necessary that he should get some assistance in restoring the Temple.

4. I presume that if the matter were laid before the King of Burma, His Majesty would have no objection.

I have the honour to be,
SIR,
Your most obedient Servant,
E. J. BARTON,
Magistrate and Collector.

[*Exhibit C* (12)]

No. 971.

FROM

E. J. BARTON, ESQ.,
Magistrate and Collector, Gaya,

TO

THE COMMISSIONER OF THE PATNA DIVISION.

Dated Gaya, 5th September, 1878.

SIR,

WITH reference to your letter, No. 221R., of the 31st ultimo, disallowing my recommendation for entertainment under Mr. Mills, the District Engineer, of a qualified officer to superintend the repairs of the Burmese Temple at Bodh-Gaya, I have the honor to submit that the work of repair to the Temple at Bodh-Gaya, in question, is by no means easy. The mouldings of the cornices, the entablatures of the columns, the statuary of the Temple, and the brick and *ashlár* work peculiar thereto, require the close application and undivided attention of a well-qualified and experienced engineer, with both a theoretical and a practical knowledge of architecture.

2. I beg to state also that many scores of images of Buddha, moulded in Portland cement, have to be made.

3. Mr. Mills' time will be fully occupied next year on the District Roads. An inspection of the next year's road-cess budget of this district will show you the important works, both "original" and "repairs," which Mr. Mills has got in hand. He can at best only inspect and generally superintend the works at the Bodh-Gaya Temple. General supervision of this kind by a man not on the spot, and who only goes occasionally there, affords opportunities to the workmen to do and to conceal bad work.

4. As a matter of equity, I beg to point out that the District Road-cess Committee pay the entire salary and allowances of Mr. Mills, and have a right to call on him to devote his whole time and attention to their own roads and bridges. Mr. Mills has also been put in charge of another heavy piece of work, which is extraneous to his own duty, namely, the drainage of this town under the Municipal Committee.

5. The extensive, elaborate and difficult works of repairs which are about to be carried out at the Buddhist Temple, require that a qualified and an experienced officer should be constantly on the spot to carefully watch their general progress and their details. I therefore again beg you will be good enough to move Government to reconsider the whole matter, and so allow a competent Superintendent of Works. Failing this, the Government might be requested to get the repair works of this temple executed by the agency of their own Engineers in the Public Works Department.

I have the honour to be,

SIR,

Your most obedient Servant,

E. J. BARTON,

Magistrate and Collector.

[*Exhibit C* 13.]

NO. 2046.

FROM

C. E. BERNARD, ESQ.,

Officiating Secretary to the Government of India,

To

THE SECRETARY TO THE GOVERNMENT OF BENGAL,

Revenue Department.

HOME DEPARTMENT.
Public.

Dated Simla, 9th November, 1878.

SIR,

WITH reference to the correspondence ending with your letter to the Foreign Department, No. 594F., dated the 20th June last, on the subject of the restoration of the old temple at Bodh-Gaya, I am directed to communicate the following order :—

2. The main points to be considered seem to be (1) what amount of work is absolutely required for the future stability of the building, and (2) whether the King of Burma should be asked to contribute towards the repairs.

3. Looking to the account of the present ruinous state of the buildings, as given in Mr. Mills' letter, No. 37, dated 23rd April, 1878, the Government of India think that the whole of the outer casing of the temple should be secured from the effects of the weather for the future, by laying all the course in lime mortar. If this be done, the building would be preserved for several centuries to come. There will be no difficulty in restoring the niches, as they can be copied from the unbroken portions of the building. But the Government of India consider that it would be a mistake to attempt the restoration of the statues. A much better plan would be to place in all the lower niches a certain number of the Buddhist statues which have been found in such numbers among the ruins. These were the offerings of pious Buddhists of former days, and are of considerable antiquity. Their setting up would involve little or no expense, whereas the restoration of hundreds of stucco figures by skilled workmen would entail a very large outlay.

4. Mr. Mills estimated the cost of the repairs, including the restoration of the stucco statues, at three lakhs of rupees. But by restricting the repairs to the outer casing of bricks laid in mortar, the actual cost would probably not exceed a lakh and a half of rupees, and under Rule VI of the Provincial Service Rules, this amount should be provided by the Government of Bengal from its provincial assignment.

5. The question of new buildings proposed to be erected by the Burmese appears to rest on quite a different footing. Those buildings are required solely for the accommodation of Buddhist priests, who are to make daily offerings at the Great Temple, which was originally erected over the diamond throne of Buddha. The cost of these new buildings may, therefore, be properly borne by the King of Burma, and in order to prevent difficulties and disputes hereafter, the Government of India agree with the Collector of Gaya in thinking that the new buildings should be entirely detached from the objects of worship. The position of the new buildings to the westward of the Great Temple, as proposed by the Mahanth of Bodh-Gaya, is quite unobjectionable.

I have the honour to be,

SIR,

Your most obedient Servant,

C. E. BERNARD,

Officiating Secretary to the Government of India.

No. 3039.

Dated Calcutta, 9th December, 1878.

REVENUE DEPARTMENT.
Miscellaneous.

COPY forwarded to the Commissioner of Patna with the intimation that the Public Works Department of this Government will henceforth deal with the case, and issue the necessary orders on it.

By order of the Lieutenant-Governor of Bengal,

H. H. RISLEY,

Under-Secretary to the Government of Bengal.

Memo. No. 403R.

PATNA COMMISSIONER'S OFFICE,
Dated Bankipore, 18th December, 1878.

REVENUE DEPARTMENT.

COPY forwarded to the Collector of Gaya for information and guidance.

By order of the Commissioner,

DURGA GATI BANERJEA,

Personal Assistant to Commissioner.

[*Exhibit C* 14.]

1878-79.

Fly leaf—Collector's Office, General Department.

Collection—XIII, Miscellaneous.

No. of File—22.

Subject—Bodh-Gaya Temple.

B papers destroyed.

Serial No. of Paper.	From whom received or to whom addressed.	No.	Date.	Enclosure.	Class of Paper.
1	From Commissioner ...	1219	29th June 1878 ...	*Nil.*	A
2	" District Engineer, Gaya	199	23rd July ...	"	A
3	To Commissioner ...	920	24th July ...	"	A
4	" Dr. R. L. Mitter ...	814	15th August ...	"	B
5	" Commissioner ...	844	19th " ...	"	B
6	From Commissioner ...	194R	17th " ...	"	A
7	To Commissioner ...	142	19th " ...	"	A
8	From Dr. R. L. Mitter ...	......	19th " ...	"	B
9	" Bengal Government ...	891	23rd " ...	"	B
10	" Commissioner ...	221R	30th " ...	"	B
11	To Commissioner ...	971	5th September ...	"	A
12	From District Engineer ...	4	15th October ...	"	B
13	To Dr. R. L. Mitter ...	1186	17th " ...	"	B
14	" Commissioner ...	1224	24th " ...	"	B
15	From Dr. R. L. Mitter ...	......	22nd " ...	"	B
16	" Commissioner ...	403	18th December ...	"	A
17	To Commissioner ...	1594	20th " ...	"	B
18	From District Engineer, Gaya...	192	20th January, 1879...	"	B
19	" Commissioner ...	473R	25th " " ...	Forwards Bengal Office Memo. No. 3040, dated 9th December, 1878.	A
20	" " ...	487R	1st February ...	*Nil.*	B
21	" " ...	468R	24th January ...	"	B
22	" " ...	426	2nd " ...	"	B
23	" District Engineer ...	1685R	7th " ...	"	B
	" " " ...	117	11th " ...	"	B
24	To Commissioner ...	1905	26th " ...	"	B

[*Exhibit C* 15.]

To

E. J. BARTON, Esq.,

Magistrate and Collector of Gaya.

Bodh-Gaya, 2nd January, 1879.

DEAR SIR,

I DO myself the honour of sending for your perusal and your marginal notes, remarks, and suggestions, and kind return early, a memorandum for Government I have prepared on the Bodh-Gaya Temple. I send it to you not merely because you are the officer entrusted with the management of the District, and therefore entitled to be kept acquainted with the broad features of any proposal of public interest or utility, but the more willingly because I believe you take an interest in the matter.

I shall feel gratified if my views meet with your approval.

Yours faithfully,

J. D. BEGLAR.

[*Exhibit C* 16.]

No. 2453

FROM

THE MAGISTRATE AND COLLECTOR OF GAYA,

To

J. D. BEGLAR, ESQ., C. E.,
Archæologist.

SIR,

IN reply to your demi-official of 2nd instant, I have the honour to state that I have perused with interest your careful and well considered note on the Temple of Bodh-Gaya.

2. I do not enter into any controversy as to whether the structure drawn on the plan of Dr. R. L. Mitra is the same as that desired by the Chinese traveller Whachauy, and whether it is consistent or not with the spirit of ancient architecture. I am mainly interested in seeing something done towards preventing the present remains of Bodh-Gaya from falling down completely. I presume more money is required than the Government could give to restore it according to Dr. Mitra's plan, together with the porch and the two pavilions. If Dr. Mitra's plan could not be carried out for want of money, it is useless for me to discuss whether the architecture is archæologically and historically correct or not. The stage at which the question has now arrived is that the Government do not now engage to re-construct, but to conserve and preserve as much of the temple as remains.

3. It was complained that the Burmese who some time ago began the repair of the temple were working on no scientific plan, and that they were injuring rather than improving the building. They swept away many of the old land marks till few things of ancient date can be traced on the area on which they worked. Asoka's railing near the temple, the courtyard of the temple, and the terrace round it, have been either demolished, injured, or changed. They also plastered over many of the inner walls of the temple in which there were niches with small figures of Buddha. It was this disregard on the part of the Burmese of the ancient features of the temple which mainly induced the advisers of Government to take the work out of their hands. It is now, I believe, settled that only what is necessary to preserve what remains of the structure of the temple shall be done.

4. I am no authority on questions of this kind. I have, however, twice examined the structure, and I think I am right in saying that the bricks which constitute the building have been placed without any regard to bond, and that mud is the only cement issued. There is, of course, a risk of an old and decayed brick building of this kind coming down bodily when an attempt is made to re-construct it.

5. I see that you recommend that the old bricks may be used which may be found in the surrounding ruins. Your recommendation is based on two assumptions, *viz.* (1) that sufficient bricks can be found on the surrounding mounds; (2) that when found, they will be unbroken and fit for building purposes. I presume that the correctness of these assumptions could only be proved by digging up the mounds.

6. I understand you to propose that the ground immediately around the temple should be dug down to a depth of 4½ feet in the hope that remains may be found of the *stupas* and small temples which Hiouen Thsang saw around the temple. To this proposal of yours I see no objection, provided the necessary funds are forthcoming.

7. I understand you to propose the isolation of the Peepul Tree. I do not think this necessary. I believe that the isolation of the Tree is not indispensable to the stability of the temple, and would be objected to by the Hindu community.

8. Your proposals about the drains seem to be quite unobjectionable. I have no doubt water has had its influence in disintegrating the masonry, and that its deleterious influence has been all the greater as the bricks have been built without bond.

9. I cannot help doubting the accuracy of your belief that you will be able to get a sufficient number of useable bricks in the rubbish heaps for your proposed works of conservation. I am afraid you will find that most of the bricks have been broken into fragments, too small to be used again.

10. I beg to return your memorandum in original.

I have the honour to be,

SIR,

Your most obedient Servant,

E. J. BARTON,

Magistrate and Collector.

[*Exhibit C* 17.]

Office Memo. No. 3040.

To

THE SECRETARY TO THE GOVERNMENT OF BENGAL,
Public Works Department.

Calcutta, the 9th December, 1878.

REVENUE DEPARTMENT.
Miscellaneous.

THE undersigned is directed to forward to the Public Works Department of this Government a copy of a letter from the Government of India, Home Department, No. 2046, dated 9th November, 1878, with copies of the papers noted in the margin,* regarding the repairs and restoration of the Old Temple at Bodh-Gaya, and to say that in 1875, His Majesty the King of Burma obtained through the British Resident at Mandalay the permission of the Government of India to execute certain repairs to this temple, which had fallen into a state of ruin, and to construct certain new buildings on the adjacent grounds for the accommodation of a number of Buddhist priests who wished to settle there for the purpose of performing religious services at the shrine. The works proposed to be undertaken were specified in a letter from the Burmese Minister of Foreign Affairs, a copy of which was forwarded to this Government by the Government of India, with the Foreign Department's letter No. 2725P., dated 8th October, 1875, which directed this Government to cause every reasonable facility to be given to the Burmese official who should take charge of the work, provided there was no objection on the part of the Hindus, who also possessed shrines at the place, to the execution of the projected works.

* Proceedings of the Political Department :—
Nos. 119-122 B for November, 1875.
No. 62B and Nos. 129-30, B for December, 1875.
No. 46B, January, 1876.
Proceedings of the Financial Department :—
A. P. Colln. I, Nos. 17-18 A, December, 1877.
No. 16 17 B. April, 1878.
Proceedings of the Revenue Department :—
A P. Colln. I, Nos. 18 21 B, May, 1887.
Nos. 25-32 B, July, 1878.
Nos. 33-36 B, August, 1878.
Nos. 37-41 B, September, 1878.
A letter from the Commissioner of Patna, Nos. 1.026 B, dated 31st October, 1878, with enclosures and endorsement No. 2777, dated 13th November, 1878.

2. A party of Burmese officials and workmen arrived at Gaya, and the local officers of this Government were instructed to render whatever assistance might be required by them, and to ascertain and dispose of any objections that might be raised by the Hindu Mahanth, who held possession of the grounds adjoining the Buddhist Temple. This was done by Mr. F. M. Halliday, then Magistrate and Collector of Gaya, who obtained the consent of the Mahanth to allow the Burmese to proceed with the work, provided the Hindu temples and idols were not interfered with. The Burmese gentlemen commenced the work and made considerable progress in clearing the ground and erecting a wall round the yard of the temple, when in May, 1877, it was brought to the notice of Government that the manner in which the work was being done was likely to impair the archæological interest attaching to the temple, that no system had been followed by the Burmese, and that the so-called restorations of the old architectural ornaments of the temple were of a most destructive and indiscriminating character. The Burmese workmen were then requested to take no new work in hand which was not included in the programme of operations sanctioned in 1875, and Dr. Rajendra Lala Mitra, Rai Bahadur, the well-known archæologist, was requested to visit Bodh-Gaya to inspect the work done by the Burmese and to report on it, as well as on the way in which they had disposed the old sculptures and architectural stones exhumed by them in clearing the grounds. Dr. Mitra visited the place in September, 1877, made the necessary enquiries, and favoured this Government with a detailed report on the subject, in which he remarked that the Burmese gentlemen, who had charge of the work, had no knowledge of architecture or of the historical aspects of the temple, and that the mischief they had done by their misdirected zeal was serious. The demolitions and excavations already completed by them had swept away most of the old land marks, and nothing of ancient could be traced on the area upon which they had worked. Dr. Mitra pointed out that every possible care should be taken to prevent the Burmese gentlemen from doing anything which would alter or obscure the historical features of the monument they had taken in hand, and that properly qualified men should be employed to supervise their work.

3. Under these circumstances, this Government found it necessary to move the Government of India to obtain the consent of the King of Burma to place his workmen under the control and supervision of an officer to be selected by this Government, and on receipt of a reply approving of the proposal, it was arranged that the work should be carried on by the Burmese under the superintendence of Mr. C. A. Mills, District Road Engineer at Gaya, in general accordance with such instructions as Dr. Rajendra Lala Mitra might give, with regard

to the restoration of the architectural decorations and the proper dispositions and repair of the ancient sculptures found at the place. Orders were issued accordingly to the local officers, and Dr. Mitra was requested to give the necessary directions, and to have drawings and photographs prepared for the guidance of the workmen, the necessary funds being advanced to him from time to time.

4. It afterwards appeared from reports submitted by the Commissioner that the duties which Mr. Mills had to perform in connection with the construction and maintenance of the District roads and the Municipal drainage of the town at Gaya, left him little time to devote to any other work. It was, therefore, suggested by the Collector and the Commissioner that either the work at Bodh-Gaya should be entrusted to an Engineer Officer of the Public Works Department, or that a properly qualified officer of the rank of Sub-Engineer should be appointed to take the immediate charge of the work, under the general superintendence of Mr. Mills. But the latter arrangement, which was preferred by Government, could not be carried out without increase of expenditure, and it was not known whether the Burmese authorities were ready to provide the funds. In the meantime, the local officers applied for funds to collect materials for the work, and represented that owing to the ruinous state into which the building had fallen, the projected works would cost far more than was originally expected. They estimated the probable cost to be not less than half a lakh of rupees, and this Government again moved the Government of India to ascertain if the Burmese authorities were aware of the extent and cost of the repairs necessary to the preservation of the building, and were ready to meet the cost of pushing on the work vigorously. The Government of India in reply now directs that only the amount of work absolutely required for the stability of the building should be done in the manner specified in their present letter,* and at an outlay of Rs. 15,000 to be provided by this Government from the provincial assignment, and adds that the Burmese will be called upon to pay the cost of the new buildings to be erected for the residence of the priests to the westward of the Great Temple. The Lieutenant-Governor in this Department consider that the case should now be transferred to the Public Works Department, and that Departments is accordingly requested to deal with it, and to issue the necessary orders for giving effect to the views of the Government of India.

* Home Department No. 2046, dated 9th November, 1878.

A. MACKENZIE,
Secretary to the Government of Bengal.

No. 32M.

COPY of the above, with enclosures (to be returned), forwarded to the Superintending Engineer, North-Western Circle, with reference to this office, No. 185M., dated 26th June last, with a request that he will, in communication with the Collector and Mr. Mills, report what is actually required to ensure the stability of the building.

By order of the Lieutenant-Governor of Bengal,

FORT WILLIAM,
The 16th January, 1879.

F. H. WEEKS,
Offg. Asst. Secy. to the Govt. of Bengal, P. W. D.

No. 33M.

COPY forwarded to the Commissioner of the Patna Division for information with reference to this office No. 184M., dated 26th June last.

By order of the Lieutenant-Governor of Bengal,

FORT WILLIAM,
The 16th January, 1879.

F. H. WEEKS,
Offg. Asst. Secy. to the Govt. of Bengal, P. W. D.

Memo. No. 473R.

PATNA COMMISSIONER'S OFFICE,
Bankipore, the 25th January, 1879

COPY forwarded to the Collector of Gaya for information in continuation of this office No. 403R., dated 18th ultimo.

By order of the Commissioner,
DURGA GATI BANERJEA,
Personal Assistant to Commissioner.

SHOW this letter to Mr. Mills.

4th February, 1879.

E. J. BARTON.

SEEN and returned.

9th February, 1879.

C. A. MILLS.

[*Exhibit C* 18.]

Fly leaf—Collector's General Office.
Collection—XIII, Miscellaneous.
No. of File—22.
Subject—Bodh-Gaya.

Serial No.	From whom received or to whom addressed.	No.	Date.	Enclosure.	Class of Paper.
1	From Superintending Engineer, North-Western Circle ...	2006	19th July, 1879 ...	......	A
2	To Ditto ditto ...	1128	6th Aug., 1879 ...	......	A
3	From Executive Engineer, Patna	5393	4th Dec., 1879 ...	......	B
4	" Ditto ditto ...	5447	8th Dec., 1879 ...	......	B
	To Ditto ditto ...	2286	13th Dec., 1879 ...	......	...
5	From District Engineer, Gaya ...	240	18th Dec., 1879 ...	......	A
6	" Mr. Beglar	D. O.	2nd Jan., 1879 ...	......	A
7	To Ditto ...	2453	....	......	A

B. destroyed.

[*Exhibit C* 19.]

No. 1885.

To

THE CHIEF ENGINEER, BENGAL.

Dated Dinapore, 9th July, 1879.

SIR,

IN reply to your No. 32M., of the 16th January, 1879, with reference to the restoration of the old temple at Bodh-Gaya, I have the honour to report that I have just inspected the old temple of Bodh-Gaya, accompanied by Mr. Windle, Executive Engineer, Patna Division, with a view to furnish Government with the information called for in their letter under reply.

2. The present state of the building is the same as explained by Rai Rajendra Lala Mitra, Bahadur, in paras. 9 and 13 of his letter, dated 31st October, 1877, except, perhaps, that the base round the temple on the south side is in a worse condition than the lower portions of the northern and southern, as the outer facing of brick-work with mouldings, &c., have bulged slightly, and may have to be taken down. The building is in such a state that the present rain may have a great effect on it, and cause considerable damage. If the building is to be restored, the sooner the work is taken in hand, the better.

3. The following I consider is the work that must be done to ensure the stability of the building :—

1st.—The basement on the terrace round the temple to be repaired and made quite secure ; the work to be done is chiefly on the south and east faces.

2nd.—The pores on the eastern face and the large opening above it should be made quite secure.

3rd.—All four façades of the temple should be made quite watertight and built up with masonry where necessary.

4. The cost of the work must depend upon how it is carried out. If repairs are made with plain masonry, and only the work noticed in para. 3 executed, then it should not be excessive, and properly Rs. 15,000 might suffice ; but if the work proposed by Rai Rajendra Lala Mitra, Bahadur, is to be done, and the architectural features of the building maintained, and all masonry in repairs and restoration to be of the best pukka, then it will certainly not cost under Rs. 50,000.

5. The work is not of the simple character Government had been led to suppose. The building being 160 feet high, will require an expensive and well-constructed scaffolding to stand two seasons, if necessary, to allow free access round the building as the work progresses. So that the different courses and mouldings can be tested that they are on the same level all round, and each position of the cave as it is repaired must be tested that it is quite true. Of course, if the south and west facades are to be repaired with plain masonry and plastered over, the task of restoring the temple will not be nearly so great, although an expensive one. The

work will have to be commenced at the base and carried on upwards, and the person in charge must deal with it to the best of his judgment as the work proceeds, for instance, where any portion of the wall bulges, he must decide whether it will be safe to leave it or whether it must be removed. Of course, the less the original structure and mouldings are interfered with, the better, and there is this fear with the building, that in removing any portion no one can tell where the trouble will end, as the interior masonry is to fall back without any bond.

6. The bricks used vary considerably in size and the thickness from 2 to 3 inches, so to preserve the courses and bond and make a best point of it, bricks of the different sizes as required should be burnt. Scaffolding will still be required.

7. I consider the work is one requiring the closest supervision if it is to be restored as originally constructed, and if there are funds sufficient to allow of the work being pushed on I shall recommend that a Second or Third Class Executive Engineer should be deputed to look after it; but if this cannot be arranged for and only an upper subordinate can be spared, he should have associated with him a native architect or one accustomed to the description of work. In either case he must be an intelligent officer, and one likely to take an interest in the work.

8. I am afraid the repairs or restoration could scarcely be completed in seven months, as stated in some part of the correspondence, but if from first to last it is completed in one year, I should consider it very satisfactory.

9. In my opinion, if any money is to be spent on restoration, it would be advisable to give the larger sum and have it properly and thoroughly well done.

11. In conclusion I would observe that no detailed or approximately correct estimate can be prepared without suitable scaffolding, so as to be able to obtain access to all parts of the building.

12. The original correspondence is herewith returned.

L. T. S.

[NOTE.—This is some rough unauthenticated copy of a letter, the writer an official, his official designation being unknown. It has been found in the Bodh-Gaya file, and relates apparently to the year 1879.—D. J. M.]

[*Exhibit C* 20.]

No. 2006.

FROM

THE SUPERINTENDING ENGINEER, NORTH-WESTERN CIRCLE,

TO

THE MAGISTRATE AND COLLECTOR OF GAYA.

Dated Dinapore, 19th July, 1879.

SIR,

I HAVE the honour to forward my report in original (to be returned) regarding the present condition of the old temple at Bodh-Gaya, and request the favour of an expression of your opinion as to whether you agree with me in what is actually required to ensure the stability of the building and on other remarks made in the report.

2. As your District Engineer has had a good deal to do with the building, you might consult him in forming your opinion.

I have the honour to be,
SIR,
Your most obedient Servant,
L. T. STEWART, COL., R. E.,
Superintending Engineer, N.-W. Circle.

[*Exhibit C* 21.]

No. 1128.

FROM

THE MAGISTRATE AND COLLECTOR, GAYA,

TO

THE SUPERINTENDING ENGINEER, NORTH-WESTERN CIRCLE.

Dated Gaya, 6th August, 1879.

SIR,

I HAVE the honour to acknowledge receipt of your No. 2006, of 19th ultimo, giving cover to a draft letter addressed to the Chief Engineer, Bengal, containing proposals for the repair and restoration of the Buddhist Temple at Bodh-Gaya, and asking me to express my opinion on the subject in consultation with Mr. Mills, the District Engineer.

2. In reply, I beg to state that the temple was inspected by Mr. Mills in April, 1878, with a view to see the nature and extent of damage done, and the remedial measures that were necessary.

3. Considering that portions of the building are in a very ruinous and dilapidated state, it will require no inconsiderable sum of money to put it in thorough repair. The temple is of a peculiar construction. The masonry cement in the interior is of mud only and bricks have been placed without any regard to bond. This peculiarity, as you have already noticed, adds still more to the difficulty. It is, therefore, advisable that no work, unless absolutely necessary, should be taken in hand, as from the nature of the structure it cannot be stated what troubles may arise while the work of restoration is in progress. Much must depend on the judgment and tact of the Engineer entrusted with the work. Indeed, the safest course would be to strictly confine ourselves to the work of repair, and interfere as little as possible with the original building. Mr. Mills seems to think that no repair, unless in the shape of an outer coating of masonry impervious to rain, would be of any real use. The water, once penetrating, would force the joints and damage the brick-works.

4. The works proposed in para. 3 of your letter to the address of the Chief Engineer, I consider sufficient to secure the stability of the building. I, however, notice that you have made no mention about the rebuilding of the porch and of the central and side pavilions over it, or as to whether the niches are to be left empty or not, in case you intend to restore the building to its original appearance.

5. I quite agree with you in thinking that if repairs are effected with plain masonry the costs will be less; but if it be decided to preserve the ornamental work the expense will be considerable. It, however, rests with the Government to determine whether the architecture mouldings are to be preserved or not.

6. The necessity for a scaffolding is indispensable in the building, which is 160 feet high.

7. The work being a difficult and intricate one, should be entrusted to an able and efficient engineer, with a suitable establishment at his disposal.

8. Mr. Mills, who has been consulted, says:—

"The opinion given by the Magistrate in his letter coincides with mine, and I have always held that a special man should be given for the work.

"I should always consider it to be a great pity if the architectural features of the building were ruined by a hideous plain masonry wall. I think they should be preserved at any cost. I am also of opinion that this could be done for about half a lakh of rupees."

9. The enclosure of your letter under reply is herewith returned.

I have the honour to be,
SIR,
Your obedient Servant,

E. J. BARTON,
Magistrate and Collector.

[*Exhibit C 22.*]

FROM

J. D. BEGLAR, ESQ., C. E.,
Late Executive Assistant of Monuments,

To

THE MAGISTRATE AND COLLECTOR, GAYA.

Bodh-Gaya, 2nd August, 1884.

SIR,

BEFORE leaving this place—which I shall in a few days—permit me to place on record some notes that may be of use, and to request your kind sympathy and effort in preserving what Government has spent a large sum of money to conserve, and in which personally I take a great interest.

I have tried to secure the better sculptures from being carried off by pilgrims and tourists by placing them as far as I could in not easily accessible places, or, where accessible, in such conspicuous places, and so arranged, that the loss of any one would be instantly perceived. Mr. Keddie has continued to employ the chowkidar I had employed for reasons of policy, *viz.*, the *pujari* of the temple, Ganesh Singh, but after my departure he will have little power to secure sculpture from the depredations of the more powerful native visitors and of European visitors if they be so inclined. A notice in large print in English and vernacular painted on a board and conspicuously set up on your authority and with your signature, would, I trust, greatly deter people from plundering the place, while a few instructions to the police to keep a watchful eye, and to instruct the village chowkidars to promptly bring any case of plunder to notice, would very materially help to secure them from plunder.

In the godown attached to my bungalow are a large collection of fragments. They were collected for the sake of their inscriptions, yet unread and unexamined. I have not time to do so now, but I intend, with the permission of the Lieutenant-Governor, to be allowed to come once more (at my own cost) to examine them. The fragments are of absolutely no value, except for the inscriptions whch may or may not be of interest until they are examined. Let me earnestly pray you to take measures for their safety. If my bungalow is to be kept up, the khansama or chowkidar of the bungalow may be directed to look after these, as they are of no intrinsic value, even as sculpture. If a good lock be put on the door, their safety is assured.

In a detached godown are a large number of earthen casts of the old plaster ornamentation of the temple. I wrote long ago, and spoke about measures for securing them or sending them to the Museum. No notice was taken of my representations, but it is not impossible that some day some one more alive to their value may move to enquire about them. The roof is leaky, and they have partly melted and are melting away. I have no funds to save them by repairing the roof. They were made over to the Executive Engineer, Patna Division, but as no employé, not even a chowkidar of that Division is now here (since they removed my office furniture and records), it would be better if the bungalow khansama or chowkidar were instructed to look after them also. In case you are prepared to tell him so, I will remove them from the leaky godown, and place them in an unleaky room which the removal of my office has rendered available, and a lock on the door would secure their safety.

In the courtyard of the temple are a number of the sacred trees of the various previous Buddhas. I had planted nearly every variety of the known 24, but some have died. Of those alive some are already high enough to be safe from cattle, but several are not. These I have secured by circles of earth walls ; but an order from you excluding cattle from the court of the temple would more effectually save them than any number of walls.

The drainage of the platform of the temple, or first floor, consisting of the open terrace and the four subordinate temples round the main central shaft, is effected by iron pipes let into the masonry on the east and west side. The inlets of these pipes are secured by perforated plates of copper, as I had had several times to extract most incongruous articles—bamboos, plants, stones, brick, mud and wood—mischievously or wantonly thrown and forced down the piping by boys and native visitors. But the perforations are apt to get clogged by the feathers and droppings of the birds which make their nests in the shelter of the temple ornaments, and an order to the chowkidar to keep them clean is essential to the stability of the foundation of the temple. The drainage of the entire courtyard and of a great portion of the surrounding lands is effected by an underground covered drain. This drain is not straight, but has three heads due to the necessity of respecting vested interests, the necessity of not offending the Mahanth and the unfortunate manner in which portions of the work were executed. The entire tank works in fact were never contemplated, nor funds provided, till long after the drain as originally divided had been completed into this main channel, pouring in the water from various underground side drains. It is necessary occasionally, say, twice a year, to clean out the main and minor underground drains, as boys take a delight in rolling or throwing in broken bricks and stones into them through the grating.

Near the final outlet of the main drain stand a few huts, and the occupants throw all their house sweeping and refuse into the open drain, just about the mouth or outlet of the main covered drain. The result is, the drain gets completely blocked, and the temple flooded. This might be prevented by an order on the village chowkidar to take cognisance of who are the parties given to such a practice, and a simple threat from the Magistrate would probably prevent their doing so in future ; otherwise they may be bound down not to do so. I had every year to clean out the outlet, where an accumulation of straw, potsherd and ashes generally four feet high effectually blocked the outlet.

During highest floods of the river, the court of the temple will get flooded. As the level of the court is below the level of the recorded flood of 1812 (I think that is the year, but my papers are gone and I cannot be sure), this need cause no alarm, as it will only last a few hours. There was no one way of preserving the ancient features and at the same time giving absolute security from flooding except by expensive sluice gates for which funds would have been necessary. There will, in case of recurrence of such a flood as is above noticed, be a foot of water over the masonry lower terracing round the temple ; it will not get into the temple itself.

The tank attached to the temple was dug and the ghat built by Gosain Belpat Gir as marks of loyalty and respect to Sir Ashley Eden and the present Lieutenant-Governor on their visits to the temple. Government contributed nearly half the expense. The tank was intended as a reservoir for drinking water which, when the river is dry during May and June, is scarce and not good in the village wells. The tank has numerous springs, which copiously flowed even in June, and gave much trouble in being got under to allow excudation to go on. The tank consequently will always have a good supply of good water. But at present the whole village wash their clothes and themselves in it, and the water is most filthy. Pigs and cattle too are brought in and washed therein, which I have been unable to prevent, and as the tank had not yet been filled till I made over charge, I was indifferent about it, intending to take measures to suppress the practice after the high flood of the river had been allowed to pour into the tank and purify its waters; but I am going and the flood has not yet come. I earnestly represent that measures be taken to prevent the universal bathing and washing of dirty men and of cattle in the tank, and the flood, whenever it comes, if only of average height, will itself pour into the tank, establish a current and subsidence and leave the water perfectly pure and wholesome; perhaps the village chowkidars could do much to prevent people bathing in the tank. The Gosain, who gave more than half the funds for the work, has repeatedly requested me to appeal to you to kindly take measures for keeping the water clean for drinking purposes.

A large number of fragments of sorts of sculpture lie in the compound and round the walls and elsewhere. These are of no interest and importance, but some are in good preservation and may either be sent to the Museum in Calcutta or elsewhere, or preserved in the Gaya Institution, where I noticed several fine pieces of sculpture are already being taken care of.

From past experience, I can say that this temple is one of the places which travellers from Europe are almost certain to visit, to say nothing of Burmese, Japanese, Ceylonese, Nepalese, Tibetans and Siamese. Chinese pilgrims have not yet come, but probably will. For the more distinguished of these travellers as chief high priest envoys, some shelter more convenient than the leaky and open Burmese Dharamsalla is a necessity. If kept up as a dâk bungalow, even the receipts must probably pay for the keep of a khansama; if only kept as a road-cess bungalow, it would on your authorisation be available for the accommodation of European travellers, lady visitors, and of the more distinguished foreign Asiatic visitors, several of whom have in past times, with the consent of Government and accompanied by Government officers, been allowed to visit the place. If kept as a road-cess bungalow, a chowkidar, who could also cook, and furniture would be desirable.

The roof of the bungalow leaks in several places, and as the walls are *katcha*, if not repaired, the bungalow will soon collapse. It has not been repaired since it was built (except petty repairs at my own cost); the fine large verandah of the office will also speedily come down if not repaired, as also the roof of the servants' quarter. If the bungalow is to be kept up, repair of however slight a nature, if only to stop the leak, is essential.

Sometime ago, I think about the time your predecessor, Mr. Boxwell, was just going away, I sent a list of my furniture, offering them for sale at moderate cost, for the use of the bungalow, and no reply has been given to me as yet. I am now going, and I again send you a list of what is available, which, if you will take over, I will leave here and make over to any one you appoint; but if you decline, I will pack up, as I am going. I can only give you scanty time for reply for this. I trust you will excuse me. I will await your reply till noon of Monday next.

Lastly, the grounds on which the bungalow stands are rented from the Mahanth at an amount of Rs. 8, and rent has been paid to him up to May. The various small buildings outside the compound walls and office alignment except one small shed are all the property of the Mahanth.

I have the honour to be,
SIR,
Your most obedient Servant,
J. D. BEGLAR.

No. 1035.

FROM

G. A. GRIERSON, Esq.,
Officiating Magistrate and Collector, Gaya,

To

COUNT CHARLES LAMKOROWSKI.

Dated Gaya, 30th March, 1889.

SIR,

I AM informed you have taken away from Bodh-Gaya a number of carved stones belonging to that place, which are either the property of Government or of the Mahanth of Bodh-Gaya. I shall be obliged by your returning them by the bearer, as no one has any right to take them away without my permission.

In case they are not returned, it will be my duty to prosecute you under Section 403, Indian Penal Code.

Yours faithfully,

G. A. GRIERSON,

Officiating Magistrate of Gaya.

Telegram.

FROM

THE MAGISTRATE AND COLLECTOR OF GAYA,

TO

THE DEPUTY COMMISSIONER OF POLICE, CALCUTTA.

Dated 31st March, 1889.

A FOREIGNER, Count Charles Lamkorowski, left this on twenty-ninth for Calcutta. Believed to have taken away a number of carved stones from Bodh-Gaya Temple. These are Government property. Please get them back and send them here. Letter follows.

[*Exhibit F* 1.]

FROM

J. R. BERINGTON, ESQ.,

Assistant District Superintendent of Police,

TO

THE DISTRICT SUPERINTENDENT OF POLICE GAYA.

Dated Gaya, 2nd April, 1889.

SIR,

WITH reference to your letter, dated the 31st instant, ordering me to enquire and report on the matter of some carvings having been taken away from Bodh-Gaya, I beg to say that I proceeded to the place on the morning of the 1st instant, and from enquiries I made, it appears that about three days ago a "Sahib," accompanied by his bearer, went to Bodh-Gaya. After having seen the temple he went up to the bungalow, and seeing some stone carvings lying about he asked the bungalow chowkidar, through his bearer, whether these might be taken away, and upon the chowkidar saying they might, he took a few of them away with him.

I questioned the chowkidar, and he stated that he had orders from the Magistrate not to allow anybody to take carvings away, but this he thought applied to the temple and the bungalow, which, he said, was Government property. As these carvings were taken from a piece of waste land to the north of the bungalow, which he (the Chowkidar) said did not belong to Government, he thought the "Sahib" had a right to take the carvings. The chowkidar pointed me out the exact place from whence he said the carvings had been taken, and I have made a rough plan at the end of this report, showing the temple and the bungalow. The Magistrate of the District, Mr. Grierson, has also stated that the land undoubtedly belongs to the Mahanth of Bodh-Gaya, and not to Government, and the chowkidar has also stated that the land belonged to the Mahanth. From the above enquiries it appears that the carvings were taken from off land, which belonged to the Mahanth of Bodh-Gaya.

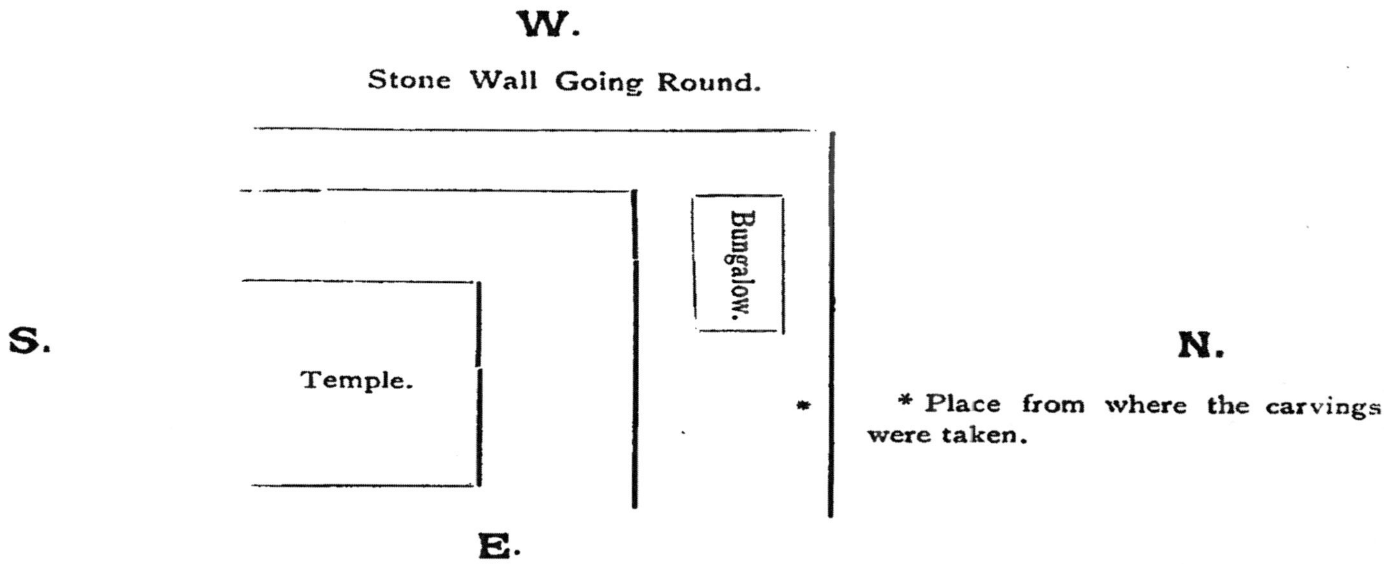

I have the honour to be,
SIR,
Your most obedient Servant,

J. R. BERINGTON,
Assistant District Superintendent.

[*Exhibit F* 2.]

Memo. by the District Superintendent of Police.

Dated 2nd April, 1889.

FORWARDED to the Magistrate. The chowkidar has no written orders, and I do not know how much is Government property and how much private property. To prevent mistakes in future, some definite orders should be issued to the custodian, as well as to the Bodh-Gaya Police.

H. N. HARRIS,
District Superintendent of Police.

[*Exhibit D* 54.]

No. 1077.

FROM

G. A. GRIERSON, ESQ.,
Officiating Magistrate and Collector, Gaya,

To

THE MAHANTH OF BODH-GAYA.

Dated Gaya, 3rd April, 1889.

SIR,

IT has been brought to my notice that visitors to Bodh-Gaya are in the habit of carrying away images and carved stones, which they find lying about on land in your possession.

I am sure you would not permit this if you knew it. On your letting me know that you may wish me to do so, I shall tell the Police not to allow it.

I would suggest that you should collect all these carved stones, and put them in a safe place in charge of the bungalow chowkidar, as they are very valuable.

I shall be obliged by an early reply.

I have the honour to be,

SIR,

Your most obedient Servant,

G. A. GRIERSON,

Officiating Magistrate and Collector.

FROM

MAHANTH HEM NARAYAN GIR, OF BODH-GAYA,

TO

THE MAGISTRATE AND COLLECTOR OF GAYA.

Dated Bodh-Gaya, 20th April, 1889.

SIR,

IN reply to your No. 1077 of the 3rd instant, directing me to collect the images and carved stones lying about on the lands, I have the honour to bring to your honour's kind notice that, in obedience to your honour's order, I collected the images and carved stones lying about on the lands in different places here and there.

I informed you of having done so through my servant. I have since then, according to your verbal directions, stored them all at my *math* in Bodh-Gaya for safe custody. I now request that you will be pleased to supply me with a written order for keeping the images in my *math*, for future reference.

I have the honour to be,

SIR,

Your most obedient Servant,

HEM NARAYAN GIR,

Mahanth of Bodh-Gaya.

No. 1230.

FROM

G. A. GRIERSON, ESQ.,

Officiating Magistrate and Collector, Gaya,

TO

MAHANTH HEM NARAYAN GIR OF BODH-GAYA.

Dated Gaya, 22nd April, 1889.

SIR,

WITH reference to your letter, dated 20th instant, I have the honour to say I shall visit Bodh-Gaya as soon as the hot weather is over, and will then talk personally to you on the matter.

I have the honour to be,

SIR,

Your most obedient Servant,

G. A. GRIERSON,

Officiating Magistrate and Collector.

To

THE DEPUTY COMMISSIONER OF POLICE, CALCUTTA.

Dated Gaya, 7th May, 1889.

DEAR SIR,

YOUR demi-official of the 16th of April. I am obliged to you for the trouble you have taken. I think that it is unnecessary to take any further step in the matter. Will you kindly forward me the three stones which were found in the bungalow compound, and which are in your custody? They are Government property, and the chowkidar will have to be punished.

Will you kindly convey to the Consul for Austria and Hungary that I am quite sure that Count Lamkorowski took away all the stones in perfect good faith? Indeed, the chowkidar admits having told him that he might do so.

That, however, does not prevent the stones being private property, those within the bungalow compound belonging to Government, and those without it to the Mahanth of Bodh-Gaya. The chowkidar had no authority whatever to permit their removal. It is easy to admit that the present affair is trivial, but Mr. Heilgers will understand what would be the consequences if any one of the constant stream of visitors carried away twenty stones from Bodh-Gaya.

A series of trivial incidents would become an evil of very great magnitude.

For this reason the Mahanth of Bodh-Gaya and Government are very zealous about the removal of so much as a single stone from the place. Effectual precautions are being taken for the future.

Yours sincerely,

G. A. GRIERSON.

Order by the Magistrate.

THE chowkidar of the bungalow at Bodh-Gaya is strictly forbidden to allow any person whatever to take away stones or images of any kind from the precincts of Bodh-Gaya Temple or bungalow, or the vicinity, without the permission of the Magistrate of the District.

If any are taken away, the matter will be very seriously dealt with, as all these stones and relics are private property.

The chowkidar will be liable to imprisonment if he permits any to be taken away.

GAYA MAGISTRACY,
The 11th May, 1889.

G. A. GRIERSON,
Officiating Magistrate.

[*Exhibit D* 55.]

No. 2282.

FROM

G. A. GRIERSON, ESQ.,
Officiating Magistrate and Collector, Gaya,

To

THE MAHANTH OF BODH-GAYA.

Dated Gaya, 10th July, 1889.

SIR,

IT appears from the report of the Chowkidar of Bodh-Gaya that the Burmese bungalow at Bodh-Gaya requires immediate repair.

I would suggest the propriety of your repairing it, and shall be obliged by your doing so.

I have the honour to be,

SIR,

Your most obedient Servant,

G. A. GRIERSON,
Officiating Magistrate and Collector.

Order Book No. 33, dated 25th July, 1889.

MR. MADDOX is placed in charge of the Bodh-Gaya Temple and bungalow. He should visit it once a month and see that the drains are kept clear, and that the other things insisted upon by Mr. Beglar are carried out.

He should also see that the bungalow is kept in water-tight repair, and that the *chaityas* and other stone relics are not carried away. He may spend any small sums from contingencies for necessary repairs, and the Mahanth's *Kandu* should be promised two rupees *bakhsheesh* at the end of the year if he keeps the roof of the bungalow water-tight.

He will also have cheap pole pankhas prepared at once for the principal rooms in the bungalow, and set up in it. The Nazir of Mr. Keddie will help him about this, and the costs met from contingencies. The pankhas are wanted at once.

G. A. GRIERSON,
Officiating Magistrate.

P. S.—An inspection book might be opened and kept at the bungalow in charge of the chowkidar.

No. 2518.

FROM

G. A. GRIERSON, ESQ.,
Officiating Magistrate and Collector, Gaya,

TO

THE SUPERINTENDING ENGINEER, SONE CIRCLE.

Dated Gaya, 25th July, 1889.

SIR,

IN forwarding you a copy of a letter of Mr. Beglar's, dated 2nd August, 1884, to the address of the Magistrate of Gaya, and in continuation of our conversation on the subject, I have the honour to draw your attention to the very unsatisfactory state of affairs which exists relating to the Bodh-Gaya Temple.

See *ante*, page 25.

2. The temple with the bungalow and grounds attached is in charge of the Magistrate of the district. He is represented on the spot by a chowkidar on five rupees a month, who has sole charge of this beautiful historical fabric, the repair of which have cost Government thousands of rupees.

3 I need not point out to you the great historic and religious interest which attaches to this building. The large sums of money spent on it by Government are sufficient to show that it is cognisant of all this. It seems, however, to have been forgotten that such a building cannot be left alone to the mercies of a venal chowkidar. Continual petty repairs are necessary to prevent the building again falling into decay, and these repairs are not within the power of the Magistrate to carry out. The Magistrate is given no money for the purpose, and if he had the money, he has not sufficient skilled supervision at hand to spend it properly.

4. Besides this the many *chaityas* and stone relics about the temple are liable to be stolen. Some of them have certainly disappeared, and when there are hundreds of them lying about uncatalogued, it is impossible to hold the chowkidar responsible. The other day an Austrian Count visited Bodh-Gaya, and went off with 20 or 30 stone relics, which he had picked up there, and I had considerable difficulty in recovering those belonging to Government.

5. The temple itself is also falling into disrepair. I have no one to look after the underground drains properly. Salt exudations also are destroying the plaster; this you have yourself seen. Villagers are encroaching on temple land.

6. For these reasons I consider that the Magistrate of Gaya is not the proper person to be in charge of the temple or its connected buildings. He has no money, no appliances, no technical skill at his command for keeping it in order. I therefore strongly recommend that it be taken over by the Public Works Department.

7. I think that it would be by no means out of the way to expect that Government should expend something every year in keeping in order an historical monument which has cost them a great deal already. I think that there should be appointed to the building a permanent custodian of the Sub-overseer grade, whose whole duty should be to guard the various *chaityas* and the like, and to carry out repairs year by year when necessary. He would be like the clerk of the works of any large English building.

8. A catalogue of the *chaityas* and other images should also be prepared.

9. Besides those already fixed *in situ*, there is in a roofless disused godown a heap of unexamined relics in charge of the chowkidar, which is freely drawn upon by sight-seers. It was used as a kind of mine for globe-trotters till I tried to put a stop to it by ordering that none were to be taken away without my written permission. I fear, however, that my order has had little effect beyond raising the price of these fragments.

10. In addition to this, almost every month new fragments of sculpture and statuary, often of considerable archæological interest, are dug up in the vicinity of the temple. Some of these used to be carried away by visitors, and others were used by villagers for currystones, well-lever counterpoises and the like. At my suggestion the Mahanth has stopped this, and collects all such stones in a godown as they are found, till proper arrangements can be made for their arrangement and display.

11. Considering that Government has spent so much money on this already, I think it might well complete its task by erecting a building to receive and properly display these carvings. I have no doubt that the Mahanth would contribute towards its cost. The carvings would be properly catalogued and placed in charge of the custodian.

I have the honour to be,
SIR,
Your most obedient Servant,
G. A. GRIERSON,
Officiating Magistrate and Collector.

No. 4450.

FROM

C. W. ODLING, ESQ.,
Superintending Engineer, Sone Circle,

TO

THE MAGISTRATE AND COLLECTOR OF GAYA.

Dated Arrah, 22nd October, 1889.

SIR,

WITH reference to your letter No. 3273 of the 14th instant, I have the honour to say that the Commissioner of Patna has expressed his concurrence with the views expressed in your predecessor's letter No. 2518, of the 25th July last, and I have asked him to represent the matter to Government which he has agreed to do. I have entered a sum of Rs. 500 for repairing the temple in the Public Works Budget estimate for 1890-91.

I have the honour to be,
SIR,
Your most obedient Servant,
C. W. ODLING,
Superintending Engineer, Sone Circle.

No. 478 AY.

FROM

THE GOVERNMENT OF BENGAL,
PUBLIC WORKS DEPARTMENT,

TO

THE SUPERINTENDING ENGINEER, SONE CIRCLE.

Dated Calcutta, the 11th February, 1890.

ARCHÆOLOGY.

SIR,

WITH reference to your predecessor's letter No. 3461, of the 6th August, 1889 addressed to the Commissioner of the Patna Division, on the subject of the Bodh-Gaya Temple, I am directed to forward for your information the enclosed copy of a letter* to the Commissioner, communicating the sanction of the Lieutenant-Governor to the proposals made by Mr. Odling. You should instruct the Executive Engineer to take over charge of the building.

* No. 456AY, dated the 8th January, 1890.

2. The entertainment of a subordinate of the Sub-overseer class, on a salary of Rs. 40 a month, to act as custodian of the premises is sanctioned. The watchman now employed on a salary of Rs. 5 per mensem will be transferred to the Public Works Department, and his entertainment is also sanctioned with effect from the 1st April next.

3. The custodian should make a catalogue of the loose carvings which are reported by Mr. Grierson to be at present stored in a roofless shed, and the *chaityas* and pieces of sculpture and other relics found in the vicinity of the temple should also be catalogued, and unless he has received special permission to do so from this office, no one should be allowed to remove anything from the temple or the surrounding ground.

4. The custodian should also submit estimates for such repairs and petty works as are necessary, and subject to such supervision as you may consider necessary, carry out the works when funds are alloted.

5. I am to request that an estimate of the cost of roofing the shed in which the loose carvings are stored, and of any repairs and petty works that are now required, may be submitted.

I have the honour to be,

SIR,

Your most obedient Servant,

W. B. BESTIC.

Under-Secretary to the Government of Bengal,
Public Works Department.

Enclosure,
Letter No. 456AY.

No. 456AY.

FROM

THE GOVERNMENT OF BENGAL,
PUBLIC WORKS DEPARTMENT,

To

THE COMMISSIONER OF THE PATNA DIVISION.

Dated Calcutta, the 8th February, 1890.

ARCHÆOLOGY.

SIR,

I AM directed to acknowledge the receipt of your letter No. 697G., dated the 9th December, 1889, forwarding a copy of correspondence on the subject of the Bodh-Gaya Temple. The Superintending Engineer of the Sone Circle reports (1) that the temple itself is in good order, but that the plaster is beginning to be attacked by saltpetre, and that the drainage is not properly attended to; (2) that the Magistrate is not able to bestow on the building the constant care which it requires, and (3) that a man of the Sub-overseer class is required to act as custodian of the loose carvings which are at present kept in a godown without a roof, and are liable to be carried away, and also to carry out such repairs and petty drainage works as may be necessary. These proposals are sanctioned by the Lieutenant-Governor. The building will, as proposed by the Magistrate, be borne in future on the books of the Public Works Department, and will be in charge of the Executive Engineer.

2. The Superintending Engineer will be requested to appoint a subordinate to look after the building and submit estimates for such repairs and petty works as are necessary, and also to furnish an estimate of the cost of roofing the shed in which the loose carvings are stored. The services of the watchman now employed should be transferred to the Public Works Department.

I have the honour to be,

SIR,

Your most obedient Servant,

W. B. BESTIC,

Under-Secretary to the Government of Bengal,
Public Works Department.

Office-note by the Magistrate attached to above letter.

VERY satisfactory. Show to Mr. Barrow.

22nd February, 1890.

G. A. G.

Memo. No. 707.

Dated 25th February, 1890.

COPY of the Government of Bengal letter No. 456AY., dated 8th February, 1890, together with the Commissioner's covering memo. No. 95G., dated the 18th idem, forwarded to the Mahanth of Bodh-Gaya for information in continuation of the conversation held between him and the undersigned in July last.

G. A. GRIERSON,
Magistrate and Collector.

No. 718.

FROM

G. A. GRIERSON, ESQ.,
Magistrate and Collector, Gaya,

To

THE EXECUTIVE ENGINEER, EASTERN SONE DIVISION.

Dated Gaya, 25th February, 1890.

SIR,

WITH reference to the letter of the Government of Bengal, No. 456AY., dated 8th instant, a copy of which is hereto annexed for ready reference, I have the honour to inform you that the rent of the land on which the Bodh-Gaya buildings stand has been paid to the Mahanth of Bodh-Gaya up to the year ending 31st May, 1889. The amount of the annual rent is Rs. 8.

2. Be good enough to let me know when you will take charge of the temple, &c.

I have the honour to be,
SIR,
Your most obedient Servant,

G. A. GRIERSON,
Magistrate and Collector.

No. 889.

FROM

A. S. THOMSON, ESQ.,
Executive Engineer, Eastern Sone Division,

To

THE MAGISTRATE AND COLLECTOR, GAYA,

Dated Bankipore, the 5th March, 1890.

SIR,

WITH reference to your No. 718 of 25th ultimo, I have the honour to inform you that the temple will be taken over by the Supervisor in charge of the Gaya Sub-division P. W. Department, on the 1st April, 1890.

I have the honour to be,
SIR,
Your most obedient servant,

A. S. THOMSON,
Executive Engineer, Eastern Sone Division.

Notice of advertisement for a custodian.

WANTED, on Rs. 40 a month, a Custodian of the Bodh-Gaya Temple, in the vicinity of which he must engage to reside permanently. He must be a resident of Gaya and possess the qualifications of a Sub-overseer, to be able to supervise the repairs and look after the drainage.

Candidates should present their applications on or before the 9th proximo.

F. H. BARROW,
Officiating Collector.

25th March, 1890.

No. 1186.

FROM

F. H. BARROW, ESQ.,
Officiating Magistrate and Collector, Gaya,

TO

THE EXECUTIVE ENGINEER, EASTERN SONE DIVISION.

Dated Gaya, 18th April, 1890.

SIR,

WITH reference to your No. 1141, dated 21st ultimo, to the address of the Collector, I have the honour to say that I have selected Babu Raghuber Prosad for the post of custodian of the Bodh-Gaya Temple. He is well connected, and has some experience.

2. Full particulars about the parentage, &c., of Raghuber Prosad are noted in the margin.*

3. I request that you will be good enough to let me know what instructions you give to the custodian. I think the instructions should be based on Mr. Grierson's letter No. 2518, dated 25th July, 1889, to the address of the Superintending Engineer, Arrah. The custodian must show energy and intelligence in classifying all the remains found, and if he proves a capable man, he will find plenty to do. I would propose that he should keep a diary, and while he submitted you a copy, he could bring me the original from time to time.

* Son of Ishri Prosad; Village Kesrawan; Pergunnah Bisara; Thana Muzufferpore; District Muzufferpore; age about 30 years.

I have the honour to be,

SIR,

Your obedient Servant,

F. H. BARROW,
Officiating Magistrate and Collector.

No. 1572.

FROM

THE EXECUTIVE ENGINEER, EASTERN SONE DIVISION,

TO

THE MAGISTRATE AND COLLECTOR OF GAYA.

Dated Bankipore, the 26th April, 1890.

SIR,

WITH reference to your No. 1186, dated 18th April, 1890, I have the honour to say that the purport of my No. 1141, of 21st March, 1890, does not appear to have been quite correctly understood. Very few applications for the post of custodian at Bodh-Gaya having been received by me, the letter referred to was issued as a circular to several officers asking for the names of any persons whom they considered eligible for the post. The case has now been referred to the Superintending Engineer, Sone Circle, to whom I will forward a copy of your letter. The appointment of a custodian will, I understand, be made by this department from among the candidates who have applied for the post.

I have the honour to be,
SIR,
Your most obedient Servant,

A. S. THOMSON,
Executive Engineer,
Eastern Sone Division.

No. 1006.

FROM

THE SUPERINTENDING ENGINEER, SONE CIRCLE,

TO

THE MAGISTRATE AND COLLECTOR OF GAYA.

Dated Arrah, 24th March, 1891.

SIR,

I HAVE the honour to forward for your information a copy of a letter No. 1005, dated 24th March, 1891, addressed to the Executive Engineer, Eastern Sone Division, regarding the Bodh-Gaya Temple. I beg that on any important matter you will address the Executive Engineer, and in regard to anything urgent or not of importance, you will communicate your views verbally or in writing to the Public Works Sub-divisional Officer. I regret that when I visited the temple the Mahanth was away, but he may rest assured that the custodian and the Public Works authorities generally will scrupulously abstain from doing anything likely to give him just grounds for complaint.

I have the honour to be,
SIR,
Your most obedient Servant,

MAHENDRA NATH CHATTERJEE,
Head Assistant,
For Superintending Engineer,
Sone Circle.

Accompaniment.
Copy of Superintending Engineer's No. 1005, dated 24th March, 1891.

[*Exhibit D* 53.]

No. 1005.

FROM

THE SUPERINTENDING ENGINEER, SONE CIRCLE,

TO

THE EXECUTIVE ENGINEER, EASTERN SONE DIVISION.

Dated Arrah, 24th March, 1891.

SIR,

I HAVE the honour to say that on the 21st instant I inspected the Bodh-Gaya Temple in company with the Collector. The sites selected for the custodian's house and the small museum are approved. Care should be taken that a ditch and fence round them, where not otherwise demarcated, are kept up. I have instructed the Sub-divisional Officer to build the pillars of the museum as far as possible after the pattern of the Asoka pillars now in this temple, and I think stone capital might be procured from Dehree. I should be willing to sanction Rs. 50 or Rs. 60 extra, which I think would suffice. Before the pillars are built, large scale drawings should be submitted for your approval.

2. An estimate should be submitted early next year for ordinary repairs to the temple, and should include removing grass from the masonry. Very special care should be taken to prevent peepul trees taking root there.

3. I request that you will cause the custodian to be very fully informed of the peculiar and in some respects delicate position he occupies. The building is not the property of Government, and is only taken charge of with the consent of the Mahanth. The custodian must at all times treat the Mahanth with the greatest respect and deference, and it would, I think, be well for him to pay the Mahanth a monthly official visit, so that he may be informed of any matter in which the Mahanth desires any special course to be taken. It would be absolutely impossible to retain the custodian in his office if he gave any reasonable cause of offence to the Mahanth or the temple officials, and this fact should be thoroughly impressed on the custodian, who can with ordinary carefulness maintain a good understanding with them. This efficiency will be largely judged by his remaining on really good terms with the temple authorities.

4. The Collector, as you are aware, retains his former position of guardian on the part of the state of the temple. He should be constantly referred to by the Sub-divisional Officer in case of doubt as to touching any part of the temple, and his advice taken in all matters connected with its preservation. I am quite certain that the Collector will render you whatever assistance you may require in connection with your duties in maintaining the building.

I have the honour to be,
SIR,
Your most obedient Servant,

C. W. ODLING,
Superintending Engineer, Sone Circle.

No. 240.

Dated Gaya, 31st March, 1891.

COPY forwarded to the custodian of the Bodh-Gaya Temple for information and guidance.

G. C. MOOKERJEE,
Supervisor, Gaya Sub-Division.

Note by Magistrate on Letter No. 1005.

HEAD CLERK,—Put this up with the original correspondence about restoring the Temple. I want to see what exactly our rights in regard to it are, if they have ever been defined.

1st May, 1891. G. A. G.

[*Exhibit C.*]

Office note in reply to above.

Submitted with old correspondence 1884. Serial numbers 1 and 3 of the year will give some information on the point. The Government order of 1890, transferring the Temple to the Public Works Department, is herewith submitted.

HARAN CHUNDER BANERJEE,
Dated 4th May, 1891. *Head Clerk.*

[*Exhibit D* 57.]

No. 1134.

FROM

G. A GRIERSON, ESQ.,
Magistrate and Collector, Gaya,

TO

THE COMMISSIONER, PATNA DIVISION.

Dated Gaya, 6th May, 1891.

SIR,

I HAVE the honour to forward herewith an extract from a letter written by the Superintending Engineer to the Executive Engineer, regarding the Bodh-Gaya Temple :—

"I request that you will cause the custodian to be very fully informed of the peculiar and in some respects delicate position he occupies. The building is not the property of Government, and is only taken charge of with the consent of the Mahanth. The custodian must at all times treat the Mahanth with the greatest respect and deference, and it would, I think, be well for him to pay the Mahanth a monthly official visit, so that he may be informed of any matter in which the Mahanth desires any special course to be taken. It would be absolutely impossible to retain the custodian in his office if he gave any reasonable cause of offence to the Mahanth or the temple officials, and this fact should be thoroughly impressed on the custodian, who can, with ordinary carefulness, maintain good understanding with them. His efficiency will be largely judged by his remaining on really good terms with the temple authorities."

2. Personally I entirely agree with these instructions, which also accord with the tradition handed down from Magistrate to Magistrate as to the position held by Government with regard to the temple, and have indeed reason to believe that the instructions are founded on information given by me to Mr. Odling.

3. I should be glad to communicate the tenor of these instructions to the Mahanth himself, with whom I am on excellent terms, but before doing so, I wish to be certain of my ground.

4. I can find no paper in the office defining the position of Government in regard to the Bodh-Gaya Temple.

5. The tradition is that, as Government has spent two lakhs on the temple, it has a certain undefined right to see its preservation and protection, the Mahanth remaining the proprietor, and all that we do, being done with his consent.

6. I am not prepared to condemn this state of affairs, which has grown up naturally and works smoothly.

7. The only thing I want to be certain about is whether it exists.

8. There must have been some negotiations between Government and the Mahanth when the repair of the temple was first undertaken, and probably the rights of Government in the matter were then defined.

9. There are no papers that I can find on the subject in my office, and I shall be obliged if you will enquire from Government as to what arrangement, if any, was came to, as to the right of Government :—

(i) In regard to the temple itself.

(ii) In regard to its precincts.

10. You can understand that while hitherto acquiescing in the traditional arrangement, I am unwilling to give the Mahanth a written document confirming it till I am certain that no other arrangement has been previously made.

I have the honour to be,

SIR,

Your most obedient Servant,

G. A. GRIERSON,

Magistrate and Collector.

[*Exhibit D* 58.]

No. 297G.

FROM

C. C. STEVENS, ESQ.,

Commissioner of the Patna Division,

TO

THE GOVERNMENT OF BENGAL,

PUBLIC WORKS DEPARTMENT.

Dated Bankipore, 21st May, 1891.

SIR,

I HAVE the honour to forward copy of a letter from the Magistrate of Gaya, on the subject of certain instructions proposed to be issued at the instance of the Superintending Engineer to the custodian of the Bodh-Gaya Temple.

Before issuing these instructions, Mr. Grierson wishes to know what arrangement, if any, was come to as to the rights of Government in regard to the temple itself and its precincts. There are no papers in his office or in mine which can throw light on the subject. I therefore submit the matter for the orders of Government. It seems very desirable that the position of Government in regard to the temple and its precincts should be carefully defined.

I have the honour to be,

SIR,

Your most obedient Servant,

DHANESH CHANDRA RAY,
Personal Assistant to Commissioner,
for Commissioner.

[*Exhibit D* 59.]

No. 1836AY.

FROM

THE GOVERNMENT OF BENGAL,
PUBLIC WORKS DEPARTMENT,

TO

THE COMMISSIONER OF THE PATNA DIVISION.

Dated Calcutta, the 7th July, 1891.

ARCHÆOLOGY.

SIR,

WITH reference to your letter No. 297G., dated the 21st May, 1891, with which you forward copy of a letter from the Magistrate of Gaya, on the subject of certain instructions proposed to be issued to the custodian of Bodh-Gaya Temple, and requesting that the position of Government in regard to the temple and its precincts should be clearly defined, I am directed to say that the question has never yet been decided, and that the Lieutenant-Governor would like the case brought before him whenever he visits Gaya.

I have the honour to be,

SIR,

Your most obedient Servant,

F. J. JOHNSTONE,
Joint Secretary,
to Government.

Memo. No. 333G.

PATNA COMMISSIONER'S OFFICE,
Dated Bankipore, 14th July, 1891.

COPY forwarded to the Magistrate of Gaya for information and guidance with reference to his No. 1134, dated 6th of May last.

By order of the Commissioner,
DHANESH CHANDRA RAY,
Personal Assistant,
to Commissioner.

No. $\frac{A}{333}$ G.

FROM

C. C. STEVENS, ESQ.,
Commissioner of Patna,

TO

THE MAGISTRATE OF GAYA.

Dated Bankipore, the 27th October, 1891.

GENERAL.

SIR,

I HAVE the honour to invite your attention to this office No. 333G., dated 14th July, 1891, and to request that you will be good enough to put up the case of Bodh-Gaya Temple before His Honour the Lieutenant-Governor when he visits your district.

I have the honour to be,
SIR,
Your most obedient Servant,
DHANESH CHANDRA RAY,
Personal Assistant to Commissioner,
for Commissioner.

[*Exhibit D* 60.]

No. 2498.

FROM

G. A. GRIERSON, ESQ.,
Magistrate and Collector of Gaya,

TO

THE COMMISSIONER OF THE PATNA DIVISION.

Dated Gaya, the 4th November, 1891.

SIR,

WITH reference to your letter No. 333G, dated 14th July, 1891, I have the honour to say that I have had the honour of discussing the subject with His Honour the Lieutenant-Governor during his late visit at Gaya, and His Honour is of opinion that it is not advisable to take any action at present in the matter or to disturb existing arrangements.

I have the honour to be,
SIR,
Your most obedient Servant,
G. A. GRIERSON,
Magistrate and Collector.

[*Exhibit D.* 3.]

FROM

COLONEL H. S. OLCOTT,
Honorary Director and Chief Adviser,
Maha-Bodhi Society.

TO

D. J. MACPHERSON, ESQ.,
Collector, Gaya.

Gaya, 6th February, 1893.

SIR,

FOR your information I beg to report my arrival, in my capacity of Honorary Director and Chief Adviser of the Maha-Bodhi Society, in company with Mr. H. Dharmapala, Honorary

General Secretary of the same, for the purpose of inspecting the Buddha-Gaya Maha-Bodhi Temple property, and of negotiating with the Mahanth for the acquisition of the religious custody of the shrine for the Buddhists of the several nations professing that religion. I had a preliminary talk with the Mahanth yesterday, through Babu Bireswar Singh, of Patna, as interpreter, and regret to say that I received no encouragement to hope that he would either sell or lease the property, or consent to the erection of a monastery or rest-house for the use of Buddhist Bhikshus or pilgrims. I gave the Mahanth to understand that the Maha-Bodhi Society, as the representative of the Buddhists, would not take or countenance the taking of any step which could infringe any proprietary right which he or his organisation might lawfully claim in this shrine, but that we should endeavour to act with him in a spirit of perfect equity. This same assurance I wish to give yourself and your official superiors.

As it was evident that the further stay of the Bhikshus in the Burmese King's Buddhist rest-house was not approved of by the Mahanth, and that to keep them there after the murderous assault made upon them on Friday evening last by parties until now unidentified, would subject them to its repetition, perhaps to the peril of their lives, I have arranged for their removal to safer quarters in Gaya, under reservation of any legal rights which the Buddhists may be found to have for the peaceful practice of their religion at their most hallowed shrine.

I am glad that the issue is a purely personal one of the Mahanth's proprietary interests, and that a good understanding exists between the Buddhists and the leading Hindus of Gaya.

I am, Sir,
Your obedient servant,
H. S. OLCOTT.

[*Exhibit D* 22.]

No. 6 P. D. Political Branch.

FROM

H. J. S. COTTON, ESQ., C. S. I.,
Chief Secretary to the Government of Bengal,

TO

H. DHARMAPALA, ESQ.,
General Secretary, Maha-Bodhi Society, Gaya.

Dated Darjeeling, 5th May, 1894.

SIR,

I AM directed to acknowledge the receipt of your letter, dated 14th April, 1894, and, in reply, to inform you that the Bengal Government is not in a position to give encouragement to any negotiations for effecting the transfer of the Bodh-Gaya Shrine to the Maha-Bodhi Society. There is perfect freedom of worship for all Buddhists at Bodh-Gaya, and the Hindu Sannyasis, who have held the place for over five centuries, are ever ready to meet all reasonable requirements of worshippers. Any well-grounded complaint that difficulties were imposed, would meet with ready attention and redress at the hands of the Bengal Government, but the Lieutenant-Governor can undertake no measures for the furtherance of the general objects of the Maha-Bodhi Society.

I have the honour to be,
SIR,
Your most obedient servant,
H. J. S. COTTON.
Chief Secretary to the Govt. of Bengal.

Memo. No. 233.

FROM

BABU KALI KUMAR RAY,
Overseer, Gaya Sub-Division,

TO

THE EXECUTIVE ENGINEER, EASTERN SONE DIVISION.

Dated Gaya, 26th May, 1894.

SIR,

I HAVE the honour to forward herewith in original a report of the chowkidar of the Bodh-Gaya Temple. The chowkidar reports that seven images was removed by Jaipal Gir,

Kothari of the Mahanth of Bodh-Gaya, from the main room of the temple, on the 17th instant, These are not ancient images, but Buddhist idols placed by pilgrims a few years back. The *Kothari* says that images of this nature belong to the Mahanth, being offerings made by pilgrims. Your orders are solicited whether any steps should be taken to recover the images, or whether the Mahanth can deal with them as he likes.

I have the honour to be,

SIR,

Your most obedient Servant,

KALI KUMAR RAY,

Overseer, Gaya Sub-Division.

No. 1684.

Dated Bankipore, the 28th May, 1894.

COPY forwarded to the Magistrate of Gaya for information and favour of such action as the Magistrate may consider necessary.

A. S. THOMSON,

Executive Engineer.

Orders thereon by Magistrate.

TO

BABU RAM ANUGRAH NARAYAN SINGH,

Deputy Magistrate.

THIS is a most serious matter in view of present circumstances and I request you at once to be good enough to proceed to the place and make a special enquiry and report the result. Please record the evidence judicially.

30*th May*, 1894. D. J. M.

RAM ANUGRAH BABU, after I wrote the above, consulted with me about this. The result was that I instructed him not to take further action until I had sent for and myself examined the chowkidar. I recorded his statement last night. I have also written to the Mahanth to replace the images immediately. He has done so.

1*st June*, 1894. D. J. M.

Statement of Nirghin Ram, son of Sahay Ram, Kahar, of Telpamalla, Gaya Town, on solemn affirmation :—

I COMPLAINED to my superior officer, the Overseer at Gaya, that seven images, which we call Buddha images, had been removed from the temple by Jaipal Gir, the *Kothari* of the Mahanth of Buddha-Gaya. I am chaprasi of the Public Works Department appointed to look after the temple. The Overseer of the Public Works Department in charge of the temple, went on three months' leave on the 8th April, and the Overseer, Kali Babu, at Gaya, is in charge in his absence. The images were taken away on Friday about a fortnight ago at 9 or a quarter past 9 o'clock at night. Jaipal Gir came with a number of the villagers and took away the images. I tried to stop him. I said, "Don't take away the images; why are you taking them?" He replied, "They are my property, I will take them." I said, "I would go and inform my master." He said, "By the time you have gone and informed him they can be replaced, and then you will be found to have told a falsehood and will be dismissed." I could say no more. They took away the images. I was at my lodging, when they arrived, and went to the temple on hearing their voices and the noise of their shoes. Then in the morning I gave information to the police at Buddha-Gaya. The Munshi asked me if I wanted to prosecute a case. I said I would go first and complain to the Babu. Then I came to Gaya that day to report the matter to the Overseer Babu, Kali Babu. The Babu was away elsewhere, and I did not see him that day. So I got a report written and left it at his office. The head-constable was on his rounds when I gave information to the police. I saw the temple yesterday, and the images had not been replaced by them. People told me they were taken and put inside the

Mahanth's *math*, and I saw them myself being taken off in that direction. The images were in the temple since before my employment there. I have been employed there for over two years. During these two years they were never removed from the temple. Two of them used to be on one side of the great image of Buddha and five on the other side.

That was in the shrine on the ground floor. I did not see the Mahanth on the day they were taken, or next day.

I complained about the matter to the Overseer, because the temple and things were under my charge, but the Mahanth's people keep the key of the temple.

D. J. MACPHERSON.

31*st May*, 1894. *Magistrate.*

I sent for the above chaprasi on receiving his complaint through the Executive Engineer, and have formally recorded his complaint above. I shall pass orders on it to-morrow.

D. J. MACPHERSON,

31*st May*, 1894. *Magistrate.*

The above complaint discloses an offence on the part of Jaipal Gir, the steward of the Mahanth of Bodh-Gaya. The apparent claim of right to remove Buddhist images from a Buddhist temple—from the most sacred shrine in the eyes of Buddhists of the whole world—is an entirely novel one. From facts within my own knowledge as to what was going on at the time, I have no doubt as to what was the motive for this act. The Buddhists are seeking to come to an arrangement with the Mahanth, whereby they may have greater control over the temple than at present, and in order to obtain a greater advantage over them in the negotiations and ground for extracting from them a heavier pecuniary compensation than he could otherwise reasonably claim, the Mahanth has, within the last two or three weeks, suddenly conceived the novel idea that the temple is really a Hindu one, and the great image of Buddha therein an incarnation of Vishnu. I can vouch for the fact that this is a pefectly novel idea. It was manifest, however, that the fact of Buddhist worshippers having placed images of Buddha alongside the great image in the shrine, would militate against that idea. Two days after the removal of these images, moreover, it had been arranged that an historical image of Buddha received from Japan should be set up in the temple. I had mentioned this intention on the part of those who had brought the image to the Mahanth about a month before, and he had no objection then to this, so long as it was not made of metal (*dhatû*) such as gold or silver, as if it were of intrinsic value, dacoits might be tempted to steal it, and he, as custodian of the temple, might be held responsible. This image, however, was not of metal at all. Nothing more occurred until the 17th, the day on which the images were removed from the temple. On the morning of that day one of the Mahanth's disciples, Ramkaran Gir, and a Muhammadan agent of the Mahanth's, came to my house with a copy of the *Indian Mirror*, announcing that the image was to be set up on the 19th, and with a verbal complaint to the effect that they were much perturbed (*ghabrao*) over this. I told them that if they had any representation to make, they must do so through the Mahanth, with whom the matter had already been arranged. The Mahanth came to me at 8 o'clock the same evening, *i.e.*, about the time when his steward was removing the images, and stated that if he allowed the image from Japan to be placed in the temple, his *chelas* might turn him out. There was no time to discuss the matter with him at that hour, and I told him to come next morning, which he did. I then told him that he and Dharmapala, who had arrived with the image, should meet and arrange matters. They met, but no arrangement was come to, owing to the attitude the Mahanth took up as to the necessity for the *prânpratishta* ceremony, which would be equivalent to making the image a Brahmanic deity. As a breach of the peace was apprehended after the withdrawal by the Mahanth of his consent, the image was not placed in the temple. The right of the Buddhist pilgrims who had come to worship in the temple on the night of the 19th May, the anniversary of the birth of Buddha, and the holiest night in the year in the eyes of Buddhists, was, however, enforced.

This recital of what was going on at the time, illustrates the motive with which the images were removed. I did not learn of their removal until I received the chaprasi's complaint through the Executive Engineer, Bankipore, on the 30th May.

The object with which the images placed by Buddhist pilgrims were removed was, in view of all the circumstances, to cause wrongful gain to the Mahanth in connection with negotiations contemplated by the Buddhists for obtaining greater control over the temple. The removal was therefore "dishonest" in the eye of the criminal law. It was also misappropriation, as there was no meaning in their being anywhere else, than in the shrine where the Buddhist worshippers had put them. Jaipal Gir could, therefore, be charged with criminal misappropriation under Section 403, and with theft from a building under Section 380, of the Penal Code. More than this, the removal of these Buddhist images from a Buddhist place of worship constituted a defilement of that place of worship, with the knowledge that it would likely be considered by Buddhists an insult to their religion, an offence under Section 295 of the Penal Code.

I had contemplated issuing process against Jaipal Gir under those sections, but I thought it advisable to give the Mahanth an opportunity of receding from the position he apparently sought to take up. I therefore wrote to him a letter, informing him of what had come to my notice, and requesting him to cause the images to be replaced at once. He has complied with this request, but seeks to justify the removal by alleging that he has always been in the habit of taking such images placed there recently as offerings by pilgrims, together with presents and fees. I have informed him that he has no authority to remove images or other votive offerings of any kind, not being of a perishable description, that may be placed by Buddhist worshippers in the temple.

Under the circumstances, I do not think it necessary to proceed further with this complaint, and I dismiss it under Section 203 of the Criminal Procedure Code.

D. J MACPHERSON,
Magistrate of Gaya.

9th June, 1894.

FROM

D. J. MACPHERSON, ESQ.,
Magistrate and Collector of Gaya,

TO

MAHANTH KRISHNA DAYAL GIR OF BODH-GAYA.

Dated Gaya, 31st May, 1894.

SIR,

I HAVE the honour to inform you that I have just received information through the Executive Engineer, Bankipore, to the effect that your *Kothari* Jaipal Gir removed seven Buddhist images from the Temple of Maha-Bodhi on the evening of the 17th instant. I therefore request you to be good enough to cause them to be replaced in the temple in the position they were in before, within a couple of hours of the receipt of this letter, and intimate to me by the bearer of this that you have done so. I beg to point out to you that it was your duty to have reported to me, immediately on its coming to your notice, that these images had been removed.

2. I enclose a Hindi translation of this letter for your information.

I have the honour to be,
SIR,
Your most obedient Servant,

D. J. MACPHERSON,
Magistrate and Collector.

Translation of letter from Mahanth to Collector in reply to above.

TO

HIS HONOUR THE COLLECTOR OF GAYA.

Dated 13th Jaisto, 1301 *F.S.* (*1st June,* 1894.)

CHERISHER OF THE POOR, HAIL!

I BEG to state that I have received the letter sent through Nazir Baijnath Singh. I have been acquainted with your orders and carried them out.

I beg to submit that the Engineer's report that the images were removed is correct (*thik*), but you have not been made aware whether the images that were removed were old or new ones. So I beg to acquaint you that these images were new ones presented as offerings (*chadhas*). Such images with presents and fees have always been brought. I have never removed any of the old images, and I do never bring any such images. If any of the old images were removed, I should have certainly informed your honour. If you issue any other sort of instructions now (*ab*) I shall carry them out. You are my lord and benefactor. Please pass such orders that may not be prejudicial to my interests (*haqq*).

The Nazir reached me at 5 A.M., but as my Dewan and agent were absent, so there was delay in getting them. I gave reply at half-past ten.

KRISHNA DAYAL GIR,
Mahanth of Bodh-Gaya.

Extract from Nazir's report to Magistrate.

Dated 1st June, 1894.

THE reply to my letter was ready by 10-30 A.M., when he made it over to me and told me to see the temple again, stating that the images have been placed there. One of his servants and *Kothari* with one image accompanied me on going to the temple. I found that six images, three on each side of the large image of Buddha, covered with a cloth, were placed, and the seventh was placed there in my presence on the north side of the large image.

After seeing the temple, I made enquiry about the Overseer, Bepin Babu. He is absent on leave since April 9th, 1894. I hear he has taken leave for three months.

BAIJNATH SINGH,
Nazir.

FROM

D. J. MACPHERSON, ESQ.,
Magistrate and Collector, Gaya,

TO

MAHANTH KRISHNA DAYAL GIR, OF BODH-GAYA.

Dated Gaya, 3rd June, 1894.

SIR,

WITH reference to your reply of the 1st instant to my letter of the 31st May, regarding the removal of images from the Maha-Bodhi Temple, I have the honour to inform you that you are not authorised to remove images or other votive offerings of any kind, not being of a perishable description, that may be placed by Buddhist worshippers in the temple.

2. I believe that you are aware that the images which were removed on the occasion referred to had been in the temple for two or three years at least, and some of them for a longer period.

3. A Hindi translation of this letter is annexed for your information.

I have the honour to be,
SIR,
Your most obedient Servant,
D. J. MACPHERSON,
Magistrate and Collector.

Note by Magistrate on the above correspondence.

THESE letters here are important, and must be carefully preserved as A papers—
Collector to Mahanth, dated 31st May, 1894.
Mahanth to Collector, dated 13th of Joisto, 1301 F. S., *i.e.*, dated 1st June, 1894.
Report of Nazir who took the letter, dated 1st June, 1894.
Collector to Mahanth, dated 3rd June, 1894.

9th June, 1894. D. J. M.

Magistrate's Office-note.

CORRESPONDENCE of 1876 and 1877 is very important, but I see from the endorsement of Commissioner's No. 20R, dated 15th April, 1878, that there was apparently no correspondence through the Collector since Commissioner's letter No. 387R, dated 21st January, 1876, which is in the file. In the interval Dr. Rajendra Lala Mitra submitted apparently direct Government and important report on the state of the buildings on the 31st of the October, 1877.

There is in the file an important letter of Mr. Halliday's, No. 1177, dated 8th December, 1875, but what is also of much importance, namely, the Mahanth's letter on which it is based (presumably in the vernacular), is not in the file.

8th June, 1894. D. J. M.

No. 435G.

FROM

D. J. MACPHERSON, ESQ.,
Magistrate and Collector, Gaya,

TO

THE EXECUTIVE ENGINEER, EASTERN SONE DIVISION.

Dated Gaya, 9th June, 1894.

SIR,

I HAVE the honour to request the favour of your supplying me with any instructions that may have been issued by your department with reference to the position the custodian, who is maintained by your department at Bodh-Gaya, occupies in relation to the Temple of Maha-Bodhi and the Mahanth of Bodh-Gaya. The favour of a very early reply will oblige.

I have the honour to be,
SIR,
Your most obedient Servant,
D. J. MACPHERSON,
Magistrate and Collector.

No. 1860.

FROM

THE EXECUTIVE ENGINEER, EASTERN SONE DIVISION,

TO

THE MAGISTRATE AND COLLECTOR OF GAYA.

Dated Bankipore, the 11th June, 1894.

SIR,

WITH reference to your No. 435G, of the 9th instant, I have the honour to forward herewith copy of Bengal Government No. 478AY, of 11th February, 1890, to the Superintending Engineer, Sone Division, and Superintending Engineer's No. 1005, of 24th March, 1891, regarding the instructions issued to the custodian of Bodh-Gaya Temple.

See *ante* pp. 33 and 37.

I have the honour to be,
SIR,
Your most obedient Servant,
A. S. THOMSON,
Executive Engineer.

[*Exhibit D* 23.]

No. 654 P. D., Political Branch.

FROM

H. J. S. COTTON, ESQ., C.S.I.,
Chief Secretary to the Government of Bengal,

TO

H. DHARMAPALA, ESQ.,
General Secretary, Maha-Bodhi Society, Gaya.

Dated Darjeeling, the 22nd June, 1894.

SIR,

WITH reference to your letter, dated the 15th June, 1894, to the Private Secretary to His Honour the Lieutenant-Governor, I am directed to inform you that the Government must decline to exercise any influence with the Mahanth of the Bodh-Gaya shrine, and can pass no other orders than those already communicated to you in my letter No. 6 P.D., dated the 5th May last.

I have the honour to be,
Sir,
Your most obedient Servant,

H. J. S. COTTON,
Chief Secretary to the Government of Bengal.

No. 7E.

FROM

MAHANTH KRISHNA DAYAL GIR OF BODH-GAYA,

TO

THE MAGISTRATE AND COLLECTOR OF GAYA.

Dated Bodh-Gaya, the 13th—16th June, 1894.

SIR,

WITH reference to your letter dated the 3rd of June, 1894, intimating to me that I am not authorised to remove images or other votive offerings of any kind not being of a perishable description that may be placed by Buddhist worshippers in the temple, I have the honour most respectfully to submit that I and my predecessors in office have been exercising absolute control over such images or votive offerings from time immemorial, and that my right in this behalf has been never questioned, and that I, as proprietor of the Maha-Bodhi Temple, have such a right under the law, and under the circumstances I have been advised to request the favour of your kindly not interfering in matters which involve questions of civil rights. At the same time I, as a loyal subject of Her Most Gracious Majesty the Queen-Empress of India, am quite willing to obey any just and equitable order that may be passed by the Government at your recommendation.

Hoping earnestly that you, as my best patron, will do all that is necessary for the maintenance of my just right and title, and as a dutiful Mahanth, praying for ever for your welfare,

I remain,
SIR,
Your most obedient Servant,

KRISHNA DAYAL GIR,
Mahanth of Bodh-Gaya.

Note on the above letter by the Magistrate.

THIS reached me the day I went on leave. I annex a memo. of the reply I would recommend should be sent. The Mahanth before sending this cover asked me (verbally) to cancel mine, but I refused to do so, and suggested that he could send in a protest which, as he wished, could be investigated after my return from leave.

28th June, 1894. D. J. MACPHERSON.

No. 1556.

FROM

E. G. DRAKE-BROCKMAN, ESQ.,
Officiating Magistrate and Collector, Gaya,

TO

MAHANTH KRISHNA DAYAL GIR OF BODH-GAYA.

Dated Gaya, 11th July, 1894.

SIR,

WITH reference to your letter No. 7E, dated 13th—16th June, 1894, I have the honour to inform you that I am not prepared to admit any proprietary right on your part over the Maha-

Bodhi Temple as against the Crown, or any right to interfere with votive offerings that may be presented at the shrine, unless merely as a custodian. At the same time the matter may, if you wish it, be investigated further later on, as arranged on the occasion of your last interview with Mr. Macpherson before he went on leave, and meanwhile your protest will be noted.

I have the honour to be,
SIR,

Your most obedient Servant,

E. G. DRAKE-BROCKMAN,

Officiating Magistrate and Collector.

Note by the Officiating Magistrate on the above letters.

THE letter of the Mahanth, No. 7E, dated 13th—16th June, 1894, should be docketed. Also the petition of Mr. Dharmapala, and Mr. Macpherson's note should be put in this file.

14th July, 1894.

E. G. D.-B.

[NOTE.—The following is the text of the petition of Mr. Dharmapala and the note of Mr. Macpherson referred to above and in the ensuing correspondence.]

Petition of H. Dharmapala to the Magistrate of Gaya, dated 12th June, 1894.

To His Worship D. J. Macpherson, Esq., District Magistrate, Gaya.

The humble petition of H. Dharmapala, General Secretary of the Maha-Bodhi Society.

SHEWETH,—That the Maha-Bodhi Temple at Buddha-Gaya is the central shrine most sacred to the four hundred and seventy-five millions of Buddhists throughout China, Japan, Siam, Burma, Ceylon, Arakan, Tibet, Chittagong, Nepal and other places. To them, your petitioner submits, the site is as sacred as Jerusalem is to the Christians, Mecca to the Musalmans, and Benares to the Hindus.

2. That the Maha-Bodhi Temple was in utter ruins till 1876, when the Government of King Mindoon Min of Burma commenced to repair it, but, in the interest of archæology, the then Lieutenant-Governor of Bengal, His Honor Sir Ashley Eden, interfered, and had the restoration completed at great cost to the British Government. The place has ever since risen to eminence, owing to the great facility of travelling caused by the opening of the Patna-Gaya State Railway, attracting great many visitors from different parts of the world, as well as pilgrims from all Buddhist countries, who are actuated with the religious devotion and fervour of paying their respect to that most hallowed spot where Prince Sakya Singha sat in meditation, and at last founded the religion which now sways the destiny of one-third of the whole human population.

3. That ever since the temple has been restored, the Buddhists have been freely worshipping in the temple, setting up images, bells, flag-staffs, and performing other rites in accordance with their religion, and the former Mahanth of Budh-Gaya never interfered and objected to the same being done.

4. That Krishna Dayal Gir, the present Mahanth of Budh-Gaya, ascended the *Mahanthi Gadi* of the Budh-Gaya Sannyási Math in February, 1892, and unfortunately he has ever since taken an antagonistic attitude towards the Buddhists in general and your humble petitioner in particular.

Notes on a petition, dated the 12th June, 1894, filed before the Magistrate of Gaya by H. Dharmapala, General Secretary of the Maha Bodhi Society.

THIS petition was filed before me on the 12th instant by H. Dharmapala, General Secretary of the Maha Bodhi Society, with the main object of being accorded permission to set up in the Temple of Maha-Bodhi at Bodh-Gaya an historical image of Buddha, which had been entrusted to him for the purpose on the occasion of his passing through Japan recently on his return from attending the "Parliament of Religions" at Chicago. It had been arranged, with the consent of the Mahanth of Bodh-Gaya, that this image was to be placed in the Temple on the 19th of May last, but in consequence of a very threatening attitude of opposition adopted by the Mahanth and his followers at the last moment, I found it expedient in the interest of the peace to inform Mr. Dharmapala that he should postpone doing this, unless in the meantime he was able to convince the Mahanth that it in no way infringed on any supposed rights that the latter claimed in connection with the temple, and obtained a renewal of his consent. Not having succeeded in this, he has now filed the present petition with a view to its being declared that the Buddhists have an absolute right of worship, irrespective of the Mahanth's consent, to set up the image in the temple. This is claimed as involved in the right of freedom of worship in the temple which the Bengal Government have recently declared that the Buddhists possess (*vide* the Government letter of the 5th May, 1894, quoted in para. 12 of the petition). The opportunity is taken of pressing one or two other matters which are held to be implied in the right of free worship, namely, to establish and set up images, &c., in the temple, and to attach Buddhist priests to the shrine who would have access to it at all times, without having to go at all to the Mahanth, who keeps a lock on the door of the temple.

2. The following is a statement of the circumstances, which give rise to the present petition.

3. About the middle of April last, Mr. Dharmapala visited Gaya on his return to India, and informed me that when passing through Japan, he had been entrusted with an historical image of Buddha, which he was commissioned to have set up in the Temple of

5. That shortly before the temple was restored under orders of the benign British Government, King Mindoon Min of Burma (King Thibaw's father) purchased a piece of land, west of the temple compound, from Mahanth Hem Narayan Gir, the preceptor and predecessor of the present Mahanth, and built a small building (now called the Burmese rest-house) for the permanent residence of Buddhist priests, who were sent out here to officiate at the daily worship which was carried on three times a day; and the Burmese priests resided in the house and officiated at the religious service, till one of them died there and was buried at Budh-Gaya, his tomb or *stupa* being just south of the Burmese rest-house, and the others left the country on account of political unrest caused in Burma by the death of the old King and the accession of King Thibaw. That your petitioner also stayed with a Japanese priest at the Burmese rest-house for nearly three months from January to March 1891: and that there were other Buddhist priests who permanently resided there, and regularly officiated at the daily services from July 1891, to January 1893, when some of them were brutally assaulted by the retainers and servants of the present Mahanth.

6. That the late Mahanth Hem Narayan Gir, who was himself a learned man and Sanskrit scholar, was always friendly to your petitioner and the Buddhists, and had leased out to your petitioner one bigha of land west of the Burmese rest-house for its extension, and your petitioner had built a kitchen and a latrine for the use of the priests, but the present Mahanth, who is bent upon cancelling the lease by refusing to accept the rent, has pulled down the additions made on the land after the priests had left the place after the assault.

7. That the Buddhists of Japan having come to know that the original image of Buddha in the second storey in the Buddha-Gaya Temple was removed to the forest of Rajgir by the Buddhist priests in the temple in the 12th century A. D., through fear that it might be destroyed by the conquering Mussalmans, and also having come to know that the image that is placed there at present is not the original image, but one set up by Mr. J. D. Beglar after the temple was repaired, and of course, without any ceremony prescribed by the Buddhist code of religion, they, on behalf of the whole Japanese nation, presented to the Maha-Bodhi Temple a very historic image of Lord Buddha, carved by the great artist Sadatomo of Nanto, by command of the ruling Shogun Minamoto Yoritomo, 700 years old, and entrusted your petitioner with it to have it placed with due religious rites and ceremonies on the second floor of the temple in your Worship's presence. They also entrusted him with a letter to your address, requesting your Worship to take charge of the image and have it placed in the temple, and your petitioner has already presented to your Worship the original letter in Japanese character.

8. That in the month of April last, Mahanth Krishna Dayal Gir himself admitted before your Worship that he had no objection to the image in question being placed in the temple, provided that it was not a metal one, on the ground that it might be stolen, and he may be held responsible for the loss or theft; and consequently your petitioner, with your Worship's permission and consent, made all preparations, and underwent some expense to take the image in procession from Gaya to Budh-Gaya with fitting pomp and grandeur, and fixed the full-moon day of Baisak (19th May, 1894,) which is the holiest day in the Buddhist calendar, this being the anniversary of Lord Buddha's birth as well as of his attaining supreme enlightenment under the Bodhi-tree at Budh-Gaya, and also of His entering Nirvana, and your Worship was informed of the date. That on the 17th of May last, when all the arrangements were nearly completed, and when the High Priest of Japan, who had come out to India on a pilgrimage, had consented to officiate at the enshrining of the image in the temple, and had arranged to arrive there on that date, the Mahanth refused to allow your petitioner to set up the image in the temple, and

Maha-Bodhi in my presence. He stated that a Japanese letter to my address accompanied the image, in which I was requested to take charge of it, and see it placed in the second storey of the temple. I requested Mr. Dharmapala to obtain for me an English translation of the letter, but this has not yet been got, and the letter is still with him. The Mahanth came to see me at the same time, and I informed him of the image that had been sent from Japan to be placed in the second storey of the temple, and enquired if he had anything to say about the matter. The Mahanth informed me that he would have no objection so long as the image was not of metal (*dhatu*). When I asked him what was the objection to a metal image, he replied, that one of gold or silver might be stolen by dacoits, and that he might be held responsible for it. I did not at the time know what material the image was composed of. However, this was the only objection of any kind the Mahanth hinted at, and I took it as implying that he consented to the placing of any other image in the temple and informed Mr. Dharmapala of this. As the image is one of sandalwood, Mr. Dharmapala assured me that everything was all right, and arranged to set up the image on the full-moon day in May, *i.e.*, the 19th of May, as being the anniversary of the birth of Buddha and also of the day on which he obtained enlightenment under the Bodhi-tree at Maha-Bodhi.

4. Mr. Dharmapala, who was away from Gaya from the time when I saw the Mahanth, returned on the 17th of May, bringing the image with him. The Mahanth himself was away in the east of the district for about ten days until that date also. On the morning of the 17th of May, one of his disciples and a Muhammadan mukhtear of a very inferior status came to me with a copy of the *Indian Mirror*, and said they were alarmed about a paragraph in it, to the effect that the Buddhists were going to set up a great image in the temple with some ceremony on the 19th. I declined to discuss matters with them, and said that any representation on the subject must come from the Mahanth personally, with whom I said the matter had, however, already been arranged. The Mahanth himself came to me at 8 P. M. that evening; and it was evident from his tone and conversation that his disciples had been working upon him, and that he and they were afraid from the importance that was apparently being attached to the setting up of the image, that it was part of a surreptitious attempt on the part of the Buddhists to oust him from the temple altogether.

I learned, a day or two after, that one or two Bengalis in the town of Gaya had put the Mahanth up to this, in order to make capital out of it. I assured the Mahanth that as regards the question of general control over the temple, the Buddhists had no intention of doing anything that would be prejudicial to his interests, if only he would discuss matters with them in a reasonable spirit, with a view to an amicable arrangement; and I reminded him that he had had no objection to the image being set up, so long as it was not made of metal, which it was not. He replied that his disciples were agitated and dissatisfied at this. But I said he ought to explain matters to them. I had no time to discuss things further with him at that inconvenient hour and directed him to come back in the morning. When he returned, he said it was Mr. Dharmapala's duty to have gone personally to him to obtain his consent to the setting up of the image; and I told him I would instruct Mr. Dharmapala to go and discuss the matter with him, and that, until matters were cleared up between them, the image would not be allowed to be put up.

5. Mr. Dharmapala, as requested by me, went to the Mahanth, but the latter insisted on the unreasonable condition that the *pranpratishtha* ceremony must be undergone before the image could be placed in the shrine, which would be equivalent to constituting it a Brahminical deity. As no arrangement could consequently be come to, the image could not be taken to Budh-Gaya on the 19th. Indeed, considerable preparations were made by the

collected a large band of armed men to resist the procession; that when the matter was brought to your notice, your Worship immediately ordered your petitioner to postpone the ceremony, and the enshrining there was accordingly suspended, and the image, which is a mastepiece of Japanese work of art, is still lying in your petitioner's hands in great danger of being damaged.

9. That the said Mahanth on the full-moon day of Baisak last actually locked the doors of the Maha-Bodhi Temple, and the gate was barred against all Buddhist pilgrims; and that some pilgrims, who had come from Ceylon, had to proceed from here to Budh-Gaya under a special police escort, ordered by your Worship, and that instructions from your Worship to the Budh-Gaya Police were necessary to procure safety for the High Priest of Japan, who had gone to worship at Budh-Gaya, and that, notwithstanding the above arrangements, your petitioner was, on account of the personal animosity that the Mahanth shewed towards him, constrained to forego the right of worship in the Budh-Gaya Temple, on the holiest day of the year.

10. That it is evident from what is stated above that the attitude taken by the present Mahanth of Budh-Gaya Math is becoming more inimical and aggressive day by day, and unless your Worship kindly intercedes in the matter, your petitioner is afraid that the Buddhists' right of free worship in the temple will practically, and to all intents and purposes, be taken away from them by the Mahanth.

11. That in his letter No. 6 P. D., Political Branch, dated Darjeeling, the 5th May, 1894, the Chief Secretary to the Government of Bengal assured your petitioner "that there is perfect freedom of worship for all Buddhists at Budh-Gaya, and the Hindu *Sannyásis* who have held the place for over five centuries are ever ready to meet all reasonable requirements of worshippers. Any well-grounded complaint that difficulties were imposed will meet ready attention and redress at the hands of the Bengal Government."

12. Your petitioner most humbly and respectfully begs to submit that there can be no "perfect freedom of worship for all Buddhists," until the Buddhists are allowed to keep their own priests to officiate and preside at the daily worship which is to be carried on three times every day, to go in and out of the temple freely at all hours and pass some special nights within the temple, chanting prayers and reading religious books, to burn incense, &c., at the altar, to embellish and decorate the place, to enshrine images, to hang bells, and to perform other rites in accordance with their own religion, and not to be dictated to by the Mahanth, who is a Hindu Saivite, at what time and in what way they are to conduct their religious worship there.

Your petitioner, therefore, most respectfully approaches your Worship, who is the representative of the Government in this district, with this petition, and humbly prays :—

(1). That the Mahanth of Budh-Gaya Math may be ordered not to interfere with your petitioner in setting up the aforesaid image of Lord Buddha, presented to the Maha-Bodhi Temple by the Japanese nation, with befitting rites and ceremonies;

(2). That the Buddhists' right of perfect freedom of worship in the shape of flowers, scents, &c., and in the suitable embellishment of the temple and its precincts by setting up images, bells, flagstaffs, &c., may be practically enforced;

(3). That the presence of Buddhist priests to officiate at the worship of Buddhist pilgrims being *absolutely* necessary according to the dictates of the Buddhist religion, their presence in the temple for this purpose and for the daily worship of Lord Buddha, which consists of the performance of certain ceremonies thrice a day, as is done in the Buddhist Temples of Ceylon, Burma, Siam, Japan and China, be permitted without let or hindrance on the part of the Mahanth and his people;

(4). That such other or further order or orders be passed as to your Worship may seem fit to meet the requirements of the case which may seem just and proper.

Mahanth's followers in order to oppose by force the taking of the image there, and Mr. Dharmapala received information as to an intention to assault him personally, which made him so apprehensive that he thought it prudent to abstain from worshipping at the Temple on the holy night. Some Buddhist pilgrims also, who arrived at Gaya on that day, appealed to me for protection, and I had to issue an order forbidding all interference with the worship of the Buddhists at the temple, and to send down the inspector of police to the temple to enforce it. The sub-inspector got there at 9.30 P.M., and found an assemblage of people, headed by some of the Mahanth's disciples, collected at the temple. They pretended they had come there to receive alms from the pilgrims that were expected that evening: but the inspector ordered them to open the door of the temple, which was locked. They made some demur, saying it was too late, and so on. The inspector, however, insisted, and the pilgrims were able to conduct their worship in peace. It is certain that, had I not sent down some police, the Buddhist pilgrims who had come from far, specially to worship at the temple on that most holy night, would not have been allowed by the Mahanth's men to enter it on that occasion.

6. I learned subsequently from a communication received from the Executive Engineer, Eastern Sone Division at Bankipore, in whose charge the temple is, that on the night of the 19th, just about the time when the Mahanth was at my house, his steward, Jaipai Gir, *kothari*, removed from the temple, under protest from the Public Works Department peon in charge, seven images that had been placed there by Buddhist pilgrims some years before.

As soon as I heard of this, I issued a peremptory order to the Mahanth to replace the images; and he did so, but at the same time he claimed the right to take any images that might be placed in the temple. In conversation with me since, he has explained that if he does not maintain his right to take even common images, such as those of clay, he would become a loser, if the Buddhists take to placing gold and silver images there. In other words, as he himself admitted to me, he would not be able to appropriate the precious metals in them. This brings me to the crux of the whole question connected with the control of the Mahanth over the temple, and I believe myself that, if an equivalent for images and votive offerings can be arranged, the whole matter can be amicably settled. It is preposterous, however, for the Mahanth to appropriate entirely to his own use any votive offerings placed in the temple by the Buddhist worshippers. He is not a Buddhist priest, and if he has actually taken such already, as there is no doubt he has, it can only have been in his capacity as a custodian of the temple, and he can have no right to do more than simply take charge of them in the absence of any others who could do so.

7. The removal of these images was probably intended to further the novel idea, started by the Mahanth since this image question has arisen, that the Maha-Bodhi Temple is a Hindu one, and that the image of Buddha in the shrine is an incarnation of Vishnu. This, he fancies, may increase his hold on the temple, and give him an advantage he does not possess, in the negotiations with the Buddhists as regards its future control. But the theory is as foolish from the point of view of the Mahanth's own interest as it is preposterous. No Hindus have ever worshipped at the temple, except perhaps that some ignorant pilgrims may have gone to see it out of curiosity, and done reverence to the image inside.

If the temple were a Hindu one, it would have been defiled by the Buddhists' offerings of biscuits and burning of tallow-candles at the shrine, nor would a *chamar* woman ever have been allowed to sweep it. Nor does it stand to reason that the temple of an incarnation of Vishnu would ever be the special charge of a Saivite priest like the Mahanth. The tree to the south of the temple is one of the places at which Hindu pilgrims to Gaya offer *pindas*, but they do so under the auspices of the Vaishnavite Gayawal priests, and have no concern with the Mahanth.

And your petitioner, as in duty bound, shall ever pray.

H. DHARMAPALA,
Genl. Secy., Maha-Bodhi Society.

NAND KISHORE LAL,
Vakil.

Dated Gaya, the 12th June, 1894.

I have not gone into the whole question of the Mahanth's right in the temple, nor have I by me, as I write, any of the authorities that might throw light on the subject; but it will be found that the Mahanth has never had any control over the Temple itself, except since its restoration by the British Government.

When Gosain Ghamandi Gir, the founder of the monastery near by, settled here about 1590 A. D., it was not the temple, but the beauty of the spot, that attracted him. The temple was indeed in ruins and half burried, and he and his successors never made the slightest attempt to put it into order or to worship in it. The truth is that it is a sin for a Hindu to enter a Buddhist temple like this, and particularly so for a follower of Sankaracharyya, the bitter opponent of the Buddhists, like the Mahanth of Budh-Gaya. The Mahanths have, it is true, cleared a space in the vicinity of the temple where mausoleums have been erected to them, and they have converted a small temple in front of the larger one into a Hindu one, and called it that of Tara Devi, though the image in it is not that of a goddess at all.

The Great Temple is also apparently in the village of Mastipur Taradih, which was settled revenue free with the Mahanths, but I believe that in none of the grants is any mention whatever made of the temple itself. There is nothing to show that the Mahanths ever concerned themselves with it, and, even when the Burmese King proposed to do something for its restoration, no question appears to have arisen as to the Mahanth's having any right in the temple itself. A perusal of the correspondence forwarded to the Commissioner of Patna with the Bengal Government's memo., dated the 16th October, 1875, and of the reply of Mr. Halliday, the Collector of Gaya, dated the 8th December, 1875, will show that the only matters on which the Mahanth was consulted, or with regard to which he made any representations, were as to care being taken not to interfere with certain Hindu idols in the vicinity of the temple, and as to a proper agreement being executed for the land the Burmese wished for the erection of a monastery and of a *paribhaga*, or a magazine for the deposit of offerings made at the Bodhi-tree.

Practically all that the Buddhists now wish was conceded on that occasion, or would undoubtedly have been, had the idea occurred at the time that the Mahanth's consent was necessary for anything connected with the internal arrangements of the temple. Since its restoration, however, the Mahanth appears to have acquired certain prescriptive rights in connection with the shrine, principally because there was no Buddhist representative on the spot to prevent his appropriating votive offerings made at it; and his possession of the key of the *sadar* gate, in the door-way of the temple, has served to enhance his control over it.

But I do not think that it can be fairly said that he has any right of ownership as against the Crown in a temple that was an abandoned building until it was restored at the expense of the Crown.

However, as I have said, I have not studied all the facts bearing on the question; anyway, whatever prescriptive rights the Mahanth may have acquired, need not stand in the way of granting the Buddhists full control over the Temple, as they are prepared to buy up those rights, and there need be no fear that any action taken in furtherance of this object will in any way affect Hindu religious susceptibilities. All the Hindus to whom I have spoken, including the Vishnuvite Gayawal priests, say that there can be no possible objection to the temple being handed over entirely to the Buddhists, and that it would indeed be a sin for any Hindu to have anything to do with it. There was one Pandit, however, Chandrashekhar Bhatta, who sought to support the Mahanth's theory that the Buddha in the shrine was an incarnation; but he showed his ignorance of everything connected with Buddhism, when he finally said that the only objection to the Buddhists having full control over the Temple, would be that they might sacrifice animals at it which would be offensive to the Hindus. What reverence for animal life is included in the Hindu religion is usually attributed to the influence of Buddhism itself, and one of the main principles of the Buddhist religion is that there is no efficacy in sacrifice.

8. I am of opinion that the right of free worship in the Maha-Bodhi Temple, to which the Buddhists are undoubtedly entitled, may fairly be held to include the rights claimed in the present petition. These are in effect the following :—

(1.) The right to set up images and present other votive offerings in the shrine ;

(2.) The right to enter and remain in the temple at all times, irrespective of the consent of the Mahanth—in other words, to possess the key of the door ;

(3.) The right to have Buddhist priests to assist in the worship at the shrine.

9. In my last conversation with the Mahanth, however, held the day before this petition was filed, he expressed a desire that no further steps should be taken in the matter until my return from leave, as he seems desirous now of coming to an amicable arrangement with the Buddhists, seeing that he has everything to lose by not doing so. He parted with me on the understanding that I would recommend this, and I stated the same to Mr. Dharmapala. I would strongly recommend, therefore, that no order might be passed on this petition on any matter connected with the temple in the meanwhile. I am prepared to go into the whole question patiently in the cold weather.

D. J. MACPHERSON,
Magistrate of Gaya, on leave.

Bombay, 28th June. 1894.

[*Exhibit D* 28.]

No. 240G.

FROM

A. FORBES, Esq., C.S.,
Commissioner of the Patna Division,

To

THE OFFG. MAGISTRATE AND COLLECTOR OF GAYA

Dated Bankipore, the 3rd July, 1894.

SIR,

WITH reference to your No. 1575, dated 12th instant, forwarding copies of a petition filed by Mr. Dharmapala before your predecessor, and of Mr. Macpherson's note thereon, I have the honour to say that the questions involved are not such as it is competent to the local authorities to deal with. If Mr. Dharmapala wishes to pursue the subject, you should refer him for orders to Government.

I have the honour to be,
SIR,
Your most obedient Servant,

BEPIN BEHARI MUKERJEE,
Personal Assistant to Commissioner,
For Commissioner.

No. 2297.

COPY forwarded to Mr. H. Dharmapala, 2, Creek Row, Calcutta, for information, with reference to his petition, dated the 12th June, 1894, to the Magistrate of Gaya, on the subject of placing an image obtained from Japan in the temple of Maha-Bodhi.

D. J. MACPHERSON,
Magistrate and Collector.

27th September, 1894.

[*Exhibit E* 1.]

No. 1588.

FROM

E. G. DRAKE-BROCKMAN, ESQ.,
Officiating Magistrate and Collector of Gaya,

To

THE COMMISSIONER OF THE PATNA DIVISION.

Dated Gaya, 12th July, 1894.

SIR,

AT the suggestion of my predecessor, Mr. Macpherson, I have the honour to forward to you copy of a letter No. 1005, dated 24th March, 1891, issued by the Superintending Engineer, Sone Circle, to the Executive Engineer, E. S. Division, regarding the Bodh-Gaya Temple, which you will observe contains a statement implying that Government is not the owner of the temple, and is in charge of it only with the consent of the Mahanth. Mr. Macpherson was of opinion that there was nothing whatsoever to warrant this statement, and on this point reference may be made to his note, dated the 28th June, 1894, on the petition of Mr. Dharmapala, of which a copy has been forwarded to you with my No. 1575, dated 12th July, 1894. Lest this admission by the Superintending Engineer should prejudice Government on the arrangement that may be come to for the future control of the temple, it is desirable that Government should either formally repudiate it or instruct the Superintending Engineer to withdraw the letter.

* See *ante* page 37

I have the honour to be,
SIR,
Your most obedient Servant,
E. G. DRAKE-BROCKMAN,
Officiating Magistrate and Collector.

[*Exhibit E* 2.]

No. 238G.

FROM

A. FORBES, ESQ.,
Commissioner of Patna,

To

THE MAGISTRATE AND COLLECTOR OF GAYA.

Dated Bankipore, the 23rd July, 1894.

GENERAL DEPARTMENT.

SIR,

WITH reference to your No. 1588, dated the 12th instant, I have the honour to say that the opinion of the former Superintending Engineer, contained in his No. 1005, dated 24th March, 1891, is merely that officer's personal opinion, and cannot be considered as binding upon Government.

I have the honour to be,
SIR,
Your most obedient Servant,
BEPIN BEHARI MUKERJEE,
Personal Assistant to Commissioner,
For Commissioner.

To

THE MAHANTH OF BODH-GAYA.

Gaya, 26th February, 1895.

MY DEAR SIR,

I WRITE to remind you that, owing to the attitude you have taken up with regard to the Japanese image which Mr. Dharmapala placed in the Maha-Bodhi Temple, you will be held responsible for any injury of any kind befalling the image. This warning was conveyed to your men last evening, and I should have done so to yourself personally, had you not left, saying you were not well enough to stay longer where I was.

Yours sincerely,

D. J. MACPHERSON.

No. 1478.

FROM

D. J. MACPHERSON, ESQ.,
Magistrate and Collector of Gaya.

TO

MAHANTH KRISHNA DAYAL GIR OF BODH-GAYA.

Dated Gaya, the 28th—30th May, 1895.

SIR,

I HAVE the honour to inform you that a report has been sent to me, to the effect that two of the marble images on the altar on the ground floor of the temple have been damaged, one seriously, so as it has been broken off at the neck, and the other on the left shoulder. Slight damage is also reported to a finger of the left hand of the principal image of Buddha.

As you claim to be in charge of all these images, I request you to inform me how this damage has occurred. It is necessary that the images that have been placed in the temple by Buddhists should be protected from damage of every kind.

I have the honour to be,
SIR,
Your most obedient Servant,

RAM ANUGRAH NARAYAN SINGH,
Deputy Magistrate in charge,
for Magistrate and Collector.

LETTER

FROM MR. BEGLAR TO THE MAHANTH OF BUDDHA-GAYA.

Dated May 14th, 1895.

To

M. GHOSE, Esq., and H. E. A. COTTON, Esq.,

Barristers-at-Law.

Dear Sirs,

I beg to forward to you for transmission to the Mahanth of Buddha-Gaya the statement I was requested by you to prepare, setting forth the views of the Government, so far as I came to know them, and the rights and privileges enjoyed by the Mahanth till the close of my works at the Buddha-Gaya Temple.

I have put it in the form of a letter to him for my own convenience.

I beg to be permitted to add that I cannot think that a great Government, with thousands of religious endowments within its territories, can descend to the mean and oppressive measure of depriving one of the most inoffensive of the holders of one of them of his rights.

I am behind no one in wishing to see ancient monuments in India conserved, but I recognise a vast difference between conservation and confiscation.

I am, Dear Sirs,
Yours truly,
Jos. D. M. BEGLAR.

Gaya Dâk Bungalow,
14th May, 1895.

To

THE MAHANTH OF BUDDHA-GAYA.

SIR,

I AM requested by your Counsel, Messrs. Manomohan Ghose and H. E. A. Cotton, to prepare a statement showing, so far as I know, what the Government recognised and respected as your rights in the ancient Temple at Buddha-Gaya, and I comply with their request so far as I can do so from memory.

No definite written instructions were ever issued to me precisely or even approximately defining what those rights were. I have received verbal instructions only regarding them from time to time, from Public Works Secretaries and Under-Secretaries of the Bengal Government, from the Superintending Engineer under whose orders I was placed on first taking charge of the work of the repairs of the Temple, from the Magistrate of Gaya in 1871, and from the Director-General of Indian Archæology under the Government of India.

These orders and instructions, in connection with my work of conservation and restoration at the Temple, show what was then considered by the Government to be your predecessor's rights in the Temple. And certain practices ordinarily observed in the Temple, and of which I am cognizant, show what was universally, by the people there as well as by visitors and pilgrims, regarded as clearly the rights of the Mahanth, your predecessor in the Temple.

My first visit to the Temple was made during the cold season of the official year 1872-73. I was there only about a week. I then found Hindoos and Hindoos only as worshippers in the Temple and of the sacred *pipal* tree. I saw at that time certain men constantly in and about the Temple, whose business it appeared to me to have been to offer daily worship by the recitation of the *Shastras*, by the ringing of bells and blowing of conch shells, and by the offer of lights and flowers to various sculptured representations of various well-known Hindu Divinities or their foot prints, within and about the Temple, to the sacred *pipal* tree, and to certain sacred spots adjacent, not marked by sculpture.

In addition to these, they employed themselves in assisting pilgrims in their performance of the ceremonies, which sacred Hindu books enjoin on them as obligatory at Buddha-Gaya (which is situated within the sacred circuit of the Gaya *tirtha*) for the repose or deliverance of the souls of their deceased parents and ancestors. I did not consider it necessary personally to see the Mahanth on this occasion; but the *pujaris* in and about the Temple, who were undoubtedly the Gosains or servants of the *math*, referred me to the Mahanth, as the authority whose permission was necessary before they could allow me to do certain acts (copying inscriptions) in the Temple, and I accordingly sent my Hindu peon to the Mahanth and obtained the needful permission; after which no opposition has been offered to my doing any archæological work in connection with the Temple. At this time there was the usual phallic emblem of Siva occupying the central spot in the floor of the *sanctum* of the Temple, and I find I have noticed its existence in my official report printed and published by the Government in 1878. General Cunningham had also noticed it previously. There was also the statue of Buddha, regarded by the people as a statue of Bhairo (Bhairaba or Siva), on the pedestal or throne. Flowers and other offerings were regularly being made to the objects of worship within the *sanctum* of the Great Temple, as well as to the objects of worship in minor temples adjacent and to the sacred tree, at the foot of which, among other sculpture, was an ancient figure of Hara Gouri with four lines of modern Burmese inscription on its pedestal, noticed also before this period by General Cunningham, and still earlier in 1828, by Dr. Buchanan Hamilton.

My second visit to Buddha-Gaya was made at the end of the year 1879 or early in 1880, under the orders of General Sir Alexander Cunningham, Director-General of the Archæological Survey of India, in obedience to the orders of the Government of India issued to him, directing me to be sent to prepare an estimate for the conservation of the ancient Temple. This time, as extensive measurments had to be made, and scaffolding put up, which could not be done without the then Mahanth, your predecessor's, permission, I went and paid my respects to him personally, and obtained the necessary permission as well as orders from him on his Gosains and servants to help me in every way. I was allowed free access everywhere, even into the *sanctums* of every one of the Temples, into these last on taking my shoes off. I found, as before, worship being carried on daily, and the phallic emblem still occupying the centre of the *sanctum* floor of the Great Temple, and the figure of Hara Gouri (Siva and Parvati) still in its old place at the foot of the holy *pipal* tree on the Temple platform or terrace at the back. There were, however, many changes in the exterior of the Temple, owing to work done by the Burmese. The pilgrims, however, were still being assisted through their ceremonies, and used to make their offerings precisely as before. On this occasion I noticed some Burmese Buddhists among the worshippers.

I prepared the estimate and sent it in due course ; and shortly after, in connection with it, personally saw the Under-Secretary, then Mr. T. Haines Wicks, under whose immediate orders I had served in 1869. The estimate provided for the thorough clearing of the accumulated rubbish. It did not provide for securing the *samadhs* from destruction, which would have been the inevitable consequence of my proposals. General Sir Alexander Cunningham, whom I also saw in connection with the estimate, had pointed this out to me as a great defect, and had told me it was impossible for Government to accept such a proposal. I was told the same by the Under-Secretary. To both these authorities I pointed out that an estimate which should avoid this defect, and secure the *samadhs* from inevitable destruction, as the consequence of clearing away the accumulated rubbish on which they were founded, would increase the estimate by about Rs. 5,000, and I further pointed out to General Cunningham that such a measure would effectually preclude from archæological exploration an important portion of the very interesting and ancient site. I was told the orders of Government were clear on the subject, and my business was to obey. About this period I was re-transferred back from the Archæological Department, to which I had been lent ever since 1871, to the Public Works Department of which I was a substantive officer, to enable me to be put in charge of the work of repair.

The estimate was returned to me for revision and re-submission when revised. Meanwhile I was placed in charge of the works, and ordered to begin the work of conservation of the Temple in anticipation of submission of a revised estimate and formal sanction thereof by the Government of Bengal. Before actually taking up the work, I saw the Secretary to the Government of Bengal, Colonel F. S. Stanton, under whose immediate orders I had served in 1864 as Assistant Engineer. He told me that great tact was necessary in doing the work, and he hoped I should have the tact to carry it through without any disagreeable incidents. I was told I had been selected for this work, not for my archæological knowledge alone, but also from the favorable opinion the Government had of my tact in having carried on delicate archæologica investigations for several years without a single unpleasant incident, and he warned me that I was not only to be most careful in doing nothing which would offend the Mahanth or wound the religious feelings of the Mahanth and the Gosains, but that I was to carefully avoid doing what would look as a trenching upon his rights and privileges, and that the Government would assuredly not support me in any measures which might reasonably give offence to the Mahanth or trench on his rights. Everything I might do must be done with the Mahanth's approval and consent.

The Under-Secretary gave me the same orders in effect, as did General Sir Alexander Cunningham. The same orders, but not at such length, were given me by the Superintending Engineer, General Stewart, and advice to the same effect given me by Mr. Barton, then Magistrate of Gaya ; but no written paper embodying all this was ever given to me. To enable me fully to obey these unwritten orders, I was given full independence of action. Though my accounts, for reasons of economy, were submitted through the Public Works Division of Patna, the Executive Engineer was distinctly informed I was not under his orders. I held my executive charge directly under the Superintending Engineer, Western Circle, who exercised a very light control over me. I corresponded directly, both with the Director-General of the Archæological Survey of India, General Cunningham, as well as with the Bengal Secretariat, demi-officially, and with the full knowledge of the Superintending Engineer; and I never did anything of importance without consulting both General Cunningham and the Mahanth, your predecessor; and only after I had their approval was any matter of importance formally and officially sent up to the Superintending Engineer for his approval, where such approval was necessary.

As a matter of fact, there never was a case of disapproval of any of my proposals or actions so sent up or reported, except in regard to the north wall of the Temple; and this was due to the strong opinion and action of the then Divisional Commissioner, Mr. (afterwards Sir John) Edgar. The Lieutenant-Governor, Sir Ashley Eden, however, on personally visiting the Temple, approved of my proposal even in this matter, and it has been carried out since. The most delicate part of my work was naturally the repair of the *sanctum* of the Great Temple, where repair work could not be done without suspending the performance of the daily worship. I represented the matter to your predecessor, and he, after satisfying himself that it was absolutely necessary for the work of repair to remove the phallic emblem from the centre of the *sanctum* floor of the Great Temple, gave the necessary orders for its removal elsewhere. He also, on the same occasion, and for the same reason, authorised me to remove, and when subsequently the removal was found impossible, to destroy the brick and mortar gilt figure that occupied the throne on the great pedestal in the *sanctum* of the Temple. He also formally suspended the daily worship within the *sanctum*, and made it over to me for the necessary repairs. When the repairs were well advanced, I looked out for a figure to take the place of the one destroyed. I represented the matter to the Mahanth, and he and I went round and examined all the figures in the *math* as well as in and about the old Temple grounds to make a suitable selection. I selected the figure which is now in the *sanctum*. The Mahanth would have preferred another; but on my representing to him that no other figure that could be obtained was large enough to suit the throne, he, with some reluctance, agreed to give me the figure that I wanted. The Lieutenant-Governor and Sir Alexander Cunningham also saw and approved the figure on their visits; and the Mahanth permitted me to remove it. It was a figure which, under the name of Bhairon, was then being worshipped. It had the red vermilion *tilak* on, and, in giving me the statue, the Mahanth insisted that the *tilak* should not be washed off, however much I might clean the rest of the statue. The statue needed very heavy cleaning, owing to the lime-mortar in which it had been partly embedded tenaciously sticking to it, and in the process the *tilak* did somehow get washed off. The statue was installed on its throne in the *sanctum* by the Mahanth himself. He used to come occasionally and see the progress of the work, and it was arranged that I was to make everything ready for the setting up of the statue and give him information the evening previous to the day it was to be set up. I made every arrangement, and slung the statue on the spot it was to occupy, and having everything in readiness, sent him the information. He came with his principal Gosains next morning, and while I superintended the working of the machinery, his hand, in seeming, guided the movements of the statue till it was safe on its throne in the desired position. I then left the place, not wishing to intrude any further in any ceremony he may have wished to perform. Next morning the Mahanth sent me the usual *dali* of sweets, fruits and eatables, which, as I had discovered during my stay, he made it a custom to send me after each important ceremonial. I knew by this that he had performed what he regarded as an important ceremony, from which delicacy, as well as some feelings of religious scruple, had induced me to absent myself. When I again saw the statue, it was on its pedestal. It had the vermillon *tilak* on. I believe it was put on by the Mahanth himself. I have still, I believe, a photograph wherein the *tilak* can be seen. The statue was in a few days partially gilt by pilgrims sticking bits of gold-leaf on to it as offerings. I completed the gilding with gold-leaf, which at my representation the Mahanth sent me. The leaf-gold was laid on, so far as I remember, by his men. I did this, as the patch work gilding was very unsightly, and I wanted a good photograph of the statue. After the setting up of the statue, I did not enter the *sanctum*, and ordered my Muhammadan workman not to do so, except under exceptional circumstances, and with the approval of the regularly-appointed Mahanth's *pujari* or other known member of the *math*. In short, I returned to my old custom, which I had followed, while the old statue and the phallic emblem were unremoved, during the period while repairs were going on inside. After the Mahanth had made over the *sanctum* to me, I asked no one's permission. I had the right to enter during that period, and every statue of note within the Temple, including the exceedingly fine one of Buddha, now known as Mayadevi, on the pedestal of the upper chamber, was placed by me where they now are, after consultation with and approval of both General Cunningham and of the Mahanth, your predecessor. I suggested to the Mahanth the desirability of setting up the figure on the pedestral of the upper chamber, but he refused to instal a figure or make the chamber and it a place and object of worship. The chamber never had had a figure on the pedestal before. I had seen none even in 1872-73. General Cunningham had never seen any, though both of us had seen the pedestal. The Mahanth had allowed me to use the chamber as a store godown to store the enormous coils of manilla ropes and chains and the other tackle used on the works, down to the day they were sold under Government orders. His refusal was perfectly consistent with his refusal to plant the *pipal* at the back of the Great Temple. In both cases he refused to set up new objects of worship. General Cunningham and I planted the *pipal* at the back of the Temple. As regards minor statues, the Mahanth had given me full discretionary powers to set them up where, when, and how I liked outside the Temple, but he had never given me nor any one else power to set up what I or they chose inside the Temple. Conspicuous instances of this reservation came under my notice, when two well-to-do pilgrims, one a Japanese and one a Ceylonese, desired to set up memorial tablets. Both had made fairly valuable offerings in the *sanctum* of the Temple where they went to worship—the Ceylonese especially—and they wanted records of their visits and offerings set up within the Temple. The Mahanth, whom I consulted, refused permission. The Ceylonese gentleman took his refusal with a good grace, and the Mahanth took some interest in seeing his offerings set up in a suitable and conspicuous place outside. The Japanese took it very ill. He tried to get some of the Gosains to do it for him, and failing in this, he tried to bully me. He discovered his mistake very quickly. I directed it to be set up in an obscure place (as it deserved, being unsightly and cut on an irregular shapeless bit of stone), and the Mahanth declined to over-rule my orders on this matter. In all matters of work exterior of the Temple and in the grounds, he, the Mahanth, had, after we came to know each and respect each other, given me full power to use my judgment, and I used it: but over the *sanctums* of the various Temples and over the statues, which were objects of worship, he never gave me any power.

When I first came to Buddha-Gaya, there were no bricks ready to execute the repairs with, but I knew plenty of bricks would come out of the excavations I would make. The very first thing to be done, of course, was to get the Mahanth's permission to carry on excavations. He readily gave it. I think Mr. Barton, the Magistrate of Gaya, wrote to him on the subject. Whether he did or did not, the Mahanth, your predecessor, without any hesitation, gave me permission, but only for the ground within the Burmese enclosure-wall—an enclosure-wall no longer existing. I undermined it with the Mahanth's full permission, and it fell, since it was built on accumulations of old *débris* and ruins. I then spoke to Mr. Barton, the Magistrate, about the bricks, requesting him to try and obtain the Mahanth's consent to my using them for the repairs of the Temple. Mr. Barton said he would write, and if he did so, no doubt his letter will be among your *math* archives. I was personally very friendly with the then Deputy Magistrate, Rai Bahadoor Bimala Chunder Bhattacharjee, a man well and favorably known to Government, and, as it happened, also favorably known and deservedly highly respected by the Mahanth. I got him to go to the Mahanth and procure me his consent to the use of the dug-out bricks by me. I also simultaneously sent my contractor (a Brahman) on the same errand, and through their mediation, the permission to use the dug-out bricks, which I sought, was given me, but the permission strictly confined me to their use in the Temple. In consequence of this, my bungalow, now the inspection bungalow or the rest-house, was estimated for and built of unburnt bricks. The estimate was approved and sanctioned by the Government, and the Government knew that it was this restriction imposed by the Mahanth on the use of the dug-out bricks that compelled me to send in an estimate for building the house of unburnt bricks.

After a short time your predecessor saw that I really had no intention of treating him without due consideration or of trenching on his rights and privileges, or of giving him offence, or of wounding his religious feelings ; and he then readily, at my request, gave me full permission to utilise the bricks, which were unfit for use in the Temple repairs, on any work I chose. More than this, as the bricks I got from the excavations within the Burmese enclosure were not enough, I asked for and immediately received permission to dig into his land at Bakror across the river, and to utilise the bricks dug out from it in the repair of the Temple. I must have used over a thousand rupees worth of bricks dug out of Bakror, and I was further permitted to dig where I chose, provided I did no injury to his property, and I have from time to time used this provilege given me. It was at this time that, taking advantage of your predecessor's kind permission to utilise, for any purpose whatsoever that I chose, all the sculpture and all the bricks that I dug out, which would not be needed for use in the Temple repairs, I built the office, the *surki* and mortar sheds, the sculpture sheds, the boundary walls of the inspection bungalow, and its well, and a great many other little things ; and I used the permission in regard to the sculpture by sending some choice collections selected by the then Curator of the India Museum, Dr. J. Anderson (with the approval of the Bengal Government) to the India Museum, partly to be kept there, partly for exchange with European Museums.

That it never was the desire of the Bengal Government to set up any claims to the control of the Temple or to ignore the rights of the Mahanth, your predecessor, appears to me clear from the consistent attitude of the Government and of the Lieutenant-Governor of Bengal. When the progress of the excavations had been such as to cause the falling down of the Burmese enclosure wall and to disclose the existence of most interesting monuments burried under the yet undug portions of the high ground round the Temple, I attempted to secure your predecessor's permission to extend the area of the excavations. He agreed as regards the east and north, but steadily refused as regards the south and west, because he had tenants settled on those lands. The tenants were willing and had agreed to accept compensation and remove, but your predecessor refused to permit me to extend the excavations nevertheless, and in this difficulty I put the matter before His Honor the Lieutenant-Governor during his visit in 1881. He was so pleased with the work he saw and, I flatter myself, with the tact with which it had been managed, that he then and there at once requested the Mahanth, who was present, having come to do honor to His Honor Sir Ashley Eden, and was going round the works with His Honor, in favour of my request, but he demurred, though very respectfully. I was present and acted partly as interpreter between them. Though Sir Ashley Eden spoke Hindustani very well, there were words here and there used by the Mahanth which needed an interpreter. On the Mahanth demurring, Sir Ashley Eden pointed out to him that he need have no hesitation in giving his consent to the measure, since, by doing so, he would improve his own property besides benefiting the cause of knowledge. "The whole will remain your property, Mahanthji," he said, in effect, "and you will lose nothing by it ; all that is being done is improving your property, which will remain as much yours after the work is done as before ; the *Sarkar* has no desire either to lessen your rights or to put you under compulsion to give, but if you will not give, it is your own property you will injure, and I shall be sorry, and learned men will be sorry and not think well of you." On this the Mahanth expressed his willingness to give, and Sir Ashley Eden immediately asked me how much I wanted to extend the excavation. On my pointing out what I wanted, he refused to permit such a great extension of the excavation as would have quite satisfied me, since such an extension would have caused the destruction of the existing Burmese rest-house; and he only asked for so much extension of my excavation as is now included in the present boundary walls, a request which the Mahanth granted then and there, and the limit was roughly marked out at once.

In the entire period during which I have any personal knowledge of Buddha-Gaya Temple, I have seen one solitary instance (except the present one) where the right of the Mahanth to the control of the worship or of the offerings of the visitors or pilgrims has been contested. The Mahanth's *pujaris* have always performed their *puja* in their own way by reading of *Shastras*, by ringing of bells and blowing of conch shells, by offerings of flowers, of vermilion *tilak*, and of *bel* leaves, and in the case of the emblem of Siva, by libation of water, by offerings of the red powder on the festival of the *Holi*, by the burning of lamps fed with *ghi*. I have seen Burmese pilgrims and other non-Hindus drape the great statue with the permission of the Mahanth or the *pujaris*. I have seen all offerings made by the pilgrims, whosoever they may have been, taken by the Mahanth or by his regularly appointed *pujaris* or servants, and with the full knowledge of the donors. I saw a few days ago the great statue in the *sanctum* draped. It is a common thing to drape Hindu statues, and may be seen done in scores, in hundreds of Temples, all over India. With the exception of the present audacious attempt, I have neither seen nor heard of any attempt made in Buddha-Gaya (or anywhere else) during my service, to set up any object of worship within a Temple, in actual use as a place of worship, in opposition to or without the full approval and consent of the sacerdotal authorities in charge of Temple. I feel certain in no church, in no *masjid*, in no place of worship of any cult, would such a thing be attempted or be tolerated for an instant, if attempted. I have seen many ancient places of worship, perhaps eighty per cent. of the most important of each cult in Northern India, and there is not a single ancient place of worship still in use as a place of worship, whether it be a Temple of one cult appropriated by another, or whether it be a Temple in which is still maintained unaltered its original cult, where I have heard of a pilgrim or a visitor (whether worshipper of the cult or not) attempting to set up an object of worship without the full knowledge and consent of the ministers conducting the current worship in the Temple, nor have I seen any instance, or come upon evidences of such an attempt in the past, in the whole of my life. Bigoted and religiously intolerant Governments have after conquest done such acts, but no private individual ever has in India within my knowledge. The solitary instance alluded to, where I have seen the authority of the Mahanth attempted to be set aside, as regards the control of offerings made, was in the case of a Nepalese pilgrim to Buddha-Gaya. This man affecting strong religious feelings, took up his residence (as you may remember) within the *sanctum*, and was tolerated by the *pujaris* out of their good feelings for his enthusiastic devotion to a cult, different indeed from that practised in the Temple, but nevertheless one in which the object of worship was pictured in one of the many forms in which the Infinite Formless is worshipped according to the Hindu cult. The man was tolerated till he developed his real desire and object in assuming such unusual devotional zeal by laying hands on the pilgrims' offerings. On this becoming known, he was promptly turned out, and he on his part was equally prompt to lodge an informal complaint before the Magistrate, Mr. Boxwell, well known for his learning and for his sympathy with Buddhism generally and the Nepalese Buddhists in particular. Mr. Boxwell, greatly excited, came to Buddha-Gaya, bringing the Nepalese with him, and insisted on the man being allowed to worship in the Temple if he chose; but it did not take many hours for Mr. Boxwell to find out that his *protégé* was more anxious about the material offerings of other pilgrims than of his own spiritual ones, and he was ignominiously dragged out of the Temple, made to disgorge the coins he had taken, and warned not to try that trick again! I was in Buddha-Gaya then, and Mr. Boxwell showed his kind feelings to the Nepalese generally by bearing the cost of the man's food after he knew him to be an impostor, until the man gave up as hopeless his bright idea of installing himself as the master of pilgrims' offerings in the Temple on the strength of the known sympathy of that kindest and warmest-hearted of Magistrates of Gaya, Mr. Boxwell, and of his own priestly rank. Your predecessor was well aware of the share I took in exposing the true greed of this unscrupulous impostor under the cloak of religion, and he never resented the small charity I showed to the man after I had helped to expose his fraud and hypocrisy. In fact, if my memory serves me right, your predecessor gave him the usual charity which the *math* offers to all poor who need it, without distinction.

That I had rightly apprehended the view of the Government in regard to my scrupulous observance of unwritten and undefined rights and privileges of the Mahanths of Buddha-Gaya, is evidenced by Sir Ashley Eden's letter, dated 10th March, 1882. It is an unofficial autograph note, and says, "I need hardly assure you of my appreciation of the admirable manner in which you have given effect to the wishes of the Government." In the matter of the work entrusted to me, I am not vain enough to think that I possessed or now possess exceptional engineering talent, but I did and do possess exceptional tact, due to my intimate knowledge of religious feelings among Indians, a knowledge earned by me by years of devotion to that study in books and in existing monuments and among a living people.

Successive Lieutenant-Governors of Bengal have shown their value of my just appreciation of the right relation between a civilised Government and the religious movements and feelings of its subject people, by entrusting to me the conservation of every monument of note in Bengal, so long as the Government of Bengal had funds to spare for the purpose. Sir Augustus Rivers Thompson ordered the conservation of the buildings in the ancient fort of Rhotas Garh on the express but unwritten condition that I was to carry it out. Sir Ashley Eden further showed his appreciation of my views by taking the work of the conservation of Sher Shah's tomb out of the hands of the Irrigation Department and giving it to me, and Sir Steuart Bayley by entrusting the work at the still sacred shrines in Gour in Bengal to me. When the works at Buddha-Gaya were coming to an end, the curator of ancient monuments in India, Major (now Colonel) H. H. Cole, expressed anxiety as to the future of buildings preserved at such cost, and the Bengal Government asked me to make suggestions as to their custody and their safety in future; and I believe my views were adopted in the main. I cannot, in the absence of any official records and at this distance of time, precisely repeat what I then said, but I have no doubt of the principles, since I hold them still. They are the result, no doubt, of my study of the laws regulating the safety of work of national interest and importance in Europe, and of my long study of Indian Archæology.

Briefly stated in a few words, it is this:—

Liberty of action, full and complete, to the *de facto* possessors of the monuments in every lawful matter, with one solitary proviso, a proviso necessitated by its forming no part as yet of a legislative enactment, but which no doubt soon will, namely, that they shall do no act which will lessen or destroy the value of such monuments, as works of art, or as unimpeachable historical records of the past.

This is all that the Government, as a civilised Government, is bound to do, and more than this it has no power of doing, unless it chooses to abdicate its high position of observing religious and civil equality among all its Indian subjects; this and no more.

I remain,
Dear and respected Mahanthji,
Your most obedient Servant,
Jos. D. MELIK BEGLAR.

GAYA DÂK BUNGALOW;
14*th May*, 1895.